JOHN McGAHERN:
A WRITING LIFE

by John McGahern

fiction

THE BARRACKS

THE DARK

NIGHTLINES

THE LEAVETAKING

GETTING THROUGH

THE PORNOGRAPHER

HIGH GROUND

AMONGST WOMEN

THE COLLECTED STORIES

THAT THEY MAY FACE THE RISING SUN

CREATURES OF THE EARTH: NEW AND SELECTED STORIES

non-fiction

MEMOIR

LOVE OF THE WORLD: ESSAYS
(edited by Stanley van der Ziel)

THE LETTERS OF JOHN McGAHERN
(edited by Frank Shovlin)

plays

THE POWER OF DARKNESS

THE ROCKINGHAM SHOOT AND OTHER DRAMATIC WRITINGS
(edited by Stanley van der Ziel)

JOHN McGAHERN

A Writing Life

FRANK SHOVLIN

faber

First published in the UK and USA in 2026
by Faber & Faber Limited
The Bindery, 51 Hatton Garden
London EC1N 8HN

Typeset by Faber & Faber Limited
Printed and bound by CPI Group (UK) Ltd, Croydon, CR0 4YY

A CIP record for this book
is available from the British Library

ISBN 978-0-571-37565-3

MIX
Paper | Supporting responsible forestry
FSC® C013604

Printed and bound in the UK on FSC® certified paper in line with our continuing
commitment to ethical business practices, sustainability and the environment.
For further information see faber.co.uk/environmental-policy

Our authorised representative in the EU for product safety is
Easy Access System Europe, Mustamäe tee 50, 10621 Tallinn, Estonia
gpsr.requests@easproject.com

2 4 6 8 10 9 7 5 3 1

For my parents

Some day men will understand what it was that made this great artist so great, the fact, namely, that he was a worker who desired nothing but to participate with all his powers in the humble and difficult existence of his medium. This implied a certain renunciation of life; but just by the patience of such renunciation did he win life.

RAINER MARIA RILKE, *The Rodin Book*

Contents

Acknowledgements

This book, though begun in Liverpool in 2018, was mostly written in the woods of North Carolina thanks to the generosity of the National Humanities Center (NHC), where I had the good fortune to hold the M. H. Abrams Visiting Research Fellowship for 2024–25. The NHC's profound respect for scholarship in the humanities and superb bibliographic resources meant that I could not have asked for a better place to work. The comradeship of the other fellows – too many to mention here – was a crucial prompt to thought and kept me buoyant on the harder days. That my landlords, Dan and Elizabeth Nord, quickly became my good friends helped me to feel at home in nearby Carrboro, allowing me to live a life of quiet scholarly intensity surrounded by birdsong. My wife, Maura, and children, Frank and Beatrice, put up cheerfully with my absence, allowing me to push on with the necessary work.

Patrick O'Sullivan read this manuscript both piecemeal over many years and in full towards the end. Over more than three decades he has been my one trusted reader, and this biography would be weaker without his intercessions and always sage advice. If infelicities of expression have survived this scrutiny, they are entirely my responsibility. Several undergraduate interns did Trojan work for me over the years 2018–23, and I wish to register my gratitude to them: Cheri Kelly, Lauren Price, Richard Snowden-Leak, Honor Wilson and Molly-Anne Yarwood. My colleagues at the Institute of Irish Studies were at all times encouraging – their knowledge about varied aspects of Irish life has been a sustaining part of my work over many years.

A great many people helped me in various ways over the years of working towards a life of John McGahern, and I would like to mention them here, although several of them, sadly, have not lived to see the book completed: Laura Albery and Rich Waterworth, Nicholas Allen, Paul

Bailey, Patrick Boner, Frances Byrnes, Niall Carson, Michael Carter, Michael Chang, Dónal and Dolores Cleary, Jonathan Coleman, Tim Pat Coogan, Alain Delahaye, Linda de Nazelle, Des Dockery, Peter Dolan, Keith Duggan, Martin Dyar, Joanne Elliott, Susan Elliott, John Foley, Roy Foster, Tom French, Patrick Gaul, Luke Gibbons, Mick Gibbons, Seán Gibbons, Michael Gorman, John Grant, Cliff Greenblatt and Stephanie Judd, Nicky Grene, Mike Griffin, Patrick Griffin, Bill Hamilton, Skip Hays, Marie Heaney, Ian Jack, Ollie Jennings, Linck Johnson, Neill Joy, Mary Keelan, Frankie Kelly, Joe Kennedy, Miles and Bláithín Kennedy, John Kenny, Declan Kiberd, Philip King, Enda Leaney, Hermione Lee, Anne-Claire Leydier, Kathleen MacMahon, Treasa MacManus, Breandán MacSuibhne, Gregg McClymont, Maev McDaid, Brendan McGurk, Kate Marsh, Sam Milne, Chris Morash, Richard Murphy, Bob Nelson, Andrew Newell, Clíodhna Ní Anluain, Deirdre Ní Chonghaile, Brian Ó Conchubhair, John O'Donoghue, Uinsin O'Donovan, Tom O'Grady, Pat O'Keefe, Thomas O'Malley, Ciarán O'Neill, Stephen O'Neill, Carina O'Reilly, Fran O'Rourke, Fintan O'Toole, Tom Paulin, Susan Reed, Trevor Rice, John Rogers, Maija Salokangas, Denis Sampson, Seán Sexton, Pete Shirlow, Tony Swift, Richard Taylor, Colm Tóibín, Niall Walsh, Eibhear Walshe.

Special thanks must be reserved for a number of people who helped me repeatedly and enthusiastically. Barry Houlihan was always on hand at the University of Galway to answer questions or to locate documents in the John McGahern Papers. Liam Kelly was unstintingly generous in sharing both his memories of McGahern and his knowledge of Leitrim life. Shep Ranbom's photographic recall of McGahern's teaching at Colgate in the 1970s proved an invaluable resource. Equally, Bob White's insights into Newcastle in the mid-1970s allowed a richer understanding of John and Madeline McGahern at a particularly contented time in their lives.

Quotations from Thomas Kilroy's letters are courtesy of the Thomas Kilroy Archive, University of Galway Library and Estate of Thomas Kilroy. The lines from 'Shancoduff' by Patrick Kavanagh are from

Collected Poems, edited by Antoinette Quinn (Allen Lane, 2004), by kind permission of the Trustees of the Estate of the late Katherine B. Kavanagh, through the Jonathan Williams Literary Agency. Quotation from Douglas Stewart's 'The Silkworms' is reprinted by arrangement with the Licensor, The Douglas Stewart Estate, c/o Curtis Brown (Aust) Pty Ltd. Quotation from W. H. Auden's 'Short Ode to the Cuckoo' is reprinted by arrangement with the W. H. Auden Estate, c/o Curtis Brown, Ltd.

For over a decade, since I first started editing *The Letters of John McGahern* and later began to write this biography, Madeline McGahern and Luke Dodd have played an essential part in my work. I have spent many hours over the years in conversation with Madeline about her husband and the times they lived through. Without her, this book could not have been written. Luke helped bring the biography out into the light in more ways than can be listed here, though I remember especially fondly one July day walking with him for hours through London's East End in the footsteps of John McGahern.

PROLOGUE
A Match

What part does luck play in the whole shemozzle?
JOHN McGAHERN, 'The Creamery Manager'

Back then, George Best was John's favourite player. How could he not be? A fellow Irishman with dazzling ball-control skills, film-star good looks and hair so thick and dark that John christened him Blackie. He would recall the Belfast man for a French newspaper on the eve of Ireland's encounter with England in Stuttgart at Euro 88: 'Black haired young devil, he had the genius for transforming a simple move into pure grace.' John's exile to London in the wake of being dismissed from his Dublin teaching job for publishing *The Dark* in 1965, while painful, carried some advantages, not least the chance to see in the flesh one of the greatest footballers ever to have played the game.

> I especially remember one late game at White Hart Lane, under persistent drizzle that misted the spotlights. Best was closely followed by two defenders and managed, thanks to a startling act of dribbling with his back to the goal, to keep control of the ball. Then, with the tip of his boots, he chipped it over his opponents, caught it himself behind their back and in front of the public who could barely believe it, the ball went like a thunderbolt into the net. Such magic gave you wings.

Whenever Best travelled to the capital, John tried to be there, so to have Manchester United playing West Ham on his East End home patch this early in the season was an occasion not to be missed. That Saturday, as London's summer tailed off unremarked, the weather slightly colder than normal, match day brought enough sunshine to keep the crowds cheerful as they poured out of Tube stations, past pubs and onward to football grounds across the city.

The date was 2 September 1967. Through the spine of the West Ham team ran those Englishmen who had achieved sporting immortality the previous year in winning the World Cup across town at Wembley, a victory made sweeter by beating their German foes in the final. Just twenty-five years earlier, the Luftwaffe had been raining high explosives down on London, a post-war city, with bomb sites and dereliction still in evidence, especially across the East End and the neighbourhoods around West Ham's Upton Park.

Hammers fans, as they made their way into the stadium, did so with a trepidation unusual for such an accomplished club, captained by England's blond hero Bobby Moore. The previous Tuesday night, they had conceded 3 at Burnley's Turf Moor, and today they were facing the league champions, Manchester United, who, four months earlier, had humiliated them 6–1 in this very stadium, one of the club's worst ever home defeats. Revenge would have to be extracted, and club authorities were keen to keep any sense of grievance on the pitch and out of the stands. Those compiling the match programme felt it necessary to fire a warning shot inside the back cover under the title 'Soccer Hooliganism': 'We have signified our intentions to back prosecution whenever the police consider it justified, and would mention that following our match v Sheffield Wednesday three local youths were fined £30 at East Ham Court for using threatening behaviour and insulting words.'

Michael Green, in his *Sunday Times* column the next day, bemoaned the increasing violence around England's football grounds. There had been trouble at Elland Road after the Leeds captain, Billy Bremner, was sent off; at Bramall Lane, in the Sheffield derby, managers and players shook hands 'to show everyone what great pals they were . . . The result', remarked Green: 'five people were taken to hospital, and dozens more thrown out of the ground.' At Upton Park, twenty youths were removed. 'I find all this a bit pathetic', concluded Green, 'in a nation supposed to be famous for its pipe sucking calmness.'

Among West Ham's players that day alongside captain Moore were his international teammates Martin Peters and Geoff Hurst, as well as a new generation of exciting youngsters who would soon become household names: Billy Bonds, Trevor Brooking, Harry Redknapp. A potent mix of proven winners and new talent, the Hammers dominated the opening half, denying the visitors even a single shot on goal.

Manchester United had been transformed into the best team in the country under the managership of Matt Busby, who had done an extraordinary job of rebuilding the club after his so-called 'Busby Babes' had been wiped out in an air crash on a freezing February night in Munich nine years earlier. Though having got off to a shaky start, the season would end in glory, with United becoming the first English side to lift the European Cup, with a squad full of stars like Bobby Charlton, George Best and Denis Law.

Within the first minute, West Ham had United on the back foot, their stocky striker Brian Dear briefly knocking out Manchester's keeper Alex Stepney in a robust challenge. George Best, United's twenty-one-year-old star number 7, seemed anonymous, uninterested. Nobby Stiles and Bobby Charlton worked hard just to stem the West Ham tide, the best they could do to shoot occasionally from long range. The afternoon looked very much like being the London club's day: a free kick got spilled by Stepney, with the ball rolling free towards the line, but Bill Foulkes intercepted at the last moment. Then Dear rattled the crossbar. United had been overrun and were fortunate to be still in contention when the halftime whistle blew. Fans left their seats, scuffles and fights broke out, Mancunians seething with frustration, Hammers with their tails up. Police, primed for trouble, weighed in as the British Legion Band played on.

The second half began with West Ham in the same dominant form. Twenty-year-old Harry Redknapp ran straight through on goal, ball at his feet, only to be denied by a great save from Stepney. Fans of the claret and blues were becoming increasingly nervous, knowing that the longer their dominance lasted without a goal the more likely they were to be caught on the break. United had not buckled, and, worse still for West

Ham, Best had woken up, swinging a pass to Brian Kidd, who spurned Manchester's first real chance of the game.

After the breakdown of yet another Hammers attack, United full back Tony Dunne countered and crossed into the box, where Charlton touched it down to Kidd, who, with Bobby Moore bearing down on him, let loose with United's first shot on target of the game. Entirely against the run of play, United had taken a 1–0 lead. Within five minutes, Charlton again unpicked West Ham's defence, holding the ball up before releasing an inch-perfect pass to David Sadler, who had looped around to his left. Sadler fired his shot past Bobby Ferguson into the opposite corner of the goal: two shots, two goals, the game turned on its head.

The Londoners' hard work eventually paid off when Martin Peters converted from a Harry Redknapp corner. But the score felt like a consolation as United had the momentum. George Best, now energised, was slashing through the heart of West Ham's midfield. The brittle right side of the home team's defence opened up again to Pat Crerand, who, wrote one journalist, 'sauntered through it, tacked round Ferguson like a yacht around a buoy, and laid on the third goal for Ryan'.

Just like that, it was 3–1 to United in what was West Ham's game in every way except for the final score on the board. 'How do you begin to explain the inexplicable?' asked Brian James's 'Diary of a Strange Match' in Monday's *Daily Mail*.

The result was of little concern to one couple who walked out of the ground. For Madeline Green, a tall, graceful, thirty-two-year-old American, it was an interesting cultural experience, an entertainment, the first football match she had ever attended. A strong swimmer and enthusiastic table-tennis player, she generally disdained team games. For John McGahern, intense, preoccupied and two weeks Madeline's junior, it was sport, a distraction from his daily life as a struggling and unhappy substitute teacher in a large Chingford primary school, part of the ever-burgeoning London-Irish community. For both of them, it was an unorthodox date that would change the course of their lives as unpredictably as those Manchester goals had settled the day in Upton Park.

As the pair left the stadium that September afternoon, almost two hours of silence behind them, such was John's concentration on the football, their interest in each other was reaching a peak of intensity. They walked together for hours through London without thought of time or destination, eventually crossing the Isle of Dogs and then strolling beneath the Thames through the Greenwich foot tunnel, emerging at the splendour of the *Cutty Sark*. Along the eastern horizon, darkness was settling; upstream London's lights pierced the dusk.

John had been frank on the long evening walk about the mess that was his life: a failing marriage, grinding disappointment at work, a lack of time to write. As the pair leant over the Thames balustrade, John commented regretfully that it was a pity they could not be together, to which Madeline – herself now certain that something fortuitous and real was within their grasp – replied that she saw no reason why not.

Luck had entered their world unannounced and would have to be seized.

INTRODUCTION
To Write a Life

> I think it is very strange that I am a writer at all.
>
> JOHN McGAHERN

The Pornographer is the only one of John McGahern's works to give us a lecture on the art of composing biography. Standing at the bar of the Elbow Inn, the unnamed pornographer at the heart of the novel receives feedback from his eccentric editor, Maloney, about a piece he has submitted describing the sexual adventures of the Colonel and Mavis on a Shannon cruise.

Maloney starts to generalise:

> I can see how you've fallen between two schools. You should have written it as plain biography, with copious, boring footnotes. That way no one would doubt you. No one has the faintest idea as to why we exist but everybody is mad for every sort of info about other existences. That way they can enjoy their own – safely. You can't beat life for that sort of thing.

As so often with this writer, levity becomes the gateway to high seriousness. John McGahern thought such questions had to be faced. How can one map the life of any other individual, never mind try to construct an accurate biography of a quiet, private man who spent so much of his writing life avoiding the literary world?

John's preferred place to write for most of that life was a small room in his Foxfield, County Leitrim, home: 'a monk's cell of two by four metres', as the French man of letters Michel Déon remembers this space. John was candid about certain convictions during an interview given to Ciaran Carty, then a *Sunday Independent* arts journalist, in 1978. As his interviewer discerned, this writer did not believe external environment guarantees artistic merit:

> 'Where anyone lives is an accident.'
>
> 'If you happen to live on the moon, you'll learn to love it. It's the quality of the love of the place and not the place itself that matters.'
>
> 'I'd be against the idea that it is better to live in one place rather than another. I don't think it matters. You don't change your life by changing the externals of it.'
>
> 'The world that you write of is inside your head and you can take that anywhere.'

Carty drew out John on this theme:

> Of course he doesn't think in terms of having come home. He would consider it an insult to be called an Irish writer.
>
> 'I know that the colours, the sky, the particular qualities that I inherit are naturally Irish, but I feel that if one doesn't belong to the human kind first, one would be a very poor writer indeed.'

This particular artist believed not only in the desirability of a private life but also in the inevitability, the Proustian inevitability, of a secret life.

His personal library was kept on plain, unvarnished shelving at one end of his study. At the other end was a small window overlooking the beautiful and ever-changing waters of Laura Lake. When I first stood in this room, some eight years after John's death, I asked Madeline, rather naively, if he looked out of that window as he wrote. She smiled at this idea and pointed to the bare plaster to her left: 'He closed the curtains and wrote at a plain desk facing that wall.'

John carried this preference wherever he went. As was likewise stated to Carty in that 1978 interview: 'All a writer needs is a cell, to face a wall. You create your own country, your own weather in front of a blank wall and the wall has always been the same, whether in Paris, Spain, London or here.'

Two photographs made up the only decoration in the room. The first was a small black-and-white card of the Marx Brothers in all their zany pomp, a welcome gift to John from Paul Bailey, the English novelist and biographer who had been his predecessor as the Northern Arts Fellow in Newcastle upon Tyne, where John spent two happy years in the mid-1970s.

The second one formed part of a newspaper article that appeared in the *Irish Times* of 25 March 2000 and features a smiling handshake between two men, Thomas Whelan and Patrick Moran. Despite having pleaded innocent, the two of them know they are shortly to be executed for their part in the events of November 1920's Bloody Sunday. Behind and between the two men stands a grinning auxiliary cadet, Lester Collins from New Zealand. Whelan, a twenty-two-year-old from Clifden, was hanged alongside Moran, a Roscommon man who turned thirty-three on 14 March 1921, their execution day.

For a period in the 1940s, John would attend Knockvicar National School with Moran's nephew Tommy. He subsequently borrowed the name 'Patrick Moran' for the central protagonist of his third novel, *The Leavetaking*, and referred to Moran's heroism in his 1987 screenplay, *The Rockingham Shoot*. John is thinking of this local legend when using a wartime execution to introduce a note of fear and violence into 'Korea', his early story about the poisonous relationship between a father and a son. Rather than hanging the two IRA (Irish Republican Army) men, he has them face a firing squad: 'The officer dispatched the boy with one shot from the revolver as he lay face downward, but he pumped five bullets in rapid succession into the man, as if to pay him back for not coming to attention.'

The condition of waiting for our end is not restricted to historical circumstance. This factor is a universal human bind, as the narrator of 'Sierra Leone' realises at the height of the Cuban missile crisis, as Soviet vessels steam towards their Caribbean destination: 'It was the stillness that was unreal, the comfortable sitting in chairs with drinks in our hands, the ships leaving a white wake behind them on the screen. We were in the condemned cell waiting for reprieve or execution, except that this time the whole world was the cell.'

John's decision to keep these two photographs around him as he wrote in the intense silence of that small room tells us a good deal about the man and his wry, stoical personality. They are small clues to a writer's life, the sort of hints that John himself was wary of interpreting when entering into the realms of the creative imagination. Writing to a new-found friend, the writer Mary Lavin, from his sister Rosaleen's terraced Leytonstone home in the late summer of 1960, John turns with frustration to a particular form's shortcomings:

> There is a definite and growing movement to upset the critical pretentions of our age. Especially the authoritative biography lark. Marie Nordlinger has shown up inaccuracies in Painter's Proust. Ellmann too. 'How little do we know about ourselves. How little do our friends know. Who has the right to say or judge.'

Manchester-born Nordlinger (Madame Riefstahl) was a friend and a correspondent of Marcel Proust, whom she first met in Paris in 1896. She assisted him with his translation into French of John Ruskin's essays 'The Bible of Amiens' and 'Sesame and Lilies'. Both of these works became, for John, an artistic touchstone. The first volume of George D. Painter's *Marcel Proust: A Biography* and Richard Ellmann's magisterial *James Joyce* had both been published the previous year to widespread critical acclaim. But John had his doubts and was impressed by Riefstahl-Nordlinger's critique of Painter. Her essay 'On Reading "Marcel Proust: A Biography"' appeared in the June 1960 issue of *X: A Quarterly Review*. This smart London magazine would go on the following spring to publish John's first work. Riefstahl-Nordlinger condemns Painter's descriptions of the part she played in Proust's Ruskin translations as 'inexact, misinterpreted or wholly fictitious', thereby adding grist to John's mill of scepticism.

Returning to this topic thirty years later, John retains his doubts: 'Even Ellmann's life of Joyce can be profoundly depressing. One admired the scholarship and the detail, but it didn't illuminate the work for me. One felt one was being dragged through a thousand newspapers.' His recurrent suspicion of the form as a valid means for understanding any writer's work was guided by Proust, consistently one of his greatest influences. Reviewing John Halperin's *Novelists in Their Youth*, John summoned this exemplar:

> In the great critical fragments that make up *Contre Sainte-Beuve* Proust states clearly that he sees the biographical method as essentially idle, since the recognizable, everyday personality of the artist bears, at best, an uncertain relationship to the inner spirit that creates what he calls *le moi profond*, which operates according to its own mysterious laws, a variant of Flaubert's 'God in Nature': and he asserts that to argue from the former to the latter is foolish. In fact, in the short, brilliant essay *On Reading*, Proust goes further and dismisses the biographical method as one of the many pleasant forms of moral idleness.
>
> The modern fashion for biography has overtaken Proust's position, but it hardly invalidates it.

John did not relent in this review's conclusion, insisting as so often on the alchemical nature of art, on its secrecy and unknowability:

> Thinking of the enormous publishing and academic industries that now surround true original work – the Collected Letters in several volumes, the Biographies, the Studies – I wonder if the overall result is not to turn those works back into the confusion and trivia and brittleness out of which they somehow contrived, magically, to emerge. We do not need knowledge of Shakespeare's 'obscure hurt' to enjoy or suffer with Falstaff or Ophelia or Hamlet or Lear.

On Reading, John's favourite of Proust's essays, is ever the pivot for a generalised dismissal.

There were exceptions to this critical inclination. Fred Kaplan's *Henry James: The Imagination of Genius* was admired, as was Hermione Lee's *Virginia Woolf*. And such an exception could also be made in personal terms. John's advice, when Kate O'Brien's biographer Eibhear Walshe asked for help, was direct:

> I have read the biography and feel it would be a mistake to publish it as it stands. It seems to me that it falls uncertainly between biography and criticism. I think the long accounts of the novels should go, and be only referred to in passing to illuminate something in the life. And the life should be much more fleshed out, the places she lived in, the people she knew . . . For instance, how did she go through all that money? We can suspect but there are too few details.

This perspective is all somewhat more nuanced than the public position of the man who disliked Ellmann's *James Joyce* for its overly literal and newsprint-focused bent. John suggested that he meet Walshe in the Central Hotel, Dublin, where he went through the entire draft over three hours and provided a close reading, saying there were too many shades of the lecture hall. Walshe recalled the encounter in warm terms: 'generous, thorough and a lesson in how to create character in a biography'. He revised extensively, leading to the production of a tighter, more finished book.

Four years after John's death, one commentator made some preliminary notes on what would be needed should an account of the writer's life be undertaken:

> The way one views the legitimacy of a biographical approach to John McGahern's fiction should depend on more precise attention to the facts than has been commonly practised thus far in the related criticism and popular reception. While it was inevitable that John's own experience would have been to the forefront of his mind when writing *The Barracks* and *Amongst Women* and other related narratives, the potential parallels with Frank's life must be viewed cautiously. *Memoir* has naturally initiated a whole new set of temptations to see the life through the prism of the work and vice versa.

A particular question should be posed. Since John had gone to the trouble of publishing an account of his own life through the 2005 *Memoir*, do we really need a biography? He does go into some detail, notably enough, about his family life, his father's absences, his move from school to school as a boy as his mother sought to continue her life as a primary-school teacher at a time when married women remaining in the profession was becoming increasingly unusual. Readers and reviewers, when the book appeared, tended to admire most the affectionate accounts of precious times spent alone with his mother walking the Leitrim lanes.

John always maintained that he conceived the work, for all the attention given to the mother–son relationship, in an attempt to understand his mercurial father. But *Memoir*, for all its emotional power, leaves the reader wishing to know more. Most of John's adult life – his emergence as a major talent, his successes and his failures – gets skipped over, as though these events were of little consequence. The man remains hidden.

Given the near total lack of books, and of an intellectual tradition, in his upbringing, John often wondered about how and why his creative life had unfolded. He said in a 1985 interview: 'I think it is very strange that I am a writer at all.' This biography's purpose is to explain how an Irish country boy, growing up in such a world, became one of the great fiction masters and prose stylists of the twentieth century.

On the appearance of *Amongst Women* in 1990, an English journalist summarised:

> His reputation is a puzzle. In Ireland he is still notorious as a banned writer, and treated with wary respect by the literary world. In France he is revered, all his books available in translation. On the international academic circuit he is a ubiquitous and controversial speaker: unselfconsciously he namedrops a breakfast with Susan Sontag, a conference platform shared with Salman Rushdie and Bruce Chatwin during their legendary convergence in the Australian outback. But in England he is virtually unknown.

Twenty years after his death, John McGahern remains a treasured figure in his homeland but is still not read as widely as he ought to be in Britain, America and beyond. Even in Ireland he tends to be misunderstood, remembered either as a pioneering truth-teller, a breaker of sullen, post-Independence censorship culture, or as a kindly farmer, a country man who happened to have a talent for writing.

But John McGahern, first and last, was actually a great artist in the high European tradition of Stendhal, Flaubert, Yeats, Pirandello, Proust, Rilke, Joyce, Beckett, Camus.

I

Cold Shadow
1934–53

> To grow up is to come to the realisation that you have no mother, but lie there alone, unsleeping.
>
> HALLDÓR LAXNESS, *Salka Valka*

The worst was over now. Standing there, in the cold Donegal morning, a breeze coming off the lake, arms outstretched in memory of her crucified Lord, Sue McManus had come through the long, sleepless night of penance, rounding the Lough Derg basilica, repeating the Hail Mary, Our Father and Creed so many times that they became indistinguishable one from the other and from the hum of hundreds of prayers caught in the flickering candlelight.

She had decided to make the three-day pilgrimage in preparation for her marriage later that summer. The following day, she would catch the boat back to the shore, having endured sleeplessness, starvation and the pain of nine barefoot stations around the island's monastic ruins and inside the still-new octagonal basilica, so thick with pilgrims that penitents, in the moist warmth of their mingled breath, fainted but did not fall.

Summer 1932. The pilgrimage was at the height of its popularity. In June, Dublin had hosted the Eucharistic Congress to commemorate the coming of Saint Patrick and 1,500 years of Christianity in Ireland. The country would not see such crowds again until the papal visit of 1979, the year in which Sue's soon-to-be-firstborn child would publish his fourth novel, *The Pornographer*.

For this devout young Leitrim woman, wanting to mark the times with a visit to Saint Patrick's Purgatory was a natural impulse, especially now that her life was at a crossroads, her single days drawing to a close.

On this morning, escaped now from the stifling foetid air of the church, she could pray purely and with intensity. She had confessed her sins, moving from exhaustion to elation, a lightness of head brought about by fasting and sleeplessness. And here she looked straight ahead, repeating the central prayer, her back to the cold grey stone of Saint Bridget's Cross: 'I renounce the world, the flesh and the Devil. I renounce the world, the flesh and the Devil. I renounce the world, the flesh and the Devil.'

* * *

Asked once to recall the overriding impressions of his childhood, John McGahern provided a memorably sensuous portrait: 'A lurid light, always. Especially the red light burning in front of the picture of the Sacred Heart. A smell of sour potatoes – whole cargoes of them would be boiled, and the leftovers kept for the pigs and hens.' This Ireland had changed little in a century: a poor, rural country of limited opportunities.

> There were very few luxuries of any sort; Ireland in the 1930s was essentially a nineteenth-century nation, with nineteenth-century sights: horses and carts on the road; people cutting their own turf for fuel. Cousins of mine would have a dirt floor, even in the 1940s; I remember trying to play marbles on it. There was no electricity, it was all candles and oil lamps. We were unusual in having a radio. No-one was well-off except the priest and the doctor and the wealthier merchants. Ninety per cent of people lived in appalling poverty. But it didn't *feel* poor. The most attractive thing about Irish society then and now is its lack of class consciousness, everybody was equally badly off.

While there is no doubting the primitive living conditions of most rural Irish people at this time, it is not quite true that deprivation was equally spread. The McGahern parents, for instance, both held a pensionable state position and never had to consider emigration as did so many of their peers in the early decades of post-Independence Ireland. In the first eighty years after British withdrawal, over two million left the country.

These figures peaked in John's childhood and youth, the fifteen years after the end of the Second World War, with over half a million of his countrymen taking the boat.

John's father, Francis 'Frank' McGahern, was a Cavan man, a native of Gowna. The McGaherns were, recalls John, people who 'set great store on looks and maleness and position'. Born in 1901, Frank was the only child of John McGahern and Brigid Leddy and was brought up almost solely by his mother, attending national school and also receiving some secondary education at the Latin School in Moyne, County Longford. '"I was in the eighth class in Moyne,"' the IRA veteran Moran tells his daughters in *Amongst Women*. '"You couldn't go further than the eighth class without going on to be a priest."' Such a possibility never arose for a poor boy like Frank, and soon there were more pressing matters to consider than life as a cleric.

Frank was born into the revolutionary generation and could not but have been influenced by events in Dublin of Easter 1916. When war broke out early in 1919, Frank had just turned seventeen. He was quick to join the IRA, having already been a member of Sinn Féin, serving in one of the country's most active flying columns under another past pupil of Moyne, the fabled 'Blacksmith of Ballinalee', Seán Mac Eoin, in later years chief of staff of the Defence Forces, government minister and presidential candidate. Thanks largely to Mac Eoin's organisational skills, Longford had a higher proportion of IRA members than any other Irish county. John would tell friends in later years that he was named Seán in homage to this local hero.

At the conclusion of war, Frank joined the new police force, An Garda Síochána, along with many other pro-Treaty IRA volunteers. He formally signed up on 27 October 1922, aged twenty. The initial batch of recruits had begun training in February, the month after British troops left Dublin Castle, making Frank among the first guards to serve the country. The ledger detailing the particulars of these men tells us that Frank was then living in the townland of Corratober, Gowna, County Cavan, was 5 feet 9½ inches tall, with a 37-inch chest. He had no medical problems, was literate and had served as a private in the IRA. Almost every man to join up that October had also fought as a Volunteer, with a handful of others either in the Royal Irish Constabulary (RIC) or in various British regiments through the Great War.

Despite ever-present tension ('a gnawing resentment of each other's lonely and passing world'), the guards who populate John's first published novel remember these days of revolution as among the best of their lives. Their night-time chats about the new Ireland and the part they played bring them back to a source: 'the six months they spent training in the Depot when they were nineteen or twenty, in the first days of the Irish Free State'. But these memories of youth quickly sour in the face of a colder political reality:

> The British had withdrawn. The Capital was in a fever of excitement and change. New classes were forming, blacksmiths and clerks filling the highest offices in the turn of an hour. Some who had worried how their next loaf or day might come were attending ceremonial functions. There was a brand new tricolour to wave high; a language of their own to learn; new anthems of faith-and-fatherland to beat on the drum of the multitude; but most of all, unseen and savage behind these floral screens, was the struggle for the numbered seats of power.

The following decades have wrought disenchantment: 'Now they sat and remembered, thirty years later, waiting to go to their homes in the rain.'

Frank McGahern, on whom Sergeant Reegan of *The Barracks* is largely modelled, graduated from the Phoenix Park Training Depot. Posted initially to the large Edward Street garda station in Limerick, he was quickly transferred to County Leitrim. Within six months of graduating, he had been promoted to the rank of sergeant and was patrolling the highways and the byways of Ballinamore, a not unusual rise in these early days of the state for a garda recruit with military experience.

He had a reputation as a severe upholder of the law and made enemies. On one occasion, his bicycle was stolen from the Kelly house in Aughawillan, where he was courting John's mother, never to be recovered and likely thrown into a local lake. While there is a certain comic tinge to the story, this event was a serious loss.

John recounts one notable moment of regret from the Sergeant's Ballinamore career: 'During my father's stay of duty, the bank in Ballinamore was robbed at gunpoint by the Doherty brothers who had been in the IRA and fought on the Republican side in the Civil War.' Frank McGahern was in no doubt about the appropriate response to such behaviour: 'I heard him remark casually while speaking about the Dohertys that if he had been armed on the day of the bank robbery not one of them would have left Ballinamore alive. I believed him.'

After three years in Ballinamore, Frank was transferred to County Donegal, a move likely prompted in part by his developing courtship with a local Leitrim girl, Susan McManus. Born on 3 May 1902, Sue was one of a family of three girls and two boys from a mountain farm in the townland of Drumderg, five miles north of Ballinamore and almost in County Cavan.

John remembers the holding that sustained the McManus family: 'The small fields they had wrested a living from on the Iron Mountains above Corleehan Church were worse than poor.' To survive there, one had to be 'resourceful, thrifty, careful'. This world had been born out of violent necessity:

> A few boggy meadows below the house gave them potatoes, turnips, cabbage and the winter's fodder. All the names on that part of the mountain were northern – McManus, McGovern, McGirl, Maguire – many of them related. Generations earlier, some had been weavers in the north who were undercutting the established Protestant weavers. In organised violence, their looms were broken, their houses burned, and they fled west and south.

This part of the country possessed a long memory that would see generation after generation rise up against their British rulers. Those weaver refugees – known by the Leitrim locals as Ultachs – brought with them a vengeful determination that would not soon be quenched. In

August 1796, Lord Lieutenant Camden reported how the Ulstermen brought about a particular reaction: 'related their suffering and I fear excited a spirit of revenge among their Catholic Bretheren'. John's maternal grandmother, Rose Anne O'Donnell, was a first cousin of Philip Meehan, the first tenant farmer casualty of the Land War, shot by Henry Acheson on 14 June 1880, near Ballinamore. Meehan's grandfather, also Philip, had joined General Humbert's army in 1798 and was killed at nearby Ballinamuck in the final showdown of the United Irishmen rebellion.

Sue McManus was a clever girl who won the prestigious King's Scholarship, which provided funding to help with her studies as a national-school teacher at Dublin's teacher-training college for Catholic women: Our Lady of Mercy, Carysfort, Blackrock. She had previously excelled as a boarder under the Marist Sisters in Carrick-on-Shannon, a difficult period in her life when 'she was uprooted from her own class' and made to feel separate.

The Carysfort register of students for 1922–24 sees her scoring 82 per cent in Doctrine and Scripture History, a well-above-average mark reflecting a lifelong interest in the Church and a devotion to her faith that she would pass on to her children. John writes repeatedly of his mother's wish for him to become a priest, and the shadow of a religious vocation explored and discarded haunts both *The Dark* and *The Leavetaking*. The latter novel sees Patrick Moran, much like Stephen Dedalus of *Ulysses*, carry with him a gnawing guilt about his mother's final days and his failure to redeem himself in the wake of her death:

> Through the sacrifice of my life to the priesthood I'd redeem the betrayal of her in that upstairs room. For years I promised it to her memory that, 'One day I'd say Mass for her.' I'd lift the chalice in anointed hands on the altar and in the lonely rooms of presbyteries I'd be faithful to her, but when the time arrived for me to make that sacrifice I failed her once again. I wasn't able to renounce the longing to enter the mystery of the lovely and living flesh of woman, and out

> of guilt I chose second best. I followed her footsteps to the Training College.

As a boy, growing up with his mother and sisters in Aughawillan, John would serve Mass in St Patrick's Church, in whose grounds one day mother and son would lie beside each other in death. 'I have nothing but gratitude for the spiritual remnants of that upbringing', he reflects, late in life, 'the sense of our origins beyond the bounds of sense, an awareness of mystery and wonderment, grace and sacrament, and the absolute equality of all women and men underneath the sun of heaven.'

Love of God, coupled with an unbreakable faith in the Catholic Church, helped sustain Sue McManus through her all-too-brief life, and she brought the best aspects of this faith to her chosen profession. She began her teaching career in Ballinamore and went on to work later in a series of small Leitrim schools, finishing in Aughawillan. Memories of her, both as a teacher and as a woman, are invariably warm. Fr Peter Dolan, now in his nineties and living in Florida, recalls with great affection his time in her Lisacarn classroom:

> My memories of her are truly delightful and grateful, easy to recall because of the joyous delight that they provide. Naturally and good-naturedly motherly is what I best remember about her. Her appearance was always genteel, personality amiable, attitude helpful, and welcome genuinely cordial and always of assistance. One wanted to learn by reason of her pleasing and inviting personality that never displayed even a hint of impatience or anger and always displayed a ready willingness to be of help and a delight to be asked. The 'rod', then very much misused as an educational motivator, was never on display in her classroom. I do not think that she even had one or ever used one.

Fr Dolan and his brothers, though born and bred in Aughawillan, had been moved out of the school there by their father after the master had inflicted a particularly severe beating on one of the boys.

Unlike most teachers of the time, Sue eschewed corporal punishment. She had a deep love of the natural world, sincerely believing that its splendour was evidence of divine creation, a belief that informed her life and work from first to last. One remarkable document sheds light on this aspect of her character: among the McGahern Papers in the University of Galway lies a notebook titled 'The Nature Study Record Book' compiled by Sue in her final year with the Marist sisters in Carrick and containing page after page of immaculately detailed, copperplate notes on various aspects of the natural world. These notes are frequently followed by delicate pencil drawings that run the gamut from tadpole development to swallows in flight to the movement of a frog's tongue. In these lovingly composed notes one sees the sensibility of a young woman that could not but impact one day on her students and on her own children. The book was treasured by John, who signed it while a student with the Presentation Brothers in Carrick in the late 1940s and early 1950s and again while training to be a teacher at St Patrick's Training College, Drumcondra from 1953 to 1955.

His happiest childhood memories are of walking the Leitrim lanes with his mother, her acting as his instructor and guide. These memories eventually become those images with which he ends his writing life in a note of memorable lyrical sweetness:

> If we could walk together through those summer lanes, with their banks of wild flowers that 'cast a spell,' we probably would not be able to speak, though I would want to tell her all the local news.
>
> We would leave the lanes and I would take her by the beaten path the otter takes under the thick hedges between the lakes. At the lake's edge I would show her the green lawns speckled with fish bones and blue crayfish shells where the otter feeds and trains her young.

This shared love of nature between mother and son seeps into great swathes of John's fiction, coming to a peak in the late work, whether via Jamesie's boasting about being the first to hear that harbinger of spring, the cuckoo, in *That They May Face the Rising Sun* or via the heartbreaking rumination on life's fragility after Kate Ruttledge is murdered by her husband in 'Love of the World':

> A silence came down around all that happened. Nobody complained about the normal quiet. Bird cries were sweet. The wing-beat of the swan crossing the house gave strength. The long light of day crossing the lake steeped us in privilege and mystery and infinite reflections that nobody wanted to break or question.

Like Kate Ruttledge, Sue McManus was a local girl attracted to a young garda outsider, Sergeant McGahern from neighbouring County Cavan, a handsome man of military bearing, respected and feared in equal part by the small Ballinamore community. Before Frank left for his Donegal postings in 1927, he proposed marriage, and the couple were engaged.

The Sergeant served variously for five years in Buncrana, Burtonport, Doochary, Ardara and Bundoran. While McGahern was serving in Burtonport, he got some unwelcome publicity as the arresting sergeant at a disturbance during the wake of a Mr McAuley. Depending on whom one believed, this event may have involved attempts by a rowdy group of young men to rouse the corpse from his eternal rest and have him smoke a pipe. The story was so scandalous that its nature made not just the *Derry Journal* but also London's *Daily Mail* and several Scottish newspapers.

When the four accused appeared before the court charged with riotous assembly, the judge was more concerned with saving the reputation of Donegal than with the mischief that had almost certainly occurred on the night. Justice O'Halloran wondered, 'What would the people in Scotland think from that report of the savages that were living down in Burtonport?' concluding, 'Although these defendants have been guilty of most discreditable and reprehensible conduct, I wish to say with the fullest deliberation that the statements regarding it which I read in the Press myself are a gross and malicious libel on the people of this country.'

This devilment, if about as exciting as life got for a country guard, suited Frank just fine. He had a sweetheart back in Leitrim and could continue to live the life of a single young man. John tells us in *Memoir* that his father 'had dalliances with many women' (though how he knows this detail is a puzzle given how taciturn and unforthcoming the Sergeant normally was).

Whether Frank was gallivanting or not, Sue was disturbed by the increasingly embarrassing endurance of the engagement, and in May 1932, she posted the engagement ring to him in Shanaglish, County Galway, where he was briefly posted after the Donegal years. This dramatic act achieved its purpose. The Sergeant appeared in Ballinamore the next day, and preparations were put in place for an August wedding. Angered by having had his hand forced, he wrote to Sue on his return to Shanaglish, keen to return the engagement ring and regain some ground. Sue's response was characteristically firm: '"No need to talk of returning your ring. With God's help we will be married in August and then you will be giving me the one – just a plain gold band."'

The wedding took place on 10 August, not in Sue's home church of Coraleehan as one might expect but in Ballinamore, where she was living with her sister Maggie, who ran a shop at the top of the town on Railway Road. By marrying in August 1932, Sue became one of the last female primary-school teachers to escape the ban brought in by the government that year which meant that women in her position were expected to resign on marriage, a piece of legislation that lasted until 1958 and is frequently cited as evidence of an increasingly unhealthy and patriarchal turn in the young state.

One story of his father's behaviour in the period before the wedding, which John recounts in *Memoir*, bears retelling. While Sue headed for the penitential beds of Lough Derg, Frank, far from renouncing the world, wished to hold it tighter. Knowing that the end of his single days was now in sight, and fearful of the impoverished future that marriage and a traditional large family would bring, in the weeks before the big day he headed into Galway and bought himself two dozen oranges, then still very much considered an exotic treat. In one last great *non serviam* before entering into this new world, alone on a park bench he devoured the oranges one after another. The high days of the flying column were over. He would no longer be master of his own destiny.

Within six months of being married, Sue was pregnant, and on 12 November 1934, her first child, Seán (the name by which he would always be known by family, childhood friends and neighbours), was born in Mrs Dalton's Ballsbridge nursing home at 33 Percy Place. This contingency of birth allowed dust jackets in years to come to state correctly, if puzzlingly, that John McGahern was a native of Dublin. A week later, mother and child were gone home to join the Sergeant in Clontibret, County Monaghan, where he had been stationed since October the previous year. Six more children would follow. The twins, Rosaleen and Breedge, were born in Clontibret in January 1936. In May 1937, Frank was transferred again, this time to Cootehall, County Roscommon, where he spent the rest of his garda career. He would have been relieved to get a barracks closer to Sue and the children, who had returned to Leitrim as Sue taught in various schools around Ballinamore. There followed the births of Margaret (1937), Monica (1939), Dympna (1942) and Frankie (1943).

Sue spent almost her entire married life either pregnant or nursing toddlers and babies. She died as a result of breast cancer on 28 June 1944, married not quite a dozen years. Perhaps the saddest sentence in the whole of McGahern is written almost in passing, the truth of it too much to dwell over: 'She had seven children in nine years, and then she died.'

For much of the twelve years of marriage, Frank and Sue lived apart. Today, one might assume that this arrangement could be explained by poor marital relations. But the matter was not necessarily that simple. Guards were not permitted to serve in their spouses' home county, and, as long as Sue wished to work near her family, and in particular near her sister Maggie, with whom she was especially close, she would remain in Leitrim while Frank endeavoured to get stationed in a neighbouring county.

After John McGahern's death in 2006, one letter-writer to the *Sunday Independent* sought to set the record straight. 'No human being could have done more to be with his family', argued the letter.

> Everyone knows that at the time a Garda would not be appointed or left in a station where a relative of his or his spouse resided. His wife was a teacher, living among relatives. He was based in a local station but on getting married, was powerless to prevent his transfer to a station in County Monaghan.

The impression one gets of Frank and Sue's marriage from John's fiction and from his *Memoir* is one of darkness and unease, a couple who do not live together, meet irregularly and fail to understand one another. Sue was pregnant for most of their years as man and wife but reared the children alone in various Leitrim addresses connected to whatever school she happened to be attached at the time: Lisacarn, Cloone, Beaghmore, Aughawillan. John recalls those times when his father would visit as fractious: 'There was always tension when he was in the house, scolding about how money was being wasted, or the poor way the house was being run, or my mother's relatives.'

The Leavetaking offers an especially bleak fictionalised summation of the relationship, describing a night of lovemaking in the period after the narrator's mother has had a breast removed: 'she'd been warned that under no circumstances must she get pregnant. There was a risk that if any of the cancer still remained in the opening of the ductal glands it would pour into the whole bloodstream.' But on the night in question, the narrator's father, having cycled the long miles through the rain and 'starved for sexuality', cannot restrain himself: 'He meant to be careful, but moving in the warm dark flesh of the woman the male urge to inflict the seed deep within her grew and it was too late when he pulled free.' The night's events end in pregnancy and, not long after, in death, with the resultant progeny described only as 'the cancer child'. Afraid of this strange man who would make these irregular visits, the narrator inevitably made a choice: 'I started to move deeper into the shelter of my mother, away from the cold shadow my father cast.'

The depressing portrait of a sex-hungry husband determined to impose himself on his wife was not John's fixed view of the marriage.

One early, undated piece of writing in the archive titled 'The Going' paints the Sergeant in an altogether more sympathetic light:

> That their father had to push a bicycle thirty miles through the evening to light a stove and get his own supper in the married quarters of the great barracks in Galway never entered their heads, that he'd have no one to talk to when he came in off his patrol at night but the barrack orderly already crazed by the day of newspapers and boredom, nothing to look forward to but sleep in the iron bed upstairs till it was time to rise to get ready for roll call and inspection at nine.
>
> Their mother had never lived with their father for any length of time. She would not give up her teaching. She didn't refuse outright to go with him to Donegal when he was ordered there a few months after the marriage, but she found several excuses for staying. That first summer, she spent the long school holiday with him but came away in spite of him in September, and it set the pattern of their marriage. Each summer she went to him wherever he happened to be stationed, and at Christmas and Easter until the second child came; while he spread out his month's annual leave to come to her often as he could at first, and out of this compromise six children were born. But as the years went, he grew more and more embittered, full of recrimination as he began to envy the home comforts of the married men and the excitement of the younger ones going off duty to meet their girls or away on a night's adventure, while he had neither one life nor the other, just loneliness without freedom. She in her turn sought her life in the children, centring it about Jim, who had been the first child, and the only boy. So, after twelve years nothing held the marriage together but the iron chains of Catholic morality, and the responsibility of children. She was ill, too, and growing worse.

We find that same, slightly softer, viewpoint taken up at moments in *The Barracks* in descriptions of the relationship between Sergeant Reegan and Elizabeth: 'She watched him with tenderness. He was a strange person, she knew hardly anything about him, beyond the mere physical acts of intimacy. There had never been any real understanding between them: but was there ever such between people?'

After five years stationed in Clontibret, Frank managed to get a move back closer to Sue's home county, to the pretty riverside village of Cootehall in north Roscommon. This place would become the cornerstone of John's imaginative world for a substantial portion of his writing life. The village today is radically changed from the place in which the Sergeant held sway for the last twenty years of his career. Back then, Cootehall was a sleepy, beautiful riverbank enclave: 'There was a church, a post office, the barracks, a presbytery, two shops, three bars, a few houses.'

Asked by his German translator in the 1970s for some context on his fictional settings, John replied:

> My backgrounds are obvious enough, mostly the upper reaches of the Shannon, the river probably the central image. There's Dublin, London, Spain. While it's not Wonderland, neither is it Geography. I know you know this, but many do not and even at the risk of pedantry I think it cannot be insisted on enough. It is a landscape of the heart and the imagination, as different and as similar to the world it grew out of as we are to our parents.

Shortly before Sue McGahern died, in her simple two-storey house in a field in Aughawillan, the McGahern children were moved to live with the Sergeant in the stone barracks of Cootehall, and a 'shadow was to fall forever on the self' of John's life. That illness, the hope given to young Seán by his mother's initial return from hospital and short remission and then the final leavetaking and moving of the children and furniture from Aughawillan to Cootehall, are all heartbreakingly recounted in *Memoir*.

Susan McCaffrey of Clooncose, a young nurse home from war-torn London, was hired to comfort Sue in her dying days. So traumatised was John by these events that he would kick Nurse McCaffrey under the table at mealtimes when nobody else could see. Aged nine, this sensitive, intelligent boy was not permitted to attend his mother's funeral on what was to be the most significant day of his life, a moment into which, and from which, all his fiction flows:

> I watched the hands of the clock jerk to two, an hour before three, as long as the hour I had lost on the cinders, trying to keep pictures of her in the days of her life as the minutes remaining to her above clay beat away. At ten to three I was frantic. I looked that no one was looking and took the blue clock from the sideboard and weeping stole with it out to the avenue to move in the shade of the evergreens, the flat and fragrant elder blossom at the gap that she'd never watch turn to clusters of small grapes again, and close to the great oak I hid in the deeps of Lenehan's laurels to hold the cold glass of the clock to my face as it beat out the last minutes to three.

John's 'beloved', as he calls her in *The Leavetaking*, was gone. For years to come, he would seek, and often painfully fail, to replace his mother's lost love in the dream of another woman. The loss of his mother, of her quiet kindness, of her generous intelligence, was an insurmountable tragedy for her eldest child.

Life in the barracks would be cruelly different from John's Aughawillan arcadia. 'A child', he comments, 'can become infected with unhappiness.' That virus took hold in Cootehall. But without the nine years lived there, John would hardly have become a writer. As always emphasised in his non-fictional writings, he would gladly have swapped artistic success for a contented childhood and insisted that writing was an activity best avoided unless one felt compelled: 'I write because I need to write. I write to see.'

There was an inevitability that John's debut novel should be called after this building, that *The Barracks* described in minute, loving detail the daily life of a garda sergeant, his terminally ill second wife and their children. But what sort of place was the barracks, and why did it exist? That the building was even called a barracks hints at a paramilitary past when such buildings were manned by the RIC, the armed, imperial police force that kept a lid on agrarian outrage and nationalist disquiet across the country for the century from 1822 to Independence.

The RIC's eventual replacement, south of the newly imposed border, was An Garda Síochána. An admirable degree of courage and optimism went into the decision that this new force would be unarmed – much to Frank's chagrin when he missed the opportunity to gun down the Doherty brothers on Ballinamore's main street. The force was full of men like Frank, former IRA volunteers who would have been more than happy to pull the trigger on local miscreants. The decision to not have these new keepers of the peace carrying guns was an enlightened one.

There were other, less insightful aspects of the young state that John could observe *ab ovo* in Cootehall and among the lanes of north Roscommon. 'The barracks itself was a strange place', he writes of his years there, 'like most of the country at the time.' His reflection continues:

> Though the Free State had been wrested in armed conflict from Britain, it was like an inheritance that nobody quite understood or knew how to manage. The Catholic Church was dominant and in control of almost everything, directly or indirectly. In a climate of suppression and poverty and fear, there was hardly any crime and little need of a barracks in a place like Cootehall, other than as a symbol.

The frankly comic nature of having four policemen stationed in a district in which almost no crime of any significance took place was not lost on more insightful citizens and is brought to memorably hilarious life in Flann O'Brien's novel from this period, *The Third Policeman*. For John, too, this recognition gave rise to what he recalls as his first efforts at writing fiction when he would assist guards with inventing minor crimes or misdemeanours to report in what were known as 'Patrols of the Imagination'.

A glance through the Sergeant's final notebook before retirement confirms the mind-numbingly banal nature of the work involved. But the roster, on another level, is as funny as any Myles na gCopaleen column:

10/6/58: While driving my car across the bridge at Cootehall Pat Moore was standing with his bicycle. He was talking to Mr and Mrs McCabe. I blew the horn and he would not leave. I stopped & blew the horn. He moved in to his own side of the road.

7/9/58: Cautioned Michael McDonnell, Hillstreet for parking at bend his lorry ID4356. Documents relating in order.

14/9/58: Inspected Regans public house at 4pm. Tom Boland & Pat Golden in it. Both bonafide. I had suspicions F. Higgins, Cloonacarron got out the back as I saw in a field at rear of houses.

These events – or non-events, rather – were also in a sense part of the young John's experience.

That Frank had made sergeant within a year of joining the force was both a blessing and a curse. Although his rank meant a certain prestige within a small community, the quick rise also made further promotion – especially once marriage and fatherhood kept him in one place – an unlikely occurrence. The quotidian drudgery of barracks life, so ably painted by John throughout his debut novel, took its toll. The excitement of his days as a guerrilla fighter could never be reproduced or matched. Now he found himself serving a so-called Free State for which he felt no enthusiasm.

Frank McGahern applied for and was awarded a medal for his IRA service but, like Reegan, took no pleasure in its possession. Having lobbied for recognition of the part he played in the War of Independence, he was eventually, and unfairly, issued an Ordinary Service Medal when he ought to have received a Military Service Medal. Disgusted when the physical object finally arrived in 1952, with the compliments of the president of Ireland, he gave it to his children for their amusement. Like Moran of *Amongst Women*, that other superannuated IRA man, he refused to apply for an IRA pension. According to a son-in-law, Frank McGahern maintained that they 'did what they did out of genuine patriotism, not for any subsequent monetary reward'.

John lived with his father, sisters and brother in Cootehall barracks from June 1944 till September 1953. That autumn, he left to go to University College Galway (UCG) and shortly thereafter to St Patrick's College, Drumcondra to train, like his mother before him, as a primary-school teacher. For John, they were nine largely unhappy years.

In considering just how unhappy, we have to ask ourselves to what degree Young Mahoney of *The Dark* is a facsimile of young Seán McGahern. In particular, was John, like his fictional creation, sexually abused by his father? John and the Sergeant frequently shared a bed for want of space in the house. In another, adjoining, room slept his five sisters and brother Frankie. A third bedroom was kept for a maid, several of whom worked for the Sergeant in these years, never staying for long. John's description in *Memoir* of his father's sexually inappropriate behaviour towards him is a close match to the fictional relationship of the Mahoneys, father and son:

> When my father came late to bed and enquired as he took off his clothes if I was awake, I nearly always feigned sleep. He never interfered with me in an obviously sexual way, but he frequently massaged my belly and thighs. As in all other things connected with the family, he asserted that he was doing this for my good: it relaxed taut muscles, eased wind and helped bring on sleep. In these years, despite my increasing doctrinal knowledge of what was sinful, I had only the vaguest knowledge of sex or sexual functions, and took him at his word; but as soon as it was safe to do so, I turned away on some pretext or other, such as sudden sleepiness. Looking back, and remembering his tone of voice and the rhythmic movement of his hand, I suspect he was masturbating. During the beatings there was sometimes the same sexual undertow, but louder, coarser.

As a means to remove himself from these ugly interactions, John would count the boards that formed the bedroom ceiling, just as Young Mahoney does in *The Dark*.

If John is willing to leave some ambiguity about whether knowing and calculated sexual abuse took place, he is in no doubt about the pervasive physical violence faced at home by him and his siblings. Beatings were frequent, unpredictable and unfair. As John grew bigger and stronger, he determined to put an end to them. He knew where his father's .22 rifle was kept – he loaded and unloaded it many times in preparation for what he might have to do if things became intolerable. 'Each move he made', thinks the young narrator of his frightening father in 'Korea', 'I watched as closely as if I too had to prepare myself to murder.' The situation never came to that pass, fortunately, though the dynamic did inevitably finish with a violent showdown:

> Then late one evening he hit me hard without warning. There did not have to be a reason. The blows could come out of a moment of irritation or misunderstanding. As I have intimated, I suspect there was something sexual in his violence, because the blows could flare up on nothing, and afterwards it was hard to trace them to a cause. I remember feeling a wild sense of unfairness and a cold rage as I fell. I rose and went straight up to him, my hands at my sides, laughing. He hit me. I fell a number of times and each time rose laughing. I had passed beyond the point of pain and felt a strange cold elation.

As well as this last brutal encounter meaning an end to the beatings for John, the clash also gave him power to protect his siblings:

> Some weeks afterwards I found him beating one of the girls and shouted at him to leave her alone. Without thinking, he turned and struck me violently across the face. His fingers left tracks across my face, but I hardly felt the blow.
>
> 'Do that again and you're finished,' I said. I felt there was no end to what I could do if he moved. I would tear him apart, limb by limb, his nose and the sides of his mouth first. He fell back, crying. 'I reared a son. I reared a son that would lift a hand to his father. I reared a son.'

Life in the McGahern family had changed for good: 'there would never be uncontested violence in my presence in the house again.'

Having the physical power to stand up to his father was not the sole liberating factor. Growing up and going to school with the Presentation Brothers in Carrick-on-Shannon, six miles down the road, meant an increasing degree of independence. The proximity of this school, opened in 1947, was a stroke of good luck. When Brother Damien, the school's first headmaster, called at the McGahern home on a recruitment drive, the Sergeant was impressed enough to let John think of secondary education: 'I was planting potatoes with my father on Cox's Hill. I can still see Brother Damien lean his bicycle against the stone wall and come towards us across the field.'

John sat the entrance exam and won a half-scholarship worth £4 a year for five years, and he attended this small school, which generally had no more than sixty students during this period, from September 1948 to June 1953. He travelled in and out of town every day, often accompanied by his best friend Paddy Morahan. Later years would see Morahan fictionalised in 'Doorways' as Jimmy McDermott, secretary and treasurer of the Sligo-based 'Pint Drinkers' Association'. The two of them cycled via Cleheen, crossing the Shannon at Hartley before passing Clarke's Pond and then on to the Leitrim Road, with the main gates of the college directly in front of them as they entered Carrick. The boys tended to spend their spare time in the handball alley, a sport John would go on to play with some degree of skill long into adulthood.

John excelled as a student and did well in the state Intermediate Certificate exam of 1951, despite the fact that he was regularly absent from school. The Sergeant kept him home: saving hay, footing turf, digging potatoes. While John would have preferred to go to school, he also found a certain comfort in hard manual labour. This proclivity remained an aspect of his temperament into adult life, and he always liked, when living in Foxfield during later years, to break his writing day with farm work. If he was to have any hope of a good Leaving Certificate, and maybe even of the opportunity to go to university, these absences would have to cease.

John recalls another fateful day when the new headmaster, Brother Placid, came calling to the potato fields of Cootehall:

> Brother Placid took my father to one side, but not out of hearing. He said I was one of his best students and could go far, but not if I was kept from school for several weeks on the way into the Leaving. They walked away together to where Brother Placid had left his bicycle out on the road and stood talking there for some time. My father was silent when he returned to the row of ridges. We worked on until the light began to fail.
>
> As we were covering the new part of the pit with rushes, my father spoke as if he had given lengthy consideration to what he had to say. 'It seems the Brothers think they may be able to make something out of you if you're prepared to work. You better get yourself ready this evening to go to school tomorrow.'

John repaid Brother Placid's confidence with hard work and in the summer of 1953 became one of just three students, alongside Thomas Flanagan of Knockcroghery and Ed O'Connor of Roscommon Town, to be awarded a university scholarship by the County Council. Just like Young Mahoney of *The Dark*, John had found in education a means to liberate himself:

> without realizing it, through the pleasures of the mind, I was beginning to know and to love the world. The Brothers took me in, set me down and gave me tools. I look back on my time there with nothing but gratitude, as years of luck and privilege, and, above all, of grace, actual grace.

John's English teacher at the school was Frank Mannion, a Galway man who is remembered affectionately in *Memoir* as 'the ramrod-straight ex-army officer' with twin addictions to whiskey and golf. Lionel Gallagher, John's schoolmate, and son of the garda sergeant in Carrick, has vivid memories of this unorthodox presence:

> Mr. Mannion was an excellent teacher who gave us a love of literature. He was also lazy especially where the marking of essays was concerned. He set us one essay for every week-end but he was very

> selective in the way they were marked. One, or at most two, would be picked from the pile, thoroughly gone through and read out to the class on the following Wednesday. These were the cream of the crop. The rest were skimmed over and hurled at the heads of their authors with force and contempt.

Gallagher's initial spell with Mr Mannion saw his essays regularly chosen for praise. But the dynamic changed when he entered his Leaving Certificate year. Both this group, Gallagher's group, and the year below were taught together in the same room. A new boy, a year younger than Gallagher, arrived as part of the other class. This boy was someone who quickly cast the others into shade:

> In my first year in that room my essays nearly always made the grade and I fondly imagined a literary career on the horizon. In my final year only one student's work got the V. I. P. treatment as Sean had joined our class. We all realised that what he wrote was well above anything the rest of us produced and we soon ceased to compete.

The coming of the Presentation Brothers to Carrick was not John's only lucky break in these crucial adolescent years. While Mr Mannion encouraged him to read beyond the curriculum by lending him Dickens volumes from his own library, there came further good fortune. A more important source, especially in a home all but devoid of serious reading material, became the library of the nearby Moroney house. In the Ireland of John's youth, there were ever-present constraints. As he summarised the matter: 'There were few books in our house, and reading for pleasure was not approved of. It was thought to be dangerous, like pure laughter.' Patrick Kavanagh, having the eponymous Tarry Flynn of his 1948 novel summon up sins for a priest in the confessional, provides him with a telling opening gambit: 'I read books, Father.' The waking hours in this country, rather than being spent loitering over books, needed to be used practically and productively each day:

Time was filled by necessary work, always exaggerated: sleep, Gaelic football, prayer, gossip, religious observance, the giving of advice – ponderously delivered, and received in stupor – Civil War politics and the eternal business that Proust describes as 'Moral Idleness.' This was confined mostly to the new emerging classes – civil servants, policemen, doctors, teachers, tillage inspectors.

For John to meet Willie and Andy Moroney, father and son, in the midst of this dull, anti-intellectual world proved a blessing. They were among the last of Roscommon's Protestant Anglo-Irish, the owners of what might be termed a small Big House, 'surrounded by a huge orchard and handsome stone outhouses'. Sent to buy apples there as a boy, John fell into conversation with Willie about books and 'was given the run of the library'. The books John borrowed over the years of his adolescence ranged from the seriousness of Shakespeare to the racier romps of Jeffery Farnol. There were classic novels by Dickens and Walter Scott, mixed with Zane Grey westerns and 'many, many books about the Rocky Mountains'. As he elaborated: 'Every week or fortnight, for years, I'd return with five or six books in my oilcloth shopping bag and take five or six away. Nobody gave me direction or advice.' Why, John often wondered, did his stern, workaholic father tolerate these trips to visit the Moroneys? He answered his own question in striking terms:

> I can only put it down to a prejudice in favour of the gentle, eccentric Moroneys, and Protestants in general. At the time, Protestants were pitied because they were bound for hell in the next world, and they were considered to be abstemious, honest, and morally more correct than the general run of our fellow Catholics.

The Sergeant's respect for Protestants was inherited by his son, and Connacht's declining Anglo-Irish class become a staple of John's fiction, from Mrs Grey of 'Christmas' to Colonel and Mrs Sinclair of 'Oldfashioned'.

To be a writer, John insists, one must first be a reader. As his imagination developed under the sway of the Moroneys' library and the support of his teachers in Carrick, there dawned on him a sense that another life, far beyond the world of the barracks, might be possible.

The idea began germinating as he rowed alone on the river, the one place where he felt truly liberated from the tyrannies of home:

> If I didn't want to fish, I rowed into an inlet, and among the reeds and drowning leaves I read. When I woke out of the book, I would come into the drone of flies, the sudden splash of a fish, the whine of the saws deep in Oakport and the far, far distant noises of the farms. Over many days and months, gradually, a fantastical idea formed. Why take on any single life – a priest, a soldier, teacher, doctor, airman – if a writer could create all these people far more vividly? In that one life of the mind, the writer could live many lives and all of life. I had not even the vaguest idea how books came into being, but the dream took hold, and held.

A life in writing had begun.

The winning of the County Council Scholarship meant that John could now leave home and go to study at UCG. The final pages of *The Dark* are, in this respect, very close to straight autobiography except that rather than give up his place at university to join the Electricity Supply Board, as Young Mahoney chooses, John left Galway once he was offered a place at St Patrick's teacher-training college in Dublin. Catching the bus from outside Daly's on Bridge Street in Boyle, John made his way to his digs with Mrs Flaherty on Galway's Prospect Hill and formally entered the university on 7 October 1953 with a view to studying for a degree in agricultural science.

'Nobody from your house', thinks Young Mahoney, 'had ever reached a University before.' Not surprisingly, he finds it difficult to settle, to accept fully the realisation of a long-held ambition:

> You were only hours here yet, and it was not easy to keep hold of the dream, wild grass and sea and broken fish-boxes same as anywhere,

> this was the University town, but it was more solid concrete and shapes and names with the sea and sky and loneliness than any dream.

This sense of unease is brought to a head within a week of arrival when Young Mahoney is confronted with a harsh truth: the university will be no escape but offers rather a bitter, utilitarian world, a seedbed of narrow bourgeois values confirmed by one lecturer in an opening address: '"If there are any among you who have literary ambitions the evidence would seem to point to a dosshouse or a jail as a more likely place of genesis than a University."' This negative view of university life is confirmed for Mahoney twice over: by his failure to attend a freshers' dance, so overcome is he with shyness, and by his unjust expulsion from a physics lecture the following day by a pompous professor for the crime of smiling.

On 23 October 1953, having endured near-identical experiences to his fictional creation, John left the university, just over a fortnight after his arrival. The decision to take up a place in St Pat's was straightforward. Teaching, as well as having been his beloved mother's former profession, would allow him time to write in the generous holidays and after school hours:

> These were all the means I needed to follow my dream. The guilt I felt at turning my back half-heartedly – on the death in life that was the priest's choice and on that dear promise to say Mass – I was able to partially resolve by telling myself that teaching was my mother's profession and was sometimes called the second priesthood. In all this there was much confusion and ignorance as well as long suppressed adolescent emotions, but the idea that first took shape in the tarred boat among the reeds and drowning leaves under the dark Oakport woods that I would write was now as clear as a single star.

* * *

Late in life, composing *Memoir*, John asked Liam Kelly, his distant cousin and friend, to do some research. Kelly, an accomplished local historian, was happy to help in any way he could. John wished to learn about his paternal grandfather. His father's father had been airbrushed out of family lore, though John had vivid memories of his father's mother, Bridget Leddy, who lived with them in the townland of Knockanroe outside Ballinamore when his mother was teaching in Lisacarn national school.

Bridget forms one of the many superbly realised portraits in *Memoir*: 'She had been a local beauty and was vain and boastful. She was forever running down the poor land of Leitrim and its poor-looking inhabitants.' John never knew his grandfather, and neither Bridget nor her son ever spoke of him:

> There were rumours that my father was illegitimate, that his father was a bar owner in New York who had come home to marry the local beauty and returned to New York with the intention of selling the bar. The more probable history is that he was a small farmer or labourer who died soon after marrying my grandmother.

The tale of the New York barkeep, itself a version of George Moore's masterful short story 'Homesickness', is first told in *The Leavetaking*, where the narrator's grandmother and her son have been abandoned in their little coastal community. This place is an amalgam of Achill (where McGahern completed writing the novel in 1973) and a nameless Donegal village. Mother and son live in vain hope for letters from America: 'For some years small sums came regularly but there was no mention of the bar or any immediate possibility of his return and then suddenly the small sums stopped.'

In fact, the true story of the other John McGahern is stranger than fiction. John's grandparents, John McGahran and Bridget Leddy, were married on 22 November 1900. This date comes according to the Scrabby, County Cavan parish records. There is nothing odd, incidentally, about the spelling of the former's surname. Multiple versions appear in records. Their son Frank's surname, when he made the *Derry Journal* as part of the Burtonport wake case, was spelled McAhern. The couple, after they got married, lived in the townland of Kilsarn in County Cavan, and in the 1901 Census for that townland, John McGahran is said to be the head of the family. Bridget is stated to be four years older than her husband, an unusual feature for the time. While she is listed as thirty-five years old, her husband John is listed as thirty-one years old. According to the civil birth records, their son 'Francis Magaharn' was born later that year on 22 December 1901 in Kilsarn.

Liam Kelly presented this information to John McGahern: that his grandparents were married in November 1900 and that their son Francis was born in December 1901. Some months later, John informed Kelly that he had discovered new and startling information: shortly after his son was born, John McGahran had committed himself to Mullingar mental hospital. Hospital records for 1911 have him listed as resident there, suffering from 'hereditary melancholia', a condition that had affected him for the previous fourteen years and three months. Frank McGahern regularly visited his father in Mullingar while continuing to keep up the pretence that the man was no more.

By the time of the 1911 Census, none of the McGahran family was living in the townland of Kilsarn. Instead, we find Bridget McGahern to be head of the house, living with her son Francis in the nearby townland of Enaghan, across the border in County Longford. Bridget, stated to be thirty-five years old in 1901, is now, ten years later, said to be fifty-two. While she had no occupation listed in the 1901 Census, she is now listed as a seamstress, one way of getting an income at a time of want. Francis McGahern is said to be a nine-year-old 'scholar' who can both read and write.

The civil death record states that John McGahern died in Mullingar mental hospital from 'terminal pulmonary tuberculosis' on 14 April 1940. He appears to have spent more than thirty years, and perhaps nearer forty years, institutionalised.

John writes in *Memoir* about his grandmother going into 'the poorhouse' in Carrick-on-Shannon and dying there. The death certificate states that 'Bridget McGaharn' of Knockanroe, Ballinamore died in Carrick-on-Shannon District Hospital on 22 January 1939. She was described as a seventy-six-year-old widow and an old-age pensioner. She was, in fact, not a widow since her husband outlived her by fifteen months, but he had been removed from the picture long before that juncture.

What can we say, ultimately, of Frank McGahern? He had few confidants and always prioritised family over friendship. 'I was never any good at getting on with people', admits Moran in *Amongst Women*. But he was, like all of us, far from one-dimensional. He could be funny and charming; he was a decent footballer at a time when Cavan dominated Ulster. He continued to remain a loyal Breffni man as the county lorded it over the province through John's childhood and adolescence, winning the All Ireland championship in 1947, 1948 and again in 1952.

A day out in Clones for the Ulster Final was a treasured memory for young Seán, as he captures vividly in 'The Creamery Manager' when the unfortunate man of the title, having embezzled from his employer, tries to bribe the local sergeant with a trip to the big game:

> Once the seniors came on the field he started at the sudden power and speed with which the ball was driven about. The game was never close. Cavan drew gradually ahead to win easily. Such was the air of unreality he felt, of three men watching themselves watch a game, that he was glad to buy oranges from a seller moving between seats, to hand the fruit around, to peel the skin away, to taste the bitter juice. Only once did he start and stir uncomfortably, when Guard Casey remarked about the powerful Cavan fullback who was roughing up the Tyrone forwards: 'The Gunner is taking no prisoners today.'

The warmest short description of the Sergeant is left by a son-in-law:

> Team lists in *The Anglo-Celt* show him playing at left-full-back for the Gowna senior football team in 1918. He may have had a motorcycle. He was a boatman and fisherman.
>
> He could swim. He was a card player. Frank had been formed in the strong and confident folk culture of the Gowna Valley and never

> shed that heritage. He could sing. He could play the fiddle and was a useful traditional step dancer, recalling later that he had frequently engaged in the specialised activity of dancing on a kitchen door.

Frank McGahern, if all of these things, rarely revealed them to his eldest child.

The image of a young man returning dutifully if dolefully to the home farm is a recurrent one across John's work, a scenario described at its finest in 'Gold Watch', where the narrator tells his lover, 'There was more caution than any love or charity in my habitual going home. It was unattractive and it had been learned in the bitter school of my father.' Asked if he had experienced any paternal kindness as a child, the narrator is unswerving:

> 'When I was younger.' I had to smile. 'He looked on it as weakness. I suspect he couldn't deal with it. Anyhow it always redoubled his fury. He was kind, too, in fits, when he was feeling good about things. That was even more unacceptable. And that phrase from the Bible is true that after enough suffering a kind of iron enters the soul.'

2
A Secret Life
1953–60

> . . . only in Dublin could I disappear into my own
> and my secret life without being noticed.
>
> JOHN McGAHERN, *Memoir*

Located at 7 Eden Quay in Dublin's north city centre, the Astor Cinema opened on 12 March 1953 with a showing of Vittorio De Sica's *Bicycle Thieves*. The first art-house cinema to operate in the city, its glory days coincided with John's years living in or around Dublin. By the 1970s, the venue had gone over to mainstream films, eventually closing on 16 June 1984 with a double bill of *Adventures of a Private Eye* and *Screwballs*. Although the foyer was converted into a video rental shop, the auditorium lay unused and fell into dereliction. The cinema was demolished in November 2002.

In late 1953, the idea of demise entered no one's mind. The Astor was a mere six months in operation and vibrant. Just turned nineteen, and newly arrived in the city from Cootehall, John went there to see *Casque d'or*, Jacques Becker's masterful portrayal of the Parisian demi-monde during La Belle Époque. He went back and rewatched the film every day for a week. The story of an ill-fated love affair between characters Marie and Manda, played by Simone Signoret and Serge Reggiani, the plot was loosely based on an infamous 1902 love triangle between the prostitute Amélie Élie and gang leaders Manda and Leca.

From the opening scene, featuring groups of young men and women boating carefree on the Seine, to the film's tragic conclusion, *Casque d'or* is a masterpiece of French cinema. The final sequence is particularly celebrated: after Manda's surrender to the police, the film shows Marie arriving at night, with one of Leca's former henchmen, at a cheap inn in the city where she rents a room. No immediate clues are provided to the audience as to why this swerve is happening. Only later comes the revelation that the room in which she is staying overlooks the courtyard in which Manda is to be guillotined.

François Truffaut, a fervent admirer of Becker's work, had particular admiration for this scene: 'If you're at all interested in how stories are constructed, you cannot fail to admire the ingenuity of the plot, particularly the strong, oblique, unexpected way it gets abruptly to Manda's execution in a scene that is as beautiful as it is mysterious.' Truffaut concluded that the film proves an important artistic truth: 'we can look at the picturesque and bloody past and evoke it with tenderness and violence'.

Cinema provided a new and welcome refuge for this shy young man, another world into which he could escape and become absorbed. John was thirteen when he saw his first film. He and his father travelled to Dublin in late September 1948 to watch Cavan retain the All Ireland football title they had won the previous year at New York's Polo Grounds. The night before the game, they watched *Boys Town*, starring Spencer Tracy and Mickey Rooney, before witnessing Cavan beat Mayo the next day by a single point.

This weekend must have been, for both the Sergeant and his son, one of unforgettable excitement. The narrator of *The Dark* experiences cinema's charms with O'Donnell, a fellow student in Galway, during his brief stay in the city when they attend a western together. Although the narrator feels awkward when O'Donnell begins to sing along with the soundtrack, this emotion dissipates when the action commences:

> And then with relief the cowboy was running, there was silence, the cinema was lost in what was happening on the one screen. There was a feeling of being set free to share in all this running and excitement, the strong righteous man and the noble woman against the hirelings. Out on the wet street afterwards there were several heroes with gun

hand crooked and unflinching walk ready to shoot their way through to the world.

'What did you think?' O'Donnell asked.

'It was great,' you managed to say out of the choking after effect of the emotion, all pictures were marvellous, you hadn't seen enough to compare, people who said one was good and another bad had some secret knowledge.

In the mid-1950s, there were eight cinemas within a half-mile radius of the General Post Office on O'Connell Street, and Dublin was a city of enthusiastic filmgoers. John recalls this era in precisely those terms: 'I remember seeing *Julius Caesar* with Gielgud and Brando playing to full houses in the Metropole. At weekends, cinema tickets were sold on the black market.' Among those films most admired, as John developed his tastes in cinema, were Marcel Carné's *Les Enfants du paradis*, Jean Renoir's *The Rules of the Game*, Luis Buñuel's *Nazarín*, Ingmar Bergman's *Wild Strawberries*, Mikhail Kalatozov's *The Cranes Are Flying* and, in later years, William Friedkin's *The French Connection*. 'It would be a brave man', John commented in a 1987 interview, 'who would say that almost any novel was superior to *Monsieur Hulot's Holiday*.' But cinemagoing, in its passivity, could never replace reading for John as the supreme distraction: 'So much is done for you. In reading, you have to imagine your own screen. The reader's imagination is itself an artist in a way that I do not think the moviegoer's can ever be.'

Any leisure activity was a balm in the rather forbidding confines of St Patrick's College, Drumcondra. This institution, dominated by a deeply conservative church ethos, was ruled over by the black-clad dean of students Fr Johnston, a sinister presence known to the students as 'The Bat'. John remembers his experience on returning there in 2003 to be awarded an honorary doctorate: 'We were being groomed as non-commissioned officers to the priests in the running of the different parishes throughout the country, cogs in an organizational wheel, secondary to the priest in all things, including education.' The trainee teachers were treated not as men but as boarders in a strict school, with The Bat happy to mete out rough justice:

> I saw people beaten. There was a friend of mine, a very intelligent boy called Éanna Ó hEithir, a brother of Breandán Ó hEithir. He was at a table in the refectory with a rough group who worked in tunnels in Glasgow and places like that during the holidays. They were very tough and big, and there was a scarcity of food. If you had any manners you'd starve, because the food disappeared.

He further recalled: 'Ó hEithir complained that he hadn't got any food, that he had a right to complain; and I saw him get beaten up in front of the whole refectory by the Dean because he insisted on complaining.'

Despite these dark early impressions, John is characteristically unwilling to think of the Church's influence as entirely negative and could see for himself the high quality of teachers St Pat's turned out in comparison with those colleagues with whom he worked in London of the late 1960s. Though life in Drumcondra was strict and cloistered, it allowed the teenage McGahern his first taste of city life, a freedom that is recalled by Patrick Moran in *The Leavetaking*:

> Between classes and study and meals we circled the path round the football field in twos or threes or fours talking of women, the old lime trees and high wall between us and the red neon of the Drum Cinema, the growling roar of the distant city. For a few hours we were allowed out Wednesday and Saturday afternoons, and they found us in cinemas. Sunday was the one day we had completely free, though the gates were shut at ten. Sunday afternoon we went to dances, most of the girls at the afternoon dances from the girls' Training College across the city.

The training college in question was Carysfort, where John's mother had studied to be a teacher thirty years before. Even these afternoon dances had the whiff of the thurible about them: 'The queue in Granby Row that warm Sunday afternoon for the Kingsway, Matt Talbot's altar against the wall, the little wooden kneeler and statue of the Virgin dust-coated and shabby, dustcoated too the glass jars in which fresh daffodils and narcissi stood.'

The summer of 1954 saw John, like many of his St Pat's peers, labouring on a London building site alongside countrymen who had travelled in their thousands for work made possible by Britain's post-war reconstruction. A passage in *Memoir* emphasises how immersed in literature this young man had already become: 'When I walked off the boat at Holyhead to the waiting London train – and thought of Shakespeare, Milton, Dickens, all the great English writers I had read and studied – I felt awe, as if I was stepping on to sacred ground.' He would stay variously in Catholic hostels such as St Anne's on the Underwood Road or with his sisters Rosaleen and Breedge as they began to make their way as nurses in Whipps Cross Hospital, Leytonstone.

The grim world of the Irish navvy is one he captures in 'Hearts of Oak and Bellies of Brass'. The story revolves around a day on a Whitechapel building site, the dilapidated streets peopled by prostitutes and vagrants. The narrator has more education – two years of secondary school – than the others and hates to be reminded of this factor. This depersonalised world in which his colleagues are named mostly for their counties of origin – Sligo, Galway, Tipperary – sees comfort taken wherever it can be found, whether at the bottom of a pint glass in the Rose and Crown or in the brothel ('Marge and Kathleen like dying elephants in the condemned row'). All sentiment has been removed:

> There was no boredom those first days, though time was slower and there was more pain, drive to push the shovel in blistered hands with raw knee in the same time as the others, a shovel slyly jabbed against a thigh as if you've stumbled, and the taunt, 'Too much wankin' that's what's wrong,' in the way fowl will peck to death a weakened hen.

This bleakest of McGahern stories concludes with the torture of Jocko, a straying Scottish wino ('the pint bottle of violet-coloured spirit swinging wide from one pocket'). However accurate this portrayal, the approach was not for the faint of heart, with John Montague describing its effects: 'McGahern's stripped style, his emotional honesty, and his ear for dialogue make him a harrowing witness of the void which underlies a good deal of Irish, and perhaps modern, life.'

London in those summers was not all hardship and loneliness. One friendship sprouted from a chance hostel meeting with a young man from Kilkeel, County Down, named Tony Whelan, who worked in a bookshop on Old Broad Street and remembers their first encounter in the hostel that smelled of 'male sweat and boiled cabbage'. As Whelan recounted decades later, there was a meeting of minds:

> People came and went in the hostel and it was not unusual to have a new room-mate when you returned from holiday. When I got up to my room there was a fresh-faced young man sitting on one of the beds pulling on his socks. He introduced himself in a soft accent as Seán McGahern. He told me he was a student at St. Patrick's Drumcondra, a training college for teachers, and had come over to work on the buildings and earn some money during the summer. I liked him immediately and believe that he may have found in me a kindred spirit.

The friendship endured for a number of years, the men seeing a good deal of each other in Dublin and London, with John visiting Whelan's Kilkeel homeplace on one occasion. Both men had writerly ambitions, with John making early attempts at poetry. In July 1958, he sent a forlorn letter: 'I still teach in Dublin. I often fear I shall grow old among the Primers and children who care as little about learning as I do about teaching.' Along with the letter were included some poems bearing the clear influence of W. B. Yeats, Gerard Manley Hopkins and Patrick Kavanagh. Typical is this effort, which he titles 'The Spoiled Poet Takes His Ordination Vows (Temptation)':

> No faith or love ordains me:
> I take the living death with hands
> That feel no flesh or blood in cups

Worn frail from centuries of use,
Too much religion have my people
From rearing priests on stingy acres
Till they have come too priestly now
To root the bitter soil and breed.
No want of serving man of God
Bids me relinquish common ways
The comfortable closeness of flesh,
Of thigh and mouth for sodden dreams.
None but the terror of blindfold lust
Has put this chalice to my lips
That I may drain its anguish part,
The confusion of eternity.

While this poetry's quality gives us little sense of the prose master to come, the preoccupations on show remain constant in the early fiction: religious vocation, the torture of lust, failure to renounce the flesh for a life in Christ, the idea of human existence as a vale of tears. John is chary of showing his hand and concludes the letter so diffidently that he places his sign-off in parenthesis: '(I would not have sent you these only you asked; I picked them because they seem different from one another; transcribing them and comparing them with their passion they seem very slight.)'

Shortly after the composition of these prentice pieces, verse was cast aside for good, though John always maintained a love for poetry across a wide array of genres and times: Andrew Marvell, William Wordsworth, W. B. Yeats, Rainer Maria Rilke, T. S. Eliot and Philip Larkin remained particular favourites.

After graduating in the summer of 1955, John did not get a school immediately since he was unwilling to play the patronage game with The Bat. Before eventually being appointed in Athboy, County Meath, he went home to help roof a beautiful stone house in Grevisk on the road between Carrick and Boyle – part of the old Rockingham estate – that the newly remarried Sergeant had purchased.

Agnes McShera had become John's stepmother the previous summer while he was away working on the buildings in London. Though he could see that she had made a difference for the good in keeping a neat and tidy house, he worried for his youngest sister Dympna and brother Frankie. Under this new regime, he feared, they were 'confused and unhappy'. While John and Agnes would retain a veneer of civility over the years, they disliked and mistrusted each other.

The Sergeant evinced a fresh interest in John, hoping that he might persuade his eldest child to find a local school and possibly help with the land at home. 'He was at his most charming, as if he was playing a new person or part, and only in odd flashes was there a hint or threat of violence. As before, when we were in Aughawillan, he was courting me.'

At the end of the holidays, John was once again free of his father's orbit. Or so he thought. With his domestic arrangements now considerably altered, Frank McGahern considered it time to make a new will, with John as executor. A characteristically contrary document, the will sowed division among Frank's children and new bride, landing the ensuing discord in a most unwelcome fashion onto John's lap. The house and lands at Grevisk were left to Frankie once he reached the age of twenty-one. Agnes would be permitted residence during her lifetime, unless she remarried. Agnes was also left £200, as was Monica. Dympna was to get £300, Margaret £150 and Breedge £150. Rosaleen was left one shilling, and John was left nothing.

While such paternal rejection must have hurt, John was now at least earning a pensionable salary for the first time and finding his way in the world of work. O'Growney National School in Athboy catered for the girls and the boys of the area but divided the sexes, fairly typically, into two distinct groups. One of his students, Paddy Duffy, remembers the young teacher's kindness in praising an essay the boy wrote on greyhounds after attending a coursing meeting in Paddy Gilsenan's field: 'When I wrote my composition the next week for my fantastic teacher, John McGahern, I wrote of owning a greyhound which was as sleek as the wind, clear-eyed as a fox, but gentle with his prey, which his master (me of course!) always let go.' Paddy's memories are sharpened by his teacher's kindness: 'The reason I remember the line from the composition was the lovely pencil set which McGahern gave me as one of the little prizes he used to give out on a Friday morning.'

For the academic year 1955–56, John took digs in Dempsey's on Upper Bridge Street. Dempsey's restricted itself to taking in only male lodgers and housed various AI (artificial insemination) men, teachers and bank officials. Young women teachers stayed in a small hotel on Main Street, the Darnley Lodge, known to the wits in Dempsey's as 'the Four Courts'. John's story 'A Ballad' catches the boisterous, laddish nature of some of his fellow lodgers, who were in the habit of throwing shoes at the ceiling beneath his room when they came in from a night's drinking, shouting, 'the poet, the poet'.

Not owning a car like most of the others in Dempsey's, John would habitually take the bus into Dublin at weekends. He attended afternoon dances in venues such as the Metropole on O'Connell Street or the National on Parnell Square, often having to leave before the final dance to catch the last bus home. Such a life of daylight city dancing is recalled in 'Like All Other Men':

> Nurses, students, actors and actresses, musicians, some prostitutes, people who worked in restaurants and newspapers, nightwatchmen, a medley of the old and very young, came to these afternoon dances. Michael Duggan came every Saturday and Sunday. He was a teacher of Latin and history in a midlands town forty miles from Dublin, and each Friday he came in on the evening bus to spend the whole weekend round the cinemas and restaurants and dancehalls of O'Connell Street.

Those dance floors would become, many years later, the fertile jousting grounds that gave birth to the imaginative sensibilities of *The Pornographer*.

Joan Dempsey, daughter of the boarding house, has fond memories of their quiet, young lodger:

> Seán was only about 20. Mr Tom Keenan was the headmaster. And Seán, he adored my mother . . . He was always with my mother and father. He wouldn't go into the dining room, he sat in the kitchen . . . Or in the yard feeding the hens with my mother. He loved my father, Stephen. He'd go to mass then on a Sunday, she'd call him back: 'What are you doing with the big heavy boots going to mass.' And there were studs on them. Then she'd call him back again: 'Comb your hair now before you go to mass.' The hair would never be combed . . . He was a gentle, quiet man. I had a lot of AI men staying that time. He never went anywhere with them, they used to be laughing at him. He was always scribbling on a little piece of paper and one of the lads used to say, 'I think he sleeps with his eyes open.' But we didn't know, of course, who we were dealing with that time.

Two of John's stories, 'A Ballad' and 'Crossing the Line', are inspired by the year spent in Athboy, with the Bridge Restaurant standing in for Dempsey's in the former. 'A Ballad' sees the narrator sharing digs with two AI men, Cronin and Ryan, and a cavalier civil engineer and former Cavan county footballer named O'Reilly, whose alleged inappropriate and drunken sexual misbehaviour towards his pregnant girlfriend Rachael forms the central thread of the story.

The narrator, a schoolteacher, agrees to accompany Ryan out to the Gaeltacht farms, where mostly Mayo Irish-speakers had been relocated across the country under a government scheme to bolster the language: 'These people had been transplanted here from the seaboard as part of de Valera's dream; lighthouses put down on the plain from which Gaelic would spread from tongue to tongue throughout the land like pentecostal flame.' The story, one of John's funniest, ends with a sighting in Dublin several years later of O'Reilly and Rachael on Henry Street, 'both wearing sheepskin coats', accompanied by two beautiful children.

Of the other Athboy story, 'Crossing the Line', about industrial unrest in a school, John commented many years after its composition on the inevitable gap between fact and fiction.

> An old man who was a teacher there, and appears in 'Crossing the Line', came to see me recently. He was in his nineties. I looked at this story again and what interested me was how little of it was based on fact. The man that was the prototype is not like the man in the story at all. So life is of very little use to fiction; it has to be re-imagined or changed or altered in some way.

The insistence that artifice could not afford too much reality remained a constant rule.

After a year in Athboy, John moved on to teach boys at St Joseph's Christian Brothers School in Sunday's Gate, Drogheda. Though contented enough with Athboy, the move to the larger provincial town appealed. Living in Drogheda made it easier to travel by bus or by train in and out of Dublin, where he had begun studying for a night degree in 1955, ultimately graduating with a Bachelor of Arts in English, Irish and Economics from University College Dublin (UCD) in 1958.

The new post, as one of John's former students relates, proved a small revelation:

> Years later, he confessed as much, telling me that on his first day of teaching in the town of Drogheda, he had asked a head brother whether he had any advice to offer; and the simple, singular answer was: 'Bate it into them.' McGahern was the kind of teacher I imagine D. H. Lawrence to have been, sensitive to the needs of young boys, but probably ill-fitted to some of the extra-curricular institutional demands.

This moment was an inauspicious start to what would be a brief sojourn on the banks of the Boyne, prompting John to recall his own happy schooldays in Carrick-on-Shannon, where the incumbent order always remained keen to differentiate itself from other teaching orders: 'The Presentation Brothers were much more liberal and they encouraged reading.'

John continued to write, taking digs a three-minute walk from work with Mrs Byrne in Hardman's Gardens, occasionally socialising in the

Glenmorgan Café on Stockwell Lane. This business also provided lodging to single male workers, among them Stephen Dempsey, a son of John's former hosts in Athboy. Another individual resident in Drogheda at the time was Joe Kennedy, a young newspaperman from Dublin, then working on the local *Argus*. He would correspond with John in later years and publish his work in a wide variety of fora, from the *Evening Herald* to the *Sunday World*. Kennedy would form part of the inspiration for the character of the larger-than-life newspaper editor Maloney in *The Pornographer*.

John had no hesitation in applying when a job was advertised that autumn in Scoil Eoin Báiste, Clontarf – or 'Belgrove' as this school was (and still is) better known. To get back to Dublin would simplify his university studies and allow the sort of invisibility he desired, the sort always impossible in a small market town. The headmaster, Mícheál Kelleher, a deeply conservative, nationalist, teetotal Catholic, liked the idea of hiring a young man from down the country. Maloney, the headmaster interviewing Patrick Moran of *The Leavetaking*, comments in this vein when Moran says he would like to assist his younger siblings' chances:

> 'Actually, my wife remarked on that in your application. It's an old country tradition. The first out of the nest helps the others out. City people are all right in their way but they don't have those good solid traditions behind them that we who come from the country have.'

Born and raised on a small farm near Bandon in west Cork, Kelleher was appointed in 1944 and is vividly brought to life in *The Leavetaking* as the balding Maloney, a figure who offers complete commitment. Working his last day with him, Moran reflects:

> 'Old fanatical peasant I'll miss you,' I think as I watch him go towards the teachers' room, ready to rout them out of any argument into the playground at the first stroke of the bell, a little stooping as he goes, the bulge of the cane in the shoulder, obsessively stroking the bald

head. He gives the same narrow care to this school as his father must have given to the crops and cattle of their small southern farm, 'This school is me. I'll go through stone walls for this school.'

Kelleher's world view was shaped by tragedy. When he was a youngster, his father had a much-loved, mentally disabled man working on the farm – a 'duine le Dia', as he would have been known to Mícheál. This story he told to colleagues many times:

> This poor old devil went to Bandon town one day, with a horse and cart for something or other. While he was gone, he had to cross a stream to get there. Then once he crossed it the IRA blew the bridge; a band of Tans appeared and had no bridge to drive over. Meanwhile this poor devil appears with a horse and cart; they made him fill in the stones to have enough for the lorry to cross, then they shot him.

John did not share the politics of his boss, though he was capable of admiring the man's iron certainty. In *The Leavetaking*, the school headmaster enters into debate with Patrick Moran on his return from sabbatical in London about the pros and the cons of life in England, about the bitter legacy left by empire:

> 'There is great tolerance there,' I saw it was quite hopeless.
>
> 'That is because they don't have the power anymore. They'd tramp on you still if they had power. What did they do here for centuries? They tramped us into the dirt.'
>
> 'That's ended now. They've left.'
>
> 'Yes, but only when they were kicked out. They're not out of all of it yet either. But they will be one day, *buiochas le Dia*.'
>
> We were sailing into dangerous waters, and yet I loved his narrow passion, faithful to the person that he was, so alien to my uncertainty; but I was glad when he looked at his watch.

This admiration is tempered by Moran's memories of encountering, when he worked as a barman, a former British soldier:

> I grew ashamed of my own voice in its use of the general clichés, and thought of little Clapson who used to drink in the pub, tank mechanic in the Sahara. 'We never were in much danger as we moved behind the lines. The worst was the sand and the stink of flesh in the burnt out tanks. You could hear the flesh sizzle in the hot metal.' His wife, who typed at Yardleys, small and grey and infinitely gentle.

Whatever John's politics, he had nothing but fond regard for the ordinary Londoners he lived among in the later 1960s and for the Geordies he would come to know in the mid-1970s, when the Troubles were at their height back home.

Belgrove had grown rapidly from the late 1940s onwards, reflecting the expansion of Dublin's northern suburbs, with their concrete thoroughfares and rows of semi-detached houses, described in *The Pornographer* as 'the lower-middle-class roads and drives and avenues of brown-tiled semis'. Here, in this vast new suburban community, a particular future was being faced: 'A whole generation of young marrieds must have grown tired of the flap of nappies on lines and summer lawnmowers.' Located along Seafield Road, the school separated boys and girls across different buildings; over the course of John's time there, the boys were divided between juniors and seniors, with John teaching variously across ages eight to twelve.

Classes were very large. Dónal Cleary, when he arrived to teach there in 1954, began with a group of seventy-six boys in the former ballroom of Belgrove House, the original school building. By 1956, there were over 700 boys enrolled, and John commonly taught classes of over forty students. Despite the large numbers and the often makeshift, prefabricated nature of the school infrastructure, Belgrove was making a name for itself, under Kelleher's headmastership, as one of the best primary schools on the Northside.

John makes his official first appearance in the school's books on 21 December 1956, though he did not teach his first class until after Christmas. He quickly found a first-floor bedsit to rent at 57 Howth

Road in the house of the Lightfoot family, where he would continue to live until September 1964. Reports and reminiscences about Belgrove in these days and about John's merits as a teacher are mixed. The school was the recipient of a Carlisle and Blake award in the early 1960s, an honour bestowed on schools with teachers of exceptional merit only.

However, like almost every other school in the country, academic excellence was often produced through stick more than through carrot. The publication of John's letters in 2021 brought back troubling memories for one past pupil, someone who felt moved to write to the *London Review of Books*:

> The school was a cruelty house, a repurposed Victorian farmhouse with outside sheds for toilets. The sadistic culture was well thought-through: a small number of outsiders, children who didn't fit, were focused on constantly for punishment. It brought the others into line.
>
> McGahern taught in the boys' section. My friend was a pupil then. He told me that McGahern often went off-syllabus with discussions of nature and literature that lit up the imagination. He did use the cane occasionally. In *The Leavetaking*, McGahern's character remembers the 'shock of the erection I got when I first beat a boy with a cane, taking pleasure in my supposed duty.' It was that kind of school.

One of John's former students with whom I had contact could not bear to recount the cruelty suffered in that classroom, with even the short exchanges we had prompting the return of vivid nightmares. Another former student recalled happier times:

> To everyone at Belgrove, McGahern was known as Seán; he is recalled by both colleagues and pupils as a gentle, quiet man, and a gifted teacher happy to turn to unusual teaching methods. He had bulging eyes that you couldn't look away from. His hair was unusual for a man in that it was fair to red in colour and wavy, curly. He had a look of Michael Caine about him (without glasses). My most outstanding memory of Seán was that he taught everything by story and it was

> written on the blackboard. The story was punctuated by 'An Lucha' (the mouse). So at various important breaks in the story on the blackboard he would have a mouse drawn. The mouse would first appear right before the first word and then so on at important intervals throughout the story. So the point being you followed the mouse and stopped when you got to the second mouse where Seán would explain everything that was written and not go on the second journey with 'An Lucha' until you fully understood the first and so on and so on to the end where 'An Lucha' got the cheese. When I first saw 'the mouse' as 'invented' by Apple for computers I roared laughing and thought, 'Apple didn't invent "An Lucha", Seán McGahern did.'

Another past pupil I met, whom John taught for third and fourth class, left with an impression of a quiet, distant, but occasionally strict taskmaster (a 'lonely man'), always dressed well in corduroys and tweed jacket:

> I saw him once in town, leaning against a lamp post, staring into the distance, dreaming. Normally if you saw a teacher you'd scatter, so to see a teacher in this way was unheard of. His voice never changed; it was soft and haunting. He was a great man for the compositions, and you'd be let off homework if you did a good job. He was able to keep control . . . There was a line . . . There were a few headbangers. Everyone got a clatter of the cane from time to time, but Mr McGahern was very fair, very soft. I liked him as a teacher. He was a great listener.

This seventy-four-year-old man, probed about accusations made in the past on Irish radio about McGahern being a violent and cruel teacher, sat quietly for some time, summoning up boyhood memories: 'He was very fair to me. He was a gentleman.'

Several of the boys John taught in these years went on to become men of influence, notable figures in the world. Among them were the writer and film director Neil Jordan and future attorney general John Rogers.

The latter remembers an intense, sometimes detached man: 'He would stand close to the window at the top of the class staring into the field at the back of the school as it then was. He would seem very preoccupied.'

Another pupil during the 1950s was the literary critic, author and university professor Declan Kiberd, who in later years would become reacquainted with John and have him teach on a postgraduate course at UCD. He has left an affectionate account of his teacher, a presence whom he could admire, even then, for an unusual reason ('the quality of his isolation'). The young Kiberd could discern important aspects in John's make-up:

> A good teacher (like the one in 'All Sorts of Impossible Things'), he could seem suddenly abstracted, as if caught up in a world elsewhere, quite distinct from our classroom. Even when he disciplined the boys, it was often done absent-mindedly, as if some emotion was being summoned which was no sooner called up than blocked off. It was only many years later that I realised he might well have been reliving the experience of being disciplined by his own father. I also had the impression, even at the time, that the disciplinary element of teaching in those days was something he privately hated and despised.

Ultimately, Kiberd's memory is of a lonesome, somewhat isolated figure with tastes that set him apart from colleagues:

> I think that McGahern himself was lonely in Belgrove as a teacher. Whenever it was my turn (it came around once a month) to wash the cups and saucers at break-time in the teachers' room, I noticed that he usually sat apart, reading a book or listening to John Arlott's cricket commentaries on a small transistor radio.

Kiberd concludes:

> I'm sure that his pay as a junior master was low but he always generously bought books out of his own money to award boys who did well in the end-of-year exams. I still have a copy of *Fairy Tales of*

> *Germany* (signed with congratulations by one Seán Mac Eathairn) – he read each of the tales aloud to the class before entrusting me with the copy.

This gifting of books or writing equipment to students remained a constant part of John's behaviour, from young Paddy Duffy in Athboy to his master's class in UCD of the late 1990s, all of whom he presented with a copy of a collection of Alistair MacLeod stories, *As Birds Bring Forth the Sun*.

Despite Belgrove's excellent reputation and favoured location in leafy Clontarf, John could see that beneath its calm exterior lay a hidden world. The best short account of this aspect is left in a letter to another teacher, the Belfast writer Michael McLaverty, from March 1960:

> Although most of the children in the school where I teach come from comfortable homes there is a small slum in the middle of Clontarf. This year I happen to have ten from there – eight to nine years old – and what I learn shakes me. Any scar will nearly always fester. I notice how they huddle apart from the other children in the playground. It is strange that while their shoes are leaking that they can always muster money for drill costumes or a shining new red tie and blue suit for First Communion – any outward show. Why I probably tell you these things is that only to day I discovered that the sweaty smell of decay, nauseatingly strong from some of them, comes from them sleeping in their clothes. It is difficult to reconcile the desire to do nothing but write ('I intend to give up this scribbling,' Byron said in one of his letters), even a cushioned civil service life, with all the human suffering about us.

Though the lengthy holidays and relatively short working days allowed him time to write, John could see that to be true to his artistic calling he would have to leave the classroom behind. Like anyone who takes teaching seriously, he found the work difficult and draining. 'I didn't enjoy teaching', he says in one late interview. 'I'm very suspicious of people who say they do. I think that if you do anything well, or even if you try to do anything well, it's hard work and it's painful. It means taking attention from yourself and giving it to the children, in the same sense that writing is simply giving it to the words; there is a certain discipline that is pleasurable, but I wouldn't call that enjoyable.'

The iron discipline that writing fiction would require was forged in earnest at 57 Howth Road. John's bedsit and its environs become recognisably the setting of a good deal of his work over the coming years, most consistently in *The Pornographer*:

> The long velvet curtain that was drawn on the half-open window stirred only faintly. A coal fire was set ready to light in the grate. The bed with damaged brass bells stood in the corner and shelves of books lined the walls. Books as well were piled untidily on the white mantel above the coal grate, on the bare dressing table. Beside the wardrobe a table lamp made out of a Chianti bottle lit the marble tabletop that had been a washstand once, lit the typewriter that rested on a page of old newspaper on the marble, lit an untouched ream of white pages beside it.

One can speculate what books might have stood on those shelves. John continued the reading habit acquired in the Moroneys' library. While never fetishising books as objects, he consumed a wide variety of literary texts. We can say for sure that W. B. Yeats was then, and would always be, John's greatest exemplar. 'The more we read of other literatures, and the more they were discussed', he remembers of these early Dublin days, 'the more clearly it emerged that not only was Yeats a very great poet but that almost singlehandedly he had, amazingly, laid down a whole framework in which an indigenous literature could establish traditions and grow.' Rilke, too, had started to become an influence, as had Kavanagh, Beckett and Eliot. A 1954 Bodley Head edition of *Ulysses* was a valued part of the young teacher's growing library, having been introduced to Joyce in the dorms of St Pat's by Éanna Ó hEithir, that Aran nephew of Liam O'Flaherty he had witnessed being beaten up by The Bat.

Though literary censorship was then peaking, accessing forbidden writing was not difficult. That said, within this censorious world, contact with the cultural institutions of the neighbouring island remained a crucial source of nourishment: 'Britain could no longer be blamed. In fact, certain British institutions, like Penguin Books, the BBC, the *Observer*, the *Sunday Times*, the *Listener*, became our windows on the world, and without them this place would have been far darker than it was.'

Howth Road became a writing laboratory, a forcing ground of the imagination, one of perhaps half a dozen rooms where we can say for sure that the works of John McGahern came into being; it was certainly the birthplace of both *The Barracks* and *The Dark*. The room remained a part of John's storehouse of images for the rest of his life.

Of his early attempts at writing in Dublin, John recalls:

> In many ways, it was an extension of reading as well as a kind of play. Words had been physical presences for me for a long time before, each word with its own weight, colour, shape, relationship, extending out into a world without end. Change any word in a single sentence and immediately all the other words demand to be rearranged.

The Howth Road bedsit is where playing with words first started to become something altogether more serious. A particularly evocative description of the place and its coastal neighbourhood is summoned up in 'Along the Edges' of the late 1970s:

> The next Saturday he stayed alone in the room, studying by the light of a bulb fixed on a Chianti bottle, the texts and diagrams spread out on newspaper that shielded his arms from the cold of the marble top that had once been a washstand, the faded velvet curtain drawn on the garden and hot day outside, on cries of the ice-cream wagons, on the long queues within the city for buses to the sea, on the sea of Dollymount and the swimmers going in off the rocks, pleasures sharpened a hundredfold by the drawn curtain. Finally, late in the afternoon, when he discovered that he had just reached the bottom

> of a page without taking in a single sentence, he left the room and went down to the front. At the corner shop he bought an orange and sat on a bench. The sea lay dazzling in the heat out past the Bull and Howth Head.

Howth to the north, Fairview to the south, Marino, Drumcondra and Griffith Avenue to the west: these coordinates became John's compass points during the crucial years of a developing artistic sensibility and cautious first steps in the writing of fiction.

John was drawn for many years to memories of these old stomping grounds. Fairview, in particular, provided much imaginative loam, as we see in this moment from *The Pornographer*:

> Spring was late, and when it came it was more like early summer. Fairview Park was full of flowers and young men, their trousers tucked into socks, kicking footballs under the greening trees, using their cast-off clothes to mark the goals. I had played with them once. They were mostly apprentice barmen on their day off. Corporation workmen started to assemble scaffolding and ladders and then to paint the bandstand.

We find his characters back again in the bars of Fairview for 'Sierra Leone', trying and failing to remain anonymous to the barman: 'For several months I had been frustrating all his attempts to get to know us, for we had picked Gaffneys because it was out of the way and we had to meet like thieves. Dublin was too small a city to give even our names away.'

Colm Tóibín, profiling John in 1985, remarks on the work's metropolitan sense of place: 'Indeed, there is no evocation of Dublin in the 1950s and 1960s as powerful as his.' Tóibín elaborates:

> He was living in Dublin. Over and over he went to the theatre, to the cheap seats in the Gate, where Lord Longford was putting on Shaw, Chekhov, Wilde, to the Gas Company where he saw Lorca's 'The House of Bernarda Alba' maybe ten times. The library in Fairview

was good, and beside Roche's Stores there was a man who sold books from a barrow at half-price.

One of the problems with *Memoir* as a record of John's life is that it focuses almost wholly on the early days in Leitrim and Roscommon, though it does include a short, lively section on the capital city towards the end. He writes: 'The life of a teacher was permanently on view in the small parishes, and only in Dublin could I disappear into my own and my secret life without being noticed.' The importance of this city to John's imaginative development is often overlooked, but he remembers youthful times there with intense fondness. His recollections are of Dublin's thriving cultural life, not of a staid, sullen place of mid-century Irish paralysis:

> There were many good secondhand bookshops in which one could root about for hours. One book barrow in particular, on a corner of Henry Street, was amazing. Most of the books found there then would now be described as modern classics. How the extraordinary Mr Kelly acquired them we never asked. Those were times when books were discussed in dance halls as well as in bars. It was easy then to get a desk in the National Library. The staff were kind and even would bring rare books on request. There were inexpensive seats at the back of the Gate Theatre, and there were many pocket theatres, often in Georgian basements.

Through attendance at these small theatres, John first got acquainted with writers such as Pirandello and Beckett, exemplars who would both remain an important inspiration.

His liking for these lively public venues should not mislead. Nor should his memories bring us to understate just how crucial silence and solitude were to John both as a writer and as a man as he entered adulthood. The same need endured throughout his life. His thinking on the need for anonymity fell early under the influence of Rilke, who issued repeated warnings to writers trying to make their way in the world.

John's favourite of Rilke's works was his one novel, *The Notebooks of Malte Laurids Brigge*. The eponymous Malte wanders the streets of Paris recalling episodes from his aristocratic Danish past, with the author pointing to the perils of renown: 'as yet I did not understand fame, that public destruction of one in process of becoming, into whose building-ground the mob breaks, displacing his stones. Young man anywhere, in whom something stirs that makes you shiver, profit by the fact that no one knows you.' So taken was John by this book's wisdom that he made a gift of it, even when he could ill afford the gesture, to his closest friends.

Suspicion and mistrust of fame – or of any kind of recognition – remained with John. This young man found Dublin, at least for a time, the ideal place to hide in plain view. In John's most urban book, *The Pornographer*, the unnamed narrator visits his dying aunt in a cancer hospital closely modelled on St Luke's, Rathgar. He is glad to escape back, afterwards, into anonymous city life:

> The next day I put aside for what I liked doing best. I did nothing, the nothing of walking crowded streets in the heart of the city, looking at faces, going into chance bars to rest, eating lunch and dinner alone in cheap, crowded restaurants.
>
> And without any desire for meaning, in the same way as I had been surprised at her bedside, I sometimes felt meaning in this crowded solitude. That all had a purpose, that it had to have, the people coming and going, the ships tied up along the North Wall, the changing delicate lights and ripples of the river, the cranes and building, lights of shops, and the sky through a blue haze of smoke and frost.

This description of a youth aimlessly walking a city's streets owes at least as much to Rilke as it does to Joyce and is one of many such passages across John's work.

Dublin, for all the comfort of anonymity, was not always lonesome. There were other, livelier, more sociable sides:

> We went to dancehalls and cinemas and theatres; the big hurling and football matches in Croke Park, race meetings in the Phoenix Park or Baldoyle or Leopardstown; we met and talked and drank and argued in bars. In hot summers we swam in the seas around Dublin or went on excursions into the Dublin Mountains. The girls we picked up in dancehalls we courted in doorways and back alleys, and on dates took them to cinemas or out to places like Howth by the sea.

The dance hall was the key location in these years for romance and the pursuit of possible partners. John's memories of these times are full of life and energy. *The Leavetaking* exults in youth's possibilities:

> The distractions of the city quickened forgetting, the excitement of books for the first time, no longer the dull slog for exams but ways of seeing, one's own world for the first time. The laughter and argument of pubs, and late at night the dances, girls from the dances, and fumbled sex in the back seats of cars or on bedsittingroom sofas or against alley walls, wet trouser legs and the stiff grey stain that had to be sent to the cleaners.

The demand for dancing is evident in the number of venues around the city centre. There were the Ierne and the National on Parnell Square, the Metropole and Clerys on O'Connell Street, the Crystal on South Anne Street and the 4 Provinces on Upper Harcourt Street. These popular dance halls were augmented by a plethora of student hops – events run for the vets, the ags, the medics and the Irrawaddies (as the engineers were known). These student events tended to take place in the Olympic Ballroom (off Camden Street) at half the price of the more established venues.

Treasa MacManus attended many such dances in this era and worked in the same Athboy and Clontarf schools as John, though at slightly different times. She recalled for me the scene: 'huge gatherings of young, ardent people awkwardly shuffling and colliding to sometimes poor quality music. It didn't matter, the craic was often great.'

The cost of dances varied: the Metropole was the most expensive, costing up to six shillings. Its ballroom formed part of a huge building that also housed a cinema and a popular restaurant. There was always a buzz about the place, patrons queueing for cinema seats. People on dates often arranged to meet in the spacious, welcoming foyer. The Metropole attracted a wide mix, young and not so young, locals and visiting people. Occasionally one might meet guests from the Gresham and Wynn's hotels.

A certain informal etiquette, according to Treasa, got observed:

> Men tended to stand around the entrance, opposite the bandstand. Girls occupied the rows of seats to the left-hand side of the entrance. However, there wasn't rigid observance to this custom. There was a bar in the Met – not sure about other places, though I imagine they all had soft-drinks available. A girl wouldn't accept the offer of a drink unless she fancied the guy. It was unheard of, in my time, that a girl drank alcohol. However, guys recount the shock when offering a drink to a visiting Englishwoman. She ordered a gin and tonic or a brandy and port and they were broke for a week!

Treasa's recall is undimmed by seven decades' passage. Clerys was similar to the Metropole ('but without the buzz'). The 4 Provinces had the reputation of attracting 'chancy types'. The National felt traditional, and the bands there sometimes included 'The Siege of Ennis' or polkas in their repertoire. One might meet people wearing a gold fáinne or a Pioneer badge. The Crystal was a smaller venue, more intimate and chic, attracting a younger clientele. Its revolving system of lighting from the ceiling showered the dancers with all the colours of the rainbow as they waltzed around.

If you were fortunate enough to hit it off with a dancing partner, finding somewhere to extend the night was not an easy call. The Paradiso on Westmoreland Street was one possibility. Appealing to a more upmarket crowd, this option represented at the time Dublin's only late-night eating place and featured a pianist and a small dance floor. The walls of the stairs as one climbed to the dining room were bedecked with photos of celebrities: Charlie Chaplin, Grace Kelly, Eamonn Andrews, famous visiting boxers.

Occasionally, on Sunday afternoons, John would socialise in the Cumberland Hotel on Westland Row. Here he fell for a young woman who worked in Belgrove Girls' School. As the narrator in *The Leave-taking* recalls:

> Across the low flat roofs of the schoolrooms I look towards the girls' school, a nineteenth-century mansion framed in beeches. The iron stairs of the fire escape climb to the door and window where the women lunch, low in the window black hair I kissed once, woman that I loved once.

This love appears to have been unrequited. As much as John was a face in the crowd of the dance-hall scene in these years, there is little evidence of romantic fulfilment. He was a shy, awkward young man, more at home with his own company than in the pressurised atmosphere of the ballroom, in what the jaundiced narrator of *The Pornographer* calls 'the cattle light', where one's happiness depended on some random partner accepting an offer of a mineral:

> Far below in O'Connell Street toy cars were streaming past, and most of the small figures on the pavements seemed somehow comic in their fixed determination to get to wherever they were going. I saw the boxer in evening dress leave the head of the stairs. The *House Full* notice must have gone up on the easel below. It was no longer possible to see onto the dance floor, the space at the head of the steps packed with men, and men on the steps below struggled to push through. Everywhere now there was the sense of the fair and the hunt and the racecourse.

This Darwinian jostling, if not to John's tastes, possessed other aspects. If hours spent at the Metropole failed to yield a lover, this venue was where, one evening, he fell into conversation with a young Dublin man who would quickly become a firm friend and whose extended family would provide a vital social and cultural milieu.

Tony Swift was a few months younger than John, one of a large, working-class family from Carrick Terrace off the South Circular Road who had established a successful commercial signwriting business based in Amiens Street. Tony and all his brothers were educated at Synge Street Christian Brothers School, deeply read and committed to artistic pursuits. By Christmas 1957, and the end of John's first year teaching at Belgrove, he had become close enough to Tony to confide his writing ambitions. One rather delirious letter as John recovers after surgery on a deviated septum tells his friend of fears and desires. Poetry at this point is still John's primary – if still deeply private – pursuit:

> I am writing on a big, brown box beside the fire – all my precious poems and notebooks are in it. I sit here all evening after coming from the hospital, dream mad short stories and lecherous poems aloud to the bloody heart of Jesus on the mantelpiece. Then I write letters that should have been written six months ago; I'm in great form for letter-writing. I saw a half-baked poem sticking out of a book to-day and, by the loose women of Ireland, did I put it out of sight, quick.

Later in the same letter, he comments on some poetry presumably sent to him by Tony: 'I liked Kavanagh's little verse though it's tinged with sentiment.'

Patrick Kavanagh's writing life was, at this point, at a low ebb. He had disappeared off most radars after the early promise of work such as his anti-pastoral epic of 1942, *The Great Hunger*, and his 1948 novel, *Tarry Flynn*. One of the few highlights John recalled of his period of study at UCD was attendance at a series of lectures given there by Kavanagh in 1958. John was impressed by the Monaghan poet's insistence on the power of formal structure at a time when he was composing his 'Canal Bank' sonnets. Thinking about this experience in 2000, many years later, John emphasised how these lectures cut against the grain:

> And it was actually quite unfashionable to write sonnets at that time, it was the time of free verse. But he said that he thought the sonnet was the expression of the love poem. And that the fourteen line sonnet with its shapes and forms was the envelope of love, and if one wanted to write a proper letter to one's love, one had to put it into a kind of envelope.

John further acknowledged the impact of Kavanagh's formalism on his own work:

> if you can follow that, the novel or the short story or whatever it is, has actually to be put into a kind of envelope. I actually think that if there wasn't that difficulty of formality and form, that it would lose a lot of its tension; that oddly enough, it seems to me that self-expression is almost no expression.

The relative failure of the 1950s for Kavanagh was soon to change thanks to the Swift brothers. Particular thanks are due to James (more commonly 'Jimmy'). He was the eldest and became John's closest friend and influence. Jimmy Swift admired Patrick Kavanagh. Worried that the Monaghan writer's increasingly dissolute lifestyle would see his work lost to the public, he took the trouble to gather up a sheaf of poems scattered around the poet's Baggot Street flat, sending them on to his brother Patrick ('Paddy') in London, to see if he might find a publisher. The result of this noble act of artistic retrieval was the publication by Longman in 1960 of Kavanagh's final triumphant stand-alone collection, *Come Dance with Kitty Stobling*.

John's attitude to literary Dublin was not nearly as positive as his happier memories of dancing, cinema attendance and trips to Croke Park. Among his close friends, notably, there was no writer. While he respected Kavanagh's work, he disliked the man and the storied world of the Dublin writers' pub. He had a particular problem with one on Harry Street and wrote to his American editor: 'The McDaid world is such a jungle that it's impossible.' Not only in the macho bear pits of McDaid's and the Palace did John feel uncomfortable among writers. On one occasion, he met Kate O'Brien, a writer whose prose he admired, for an evening in the Hibernian Club on St Stephen's Green. The night was a failure, as he tells Tony Whelan: 'not worth describing, so many silly evenings. I find literary people bore me to almost the point of violence. You can find less and less reality in life as you grow older. But I suppose it doesn't matter a curse.'

This world is brought to life in short stories such as 'My Love, My Umbrella' and 'Bank Holiday'. In the latter story, a couple meets a barely fictionalised version of Kavanagh in a scene set in another pub on Harry Street (now Bruxelles), across from McDaid's:

> There was a sense of a cool dark waiting in Mooney's, a barman arranging ashtrays on the marble. They ordered an assortment of sandwiches. It was pleasant to sit in the comparative darkness, and eat and sip and watch the street, and to hear in the silence footsteps going up and down Grafton Street.
>
> It was into this quiet flow of the evening that the poet came, a large man, agitated, without jacket, the shirt open, his thumbs hooked in braces that held up a pair of sagging trousers, a brown hat pushed far back on his head.

After a row with the poet over cigarettes, the couple cross the road to McDaid's but quickly think better of staying:

> The door of the bar across the way was not open, and when he pushed it a roar met them like heat. The bar was small and jammed. A red-and-blue tint from a stained glass window at the back mixed weirdly with the white lights of the bar, the light of evening from the high windows. A small fan circled helplessly overhead, its original white or yellow long turned to ochre by cigarette smoke.

In one interview, John said of the capital: 'Dublin is too small a city, where the small literary world spends time self-congratulating.' But you can tell that he still holds a certain appalled fascination for Kavanagh and for the literary pub scene:

In fact, it was quite funny what one could see in the bars of Dublin at that time. Kavanagh was beating up Flann O'Brien, the author of *At Swim Two Birds* and of *The Third Policeman*, a writer influenced both by Joyce and by Beckett, but O'Flaherty, the famous novelist of *The Informer*, a nationalist, born on the Aran Islands, who was taller and stronger than Kavanagh, would often inflict on him severe punishment. In short, they all drank enormously.

John's public profile, after the publication of *The Barracks* in 1963, inevitably rose. He became more concerned about privacy, about his ability to write and to live unhindered by the intrusion of prying individuals. One letter of April 1964 to Mary Keelan, an American graduate student he had met in Dublin the previous summer, is instructive. Both are keen that their budding romance be concealed, and John remarks of his home city, 'I'm afraid I do not trust very much, this city is a village, and I'm more known than ever now. And God knows what may happen, so it's better to be free of eyes and minds not our own.'

But John did have, caution aside, a small, tight circle of friends. Having championed Kavanagh, Jimmy and Paddy Swift shortly made another vital intercession in Irish letters by arranging for the first publication of John's work. Though Tony was the Swift with whom John initially became friendly, Jimmy soon became his closest confidant and the single most important influence on John's artistic development and thinking in Dublin. This debt is acknowledged in the dedication of *The Barracks*.

John and Jimmy would meet every Friday night in the Stag's Head pub on Dame Lane over several years, switching occasionally to Mooney's of Eden Quay. Deeply read, Jimmy was, like most of John's close friends, quite a bit older. He is fictionalised as the character Lightfoot in 'Wheels' and in *The Leavetaking*, and as James White in 'Bank Holiday'. The latter story invokes fond memories of the weekend ritual:

> They met at eight-thirty on the Friday night of every week for several years, the evening interrupted only by holidays and illnesses,

proof against girlfriends, and later wives, ended only by White's transfer abroad. They met in bars, changing only when they became known to the barmen or regulars and in danger of losing their anonymity. They talked about ideas, books, 'the human situation', and 'reality and consciousness' often surfaced with the second or third pint.

John first read Proust at Jimmy's urging – only to abandon the effort, renewing it after further encouragement. Jimmy's great enthusiasm for W. H. Auden also saw John follow his lead. These pieces of advice were just two of several key intercessions.

The Lightfoots were John's landlords at 57 Howth Road. As so often, he borrowed some fragment of reality for his imaginary world. He first uses the name for a thinly veiled version of Jimmy Swift when the narrator of 'Wheels' overhears a comical conversation between two railway porters about the failed suicide attempt of a colleague:

> They'd fill the trolley, the smile dying in the eyes as they went past, the loose wheels rattling less under the load, the story too close to the likeness of my own life for comfort though it'd do to please Lightfoot in the pub when I got back.
>
> 'Looked at with the mind, life's a joke; and felt, it's a tragedy and we know cursed nothing,' he'd said last night over pints of Guinness.

Four years later, in *The Leavetaking*, we find another version of the relationship:

> Lightfoot, not my friend since he found friendship disgusting, quoting Proust that it is the halfway house between physical exhaustion and mental boredom. Only what one loves *is*, as we comically try to hang on to what must pass, and I respect Lightfoot too much to claim him for a friend against his will. The simple feeling that such as he is alive is enough to make my own life more bearable and he made that wet evening in the deathroom general for me when he spoke of his own mother. We sat at the long marble counter of The Stag's Head, the

silver clock on the slender stem crowned with antlers and the scroll of *tempus fugit*.

If Lightfoot baulked at the idea of friendship's value, John also had concerns. To rely on anyone too heavily was a weakness that could not be afforded. He reassesses, when he comes to write 'Bank Holiday', the part played by what was – outside of his relationship with Madeline – perhaps the closest friendship of his life:

> Now he could hardly remember a sentence from those hundreds of evenings. What he did remember was a barman's face, white hair drawn over baldness, an avid follower of Christy Ring; a clock, a spiral iron staircase to the Gents, the cold of marble on the wristbone, footsteps passing outside in summer, the sound of heavy rain falling before closing time. The few times they had met in recent years they had both spoken of nothing but people and happenings, as if those early meetings were some deep embarrassment: they had leaned on them too heavily once and were now like lost strength.

While the friendship would never again return to the intensity of those Friday nights, Jimmy and John remained close for many years to come, with Jimmy frequently visiting John's Leitrim home well into the 1990s.

There were two other particularly good friends acquired in the last years of the 1950s: Kevin Lehane and Tom Jordan. Lehane, thirteen years John's senior, was a cinema manager and is described by John's American editor in a letter of July 1965, in which he is mentioned as being a member of 'the John McGahern Fan Club'. Patrick Gregory was taken by the man:

> He was splendid. I called at the theater at 10 in the morning two days before my departure. Although he was on duty all that day, and free only from 7 to 9 at night, we agreed to meet for a pint before his night duty commenced. We had a pint, then another, and Tony Lennen (of the Irish Times) joined us. Kevin, realizing that the jig was up,

> phoned the theater and told them that he wouldn't be there that evening. We drank on until closing time – changing pubs from time to time, in lieu of the 'sightseeing' tour that Kevin felt he should be offering me.

The cinema in question here is likely the New Electric on Talbot Street, which doubled for a time as a late-night venue for folk music events, challenging the Grafton Cinema unsuccessfully. The New Electric was located beneath the train line, and Lehane was in the habit of giving John use of his office there as a place to write. As well as being a perfect hiding place, the space was convenient for John to go straight there from school, a short bus trip along North Strand. Lehane's office was also beside Amiens Street Station, terminus for the train to Sligo and in proximity to some of John's preferred pubs, such as Grainger's and the North Star. John learnt to judge train times by the presence of particular rail drivers whom he knew and with whom he would leave to catch the train home to the west.

Lehane became an important guide to the intricacies of Dublin's streets, its pubs and its people. He published an affectionate book about the city, made up from a series of articles originally published in the *Irish Times* in the 1950s, under the pseudonym Tom Corkery. His prologue to the book ends thus:

> The Dublin social, as distinct from the cultural, scene is very varied. It goes on all the year round and ranges from art exhibitions to horse racing to literary festivals via medical and scientific congresses. It is not to say of course that these grave and learnt conventions of the arts and sciences are designed by their organisers as social binges; it is only that they invariably end up that way. And for all her visitors the city changes its face; high-spirited in an aristocratic way for Horse Show Week, jovial in a robust manner for returning American Gaels and GAA finals, hail-fellow-well-met for the rugby internationals, long-haired and longer-winded for the theatre festivals.

John reviewed Lehane's book in the *Sunday Independent* of 4 January 1981:

> This is a lovely book. I might be tempted to refer to it as a bewk, so contagious is its idiom, were it not for the certainty of being blowed out of it by the citizens, with their inexhaustible arsenal of non-sequiturs, that come to such vivid life in its pages.

The city's film audience was one of the biggest in Britain and Ireland, second only to London in terms of tickets sold per annum. Film was the glamour medium of the time, and many cinemagoers went to the pictures two or three times a week at a wide range of venues. The Adelphi, the Carlton and the Corinthian were among the most popular city-centre cinemas. Venues such as the De Luxe (Camden Street), the Grand (Fairview) and the State (Phibsboro) added to the choice. Lehane in his writings drew on his experiences as a cinema manager, his knowledge of Dublin's pub culture and his affection for his native city. He did not indulge in urban sentimentality but wrote of the Dublin in which he lived and worked. Lehane also contributed to *This Is Ireland*, a magazine for tourists, and was the chief contributor to *Dublin: An Official Guide* in the late 1940s.

While Jimmy Swift and Kevin Lehane were friends whom John would meet regularly in the city centre, the third man he liked most in this period was a work colleague and fellow Belgrove teacher. Tom Jordan was a native of Kilrush, County Clare and a former Christian Brother who became a schoolteacher on leaving the Brothers. He and John remained close friends from the first days of working together until the end of Jordan's life, with John and Madeline frequently staying with the Jordans in Raheny and Tom and his wife Blainid coming for summer stays in Leitrim.

Jordan's experiences in the Christian Brothers, and especially of leaving the order, inspired John to write 'The Recruiting Officer', the story with which he chooses to end *Nightlines*:

> Old Cogger dithered till the day before I had to leave, but at nightfall brought home two likely fits. I picked one, and packed it,

and off we set by bus for Limerick, to all appearances two Christian Brothers going on some ordinary business, but old Cogger would come back alone.

Researching what he needed to make the story work, John had asked Jordan to put in writing memories of his final days with the Brothers in December 1945. This friend and colleague was happy to help, writing in a letter of December 1968:

> Instructions were sent to my boss to dismiss me (or maybe release me) as quietly as possible so as not to scandalise my brethren or the good townsfolk. He showed me the letter. I was to get a suit of clothes, underwear, my ticket home and £1. I told him the underwear I had would do and he raised the £1 to £5, telling me to keep it quiet or he would be called to account for it.

And so the letter continues, always walking a line between comedy and tragedy, closing with memories of his re-entry into the world after leaving the Brothers' house in Enniscorthy: 'I got off the train at Bray that day. Fear of meeting my sisters. Went into a café. I'll never forget as I started and blushed when the waitress said: Yes, Sir? First time ever called "Sir".'

The story is one of several attempts that John would make over the years to examine Ireland's troubled history of clerical and institutional abuse, starting with 'Christmas', coming to a famous apogee with *The Dark* and finishing with *That They May Face the Rising Sun*. Jordan became an important early reader of John's work and was one of only a small number of people over the course of his writing career in whose judgement he trusted.

John kept his friends notably separate, with Niall Walsh an instance of this tendency. John first met the Tullamore man in the early 1960s, when Walsh was working as a general practitioner. They became firm friends and remained so right to the end of John's life. But Walsh never once met, or knew of, Swift, Lehane or Jordan. Different pubs were used for different friends: Lehane tended to drink on the Northside; Swift, on the Southside. For Walsh, O'Neill's of Suffolk Street became the go-to watering hole. Jordan liked a pint too but was a devout family man and tended to stay in the Northside suburbs, close to his Raheny home.

Other friends John would visit in their Northside home included Dónal Cleary, a Belgrove colleague, and his wife Dolores, in whom he confided about trouble at home with the Sergeant and his younger siblings. Dolores recalls their young teacher friend sitting up late in silence, staring into the fire before walking the hour alone through the night back to 57 Howth Road.

* * *

In lots of ways, and not unsurprisingly, retirement did not suit Frank McGahern. Having moved out of the Cootehall barracks and into the stone house in Grevisk, he quickly realised that letting go of the trappings of power had led to a diminution of respect in certain quarters. 'The sum total of it is I am not Police Sergeant & they are having their satisfaction', he wrote to John in a letter of 8 January 1960, raising what must have been an appalling vista before his son's eyes:

> It is imperative that I get out of here and as soon as possible not in my interest as I have a way or means of getting out but in the interest of the family. Therefore, I request that without delay you take Monica and Margaret into your confidence get a house or flat for us in Dublin to which we can move without delay.

Although this crackpot scheme of a move to the city was quickly enough extinguished, the moment gave John sufficient pause for thought to dramatise it in 'Wheels':

> 'The one important thing I ever asked you couldn't even be bothered,' he accused.
>
> 'That's not true. When you wrote you wanted to move to Dublin, I went round the auctioneers, sent you lists, looked at places.'

> 'And you said if I did get a place and moved that you wanted no room in it.'
>
> 'I want to live on my own, I didn't want you to come thinking differently.'
>
> 'I didn't come under illusions. You took good care of that,' he accused bitterly. 'And I was foolish enough to think there might be more than pure selfishness.'
>
> I knew the wheel: fathers become children to their sons who repay the care they got when they were young, and on the edge of dying the fathers become young again, but the luck of a death and a second marriage had released me from the last breaking on this ritual wheel.

John knew that he could never happily live near his father again. But the gambit of the move to Dublin would not be the last attempt the Sergeant would make to have his eldest son firmly in his control once again.

To make matters in Grevisk more difficult still, the youngest child, Frankie, was rebelling in determined fashion, skipping school, staying out late, drinking and smoking. The Christmas of 1959 proved miserable for John as he saw for himself the deep unhappiness of his home. It would not be long before things came to a head, and, after a violent showdown between father and youngest child, the Sergeant wrote to John seeking his help in disciplining Frankie:

> I know a way with that gentleman but at least I'd have to have your approval as I would not have the approval of any of the girls. Indeed it might be well if you were present as there is always a danger of collapse owing to age and weight. It may be as well to allow him to hang about for a year or so. Indeed he might go off of his own accord and attend school, but I cannot see it happen.
>
> There is a danger of serious nervous breakdown in my case as I have all the time being [*sic*] worrying. I considered entering a mental hospital and it might be the best place in all my circumstances.

John went home to calm things down, pointing out to his father that to assault someone was a crime and visiting Frankie's school to attempt some mediation. Peace did not endure, and before long Frankie had run away from home again, turning up in Dublin to seek his siblings' help. Put on the Holyhead ferry, like so many young Irish people before and since, Frankie was soon on his way to Breedge and Rosaleen in London, where he would, after some early misadventures, make a successful life for himself.

Despite all this tumult at home and the happier distractions of Dublin's cinemas and dance halls, John was delving further into the imagination, spending more and more time alone with pen in hand. Only in writing, increasingly, could he find satisfaction. Not even his evening third-level studies held much attraction: 'the university could not give me what I wanted'. This period of gestation would shortly end, and the artistic ruminations born on the rivers of north Roscommon and nurtured on the streets and in the bars of Dublin would be shared with the world.

3
X Marks the Spot
1960–63

. . . writing is always painful.

JOHN McGAHERN

June 1962, a Mayo man walks the streets of London. He is looking for a job to supplement his meagre teacher's salary back home. The story is a common enough one, with the building sites of the British capital full of every shade of Irish navvy, some lifers, others summer migrants. On Hammersmith Broadway, he spies coming up the road on the far side a Roscommon lad he knew in teacher-training college, the best part of a decade previous.

Uinsin 'Jumbo' O'Donovan can reconstruct that moment as if recalling yesterday:

> 'Ah, there you are Mac Eachrain!'
>
> 'Ah, Jumbo . . . Will you come and have a drink?'
>
> I says: 'John, I have no money. I have to go and look for a job.'
>
> Says he: 'I've got £100.'
>
> 'Where in the name of God did you get money like that?'
>
> 'Faber and Faber.'
>
> 'Well, if you have £100, John, I'll go for a drink.'

This elderly man continued his account with a sort of delighted bemusement:

> We went up Hammersmith Broadway, into the George, and we were there for a while, and I said, 'What's this auld book about, John?'
>
> 'Ah, it's about a Barrack,' he says.

'What kind of a Barrack? Like Portobello Barrack?'

'A guards barrack,' he says.

'Who'd read a book about a fucking guards barrack?'

We had a good drink that day, between us.

O'Donovan alternates between delight at the memory and a kind of wonder at having known John at this time. 'That was the first inkling I got that he was writing at all', he recalls of his former classmate. 'A man you wouldn't notice.'

Looking back from more than sixty years out, *The Barracks* is hard to credit as a debut novel, so masterful is its prose, so powerful the emotional impact without ever having to exaggerate. The contemporary Irish novelist Deirdre Madden, when asked in 2008 to select her 'book of a lifetime', recalled the effect that *The Barracks* had on a young woman travelling through central Europe in the early 1980s: 'I remember being in a youth hostel in Austria and staying up late into the night to finish the book, and then not being able to sleep afterwards. I must have been lying awake for hours thinking about it.' Many readers will recognise this feeling, of having been moved off one's axis and pitched into the whole, quiet world of a dying woman, plagued by a burning awareness of her mortality. 'At times', writes Madden, 'there is almost something eerie about the way that McGahern's language works. The words seem to disappear and you see the thing itself, as if unmediated.' For this aesthetic to have formed so early in life strikes her as astounding: 'To develop a style with this degree of clarity and deceptive simplicity even late in one's writing career would be an achievement, so to find it in a first novel makes it all the more remarkable.'

Madden is far from the only younger writer of significance, Irish or otherwise, to recognise in this debut an astonishing sure-footedness. Andrew O'Hagan, contributing to a *Guardian* series titled 'I Wish I'd Written', offers this assessment: 'John McGahern's first novel *The Barracks* is a little masterpiece. The words are strange and beautiful; emotion passes through the sentences like clear water. There is more grace in these quiet pages than in the whole of *War and Peace*.' In sum, O'Hagan sees the book and its author as *sui generis*: 'McGahern is, in some way, in some priceless way, out on his own: his prose is richly odd, and has none of the mannered simplicity much-loved by the world's Creative Writers. He is a writer with nerve.'

Contemporaries could be no less impressed. John Montague, seven years John's senior, compared *The Barracks* to *Madame Bovary* in the poetic detail of its style. Montague saw this publication as having instigated a kind of revolution in Irish literature: 'What was new and startling was the quality of the writing; Irish provincial life had never been transcribed with such exactness before.' Certain questions naturally arise, given the stunning achievement involved. How did such mastery happen for one so young? Where does this novel in which nothing much happens come from and how does its author manage to hurt us out of our quotidian lethargy?

For Irish writers wishing to begin a publishing career in their own country at the start of the 1960s, options were extremely limited. The buoyant literary magazine scene of the mid-century had passed. Seumas O'Sullivan's death in 1958 brought about the demise of his carefully nurtured creation, the quarterly *Dublin Magazine*, a forum that had been such an important support to writers, from Samuel Beckett to Mary Lavin, since the foundation of the state. *The Bell*, first to publish Brendan Behan, Brian Friel and many other important writers, had finally closed in 1954 after several stuttering years. And *Envoy*, established in 1949 under the editorship of John Ryan, expired two years later after publishing an array of national and international stars, as well as promoting Irish visual arts.

John McGahern, looking around him in January 1960 for an Irish magazine that might take one of his stories, found only Mary O'Malley's *Threshold*, a Belfast-based quarterly and spin-off from the Lyric Players Theatre. O'Malley's theatre group had come south in September 1959 to put on a four-day run of Yeats's *Oedipus at Colonus* and *The Death of Cuchulain* in the Dagg Hall, Westland Row. John was an enthusiastic audience member. Writing to O'Malley on 17 January with the offer of a story for publication, he is tentative:

> I was born in Dublin in 1934, but was brought up in the West of Ireland, for the most time in North Roscommon.
>
> I have not appeared in print. My first novel was finished a few months back and was recommended by another writer to his publishers, Hamish Hamilton. They are still considering it.

O'Malley's response, though unknown, seems to have been a rejection. No contribution by John appears until 1962, when *Threshold* became the first Irish literary magazine to publish his work. This item is not a story but an extract from *The Barracks* titled 'Waiting', one taken from the second chapter in which Elizabeth Reegan visits a doctor's surgery. That number of the journal was guest-edited by Roger McHugh, who had taught John when he was studying for his undergraduate degree in English. The presence of other contributors such as Tom Kilroy and Tom MacIntyre made this issue all but a college magazine, showcasing new UCD talent.

The manuscript mentioned by John in his letter to O'Malley ('first novel') had been submitted to Hamish Hamilton the previous summer. As for every writer awaiting judgement, the months of anticipation dragged. 'It is a trying time waiting for some word back', John wrote to Michael McLaverty, the Belfast writer with whom he had begun a warm epistolary relationship after hearing him lecture at UCD on the merits of Daniel Corkery. 'If it was either accepted or rejected I could settle back to work again, and some peace. Perhaps, if it is published, you might do me the honour of reading it.'

The novel, titled 'The End or the Beginning of Love', never did get published and rests today among John's papers in the University of Galway. The manuscript was read and rejected by at least three London publishing houses: Hamish Hamilton, Hutchinson and MacGibbon & Kee. This last imprint, through the 1960s, was making a name for itself revivifying the reputation of neglected Irish writers such as Patrick Kavanagh and Flann O'Brien.

The eventual Hamish Hamilton rejection infuriated John, not because the verdict was a 'no' but because of the attendant critique's nature. This reader's report, calling into question the line between fiction and autobiography, proved especially hard to take. As John tells Paddy Swift in a letter of September 1960, with which he includes his other rejection slips:

> The insistence that to string a few lunatic situations into a plot is more valuable and difficult than to give passion and pattern to the lives of people being eroded out of their existence in the banality and repetitiveness of themselves and their society is the real maddening thing. I better leave it so! But the autobiography stunt! Very few of the situations in the book ever happened in my life – in that sense, it is no more mine than the Man in the Moon's autobiography; THE WHOLE BOOK owes everything to my experience, the way I suffered and was made to laugh, the people I have lived among, the landscape and the books I liked, – in that way it is as auto as I was capable of making it. But it is seldom possible to be ourselves in real life: because of the need FOR MONEY, for friends, for a beloved, or even, I suspect, because of the need to have enemies. And if you feel you must be a responsible individual in some manner, and can't or do not wish, or feel that it's not enough to be a saint, then you have little choice but to try some artifice. The common notion that you can make an art out of your life, refinements of pleasure etc, is pure moonshine as far as I see it.

The letter stands as an important early defence of John's decision to make art out of life, a far cry, he always insisted, from autobiography. That he should ultimately write and publish *Memoir* in his final years, after he had finished with the composition of fiction, is notable in this regard.

Though the multiple rejection slips stung, John's luck was about to change. Part of his reason for writing that angry letter was to ask for the return of a manuscript, an extract from the rejected novel that he had sent for consideration to the little magazine *X: A Quarterly Review*, which Swift had begun to co-edit in 1959 in partnership with the South African-born poet David Wright.

The two had first met in London in 1953 in the small bar of the Duke of Wellington at the corner of Wardour Street and Old Compton Street. Shortly after this initial rendezvous, Wright became editor of another London magazine, *Nimbus*. Via the good graces of Paddy and Jimmy Swift, this outlet received and published nineteen Patrick Kavanagh poems, thereby reviving his writing career and leading to the appearance of *Come Dance with Kitty Stobling* in 1960. This coup whetted the appetite for further publishing ventures, and in November 1959, *X* made its debut. This remarkable quarterly that mixed the literary with the visual arts was, recalled Wright, a child of Soho, a particular efflorescence: 'born in that Bohemian jungle, a society which, as I now realize, was as extraordinary as it was short-lived'.

While the chemistry that led to the brief success of *X* was primarily down to the warm working partnership between Wright and Swift, the magazine could never have got off the ground without the patronage of Michael Berry, later Lord Hartwell, the aristocratic press-baron owner of the *Daily Telegraph* and soon to be founder of the *Sunday Telegraph*. Berry, through the brokerage of Mary Hutchinson, one of the last survivors of the Bloomsbury Group, undertook to guarantee the first four volumes of *X*. As Wright recalls, Berry perfectly fitted the bill: 'proved an ideal backer – he never interfered. Indeed, I never even met him.'

Hutchinson was born Mary Barnes in 1889, and formed an interesting bridge between two eras of London bohemia. A cousin of Lytton Strachey, she married the barrister St John Hutchinson in 1910 and became a notable figure: celebrated hostess, patron of the arts, confidante of Vivien Eliot. A model for the self-confident socialite Jinny in Virginia Woolf's *The Waves*, a character who never ceases to 'move and to dance', Hutchinson was, on David Wright's account, a 'friend of practically every twentieth-century artist or writer of note, from George Moore to Alberto Giacometti and Samuel Beckett'.

She entertained in a magnificent apartment high above Hyde Park Square, a leisurely fifteen-minute walk from the Swift home on Westbourne Terrace. In later years, she hosted John and Madeline here, her reception room in the round hung with Matisse odalisques for which she had been the model. John recounted, when he became friendly with Hermione Lee, Virginia Woolf's biographer, an anecdote about Woolf's first encounter with Katherine Mansfield:

> The one person I had known was Mary Hutchinson, and found that small portrait richly accurate. She told me once that she was at the first meeting of V.W. with Katherine Mansfield. Beatrice Glenavy was also there. K.M. came dressed like a hippy, with many rings and bangles and a small cloth bag. All V.W.'s competitive jealousy fixed on K.M.'s hands. As the meeting continued it was punctuated by the sound of the rings dropping into the cloth bag.

John continues: 'I have no idea whether it was fact or "a story" but I still hear in my mind the clink of those rings falling into that small cloth bag.'

Whatever the truth of such yarns, *X* could not have happened without Hutchinson's support. One can only speculate on the arc of John's future publishing career without the impact of the magazine. But Hutchinson's patronage of the quarterly did not come without a cost. Wright recalled, 'There was not a page of the magazine that we did not have to pay for with hours of argumentation, till in the end Swift had to give up answering his telephone altogether.' Not without a certain relief did its two editors wind up *X* after seven issues.

The surrealist poet David Gascoyne introduced Paddy Swift to Hutchinson. Gascoyne, the French translator Pierre Leyris, the English renegade poet George Barker, the Irish man of letters Anthony Cronin and Hutchinson were listed on the masthead inside the front cover of *X* as 'Correspondents'. The long-standing friendship between Hutchinson and Leyris would later become important for McGahern when Mercure de France, the prestigious Parisian publishing house of which Leyris was a director, published *Nightlines*, his first collection of short stories, under the title *Lignes de fond* in 1971. Leyris provided an insightful preface.

Barker, a close friend of David Wright, counted as central to the *X* circle. Infamous for his hellraising style and unorthodox personal life, Barker was a man for whom John developed an intense dislike. A similar dynamic formed with Cronin, who had first become involved with a little magazine as assistant editor to Peadar O'Donnell at *The Bell* in its final years. Cronin became a regular contributor to *X* and was someone whom John met through the magazine in London. John was suspicious of his motives from the outset, a suspicion that grew to open hostility when he wrote a negative review of *The Dark* for the *Times Literary Supplement* (*TLS*) on its publication in 1965, at a time when it was still that paper's practice to keep reviews anonymous.

The fifth issue of *X*, in which John's work appears for the first time, carries an extract from Cronin's forthcoming novel *The Life of Riley*. This extract sees *The Bell* satirised as *The Trumpet* and O'Donnell mercilessly lampooned as Prunshios McGonaghey, the magazine's tiresome socialist editor, a figure obsessed with 'the dialectic'. Cronin gibes at his former colleague's manner: 'like a man about to address a meeting in a draughty hall'. John saw this selling-out of a former patron as characteristic behaviour from the man he would call in private 'Crony Tonin' and whom in later years he would fictionalise as Paddy Mulvey, a down-at-heel bohemian, in 'Parachutes'.

John took pleasure in recounting to his American editor Patrick Kavanagh's delighted reaction to the critical and popular flop of Cronin's novel three years later:

> When Cronin's Riley failed here I heard Kavanagh go round McDaid's: 'Phoor Cronin. Phoor Cronin. Aah, sad, sad. His ambition was to rrite a bestseller before he was forty. Med too many enemies. Phoor Cronin. Sad. And the whife'll cause trouble. Dissapointment. Were led to believe, ow there was big advances on the job. And he'll never ger another publisher. Because he wont sell 800 copies. It wont

> pay for the fucking printing even foo fum.' We talked once about the solicitor side of Cronin. And Cronin is hated inside as well as outside the ring.

John intensely disliked the little world of the literary pub, replete with its backbiting coterie, whether seen in Dublin's Graftonia or in London's Soho. His preferred shorthand for those circles was 'The Racket', and he determined to be no part of its reach.

X was unusual in its design, shaped like a menu card Swift and Wright had read in a café by Victoria Station and printed on stiff, high-quality paper. 'The unstated object of the magazine', remembered Wright twenty-five years later, 'was to make war on mediocrity'. The editors were determined to avoid insularity and provincialism, with a wide range of European writers and artists championed. Swift took charge of the art side of *X*, rejecting the faddish craze for abstraction and favouring the figurative work of painters such as Craigie Aitchison and Frank Auerbach. Likewise endorsed were the as-yet-uncanonised Francis Bacon and Lucian Freud. Of these artists, John admired Bacon's work in particular and tried to buy one of his paintings – alas, with an asking price of £600, the piece lay beyond his reach.

Just as abstract art came under sustained attack, so too did the perceived phoniness of the Beat generation: 'The beats are an amusing phenomenon. They have no more connection with literature than the men in the moon.' This editorial opposes to current phoniness an enduring counterpoint: a 'natural bohemianism of the eclectic and fastidious spirit' that has 'always been a way of life, alternative to that of society, for the artist'. This type of bohemian attitude is the one supported by *X*. The same outlook represents, the editors conclude, 'an underground mood which is of its nature detached, calmly contemptuous, possessed of the indifference of freedom'. This governing mood suited the young, unpublished John McGahern down to the ground.

Extracts from John's unpublished novel 'The End or the Beginning of Love' appeared in March 1961, in another impressive issue, dominated by seven black-and-white photographs of Francis Bacon paintings. Among its contents is a laudatory essay on the artist by Helen Lessore, director of the Beaux Arts Gallery, which had staged a solo Bacon show in 1953. Her concluding remarks move into the sort of artistic lexicon both valued by John and applicable to his work. She describes Bacon's more recent paintings in striking terms: 'of that order of reality of which Rilke spoke when he said that the angels often do not know whether they are passing among the living or the dead. There are no longer any tricks at all.' One further comment provides even more solid reason to see the essay as an influence on John's aesthetic theorising: 'Francis Bacon has at last brought out into the clear light of day images even more arresting and disturbing than any of those earlier ones.' The editors would use almost identical language when praising 'The End or the Beginning of Love' in their closing remarks:

> Mr John McGahern's prose seems to us distinguished not only by reason of its content but by the lucidity of its English and its spare and poetic qualities, which owe nothing to those stylistic mannerisms and gimmick Mandarinese that reviewers identify with 'poetic prose'. Once again it is a question of bringing the image that moves us out into the light, uncluttered by adjectival, philosophical or explanatory junk.

They note of Lessore on Bacon: 'this painter has brought the image out into the light of day in a shocking way'. That McGahern and Bacon should be linked in this way is notable. *X* admired the two men for the same sorts of artistic endeavour: that is, for their attempts to winnow abstraction out of their work and push for a more representational, figurative art.

On the subject of the image, Bacon is remarkably close to McGahern, stating in one 1962 interview with David Sylvester: 'I'm just trying to make images as accurately off my nervous system as I can.' And again, returning to the same subject in 1979: 'I'm lucky in that images just drop in as if they were handed down to me. Really, I think of myself as a maker of images. The image matters more than the beauty of the paint.'

That 1962 interview, in an even clearer parallel between McGahern's thinking and Bacon's thinking, sees the latter muse on the essential absurdity of his endeavours:

> You see, all art has now become completely a game by which man distracts himself; and you may say it has always been like that, but now it's entirely a game. And I think that that is the way things have changed, and what is fascinating now is that it's going to become much more difficult for the artist, because he must really deepen the game to be any good at all.

John's short 1966 essay, 'The Image', comes to a similar conclusion about art, describing the search for the one, clear image as 'the whole mortal game of king', a game where 'we cannot live, we can only absurdly reign'. Like Bacon, he too wishes to deepen the game, while acknowledging at the same time that literature is a luxury pursuit.

Writing many years later of his friendship with Paddy Swift and the importance of the London summer of 1960 to his growth as a writer, John remembers a particular conversation:

> As we sat in the heat and noise and drank gin, the talk turned to Stendhal – *Naples and Florence*, *Memoirs of an Egotist*, the Journals. 'It would be obscene to be anything but a romantic in this conformist age,' Paddy asserted, and I disagreed, thinking it was more a matter of temperament and background.
>
> By way of the many beautiful girls that passed along Bayswater Road, the talk turned to Balbec and the sea, to the great passage on memory in St Augustine's *Confessions*, and finally to the Image, how all artistic activity centres on bringing the clean image that moves us out into the light. On that we could agree. We could even order a large gin on the strength of it. Paddy quoted Aquinas: 'The image is a principle of our knowledge. It is that from which our intellectual activity begins, not as a passing stimulus, but as an enduring foundation.'

That the image as aesthetic keystone should have formed part of the two men's conversation will come as no surprise to anyone who has examined the seven issues of *X* at any depth, and John's indebtedness to the magazine lasted well beyond his one actual contribution.

'The End or the Beginning of Love: Episodes from a Novel' runs over ten pages of *X*, lodged between two Geoffrey Hill sonnets and a Dannie Abse poem. These four extracts bear a striking resemblance to moments that occur in *The Dark*. As in that novel, Mahoney is the central male adult character, here painted as an even more merciless brute. Unlike in *The Dark*, Mahoney's son – the novel's narrator – is given a name: Francie. Episode One sees Mahoney share a bed with his frightened and despairing son. Episode Two is less familiar: a potato-picking scene on a cold, wet, autumn evening that owes much, one feels, to Patrick Kavanagh's epic of thwarted rural life, *The Great Hunger*. Francie tries through humour and mimicry to protect his sister Josie from the worst of their father's tyrannical rages:

> 'O God, O God, such bastards of childer!' she started to mimic her father.
>
> 'It's in the County Home ye'll all finish up! In the dale coffin of the pauper! WILful waste is WOEful want,' he continued on. They roared laughing.

Episode Three sees Francie and his father walk away from the chapel after Confession and Francie admit to an interest in the priesthood. Mahoney becomes excited at the prospect of becoming his son's housekeeper, an excitement that quickly dies against the wall of Francie's silence. We are permitted one heartbreaking moment of insight into Mahoney that does not reappear in *The Dark*: 'He lifted his hand to touch Francie's shoulder and then let it fall hopelessly again. His heart was heavy with failure. In his own strange way he loved his son desperately.'

The final episode, much like *The Dark*, concerns the visit of a distant cousin, Fr Gerald, who has arranged for Josie to go into service in a shop of his parish. Mahoney and the priest dislike each other but have to go through the motions of civil speech, an elaborate dance that becomes a hallmark of John's fiction: 'The weather, crops and cattle, the luck of Ireland in having the Catholic Faith to stand up against the Communists were shuttled back and forth for two hours of crucifying boredom.' Then Fr Gerald, before leaving with Josie, takes Francie aside to urge him towards greater study and a possible future as a seminarian in Maynooth.

Throughout the ten pages, one is struck by a pervasive sense of poverty as far removed from Soho, Francis Bacon and London's swinging sixties as one could imagine. Nothing remotely like this fiction had previously appeared in *X*. Nor would anything like John's work appear there again. The passages amount to a description of an Ireland just a generation away from the poorhouse, memories of famine still present in obsessive and even violent thrift, where to be a doctor, a priest or a merchant are the only ways out besides the obvious path of emigration.

As in Kavanagh, the lack of spiritual sustenance, despite the outward shows of piety, is more damaging to the Mahoney family than any material hardship. John uses the uncompromising everyday language of north Roscommon, especially in Mahoney's speech. His calculating delight at the notion that Francie might have a religious vocation discerns a possible future for himself:

> 'It's a hard life but a good wan,' his father began. 'It or a doctor's is all there's respect for in this country and a doctor isn't for the like of us. We're not rotten enough with money and ignorance! But a priest's a good clane life and you don't have bostoons tryin' to sit on you like in the police. Begod we'd have great times when you'd be ordained.

John would continue in *The Barracks* with the experiment in direct mimicry of the speech patterns around which he was raised. But he switches for the most part, by the time he comes to write *The Dark* and onwards, to standard English.

While several rejections of his first novel had been endured prior to the appearance of sections in *X*, their publication in the journal caused an immediate stir. But there were, even before this juncture, certain possibilities in the air. The small London firm of Barrie & Rockliff, publishers of *X*, paid a welcome £40 for the extracts. The imprint approached John with a view to publishing 'The End or the Beginning of Love' as a stand-alone novel in its entirety. This company was not known for its fiction list: in 1960, its publications included subjects as diverse as eighteenth-century French porcelain, the royal residences of Great Britain and the pommel horse.

Nonetheless, when John Bunting, an editorial assistant at the firm, telegrammed John at his Clontarf bedsit on 31 January 1961, the contents of the note can only have been greeted with excitement: 'Paddy Swift gave me manuscript your novel stop tremendously impressed and want to publish but must first consult co-director stop probably too good to sell stop congratulations and admiration stop.' While this moment represented the breakthrough for which this young writer had long hoped, the situation was far from straightforward. There existed a double issue: because John had left a typescript with Paddy Swift to show whichever London publishers he saw fit; because John had been harbouring doubts over the wisdom of publishing a novel in which he had diminishing confidence in terms of its artistic rigour. Either way, John did not want to commit immediately to Barrie & Rockliff.

One Paddy Swift letter from this period apologises to John for his slowness in getting the typescript to Martin Green at MacGibbon & Kee but assures him that they are considering it: 'No question, by the way, of hawking since we only bother with the people we know. Martin Green wrote the most flattering report I've ever seen or heard of.' Green, an English writer and publisher, was an important figure among Irish writers in Soho of the 1950s and 1960s. Having co-founded the literary magazine *Nimbus*, he went on to have a leading role at MacGibbon & Kee and at Martin, Brian & O'Keeffe.

In a later letter, Swift tells McGahern that Barrie & Rockliff are keen to publish the novel. Clearly, at this point there is another manuscript in play: 'Yr. original MSS is very good & if they brought that out you could also do the other – but if you want the new one that's what you must get.' This second document is, presumably, an early draft of what was becoming *The Barracks*.

This sudden fluster of activity was brought to a halt in the most pleasing of ways when John received a letter on 15 March that would decisively change the course of his life. The letter was written by one of London's leading literary editors, Charles Monteith, of perhaps the city's most prestigious publishing house, Faber & Faber, and was addressed to John, c/o *X*: 'I was very interested in the extracts from your novel which are published in the current number of "X". If by any chance you haven't yet made arrangements for its publication I would be absolutely delighted if you would give us an opportunity to consider it.'

Attracting the attention of Faber would have been thrilling for any young writer. But their interest represented, for John, a special honour. By this point, he had developed a devotion to one of the firm's directors, T. S. Eliot, and in particular to his *Four Quartets*. He replied immediately:

> Thank you for your letter of the 14th March concerning the extracts that appeared in X.
>
> It is a first novel that was actually accepted for publication, but by then, I could not in conscience publish it without serious revision. The pieces in X are part of the revision.
>
> In the revising another novel evolved which owed nothing to the first. I felt I must leave the revision aside for a time and finish and try to publish this new work. The publishers do not seem to like this delaying and I am not happy with the position.
>
> I sent the first part of this new work to the editors of X who have just written to say that they consider it a real advance and exciting. Whether this opening (13,000 words or so) would be too slight for you to make me an offer or not I do not know. If you consider it possible, I could let you see a copy.

And so began what would prove a lifelong, sustaining working relationship.

To bury a first novel for which he had already been enthusiastically offered a contract was a remarkable decision – particularly by an author whose only publication to date consisted of a few thousand words in a niche London quarterly. The decision suggests two of John's core qualities: a steely confidence in his own writing talent and a certainty that the rejected work was so flawed that its publication would do more harm than good.

Before moving to analysis of *The Barracks* and its genesis, the possible flaws of 'The End or the Beginning of Love' deserve consideration. Many of the traits and the tropes that would one day be considered 'McGahernesque' are present: a beloved mother dying young; a brutish, frustrated father; boyhood struggles with a religious vocation; the unconquerable power of sexual desire; daily country life in Ireland of the 1950s; acutely realised portraits of the natural world. But where this manuscript differs from the later published work lies chiefly in two areas: here there is a more obvious reliance on his Irish writerly forebears – on W. B. Yeats and James Joyce, especially. Related to the Yeats homage is a romanticism that John would ultimately never permit to appear in print.

The first handwritten drafts have the central character as a boy named Jude Mahoney, a name that changes in later drafts to Hugh and finally to Francie. His best friend – in a trope that would later appear in the short story 'Lavin' – is a boy named Campbell who is more advanced, more sexually inquisitive.

The opening paragraph sees the boys idling in class as the summer holidays approach:

> After the examinations in early June the days dragged leisurely towards the long holidays. Master Butler dozed at his table, after giving the class sums which he never corrected. In the afternoon he took the classes into the playground, where the children sat on the heat-cracked ground, and read in turns passages from 'The Deserted Village' which the master slowly commented on. He was due for retirement in the coming year, and sometimes ignored the whispering

> class to stare down the long playground where cattle stood ankle-deep in the shallows of the lake, swishing viciously at the buzzing heat.

The direct mention of Oliver Goldsmith's classic poem, while uncharacteristic overall, is fairly typical of these early efforts. They tend to look too much to an Irish literary tradition, to stick too closely to stylistic tics that previous great writers had already made their own. One of the clearest examples of this indebtedness comes in Jude's adolescent struggles with lust and masturbatory fantasies, clashing with his efforts to memorialise his late and much-loved mother:

> He would take a nun: his mind laid her out on the red carpets of the altar and fiercely his mind created the shimmering, immaculate purity of her flesh and he took her body fiercely, the blood rushing madly towards her pale cheeks. But his body sickened from the orgy, his mind revolted at the last, terrible blasphemy. He was to be a priest; his voice, promising his mother to say Mass for her, her dying face on the pillows returned out of the sickroom. How could he raise his hand over her haunting image? How could he be a priest, now? Had he put down his soul among the stinking and burning damned, and would his dying face, looking with tortured yearning through the white vapours of the fiery furnace, reproach him with his sins, dwelling on the individual ugliness of each crime; he had thrown her and the blessedness of heaven away.

This passage is pure Joyce, a combination of *A Portrait of the Artist as a Young Man*'s vision of Hell, as recounted to Stephen Dedalus and his schoolmates in their retreat for Saint Francis Xavier, and the later guilt of Stephen in *Ulysses*, as he is haunted by thoughts of his dying mother and his failure to pray at her bedside. But the Joyce work to which this passage comes closest is *Stephen Hero*, the unfinished and posthumously published test run for *A Portrait of the Artist as a Young Man* that Joyce abandoned, knowing that it lacked the inner calm necessary for art to prosper and to endure. John was to learn the same lesson about his third novel, *The Leavetaking*. Like James Joyce, John McGahern realised the necessity of suppressing prentice work. Though he did, subsequently, let an admiring Monteith see 'The End or the Beginning of Love', he had no regrets about leaving the manuscript to one side.

John's savvy London editor, if willing to go along with him on this front, was more insistent on how *The Barracks* might be handled, long before the book was published. In July 1961, he wrote to John suggesting that a section of the novel be entered for the AE Memorial Award. Modelled on America's Guggenheim Fellowship, the prize was established through the auspices of the Irish Academy of Letters to promote literary excellence in Ireland and to support the finishing of a projected work. Candidates had to be born in Ireland and under thirty-five. This prize had only ever been won by poets such as Patrick Kavanagh, Richard Murphy and Valentin Iremonger, and John was understandably reluctant to let his name go forward. As he explained to Monteith:

> The literary Ireland is much a single house, without a figure of any real authority, and I've no connection with it. They are practically all either friends or enemies, I fear such confinement doesn't breed tolerance, and it'd be unlikely to be given to anybody outside. It'd be more likely to be decided on literary politics than on quality. But there's little to lose by entering, and if you feel this may not be true, I'd enter.

Six months later, John learnt to his astonishment that he had been chosen as the winner. While much of the prize money had been eaten up through having five copies of the manuscript typed for entry, there was enough left over for John and his landlord, Mr Lightfoot, to hit the bar of Harry Byrne's on the Howth Road for a celebratory pint. As John recalled nearly three decades later in the context of nomination for the Booker Prize: 'Later awards were never to be so exciting or sweet.'

Having allowed himself this brief acknowledgement of success, John quickly returned to a more characteristically reflective mode in a letter to Michael McLaverty:

> For a little while, the morning it came, I was excited as a schoolboy with the Award, and then afterwards there was the blank inscrutable face of my work that knows nothing of awards or rewards, but only faith and passion and suffering and the long availability, which we call work, will move. The most gladness my success, if so little can be called that, has brought, apart from my friend's sake, is to affirm in my bones that all success and failure are private. What happens outside that are either lucky or unlucky accidents. For all art approaches prayer.

Few letters better capture the core of John's views on the act of artistic creation. As he grew older, John remarked often – without self-pity and with a wry smile – on writing as a tough career choice. 'It would be easier to rob banks than to make a living as a writer', he liked to say.

Everything was now changing faster than was comfortable. The *Roscommon Herald* ran a news story on 10 March, picked up from the *Irish Press*, about this young, unknown contender, son of a local retired garda sergeant now living in Grevisk: 'He is a shy man and with an artist's characteristic caution he avoids discussion in detail of an unfinished work.' The Sergeant naturally got wind of his eldest son's new-found celebrity before long and wrote a grudging letter to remark upon the media coverage:

> All last week you were the topic in Cootehall but I think they would prefer if you were born in the parish or shown to have some connection with it. Mrs Henry saw your photo in the *Irish Press* and brought it to Jim in bed. She hid the name. It was a very bad photo.

John's success did not suit the Sergeant on several levels – not least because this turn of events made a homecoming and reunion between father and son ever more unlikely. He concludes the letter with a typically sly dig at his son: 'I daresay Brother Placid will take advantage of a bit of cheap advertising. Should you have told him? I wouldn't know.'

For several years prior to the emergence of John's published work, his father had been searching for a property in Roscommon that they might farm together. He asked John, when the neighbouring Rockingham estate was being divided up into 65-acre parcels, if he could act along this line ('think up a bit of influence for yourself and me'). And he wrote again when a house and 35 acres came up for sale in nearby Knockvicar, encouraging John to put in an offer:

> The price asked was not too high. I have a shrewd idea a bank would accept a deed or mortgage on the place for the other half. It might well be bought for £1,000. If you intend to stay all your life in Dublin etc. etc. you may be sure I know nothing except that individually we might accomplish little but as a team nothing might daunt us. I am not as young as I used be and so etc. etc. but I have written too much.

When this attempt to coax his son homeward failed, the Sergeant switched to suggesting that he might move to Dublin to be near his children, a prospect that horrified John and that he successfully nixed. These painful negotiations are recalled by John in 'Wheels'. Ten years later, 'Gold Watch' returns to reflecting on this fight to a bitter end:

> My father had never forgiven me for taking my chance to go to university. He had wanted me to stay at home to work the land. I had always fought his need to turn my refusal into betrayal, and by going home each summer I felt I was affirming that the great betrayal was not mine but nature's own.

Such portraits of his father and their relationship became a stock part of John's imaginative armoury from *The Barracks* onward.

Sergeant Reegan, like Frank McGahern, is a veteran of the IRA, a man who once dreamt of great things for himself and for his country, only to have those dreams crushed under the weight of a newly victorious bourgeoisie and the realities of family life:

> All his people had farmed small holdings or gone to America and if he had followed in their feet he'd have spent his life with spade and shovel on the farm he had grown up on or he'd have left it to his

> brother and gone out to an uncle in Boston. But he'd been born into a generation wild with ideals: they'd free Ireland, they'd be a nation once again: he was fighting with a flying column in the hills when he was little more than a boy, he donned the uniform of the Garda Siochana and swore to preserve the peace of The Irish Free State when it was declared in 1920, getting petty promotion immediately because he'd won officer's rank in the fighting, but there he stayed – to watch the Civil War and the years that followed in silent disgust, remaining on because he saw nothing else worth doing. Marriage and children had tethered him in this village, and the children remembered the bitterness of his laugh the day he threw them his medal with the coloured ribbon for their play. He was obeying officers younger than himself, he who had been in charge of ambushes before he was twenty.

That Reegan's glory days have vanished when he is still in his early twenties and that he has lost his first wife leave him frequently on the verge of frustrated violence. For Elizabeth, his second wife, and the existential hero of this novel, the consequences of living in this man's unfulfilled world are painful and yet this situation is a cross she carries with stoicism and grace.

While there are interesting political undercurrents at play in the novel, *The Barracks* is above all a book about consciousness and the examined life. John believed that the majority of people go through their lives without becoming conscious, and we see this view reflected via the characters of the various guards and their wives who circle about the rural barracks – unmistakeably modelled on John's Cootehall home – over which Sergeant Reegan reigns. Time is passed in idle talk, in card-playing, in listening to football matches on the radio, in repetitions that work in the blood 'like a drug'.

Prayer is used as a ritual whereby thought is shut out and darkness kept at bay:

> Then *Our Fathers* and *Hail Marys* and *Glory be to the Fathers* were repeated over and over in their relentless monotony, without urge or

> passion, no call of love or answer, the voices simply murmuring away in a habit or death, their minds not on what they said, but blank or wandering or dreaming over their lives.

Elizabeth is the only character who has awoken out of this lethargic existence, having come suddenly to consciousness through reading and her relationship with the handsome but tormented Halliday, a doctor in her hospital when she worked as a nurse in London of the 1940s:

> She was less and less awed by the conversations and people and things that had dominated her earlier life. She was already reading, getting books out of the little public library beside Aldgate East Station, beginning to see her life in its passage, it'd end and never repeat itself, and she felt it unique and all the days precious. If she lived the life other people lived, looked on it the way they looked, she'd have no life of her own. She did not want an ensured imitation of other people's lives any more, she wanted her own, and with the wild greed of youth.

For knowledge of London's East End and the world of the hospital, John drew on the experiences of his twin sisters, Rosaleen and Breedge, who lived for many years in Leytonstone, working in Whipps Cross Hospital, and in whose large, shared house on Forest Drive West John regularly stayed over the years.

The reading material that her lover lends Elizabeth ensures the final rebirth takes place: 'She had loved Halliday and counted no cost. She could feel again her excitement bringing him back the first real books she'd been ever given and crying, "But they're real! They're not stories even. They're about my life."'

What Elizabeth ascribes to Halliday's impact is pretty much exactly how John recalled his own experience with books almost thirty years later:

> A time comes when the way we read has to change drastically or stop, though it may well continue as an indolence or pastime or drug. This change is linked with our growing consciousness, consciousness that

> we will not live forever and that all human life is essentially in the same fix. We have to discard all the tenets that we have been told until we have succeeded in thinking them out for ourselves. We find that we are no longer reading books for the story and that all stories are more or less the same story; and we begin to come on certain books that act like mirrors. What they reflect is something dangerously close to our own life and the society in which we live.

Elizabeth Reegan is keenly aware of her own mortality; how she deals with that knowledge in the wake of a breast-cancer diagnosis remains the central subject matter of this debut novel. Though saddening and unflinchingly honest in its portrayal of pain and torment, this work should not be read as a tragedy, given Elizabeth's clarity of vision and maturity of thought.

As the publication date of 22 February 1963 grew close, John became nervous and worried especially about repaying Faber's confidence. He wrote to Charles Monteith: 'The most thing I'll fear for on the 22nd – after all the encouragement, and extreme kindness you showed me – is that the book will, before the strange public, justify your trust.'

Any concerns quickly proved unfounded, with a flurry of admiring reviews in the main British broadsheets. Leading the charge was Anthony Burgess in the *Observer*, a commentator who saw in the novel a brilliantly realised moment in modern Irish fiction, daringly true and clear from all sentimentality:

> I know nobody who has caught so well the peculiar hopelessness of contemporary Ireland – the empty formulae of seedy courtliness of family night-prayers; the radio Angelus; the lost rosary-beads hung on railings; the endless phatic communion which fails to communicate. This, by a very young man, is more than just promising.

The *Sunday Times* found *The Barracks* a novel 'of mesmeric power and beauty, with a wholly Irish absence of despair'. And the *TLS* was optimistic about what lay ahead: 'there is a quiet authority in his work that promises well for the future, and the publishers are not far off the mark when they describe his novel as one of haunting power'.

There were distinct nuances in perspective. If the British newspapers were excited about the emergence of a new young contender, the book's reception in Ireland was more mixed. Kate O'Brien, a writer whose work John would grow to admire and teach in later years, was in no doubt about the quality of *The Barracks*:

> Seldom do we read a first novel, and a first novel by a writer still in his twenties, in which we find full maturity of thought allied to unbroken certainty of direction. But John McGahern, it can be readily said from the evidence of this first book, is an endowed and given writer of prose fiction; and it is with a sense of rare safety that one reads *The Barracks*, page after page, from the anxious beginning to the lonely end.

The review continues in this almost wholly positive vein: 'it is difficult to find words exact enough to express my admiration of this subtle, close-woven, tender, true, poetic work'.

Benedict Kiely in the *Irish Press* was equally impressed: 'His sentences move as steadily and unhurriedly as the flow of the river past the barracks in which Elizabeth Reegan dies, and the impression they leave is of experience sincerely grappled with and of understanding and of truth known intimately.' John D. Sheridan in the *Irish Independent* – the Sergeant's newspaper – was even more enthusiastic: 'Mr. McGahren's [*sic*] descriptions tingle with life, and all his pictures are vivid and satisfying.' But Sheridan concludes in censorious mood, alarmed by the coarseness of the language:

> Some of his accounts of the affairs of the body are crude to say the least of them, the Holy Name occurs frequently, with and without capitals, and there is a fair sprinkling of one of our commonest and ugliest vulgarities. For all these too there are precedents, some of them not so distinguished and any reader of contemporary run-of-the-mill fiction will be hardened to them by now, but they strike a

> jarring note in a first novel which is marked by sensitive writing and seriousness of purpose.

The *Cork Examiner* noticed the same moral turpitude but was less inclined to forgive:

> A section of this book won the AE Memorial Award for 1962, the first work of fiction so honoured. One feels that it must have been the first section because in the middle of his novel Mr. McGahern allows one of his central characters to think back on her life as a nurse in London and the relationship she had with a young doctor. Up to that point in the novel, the story is down to earth, but at that point the earth changes to mud, and Mr. McGahern sullies his book with expressions which a London jury in a famous trial found acceptable but which a great number of others most certainly do not.
>
> It is a pity that Mr. McGahern so sullies and cheapens his work for a shock effect because this story of life in a Garda station somewhere in the West of Ireland has an authentic ring.

An attack of this sort was not unexpected. John had become anxious, finalising work on the debut novel, about possible trouble over his decision to use the word 'fucking' in print. December 1961 had seen him writing about this issue to John Montague, then editing *The Dolmen Miscellany*, an anthology featuring new Irish talent funded by the fag end of Irish Academy of Letters money, about these concerns. Having agreed to publish an extract from the forthcoming novel, Montague had raised a difficulty with word choice that John stoutly defended: 'The *fucking* can hardly cause trouble, it has no sexual significance, it only lights the breakdown of civility.'

Although Montague took this point, John's concerns were raised when the completed manuscript of the novel reached Charles Monteith. As his editor at Faber explained to John:

> We have no objection in principle to printing the word 'fucking' which is used occasionally in the dialogue and I don't think that

> nowadays there would be any legal risk in doing so in this country. I think I ought to point out to you, though, that if we do print this word it is likely to have two results which would to some extent impair the sales of the book. Some libraries and bookshops, particularly in the Provinces, do still have fairly strong objections to buying books which contain such words and expressions; and moreover, – and this is probably more important than usual in the case of THE BARRACKS – the retention of this word would of course almost certainly lead to your novel being banned in the Irish Republic. I am quite happy to leave the final decision about this to you and if you really do insist on the word going in it will go in.

John agreed to remove the word from Sergeant Reegan's dialogue but refused to excise it from Dr Halliday's self-assessment. While Faber suggested a compromise of 'f . . . . . .', John would bend no further. The offensive word, or a version of it, is uttered several times by Halliday in the published work. An instance comes in the passage where he breaks with Elizabeth, destroying her romantic hopes:

> He saw she was shocked and broken but the threads had become too involved with his own life and he couldn't stop.
>
> 'These last weeks have been nothing but torture – that I'd come to the end of my own tether and used you to get a short breather. That I used you so as not to have to face my own mess. That I seduced you because I was seduced myself by my own fucking lust.'

Two years after the *Lady Chatterley* case, to which the *Cork Examiner* review refers, had lit up the Old Bailey, there was still anxiety in London publishing circles about obscenity. Conscious of the Irish censors' reputation for zealous prudishness, Monteith decided to seek legal advice and contacted a firm of Dublin solicitors, Gore & Grimes, who wrote nervously to Faber about possible scandal among the Irish reading public.

Discussing the matter with Monteith, John is frustrated at what he sees as an overly cautious approach:

> I thought Gore Grimes letter silly and irresponsible when it arrived, he went to no trouble to find the facts, but mostly advised you and me on the use of language, his letter is all vague – 'it may be but I think' – except for the Lady Chatterly [*sic*] which everyone knows about.

Although *The Barracks*, despite its use of obscenity, did not attract the ire of the Irish Censorship of Publications Board, the novel did fall victim to the perhaps even more powerful unofficial censorship at work in the country. John recounted the book's fate on his home patch:

> When *The Barracks* was published, my aunt had a sweetshop beside the school in Ballinamore, and the priest in charge of the school removed my book from the public library in the town on his own authority. The reason was that a married couple had made love in affectionate tiredness on Christmas evening, and he took this as unfit for consumption.

John despised the environment that could give rise to such an event, but his public statements about censorship remained civil and largely dismissive.

In addition to being withdrawn from certain libraries, the book also met with hostility from some Irish reviewers (most notably, as seen, from the *Cork Examiner*). Despite these headwinds, Monteith wrote to McGahern a month after the *Examiner* review, delighted with the trajectory of the book and its author:

> THE BARRACKS really has, I think, established you as somebody to be reckoned with. Almost without exception, reviewers took the book seriously – as it deserved to be taken – and were quite clearly impressed by the talent it showed. Our sales people tell me that it goes on selling very steadily – if not spectacularly – and certainly we are altogether satisfied and happy about it. In the Irish Republic of course sales have been particularly good; and apart from one or two thick headed people – like the reviewer in the Cork Examiner – most Irish critics have really gone to town about you.

The concerns discussed by John with Monteith about the use of 'fuck' and its cognates had proved prescient, though the book avoided a ban. But the gauntlet had been thrown down, and John was now a marked man. Official Ireland would not be so forgiving the next time.

Mary Hutchinson was pleased, back in Bloomsbury, to see John's success. Positioning herself as patron, she wrote to share her feelings with this new young find, whom she had begun to consider in the same vein as the emerging Van Gogh. To mark the moment, Hutchinson took the unusual step of sending a copy of his debut novel, inscribed in notable terms:

> John McGahern, to congratulate you on the publication of *The Barracks* – your first book – a new writer's book that caused a stir – readers finding in it the essence Vincent called for; 'Live with a lofty and intimate sympathy, with strength, with intelligence' (Letter to Theo July 1880) from your friend, Mary Hutchinson 1963.

She insisted on throwing a launch party that John could not bring himself to attend.

Peter du Sautoy at Faber telegrammed his good wishes, and Rosemary Goad, du Sautoy's colleague at the press, wrote in admiration. John made grateful reply to her:

> To a certain extent I have forgotten The Barracks; the reviews, except the awful sensation of the first weekend, don't affect me, except that I wished they were so much better so that they might justify your work and faith and Charles's. I hope it doesn't lose money. They say in Dublin that it's been the bestselling novel here for years, but of course Dublin is only a small place. And it got a rave notice on the radio tonight. Some very nice letters came, and Hamish Hamilton admired it very much and said he was quite jealous. All I care much is that you won't find your marvellous effort misplaced.
>
> I am afraid my family are not reconciled and won't. I am not wanted at home this Easter. It's strange how one learns to be alone. It was such a nightmare house to grow up in too.

To have the full backing of all at Faber at this crucial moment in his emergence as a writer meant everything to John, and he would remain loyal to the firm till the end of his days. Back in Cootehall, as John indicated in his letter to Goad, the Sergeant was angry at what he unsurprisingly took to be an unflattering portrait of himself. As John informs Monteith, he told his son that he considered *The Barracks* 'an immoral disgrace' and travelled to Dublin with a relation, Fr Michael Kelly, for a confrontation.

That showdown having failed to make John see sense, he called a family conference and wondered why his eldest son could not just write about something rather further from home. John told Monteith:

> He made speeches. 'If he can write, why can't he write about South America or some of those exotic places, and he'd make more money. They ran Brinsley McNamara's father, you know, out of Delvin,' and the collar of the coat is pulled up to the ears even in sunshine, and the face assumes the proper aspect for a journey to Calvary, but no cross was ever carried with such capers of interior delight.

And the wider world of Leitrim and Roscommon was, John notes, equally hostile:

> The local bumpkins say they'll 'dip' me if I ever show my face again in Cootehall. The priests in Ballinamore removed the book from the Co. Leitrim library where my aunt lives as unfit for parochial consumption. It's such an absurd country, but from a safe distance I am as well to enjoy it quietly too.

The only comment made about the book directly from father to son is an opaque gem:

> Apologetic acknowledgment of book belatedly.
>
> The blinds being drawn and the lamp lit a certain ex Police Sergeant prefers to ponder till the lamp shows light, or signs of flicker.
>
> Daddy

4
A Calamity of Love
1960–64

Sex is difficult, true.

RAINER MARIA RILKE,
Letters to a Young Poet

Perhaps as important as the publishing opportunities afforded to John by Paddy Swift and *X* was the exciting network of friends and fellow artists that opened up. Among those figures in the circle whom John came to know over successive summers in the early 1960s were several charismatic individuals. One was the glamorous young British Indian poet Dom Moraes, who had won the 1957 Hawthornden Prize while still an undergraduate at Jesus College, Oxford and shared John's passion for cricket. Another striking personality was T. Carmi, an American-born Israeli poet of military bearing, rumoured by some to be a spy.

Elizabeth Smart, the Canadian poet and novelist, lived in a flat at 9 Westbourne Terrace, Paddington, with Paddy Swift and family in the garden flat below. Smart's flat spread over two and a half floors that she shared with her four children by the renegade poet George Barker. During term time, the children were all away at boarding school and the apartment became a meeting place for those involved with producing *X*.

Frank Auerbach, then a penniless painter, recalled Smart taking him under her wing one night in the French House on Soho's Dean Street, having made £30 that day writing advertising copy for Jaeger fashions. She fed him and let him sleep in Westbourne Terrace. Awaking in the morning, he found a pound tucked into his pocket. Smart's son Christopher recalls his mother playing a subservient role in this very male world: 'She would race around as the general factotum and handmaiden, playing hostess to make sure that the great and serious minds of the men present were comfortable and being taken care of. She was never asked to contribute to the magazine.'

John remembers with affection the summer of 1960, when Smart and her friends first became part of his life. After drinks in a Lancaster Gate bar, they would move on to Soho: 'Later we would climb the narrow stairs to Muriel's, then end the evening dancing into the hopeful hours at the Mandrake. "All Men Are False Said My Mother" was a hit that year. Elizabeth Smart played it over and over on the jukebox.'

The song recalled, Joan Baez's 'Silver Dagger', is a haunting ballad of male duplicity. Smart, who had spent her life trying to escape from the clutches of a conventional, bourgeois mother, and whose 1945 prose poem of romantic longing and heartbreak, *By Grand Central Station I Sat Down and Wept*, had achieved cult status, was twenty-one years John's senior and briefly, but blissfully, became his first lover. Over two pages in *The Leavetaking*, she is remembered fondly by Patrick Moran as the older, experienced woman who initiated him with kindness and patience: 'It was Elinor who first taught me the loveact in whatever dignity it has.'

John was grateful to have at last a well-versed and unhurried lover. Smart kept for herself the apartment's sitting room, with three great windows overlooking the street, fireplaces at each end, her bed, a writing desk and a couch for visitors. While the building, and indeed the whole terrace, was a picture of faded Victorian grandeur, the ambience presented was still mercifully far removed from the 'fumbled sex in the back seats of cars or on bedsittingroom sofas or against alley walls' recounted in John's fictional tellings of early encounters. In Smart he had found someone intelligent and mature who made few demands and with whom he knew he would not have any sort of lasting, serious relationship.

Patrick recalls his first night with Elinor in sacramental terms, that he had 'entered the rich dark mystery of a woman's body'. That they should be brought together is seen as 'blessed chance'. Elinor, in thinking about the luck of meeting as they have, enunciates a doctrine of life that had become very much John's own: 'I think life is mostly that way. Anything that is given can be at once taken away. We have to learn never to expect anything, and when it comes it's no more than a gift on loan.'

At the end of the brief affair, John returned to Clontarf and the humdrum of teaching life. He and Elizabeth remained on good terms: in March 1965, Smart's position as books editor at the fashionable *Queen* magazine allowed her to give the world its first glimpse of *The Dark*, and John could write enthusiastically to Jimmy Swift of her 'marvellous' character.

The piece was run under the title 'The Four-Letter Word' and consists of the novel's opening chapter, in which Young Mahoney is attacked by his father for using the word 'fuck'. This section is a savage, pitiless depiction of sexual humiliation that sits uneasily between an article on the band leader and dancer Victor Silvester and a photo shoot of new-season men's sporting fashion: 'Clothes for sports evolve, because violent activities make their own violent demands, as fishes and birds evolve to suit their elements.'

Founded in 1861, the magazine under Jocelyn Stevens had become a vehicle for the smart set, the younger side of the British establishment at the heart of London's swinging sixties. Smart's commissioning of the extract from *The Dark* was characteristic of her generosity towards friends. The same issue carries a series of recommendations to her readers, with MacGibbon & Kee's newly republished *Tarry Flynn* heading the list: 'Patrick Kavanagh writes beautiful nude prose with the same innocent daring with which he writes poems. He and *Tarry Flynn* are now flourishing local legends that deserve far wider and louder applause.'

More important to John than Smart's literary and artistic networks was the air of calm their affair had given him. 'It was that same gift', thinks Patrick Moran in *The Leavetaking*, 'that gave me the confidence to enter several casual and purely sensual affairs and eventually to fall into a calamity of love.' Sex, the intensity of feeling around the pursuit of love and the satiation of desire would become among the dominant notes in John's fiction now and for the rest of his writing life.

John's early unpublished fiction carries one extraordinarily dark depiction of sexual relations as unclean and corrupt. The central male character in drafts of 'The End or the Beginning of Love' is keen on a local schoolteacher, Kathleen Lynch. She permits him to kiss her in early courtship. Knowing that any expansion of a sexual relationship must come through marriage, he broaches the question, only to be told by Kathleen that she intends to become a nun. This theme would be resumed many years later in the story 'Like All Other Men'. The early unpublished novel is replete with disgust at physical life:

> 'But why don't you want to marry?'
>
> 'I don't want to; there's something dirty and disgusting about sex, something,' she shuddered with repulsion, 'unclean.'
>
> 'Yet you kissed me?'
>
> 'Yes,' she agreed bitterly, 'our animal passions blind us and carry us away. But when you think of it: another body sleeping close to yours, his flesh against your flesh all the nights of your life. It's revolting!'
>
> He understood her. They all seemed to have inherited the idea of the horrible ugliness and sewer filth of sex. It had come up before his own mind: black blood splashed against the pale skin of the loins, the stench of rotting fish, blood matted in the hair that twisted like a pile of worms, the rough edges of a yellow tapeworm moving in the blood it fed on.

John squarely blamed, for associating sex with bodily and spiritual corruption, the Irish Catholic Church. He felt that the Church, for all there was to admire, had erred grievously in attempting to remove the natural place of the sexual instinct from its teachings on human behaviour. His position on the subject is captured best in a series of reflections that remained unpublished in his lifetime and that open the 2009 collected essays, *Love of the World*:

> We are sexual from the moment we are born until we die, it grows as the body grows and fails with that body, but by then it has

> become part of the mind as well, the will and the intelligence and heart, which continues to grow even as the body fails and suffuses everything we hold precious or dear. The church I was brought up in sought to limit this powerful and abiding instinct to the functional act of procreation, surrounding it with shame and sin, as it directed this human act of becoming away from the passing world in which it is set to God and Eternity.

For the Church of John's youth, sex was degraded, shameful and to be avoided except for procreation. This emphasis, he argues, is the Church's great error, pulling down the institution into an anti-life whorl: 'I see sexuality as just part of life. Either all of life is sacred or none of it is sacred. I'm inclined to think that all of life is sacred and that sexuality is a very important part of that sacredness.' John would ponder this issue repeatedly across his work, with *The Dark*, in particular, illuminating several of the more unpalatable consequences of such an unnatural rejection. As he would soon discover, this examination proved one that his country was not yet willing to endure.

Through the early 1960s, having been gratefully initiated into the world of mature sexual love by Elizabeth Smart, John embarked on a series of romantic relationships, some slow-burning and largely platonic, others passionate and erotically charged. Among the women to whom he was drawn at this time was the New York Irish writer Elizabeth Cullinan.

A letter of March 1963 to Michael McLaverty comments on the painful difficulties attendant on publication of *The Barracks*: 'The experience of coming out in a book was ghastly; I think it'll be a long time before I can go home.' Then John moves on to happier thoughts: 'Mary Lavin is gone to Paris, will be soon to America. I often see Miss Cullinan, she is a very beautiful person. I will miss her very much when she goes home.'

A year older than John, and born and bred in the Bronx, Cullinan started work in the typing pool at the *New Yorker* in 1955 and became secretary to the magazine's influential fiction editor, William Maxwell.

Her first story was published there in 1960, and by the end of 1961, she had carved out an impressive niche for herself, with six further stories appearing in the magazine. At Maxwell's prompt, Cullinan moved to pursue a writing career in Ireland from 1961 to 1963. She became part of the Dublin literati and of Mary Lavin's salon, which gathered informally at her Lad Lane mews near the Grand Canal and at her Bective farmhouse in County Meath.

McLaverty had been keen, from the 1959 beginning of his epistolary friendship with John, to point the young man towards Lavin and her network. He made reading recommendations to John – Mary Lavin's 'The Small Bequest', Frank O'Connor's 'Uprooted', Tolstoy's 'The Death of Ivan Ilyich' – for his 'own private enjoyment'. McLaverty continued to champion Lavin – then Mrs William Walsh – and in spring 1960 John took the step of ringing her and arranging to meet. As he recounted to the Belfast writer in March 1960:

> I rang Mrs Walshe [*sic*] and she received me with great kindness. I think she is the most charming and interesting woman I ever met. She said many good things but she has the unusual gift of seeming to say everything as if she was saying it specially for whoever she is speaking with. I also found that our vision of life and writing had much in common and that – deplore it how we may – is the most exciting discovery of all.

Thus began an important early literary friendship that would lead to an exchange of letters showing the young John on occasion in thrall to this more established artistic figure. Those first meetings quickly led John, unusually, to have enough trust in Lavin to permit her to see parts of 'The End or the Beginning of Love'. The earliest surviving letter, of 9 May 1960, urges her to let him have a fully candid assessment: 'the harsh truth . . . Nothing any less is ever any good in anything.' He concludes with a flirtatious note that would typify some of these missives: 'I have great faith in you – (a strange thing for a young person to say) because I think you have remained always young. O it was a very lucky day for me to meet somebody like you. I had almost lost faith in men and women.' The following month, he allows himself to write something close to a love letter: 'I despair that those as beautiful as you must go down with the rest, that not even our love and admiration can provide them with an eternal summer.' There is no evidence to suggest that anything physical came of these epistolary niceties.

Summer sees John sharing a room with his brother Frankie in their sister Rosaleen's small Leytonstone terraced house. These months were, as we have seen through his memories of Soho and the vibrant *X* circle, a crucial period in John's imaginative development, and he is more open with Lavin about the effect the times are having on him than with anyone else (bar with Jimmy Swift, perhaps):

> I have met many artists since I came. Some of them famous. Some young and unknown. There is a strange excitement here: of vital work, of the desperate struggle against time in a desolate and hostile city, of loneliness. Life is refined down to bare essences. There is none of the easy cushions of a small town. You must vitally live or be nothing. There seems nothing but death and sex and the grapple to keep alive and understand our passing.

By autumn, John has increased in confidence, buoyed by his new literary friendships and brief affair with Elizabeth Smart. His letters to Lavin suddenly seem written by an older man giving succour to an apprentice writer. 'Why should you linger on an opinion of your work?' he asks her as she frets over the critical opinions of Frank O'Connor. 'Great work comes out of lonely conflict, far from what Byron called the enervating vapours that the stove of society gives off.' Later letters become more business-like, with talk of placing work at the *New Yorker*, of meetings with agents or of an admiration for the work of Proust, Thomas Mann and others.

The early hints of possible romantic longing for Lavin did not endure, though John did continue to visit Lad Lane occasionally, mixing with a host of writers and artists. Lavin's daughter, Caroline, who would later go on to an influential role in Irish cultural circles as a journalist and literary editor at the *Irish Times*, had fond memories of McGahern's visits to the house:

> While my sisters Valdi and Elizabeth were old enough to be downstairs, I seemed always to have been put to bed when exciting people like Frank O'Connor, Tom McIntyre, Tom Kilroy and Nuala O'Faolain were downstairs. John was the one that came upstairs to talk to me and read me Rupert Bear, conveying the impression that he was as fascinated by Rupert in his yellow trousers, red jumper and trademark scarf as I was.

At the end of his life, John could look back with wry humour at McLaverty's attempts to get him accepted into appropriate writerly circles: 'I was introduced to Mary Lavin's salon by McLaverty. He was suspicious of literary Dublin, and he thought it a safe house for a young man. I went there, mostly out of politeness, a few times. The trouble was that I wasn't on the lookout for safe houses.'

But such retrospective diminishment is not wholly accurate. Through this circle, Cullinan – or 'Betty', as she was widely known – came to meet John. She became for him a portal into the world of American publishing when she recommended his work to William Maxwell, who accepted a revised version of 'Strandhill, the Sea' under the title 'Summer at Strandhill', publishing this work in the *New Yorker* on 21 September 1963. Writing to Cullinan in praise of her eye for talent, Maxwell says, 'you must now revise your belief that you don't know how to tell a good manuscript from a bad one. You have changed. You have learned. And if you see any more of this calibre floating around Dublin, start them on their way to me.'

Joe Kennedy, John's journalist companion, recalls meeting him in Café Ritz on Middle Abbey Street, where John showed him a copy of the *New Yorker* and proceeded to declaim the story in memorable terms: 'verbatim like an actor dramatically delivering his lines'. Kennedy was astonished and impressed by the performance – even more so when

John revealed the fee of $300: 'a mind-boggling fortune to a hack such as I on 12 guineas a week and the occasional "docket" for an advertising feature!'

Cullinan's friendship with John, while close, appears to have fallen short, ultimately, of the sort of commitment she desired. Their dynamic is stylishly fictionalised in one of her *New Yorker* stories, 'A Swim', from 1965, where good times together are remembered:

> The evening had turned out happily, and there'd been others like it – evenings at Mooney's on Harry Street, where there was a bartender who looked like James Joyce, and at the pub on Sussex Road, near the Canal, which they had called the little pub, until the night there was a fight there and he was hit on the head with a bottle, and then they called it the low pub. Evenings at Jammet's, the beautiful, old-fashioned Dublin restaurant, and evenings at the Palace Grill, where people up from the country went for their tea – bacon, egg, and sausage, tea, bread and butter. During the fall they met twice a month at the State Cinema in Phibsboro for the showings of the Film Society; then through the winter and spring they watched for French and Italian pictures they might want to see that would come to the theaters on the quays, the Astor and the Corinthian.

And yet the easiness and charm of those evenings come to mark a kind of rebuke, pushing Bernadette, the story's American narrator, towards some sort of conclusive break: 'All those times, all of them aimless and happy, troubled her as they came to her now, as though buried in her memory they'd grown to a size that her mind could no longer comfortably contain.'

Jim Delaney, the Irishman of whom Bernadette is so fond but with whom she is determined not to fall in love, remains keen for her company. The friendship has endured despite an ever-present distance accentuated by a failed love affair on his part. Bernadette thinks about the strange, secret endurance of what amounts to a connection tantalisingly short of love:

> when they went out she often arranged to meet him, not have him call for her or take her home, or she'd suggest that they see each other of an afternoon rather than an evening, or in some thoroughly neutral setting, like the National Library. Above all, she never mentioned other places she went, with other people. But after a while there were none. Other attachments ended, but this one survived – survived her loving him and, later on, his falling in love with someone else. Not only did it survive that threat, it flourished on account of it, for one evening he told her about the other girl, who the night before, as on many other occasions, had left him for good. After that, their evenings were devoted to the other affair, planning his strategy, analyzing his mistakes, celebrating his victories. He would call her up to talk of it, sometimes late at night after he left the other girl home. Once he appeared on her doorstep at eight o'clock in the morning.

Over the course of a day out at the beach, Bernadette finally accepts that the friendship is causing her harm and sees that their meetings must end.

That sense of two young people seeking, but ultimately failing, to find love becomes solidified in 'Doorways', John's 1976 story that can be read as an intriguing partner piece to 'A Swim'. Here we have another seaside denouement, except now it is the unnamed male narrator who seeks to make a friendship into a love affair, only to be spurned by an attractive, but always out of reach, American woman.

Kate O'Mara is a thinly veiled fictional reconstruction of Elizabeth Cullinan who has come to Ireland to be a writer, having worked 'on a magazine in New York'. The two meet at a party thrown by Nora Moran, John's unflattering fictionalised version of Mary Lavin. They begin to see each other, but for the narrator it is a frustrating experience: 'Aimlessly, like old people grateful for mere human presence, we went out together that winter. Only once did I challenge the sexual restraint.' Kate is seeing someone else and is unwilling to take another lover, though, as in 'A Swim', there is always the vague possibility of friendship developing into something more.

For those in Mary Lavin's circle, there was an assumption that John and Cullinan were lovers. A Frank O'Connor letter to William Maxwell describes a scene at one of his Dublin soirées: 'Betty came to a party with her boy, and who should be here but an Englishman who was on the committee that gave him a prize. "So sorry," he said as he left. "He shouldn't have got it, you know, but he was everybody's second best."' O'Connor's sniffy attitude is explained by John many years later in a letter to a friend who had drawn his attention to the O'Connor–Maxwell correspondence:

> It was the one time I met Frank O'Connor and he remained in bed throughout my stay, which wasn't long. The prize was the AE Memorial. The Barracks wasn't published then. The English man was almost certainly Philip Edwards, Professor of English at Trinity. Thomas Kinsella was expected to win the AE. I had no hope and only entered at Charles Monteith's insistence. Faber offered to pay the expenses if I lost. Typing 5 or 6 copies of an unfinished novel, having it typed, was expensive then, and it absorbed most of the £100 prize.
>
> The edge to O'Connor's remark was due I imagine to a tv interview I gave on winning the prize.
>
> I was asked, 'What do you think of O'C and O'F?' It was like asking a young writer now, 'What do you think of Heaney and Friel?'
>
> I replied blithely, 'I don't think about them at all,' thinking with a young person's conceit that I had adroitly avoided the question. Elizabeth C. told me that O'Connor had watched the interview and that I couldn't have said a worse thing. So much for conceit!

'My response', John concludes, 'was an unfair young person's response and I would prefer it to have been different.'

Whatever O'Connor's opinion of John as a writer, he was wrong about the nature of his and Betty's relationship, as both 'Doorways' and 'A Swim' make painfully clear. In 'Doorways', the narrator, having had his advances spurned by Kate, leaves Dublin to holiday in Strandhill and spend time with an old friend, Jimmy McDermott, drinking pints, playing handball, walking by the sea. Kate, having broken with her now married lover, follows the narrator, and he books them into separate rooms in a beachside hotel. All seems clear now for a sexual relationship to bloom, but, as in 'A Swim', we come to an unhappy epiphany on the strand:

> We began to read but the tension between us increased rather than lessened. I saw the white tinsel of the sea thistle, the old church, the slopes of Knocknarea, the endless pounding of the ocean mingled with bird and distant child cries, the sun hot on the old stones, the very day in its suspension, and thought if there was not this tension between us, if only we could touch or kiss we could have all this and more, the whole day and sea and sky and far beyond.

The story, with several open nods to Beckett, is a study in the absurdity of human behaviour, in the folly, particularly, of trying to reach beyond individual loneliness to imagine a completed life. Such an attempt, insists McGahern's fictional world, must remain stillborn. Call this world view pessimistic, if you will. But some form of this perspective, to John, was simply the truth. He had felt the matter intuitively and deeply from boyhood onwards, with recognition finding its most accurate iteration in a letter to his youngest sister:

> Joseph Conrad, you may have read some of his novels of the sea, I think said: 'We live as we dream, alone.' Nothing else is possible, to live in the light of our longings and conscience. I used to rare [*rear*] against the petty, repetitive lives of people. It is only a waste of time, Dymphna. We have only one brief life to live; we can live no other here. So why trouble too much with how the others live? You must live your own: and what it is will come to you if you have patience: and you will need much courage and discipline. As we are we are almost nothing: but I believe we can almost make ourselves into anything. By Discipline and Work. It is a difficult, bitter way, but there is No Other. You must follow whatever your aspirations are. It

> will not matter whether you succeed or fail. What is success? What failure? Who knows?

'Doorways' brings into the light the same message. Our own efforts to put order on the world are as one with those of the tramps Bartleby and Barnaby, who inhabit the doorways of the story's title: absurd, empty, ultimately comic. 'I understood nothing,' concludes the narrator. 'Perhaps we had come to expect too much.'

If Cullinan and McGahern could never quite find a way to become lovers, there were no hard feelings in the longer run. When, in early 1971, 'A Swim' was collected in *The Time of Adam*, the book's publication coincided almost exactly with the appearance in the USA of *Nightlines*. Cullinan writes an admiring letter to John: 'I've just read "Nightlines" and I think it's a perfect book. I love and admire it completely.' She picks out personal favourites such as 'Bomb Box', 'Wheels' and 'Korea' before heaping special praise on one perhaps surprising choice: 'I think "Lavin" is the most erotic piece of writing I've ever read, thoroughly and truly erotic.' She adds that Mary Lavin is in the USA, insisting proudly that the character of the eponymous lonely pervert is named after her. Throughout this warm and chatty letter, affection and a desire for emotional honesty ring out:

> I've been involved with someone here, probably the stupidest and most typical such mess of mine and it's been a very demoralizing thing for me. I'd love to be able to tell you. It would make you laugh, and maybe it would make me laugh; it's such foolishness but such unhappiness and of a slightly different order from what I'd at least have an idea of how to deal with. Come to think of it, you probably wouldn't laugh; you'd shake your head.

'After all that', she finishes, 'you'll be glad you're across the ocean. But I'd love to see you.' Whoever or whatever was responsible for the failure of John's relationship with Elizabeth must remain moot. But the story told in 'A Swim' of a man using a woman as a sounding board and a solace in the wake of a disastrously failed love affair rings true. John's emotional life, alongside his work towards bringing *The Barracks* into print at this time, lay in turmoil.

John had fallen deeply in love early in 1962 with a woman to whom he would privately refer in later years only as 'the dark-haired girl'. Their meeting in a Dublin dance hall – probably the Metropole – is fictionalised in *The Leavetaking*. This novel revolves around, in its first half, the narrator Patrick Moran losing his mother, his beloved, as a child. Its second half circles around Moran's attempts to replace her with an equally intense object of desire: 'It was in one of the expensive dance halls in the city that we met, with bars and waiters, and where the dancers – especially the men – were seldom very young. She was tall and dark-haired, and there was about her a hard if not cruel gaiety.' So began one of the most painful episodes of John's life, one that would bring him to the brink of despair just at the point when some of his earliest writing victories were being won. There are few writers who deal with heartbreak as unblinkingly as John, and the high stakes involved in falling in love are best described in 'Along the Edges': 'We assemble a love as we assemble our life and grow so absorbed in the assembling that we wake in terror at the knowledge that all that we have built is terminal, that, in our pain, we must undo it again.' The shakiness of all human desires and aspirations has rarely been so hauntingly described.

Cullinan was not the only friend in whom John confided about the awful pain of failed love. 'I waited and waited on Tuesday evening and that was all', he writes to Nuala O'Faolain. 'Then I thought she might be ill, or some accident, but the obvious one is almost always right, the hardest one to admit.' O'Faolain recalls these times many years later in writing John's obituary:

> He had come out of childhood and youth a formidable person. He wasn't finished with suffering – he had been rejected by a woman he was mad about, and I remember how it used to hurt him when an ad came on that ran in the cinemas then – an ad for Mystic nylons, where

> a witch-like woman ran nylon stockings through her long hands. But he had already made himself.

Of the love affair itself, there is little we can know for certain except that it was brief. John's surviving letters make hardly a mention of it as it occurred. The fact that, after more than a decade's research, I still cannot name the dark-haired girl with certainty is suggestive of a liaison that was secretive even by John's cautious and private standards.

The pair probably met in March 1962 and finally broke three to four months later. First mention of the affair and its collapse comes in an early-summer letter from London to Mary Lavin, in whom John has confided:

> it was kind of you to speak to me about the affair business. It went well here for a while and it's more futile and terrible again. I go to Paris Friday, it'll probably be the last ridiculous leg of the affair, but it's hard to have the courage to endure it, when reason etc. is long gone overboard.

July sees John turning to Jimmy Swift for comfort as he flails about in the aftermath of rejection:

> These days are so crazed with suffering now that I have no calm to see anything.
>
> It'll soon be over, I say again and again all day like a prayer. I have no real hope, only it drags on and on, and I know I am coming to the end of my strength, I cannot endure much more.

Another letter follows later in the month, with John in even greater torment:

> This girl didn't write. I suffer much, especially the times before the different posts come, but it's despair now and regret, not much of the sickness and desperation of before. I go to Mass often. It's the only place these days I can find the calm to see the Mystery. It's strange, at seventeen I believed I'd rise one day to true prayer by great effort, and now I smile to see myself reduced to it. We are played strange tricks.

In September, now back in Clontarf, he puts the whole thing more succinctly to Michael McLaverty:

> I write little, except a story of the break-down of innocence in a child. I came to almost the end of my world after finishing the book. I fell in love with some one: there is little end of pain in sight; and I am too troubled most of time to get any of the calm to work.

John's failure to hold on to this first great burning love object of his adulthood is brought to painful life in *The Leavetaking*:

> It was in the warm evenings that the torture grew fine: along what seafront, a scarf binding her hair against the evening wind, was she walking hand in hand with her new lover; in what bar were they mingling memories of their previous lives; in what room was he caressingly unbuttoning her dress, she kissing his neck as his trembling hands drew the elasticized silk, and did she open her thighs to him with that low provocative laughter.

As autumn 1962 rolls on, there is less evidence of the dark-haired girl as John buries himself in the proofing of *The Barracks*. Yet December sees him hint at unhappiness in an otherwise warm note to McLaverty, apologising for failing to fulfil a promised engagement in Belfast and hoping for better times ahead. 'My life will be less a mess then', he concludes, 'and we can laugh.'

The piece mentioned in the September letter to McLaverty is what becomes 'Coming into His Kingdom', John's first published story in Ireland and one on which he had been working for several years. The piece only came fully to a head in the emotional maelstrom brought about by the intensity of the affair's brief life and death. In gifting Jimmy Swift a Faber proof copy of Stanislaus Joyce's *Dublin Diary*, John included a draft of the reworked story:

> You saw it years ago but it bears no resemblance to that now. I thought it good but when the typescript came back it did not come violently

> to life for me. Could you scribble a note when you read it and tell me if I should send it away? Tell me truly about the story, since my own judgement's gone. What you say will neither delight or shatter me, since I don't care about the work. It was written in a crazy fit and I suspect it deeply.

Swift encouraged him to go ahead and send out the story into the world. In 1963, it appeared simultaneously in the *Kilkenny Magazine* and in the Robert Rubens-edited anthology of short stories *Voices*, alongside more established names such as Doris Lessing, Jean Rhys and Patrick White.

'Coming into His Kingdom' is a study in childhood sexual awakening set in a rural Irish community recognisable as Cootehall. The story opens with a boy, Stevie, being mocked for falling on a girl, Nora, as they play a game with fellow pupils on their way home from school. 'They're in love, they're in love, they're in love!' opens the story. What these taunts mean and why they are being made is a mystery to Stevie, though he senses there is some dark and unspoken secret behind them. Over the next days, he seeks the truth through an older girl, Teresa:

> 'I don't see what harm it would do you to tell,' he pleaded.
>
> 'You'll have to grow up.' She laughed the animal laugh of her superiority. Soon she'd be a woman in her prime. Already her body was changing.

This withholding sneer prompts in Stevie unhappy memories of his mother's passing: 'He felt the same futility and confusion of everything as when his mother had gone away for ever, the terror and pain of his whole life draining away.' Eventually Teresa relents and, encouraged by the bribe of a toffee bar and the gold wheel of a clock, tells Stevie that his entrance into the world came about the same way as the bull and the cow in the field. The moment, for the boy, is one of shuddering epiphany:

> The whole world was changed, a covering torn away; he'd never be able to see anything the same again. His father had slept with his

> mother and done that to her, the same father that slept with him now in the big bed with the broken brass bells and rubbed his belly at night.

But alongside this disgust and shame comes an erotic charge, an intense sense of revelation: 'While he walked, his wondering changed to what it would be like to rise on a girl or woman as the bull rose; if he could know that everything would be known.' Like McGahern in the painful aftermath of his affair with the dark-haired girl, as the story ends Stevie can find consolation only in prayer, lending the piece its title: '"Our Father, who art in Heaven, hallowed be thy name; thy kingdom come: thy will be done on earth," broke suddenly on his lips as he gathered himself to catch up with the girl so as not to have to come into the village on his own.' From the depths of his despair, a final reworking of the story was the only writing John could summon. We can see running through it all of the preoccupations that came most heavily to bear on his writing life.

While the loss of the dark-haired girl, however painful, may have helped John into some kind of clearer recognition of his own sexual needs and their source, his attempts to overcome the residual heartache brought him rapidly into further difficulties. The 'Darina' gossip column in the *Irish Press* of Friday, 22 February 1963, carries an interview with John to mark the publication of *The Barracks*. The unnamed interviewer, Joan Kelly, was then a civil servant and a successful freelance journalist, eight years John's senior. This piece is an intriguing item, moving from high seriousness about the nature and the purpose of writing to good-humoured modesty and teasing badinage.

'One could say Mr McGahern is unassertive and lacking conceit', begins the article, 'but his apparent modesty is, I suspect, nothing but a refusal to be impressed – most of all by his own achievements.' Kelly is struck by the young writer's relaxed demeanour: 'With a casualness one might expect from a writer of comic magazines, he will lightheartedly and convincingly admit he'd prefer to be out enjoying himself rather than staying in and writing himself out.' Here, in this early interview, the first of John's career, he is clear-eyed about writing as close to an affliction. 'I've been writing since I was 17', he admits, 'but it was failure, I think, which drove me to it. Failure to find complete satisfaction in life itself.'

Kelly baulks at this notion as she sits down with a man whom she sees as the coming Irish talent, a writer who 'can boast to being an enormous success as a failure'. She points to sections of his first novel 'The End or the Beginning of Love' having been published in *X*; work appearing in the *New Yorker*; a second novel coming out that very day, with a third almost completed. Refusing to be pigeonholed or labelled, John asserts the need for artistic independence with characteristic rigour: 'Labels mean nothing. If a writer is any good he's individual, he creates his own world. If he can be really lumped together with other writers you can be sure he's no good.' This exchange is as solemn as John permits the interview to become, before pulling it back to flirtation:

> Thinking, mistakenly, that Mr. McGahern had now decided to play the game seriously, and answer my questions, I asked what his ambition was, seeing as how he had his third novel almost finished.
>
> He smiled, and said gaily: 'For the weather to get fine, and for the two of us to go out to Howth and have wine and prawns in that lovely pub on the hill, The Cock Tavern.'

Whether or not this closing exchange was meant to take the heat out of a conversation that was entering territory in which John was uncomfortable, he soon realised his professed ambition of drinks in Howth, and an affair ensued.

Sixteen years later, John's relationship with Joan provides inspiration for the painful affair between the narrator and Josephine in *The Pornographer*, beginning with carefree nights out in Dublin and ending with the birth of a child in London who is to be raised alone by his mother. Towards the end of his life, John wrote an account of what came to pass over the following year. Still reeling from his rejection at the hands of the dark-haired girl, he made it clear that he was in no state to want a serious relationship:

> She was an attractive woman and if she wished for company I was happy to meet her on that basis. After a brief time of irregular meetings, mostly for conversation and drinks and sex, she grew more involved and wanted a serious relationship. That I could not give, and I ended the affair.

Some weeks later, Joan wrote to John that she thought she was pregnant: 'She was unhappy and worried but also happy in that she thought it was all for the best and that we should be married.' They met, and John arranged for a pregnancy test through his doctor friend, Niall Walsh, which proved positive. Joan wanted marriage, which John refused. He offered to pay for an abortion, which he could arrange through his London contacts (though the procedure was not yet legal in England), but Joan made it clear that she intended to go through with the pregnancy:

> What was uncertain at this stage was whether she intended to keep the child or have it adopted. I wanted the child adopted. Since I had taken no responsibility for our relationship, I was equally unwilling to take any responsibility for the upbringing of the child, and I felt trapped. Either way, I had been culpably careless, and naïve to think that the candour I expressed as to my intentions was sufficient.

Joan decided to move to London, where she had some journalist friends, and to have the child there. John offered to give up his teaching post in Dublin and to move to London to help Joan through the pregnancy. This offer she refused since he had made it clear that his help would only be for the term of the pregnancy, and she felt that continuing to work in Dublin would be more useful.

John arranged an introduction to a friend in London, Murray Mindlin, a publisher, scholar in Ancient Near Eastern languages, and then editor of the quarterly magazine *Censorship*. John hoped Mindlin might be of help in arranging contacts. Joan preferred to move in her own networks and sent John many letters from London, none of which received a reply and none of which have survived. These communications concerned her difficulties and her social life (there was an older successful English journalist who wanted to marry her). They likewise concerned articles she was writing and temporary work taken in London as a secretary. John regularly sent money and in the school holidays visited her in London ('when it became ever more clear that our positions were irreconcilable').

Joseph Kelly was born in January 1964, and John signed the papers acknowledging paternity. Subsequent correspondence, John claims, 'became acrimonious and manipulative on both sides'. A complete impasse came:

> She insisted that I see the boy before giving it up for adoption and once I saw him that I couldn't possibly give him away. I refused to see the child. She had moved to Harrow and I sent some further monies there and then did not hear from her again for some years. There ended something I have regretted bitterly all my life.

A further fifteen years would pass before John again met Joan Kelly. This moment happened in 1979, the year, coincidentally, in which a fictionalised version of the affair appeared in the form of *The Pornographer*. Despite meeting mother and child on several subsequent occasions, John chose to play no active part in his son's life, last seeing him at a pre-arranged Dublin meeting in 1992, when they parted on cordial terms.

There is little sign of the turmoil brought about by the affair in John's letters of this period, except for writing to Michael McLaverty on 24 May 1963 – 'I do not get much work done. My life is in a bit of a mess. And I may go away from here soon' – and a week later, more stridently, to Joe Kennedy: 'I'm afraid that you met me at the most chaotic time of my life. This person will be on my hands till the end or almost the end of June. Then she goes.' That same letter returns to the theme of failure raised with Joan Kelly in their *Irish Press* interview three months earlier, as John comments on some fiction Kennedy had sent for consideration: 'I wouldn't get too worried about what you say. We all fail. No one real succeeds. We fail ourselves and we fail one another. So I don't think anything matters very much. Certainly writing solves nothing. I often curse the day I began.'

This stance is an arresting perspective from a young man who has just seen his first novel published by Britain's most prestigious publishing house and is well on the way to completing a second one. While one might read these mordant thoughts as the words of a hunted, harassed man, there is also in them a deeper truth revelatory of a more constant world view. John had not enjoyed anything about the publication of *The Barracks* other than the fact of successfully bringing his private world into the light, fulfilling the compulsion for artistic creation that drove him on.

With Joan Kelly settled in London, John was relieved to see, at the end of June, the coming of the annual long vacation from Belgrove. The trouble into which he had got himself through carelessness – the one crime for which he knew he would always be punished – had done nothing to quell the need for romantic fulfilment. That summer, a phone call from a stranger to Howth Road set him on a new path. Mary Keelan was in her third year of graduate study in English literature at the University of Chicago, specialising in medieval and Renaissance studies. As literary editor of the *Chicago Review* in this period, she had met the Dublin poet Thomas Kinsella at a campus reading. On Kinsella's recommendation, she looked up Richard Murphy during her short summer tour of Britain and Ireland. Visited by Keelan at his Cleggan, County Galway home, Murphy suggested that she try to meet John McGahern. The two Faber writers had been introduced by Charles Monteith, who had overseen the publication of Murphy's debut collection, *Sailing to an Island*, at almost the same time that *The Barracks* appeared.

Though they met for only two days that summer – wandering along Grafton Street and its environs, and among the book barrows of the Liffey quays before jumping on a bus to spend the late afternoon and evening in Howth – Keelan made a powerful impression on John, and they entered into a warm, epistolary friendship. 'Mary Kelleher', a fictionalised version of her, is the central female character in what perhaps amounts to John's only truly optimistic story, 'Bank Holiday', written twenty years later.

It was a story that changed frequently, and sometimes radically, from first draft to final published work. Early drafts include a back story of the narrator Patrick McDonough's previous disastrous relationship with a mentally disturbed woman, sometimes named Rita, sometimes Margaret, and a scene with an open razor held by this woman beneath the couple's bedsheets as she waits for her lover. Writing in January 1981 to Frances Kiernan, his editor at the *New Yorker*, he describes this piece as 'the razor story'.

As revisions continued over the best part of five years through the early 1980s, and the name of the story changed from 'The Natural Process' to 'Bank Holiday', the castration-anxiety scene disappeared, with the finished product becoming an uncharacteristically celebratory consideration of romance. In the wake of a day together at the beach, McDonough and Kelleher become lovers, and a great calm stretches out before them:

> The following days were so easy that the only anxiety could be its total absence. The days were heightened by the luxury and pleasure of private evenings, the meals she cooked that were perfection, the good wine he bought, the flowers; desire that was never turned aside or exasperated by difficulty.

John only became capable of writing in such a way in his middle age. Patrick McDonough of the story, himself fifty, is relaxed, professionally successful and bearing 'the privilege of being no longer young'. This man has acquired a certain wisdom about himself: 'When he was young he had desired too much, and so spread his own fear. Now that he was close to losing everything – was in the direct path of the wind – it was little short of amazing that he should come on this extraordinary breathing space.'

But 'Bank Holiday' is a fiction, and the happy summer days John spent with Mary Keelan in 1963 were nothing like the love affair described in the story. Yet those days did mean a great deal to John, and there ensued a year of heartfelt, sometimes passionate letter-writing that would ultimately bring the pair together again in June 1964. The first such surviving letter, dated 17 October 1963, sees John regretful about the brevity of the pair's time spent together: 'I thought you very beautiful. I was more sorry than you could know that last evening. That we had no time to go out to lots and long evenings together.'

The following month, he ruminates on the differences, as he sees them, between erotic love and married love:

> It's a world of such inherent calamity. And the thing that only a love affair exists in its tragedy, erotic love of any passion, the lunacy of the subjective dream. Marriage is a very different thing of course, a social thing, but I often dream that it gives strength, allowing the miracle of two real people finding each other in their ripeness.

And herein lies the first hint of an idea that was beginning to gain momentum in John's mind at this time: that marriage might be the solution to the turmoil that had characterised his life for too long. He could little have imagined that a year later he would bring these early thoughts to a logical conclusion, though not with Mary Keelan.

Letters continue through the autumn and winter of 1963, with reactions to the shocking assassination of President Kennedy in Dallas, and a sadness at being away from his family home for the first time ever at Christmas, his father having made it clear that he was unwelcome in the wake of what he had written in *The Barracks*. The reflections on love continue in a consistent stream, with Keelan used as a sounding board. 'All my days till a year or so, more, were a turmoil', writes John in one letter. 'I was in love without wanting it, only admitting it to myself when driven to the wall of desperation, a writer without wanting, alive without wanting. Love was a way into all kinds of destruction, mostly the will to destroy my art.' Always there is a sense of two cautious people circling each other, seeking grounds for love without destruction. 'So write to me, please', concludes one Christmas letter, 'and we may be lucky enough to love together, now that the chance is given both ways.'

In the early months of 1964, John enthuses about Kafka's 'Metamorphosis', Rilke's *Notebooks of Malte Laurids Brigge* and some work by Jean Genet and Jacques Rivière, while Mary recommends he read Dostoevsky. In February, John writes with the good news of his having won the Macaulay Fellowship, which will free him from teaching duties later in the year, allowing him to travel abroad and to write full-time. For all that good news, John warns her of his fears that she will see a much-diminished man when they meet again in the summer, his health having been broken by the writing of what is becoming *The Dark*.

In March, he returns again to the question of love and whether there is any real chance of things working out between them:

> My will is the same as yours, I want you very much, but I know too much of love not to be wary, it can be a hell around you quick enough. What I most fear is that you may find the reality – me – a long way from your dream. So is that fair answer? It's honest.

By spring, the novel is all but complete, and John is emptied: 'Drained of every strength; and just despair, and crushing weariness.' In April, his mood is rising. Plans for the couple to meet again are taking shape, with much talk of whether it is best to meet in London or Paris. On 6 May, John signs off his letter in a mood of expectancy: 'I almost hate the sight of a plane by this but I will write longer soon and in eight weeks or less we will have each other.'

Ten days later, he seems sold on Paris, though this choice, too, has its ghosts, the debris of his affair with 'the dark-haired girl' never far from his thoughts: 'the loveliest city I know, a real style, and elegance; and we can go there, and stay in a cheap hotel and go and eat in the small restaurants. I love it more than anywhere, and I was deliriously happy and unhappy there in dead days.'

The reunion between John and Mary Keelan proved, ultimately, a disappointment. After meeting up in London on 8 July, with one evening spent over dinner in the company of John's sisters, the couple travelled on to Paris via ferry and booked into separate rooms at the Hotel Celtic in

Montparnasse. Peter Lennon and his Finnish wife, Eeva (née Karikoski), acted as their informal Parisian hosts. Lennon, a native of Dublin and four years John's senior, was then working in the city as a *Guardian* correspondent. Three years later, he would direct the film *The Rocky Road to Dublin*, which includes a brief discussion of *The Dark* and its controversial banning. Made in the immediate wake of the fiftieth anniversary of the 1916 Rising, this film posed the question: 'What do you do with your revolution once you've got it?' The answer forms an unsparing critique of Official Ireland's post-colonial baggage and theocratic leanings.

Mary Keelan recalls 'Peter's almost manic introducing, involving, influencing' and his desire to see John as part of an international literary scene centred in Paris, with their fellow Irishman Samuel Beckett at its core. Peter, Eeva, John and Mary would meet up every day for late-afternoon or early-evening drinks at local cafés, followed by dinner. All of these venues had literary connections with which Lennon would regale them. He sometimes would have other artistic friends and journalists join them. This sort of networking – with many attendant drinks and cigarettes – was neither to John's nor to Mary's tastes. But they felt obliged, as guests in a foreign city, to be social and compliant.

Throughout their days together, John was intense, never relaxed, and much exercised by the fallout from Joseph Brodsky's February trial in Moscow. The young writer had been found guilty of social parasitism and sentenced to five years of exile and hard labour, his life as a poet not considered a sufficient contribution to society. John knew that his own fight with the censors was now all but inevitable. Looking back on that time in her life, Mary could see a truth: 'each of us had expectations that, in retrospect, were unrealistic if not ridiculous'. John spent every morning shut away in his room, trying to make final changes to the manuscript of what would soon become *The Dark*. And it was in her hotel room on one of these mornings that Keelan first read part of the novel, typed with annotations.

What she saw shocked her and made her feel uncomfortable, though she would never say such to John. She wondered about this person for whom she had crossed the Atlantic and connected her feelings on reading *The Dark* at that time with the sensation she got when reading Jean Genet's *Our Lady of the Flowers* in the University of Chicago library the previous spring, where this book was kept under lock and key. The feeling, remembers Keelan, was one of 'blood curdling evil'.

On Bastille Day, the Lennons were joined by a visiting Finnish friend named Annikki 'Anu' Laaksi, a native of the small western town of Lapua. Recently divorced and living in Helsinki, where she worked as a theatre producer and translator, primarily from Russian to Finnish, she was good friends with Eeva. Eeva recalls Parisian high spirits on the day: 'people were dancing in the streets, and John and Anu fell instantly under each other's spell in that atmosphere'. A flirtation quickly began, too obvious to ignore but not enough as yet for terminal damage to the fragile relationship between John and Mary.

A couple of days later, the couple took a planned train journey to San Sebastián, which they found disappointingly overcrowded with tourists, and stayed in a dingy *pensión* near the boardwalk. From there, John sent a postcard to Charles Monteith, describing the place: 'It is very beautiful here, and monstrous in some way.' He found Spanish Civil War ghosts still tangible. Worst of all, John was finding concentration difficult: 'It is impossible to get enough withdrawnness to work and I may have to go back to Dublin to finish what I have to do.'

Though the couple never argued, they went different ways at the train station, he back to Paris and she to Madrid. Mary eventually returned to France but did not see John again until in Dublin with Chicago friends during Horse Show Week in early August. Even then, she felt that something might have worked out between them. But she had to return home to be with her mother, who was unwell.

And there the relationship, such as it was, came to an abrupt end – but for one autumn letter in which John seems as confused as ever about where his life is leading: 'I often think of the summer mess, and I cannot understand, except that everything I turn my hand to seems doomed to one kind of failure or another, I cannot understand and the more I write the more confused this becomes, and I do not know anything.'

That John would be married the following month seems, at first glance, extremely surprising. But marriage had been one of his preoccupations in conversation with Mary and was much on his mind throughout their friendship. This facet of his thinking was about a sense of stability, a dream that might solve a whole array of emotional problems.

Though they never had an intellectual discussion on the subject of marriage or on the subject of children, there was much that was implied or inferred. The inarticulate and the unspoken quietly undermined their relationship in the longer run. John made up his mind – seemingly almost no sooner than it had become clear that Keelan and he were not to be together – on a crucial matter. He would marry Annikki Laaksi, with whom he entered into an intense physical relationship after parting with Keelan in the dying days of July 1964 and returning to Paris.

On John's return to Dublin, the pair began to write to each other. John was relieved when Annikki wrote to assure him that she was not pregnant. She, on the other hand, wished that she were, and wrote of her fears that she should lose him before they could be reunited. She tells him that her Helsinki flat is quiet and that he can finish writing his book while she works in the nearby theatre. By early September, they are discussing marriage alongside multiple possible travel arrangements: ship from London to Helsinki, flight from London to Copenhagen, followed by train to Stockholm and onward into Finland. John, with his customary need for privacy, prompts Annikki to swear the Lennons to secrecy about the affair, and she writes to Eeva to ask for her discretion.

John's next letter asked Annikki if she might accept having his still nameless novel dedicated to her, an honour she proudly accepted, commenting on how painful a process she knew it was for John to complete it. Two days later, she wrote of her hopes that John would be with her by 14 November, just after he turned thirty.

The chance to be together again came sooner than either had hoped for. John was now on a year's sabbatical from Belgrove courtesy of his Macaulay Fellowship and travelled to a rather dull writers' conference in Berlin, where only W. H. Auden impressed. The city itself was much more appealing than the festival, and John spent his time visiting museums and galleries. As he enthuses to Charles Monteith, 'I liked it very much, marvellous wide streets, and trees, the museum I most enjoyed was ever at Dahlem, two Vermeers you could look at all day. East Berlin was an intensification of the difference between France and Spain and the people were afraid.'

On 28 September, John flew from Berlin to Hamburg, where he caught a connecting flight for Helsinki. Finland was a revelation, a striking combination of urban wealth and modernity with rural traditionalism. 'I went down last week-end to a town in the middle of the country', he writes to Rosemary Goad at Faber, 'it was very strange, extraordinary forest and lake and timber rivers, the train crowded, life at all the stations, it seemed nineteenth century Russia.'

While Annikki worked at the theatre during the day, John reread *Ulysses* and applied for a visa to visit Saint Petersburg. The new novel was finally complete, and there was time to relax and take in the city. As he described to Monteith:

> It's rather beautiful here, everywhere inlets of the sea and a great harbour and parks, full of pine and silver birch and redberried rowan and areas of stripped rock: but the place is horribly expensive, at least twice as expensive as London, there's no poverty at all, there's a real sense of materialistic dullness and puritanism in most of the faces, and then the nation seems to get methodically sozzled as a religious duty every weekend, some of it spilling into the streets in an ugly despairing way, but sometimes comic, one against a tree on a height in the park with arms outstretched in the shape of a cross, not even a muscle moving, with fumes of spirits strong at 15 yards away, and the dusk settling into a blue freeze.

In deep winter, on 24 November 1964, John and Annikki were married in a harbourside Helsinki register office, with two porters as their witnesses. John would soon write this day into fiction:

When they were called she asked the two porters to act as witnesses, tipped them when they agreed, and they followed sheepishly to the doorway of the room and remained there during the ceremony neither fully in nor out. The mayor stood with the chain of his office on his breast behind a leather-topped desk.

When the mayor asked the man to put the wedding ring on her finger, they had none, and he looked on in disapproval as she took the silver ring with the green stone the sculptor killed in the car crash had given her, and the man put it on her wedding finger. It was with the same distaste that the mayor called the porters from the doorway to sign the certificate – but they were married. As he paid the fee she joked, 'The divorce will cost much more.'

Three weeks after the wedding ceremony, such as it was, the Sergeant wrote to wish the couple luck in characteristically contrary terms:

> I would like to get you a wedding present. Which again reminds me that I gave a dog rose bush once upon a time. I love Roses. They so very well represent life. The thorns are always there to prick but still the beautiful bloom comes again and again if we have patience.
>
> Prior to 1917 the Russian peasants had a tough time. I wonder are they much better off today, or worse. In 1920 I sang the song not thinking what it was all about – 'We'll keep the red flag flying here.' It was a kind of a slogan in our life and death struggle for political freedom.

For now, at least, John's dream of woman had come true, and his long, hard journey from childhood loss and darkness into the new stability of married love had ended.

* * *

'After the harshness of growing up,' recalls the narrator of 'High Ground', 'a world of love and beauty, of vague gardens and dresses and laughter, one woman in a gleaming distance seemed to be almost within reach. We would enter this world. We would make it true.' Asked almost forty years after his wedding day about his views on love and sexuality, John replied that his opinions on the subject would not be 'any more valid than those of Roy Keane'. Pressed on the matter and asked to consider the connections between love and death, he turned from thoughts of Ireland's forbidding midfield enforcer to France's laureate of involuntary memory:

> In erotic love Proust captures this exactly when he says that one's own sense of self passes over completely to the other and, in fact, if one is rejected it's almost like one's whole life is being rejected. It's one of the classic sentences: 'My love, I cannot live without her.' But then you have to live without her and it's almost like you have to die . . . The more passionate that is, the more terrible it's going to be.

5
Darkness Visible
1963–67

> Fame, when it came, made him if anything still
> more solitary. For Fame, after all, is but the sum of all
> misunderstandings which gather about a new name.
>
> RAINER MARIA RILKE, *The Rodin Book*

Sitting alone in his Stockholm hotel room during the opening days of 1965, having left Annikki in Helsinki to get on with her theatre work, John was sufficiently moved by the presence of a Bible to make a transcription. A note pencilled onto a hotel envelope would remain buried among his papers for the rest of his life:

> God so loved the world that he gave his only begotten Son, that whosoever believeth in him should not perish but have life everlasting. This holy Book which on its pages reveals the Way, the Truth, and the Life has been placed here by the Commercial Travellers Christian Association in the hope that through this book many a soul may get to know the love of Christ which passeth knowledge.

So began the most momentous year of his writing life, a year that would see him rejected by Official Ireland, publicly vilified, dismissed from his teaching post and pushed towards self-imposed exile. As he transcribed those words, he was thinking about the next leg of his journey to Copenhagen and pondering the production of his second novel, still at that point named 'The Pit', the proofs of which awaited him in London. Conscious of the difficulties he had with *The Barracks*, both in terms of Ireland's official censorship and perhaps more significantly in terms of the unofficial moral policing that could permit a priest to order the book's removal from local libraries, he could not but have known that what he was now working on would produce a far greater storm.

The *Dictionary of Irish Biography* notes in its entry for John McGahern: '*The Dark* is often hailed as marking the moment at which the Republic's post-Revival literature came of age.' John himself was not quite so sure of the novel's totemic stature, remarking of its birth several decades later: 'In Dublin in the winter of 1963–64 I wrote *The Dark*, too quickly.' Such a settled view could only be made in retrospect since the composition of the novel took a greater physical toll than anything else he would ever work on, representing a necessary bridge from a painful childhood past into a more mature and possibly happier future. He knew as he composed it that something startling and powerful was gestating within his imagination. John writes to Mary Keelan in the days before Christmas 1963 of what he senses will be the popular failure of *The Barracks* in the USA, where an American edition was due for publication by Macmillan early in the new year. He hints that what is to come in his next book is of an altogether more arresting character: 'What I will soon begin to make pure cannot go unnoticed.'

If John did write *The Dark* with too much speed, he did so because he needed to push through and beyond the trauma that its subject matter brought to the surface. His second novel was a book, one senses, he *had* to write if he was going to progress and mature as an artist. To an onlooker in the summer of 1963, matters seemed to be going very well indeed. Joe Kennedy called at John's Howth Road bedsit in May to write a short piece for the *Evening Herald*:

> Things are looking up for Mr. McGahern, you might say. But this young man, whose work has also won the AE Memorial Award (the first prose work to have done so), is very modest about his achievements. Mr. McGahern is certainly not one of the bedraggled Bohemian brigade. His suit – with waistcoat – had a well-cut look; in his pocket was an elegant gold watch his grandfather had once

bought in New York. A picture of The Successful Young Author? Mr. McGahern modestly denies it.

More than half a century later, Kennedy recalled that visit: 'he in good suit, sitting at dressing table. Ink bottle, N-pen (primary school issue, broad nib) preparations for writing. No casual dress then. It was as if he was getting ready to say Mass!' This description of the writer at work matches one provided in *The Pornographer*, a book whose central character also lives in a Northside Dublin flat. The ecclesiastical parallels are striking. The novel's narrator prepares for writing in a ritualistic fashion: 'I washed and changed, combed my hair, and washed my hands again a last time before going over to the typewriter on the marble, and started to leaf through what I had written.' This process occasions memories of time spent as an altar boy: 'We used to robe in scarlet and white how many years before.' Intense reverie follows:

> The wine and water and hand linen had been taken out onto the altar. The incessant coughing told that the church was full. The robed priest stood still in front of the covered chalice on the table, and we formed into line at the door as the last bell began to ring. When it ceased the priest lifted the chalice, and we bowed together to the cross, our hearts beating.

Then the narrator's reverie takes on an ironic but nevertheless epiphanic cast: 'Among what rank weeds are ceremonies remembered, are continued. I read what I had written, to take it up.' Writing, then, is a sacred occupation, a credo John would make explicit to Michael McLaverty when declaring in 1962, 'For all art approaches prayer.' Coincident with John's short Stockholm stay occurred the death of T. S. Eliot, a director at Faber and a writer John much admired. Dying on 4 January, Eliot's memorial service took place one month later at Westminster Abbey, and John attended, holding on to the Order of Service as a keepsake.

The Dark was rapidly taking concrete shape in these short winter days. 'The proofs came', he writes to Jimmy Swift, 'wide margins, it seems more attractive than the Barracks.' By mid-February 1965, John had been joined by Annikki, and they lived through the spring with John's twin sisters and their families in their large Leytonstone house, making plans for travel to warmer climes. Valentine's Day saw the couple visit Oxford, with John introducing his wife to Charles Monteith, who was a Fellow of All Souls and brought the pair on a walking tour of the colleges before having them join him at high table for supper.

Less pleasant was a March trip to Ireland with the primary purpose of introducing John's new wife to the Sergeant. The intention was to stay for a fortnight, but one night in Grevisk was enough to convince Annikki that she never wanted to visit the place again. She recalled it all vividly more than forty years later: 'The moment I entered the McGahern family house . . . I sensed the horror and the violence. It was stifling, I could hardly breathe and I refused to stay a second night in the place.'

It was not only Roscommon and Leitrim that were a failure. During three days spent in Cleggan with Richard Murphy, it rained constantly, and the capital city, too, was a disappointment, as John told his newly acquired American editor, Patrick Gregory at Knopf: 'Dublin gave Anu the sense of a city drained of its best talent for whatever that's worth.' John's hoped-for return to live in the city for a period was beginning to seem more and more unlikely.

The possibility of a happy Irish repatriation became even more distant when, on 26 March, the opening section of *The Dark* appeared in London's glamorous *Queen* magazine under the title 'The Four-Letter Word'. There could be no going back now. On 6 May, Faber published the novel, and John suddenly became – at least in his homeland – famous.

He had long dreaded this fate. This decade was the one that had begun with the *Lady Chatterley* trial, which Penguin won, a legal showdown that paid a great deal of attention to so-called four-letter words and which caused a sensation, leading directly to enormous sales for D. H. Lawrence's famously explicit novel and a general loosening of literary censorship in Britain. Some years later, Philip Larkin could joke about this moment that sexual intercourse had begun in 1963: 'Between the end of the *Chatterley* ban / And the Beatles' first LP.'

But if the grip of the censors was being loosened in the UK, the same was not yet true in Ireland. Before the end of May, *The Dark* had been seized by Irish customs officials, forwarded to the Censorship of Publications Board, and subsequently banned. The case immediately became one of the great causes célèbres of Irish censorship history. John, all too conscious of what would likely occur in the wake of the novel's publication, had made arrangements to be out of the country to coincide with the book's release. At first it seemed like Greece might prove a good hideaway, with Monteith advising on possible accommodation on the island of Thassos.

These plans were soon overtaken by the attractions of southern Spain. John and Annikki determined to settle for a few months in a borrowed house near the beautiful, and then still undeveloped, fishing village of Garrucha in Almeria to avoid the inevitable tumult around publication. On 28 April, the couple left London for Spain, slowly travelling down through France to Barcelona. Much to his delight, John happened upon a copy of the *Sunday Times* for 9 May, which carried a rave review of *The Dark* by Julian Jebb. This man would quickly become John's favourite British reviewer and later a friend to whose memory, in 1985, he dedicated his third collection of short stories, *High Ground*.

Of *The Dark*, Jebb wrote:

> it seems to me a perfectly written tour de force. Like Robert Musil's 'Young Törless' it creates a small world indelibly and without recourse to deliberate heightening effects of prose. John McGahern's gifts as a novelist are already mature with this, his second book. There are few writers in their twenties whose future work can be anticipated with such confidence and excitement.

The book could not have asked for a better start.

By mid-May, the couple had arrived in Garrucha, where a letter was waiting from Monteith with the bad, but unsurprising, news from

Ireland. 'I was more disturbed than I could have known by the seizing', admits John in his reply, though the charms of the new-found Mediterranean refuge were a consolation:

> It's a lovely house, by the sea, with a burnt mountain at the back, a few stunted olives and bread trees and small goats on the eroding rock. All kinds of meat and milk or butter are expensive; but there are marvellous fish and artichokes and wines and small peaches for almost nothing. It's a pity that you cannot come.

He closes the letter with moving gratitude: 'I have to thank you again too for the kindness and consideration you showed me ever since I first sent you The Dark, and how much I value it within my own quiet that's impossible to communicate.'

Writing the next day to Patrick Gregory, John describes the initial feelings at the book's treatment in Ireland:

> Yesterday, Friday, Charles Monteith wrote enclosing some extraordinary reviews, and the news of the seizure in Ireland, I was not taken unawares, but it was strange how sickening the certain knowledge was, and the sense of disgrace, my uncle at his petrol pumps and other sentimentalities and lunacies filling my brain.

Two days earlier, the case had been raised in the Dáil, with Brendan Corish TD, leader of the Labour Party, asking the then minister for finance Jack Lynch to make a statement. What followed reads like a Myles na gCopaleen parody:

> Mr Lynch said that the book referred to was detained by an officer of Customs and Excise in accordance with sub-section (I) of Section 5 of the Censorship of Publications Act, 1946, for reference to the Censorship Board for examination as it was, in his opinion, a book which ought to be examined by the board under the Act. The book had not therefore been seized by the Customs authorities: they would be guided by the decision of the board as soon as it was received.

Dr J. O'Connell (Lab.) – Would the Minister say whether the book in actual fact was read by the Customs officer before the seizure of the book?

Mr Lynch – That could hardly be physically possible, but under the sub-section as quoted a Customs officer may detain on importation for purposes of referring to the Censorship Board any book which, in his opinion, ought to be examined by the board. He is not required to read it. That requirement is for the Censorship Board.

Dr O'Connell – Will every new book arriving in the country be held up?

Mr Lynch – Not necessarily.

Mr Dunne (Lab.) – How could he tell this book was suspect?

Mr Lynch – I am sure Customs officers do not live in the clouds.

Mr Lindsay (F.G.) – Without reading it, how could he form an opinion?

Mr Lynch – First sight is often a great help to people.

The *Irish Times*, in an editorial titled 'The Wise Monkeys', commented on this absurd exchange: 'We do not know what action the Censors will take, but we are so bold as to declare that whoever is corrupted or depraved by this book is past redemption anyhow. Once again we are in danger of making ourselves internationally ridiculous.'

Jack Lynch's last comment about 'first sight' in the Dáil debate is interesting, and comic, in a couple of ways. First, although the printed book was banned by the Censorship Board, blind Irish fans of McGahern were free to read *The Dark* since the novel was permitted into the country in Braille. 'I am terribly glad', commented John, 'that these people, at least, will soon be free to read *The Dark*.' Second, as regards judging a book on its immediate appearance, John had deliberately made it easy for the censors, spelling out the word 'fuck' in block capitals on the opening page.

That obscenity was only the start of what amounted to a truly remarkable challenge to Irish Catholic decency. The book is the first Irish novel to describe sexual abuse by father on son, employer on employee and, perhaps most significantly for the censors, priest on boy. *The Dark* also contains many graphic descriptions of masturbation as well as a series of teenage sexual fantasies, one of which involves a priest ravaging a woman on the floor of his church, having been sexually excited by her confession.

Frankly, there was no way this book would not be censored in Ireland. The year 1965 was a time, after all, just twenty-four years since Kate O'Brien's admiring novel about convent life, *The Land of Spices*, had been banned for describing two men in 'the embrace of love', and a mere five years since the banning of *The Country Girls*, Edna O'Brien's comparatively tame affair.

Intriguingly, early drafts of the novel demonstrate that John, far from being deliberately provocative, decided to temper the extent to which he would write about sexual abuse. Chapter 3 of the published work sees Young Mahoney in bed with his father, stiff with terror as the older man strokes his son's stomach:

> The growing hotness and the sweat were the worst but it was better to lie in the arms and not listen except to the thick lulling rhythm of his voice as the hands stroked and not listen and not care. It was easy that way except for the waves of loathing that would not stay back.
>
> 'You'll kiss your father good night?'
>
> The lips closed and breath went as his arms crushed, now the repulsion of the mad flesh crushing in the struggle for breath.
>
> 'Good night, sleep well,' he said and it was unimaginable relief to be free and to suck breath in and to wipe his track off the lips.

As upsetting and appalling a scene as that is, John had considered a much more explicit depiction in an early draft, where the abused boy is named Jim:

> He didn't care much now. The hands, the rhythmic words, were a kind of pleasure, stroking, caressing; except for the increasing hotness, the sweat. But it was better to lie in the arms and not listen except to the continuous rhythm of the voice with the stroking hand and not

listen and not bother or care. Just lie there. There was an ease in lying and just been [*sic*] stroked.

As always, the voice broke in the end. 'You'll kiss your father goodnight now?'

As the lips met, his body stiffened. Thick liquid was pumping on his belly and thighs. His father quickly turned his body away, put one hand down to his own body. No more liquid was pumping on the boy now.

'Good night, Jim. Sleep well,' and the father turned away to his own side of the bed.

'Good night, Daddy.'

'Good night, Jim. Go to sleep now.'

Quietly he waited. When he was sure his father was separate he put his hand down to where his body was wet. It lay thick and sticky on his bed and when he brought his fingers up much of it was sticking to his fingers, it was too thick and sticking to be piss, he could see it in the dark but it had a strange smell. With part of his nightshirt he dried it away. It must have come from his father, it couldn't have come from anywhere else, but he'd never known it before.

For whatever reason, John decided against presenting the abuse in such openly sexualised fashion. It is not possible to say whether this decision stemmed from an awareness of the censors, from a personal stylistic motivation or from an attempt to cauterise a wound: writing the novel was a deeply painful affair, one that took a heavy toll on John's health. 'I feel as if I'll never write again', he confesses to Mary Keelan in April 1964. 'Drained of every strength; and just despair, and crushing weariness but I complain far too much.'

On finally finishing the novel a fortnight later and sending off the manuscript to be typed, he admitted to Charles Monteith: 'I feel pretty lousy, I had almost to fight for my life in it.' His health had been deteriorating – intense nightmares, hair falling out, dramatic weight loss – right throughout the book's composition. In one phone call with

Mary, he told her that a doctor had prescribed taking long bus rides, staying on until the end of the journey and then returning, over and over, just riding the bus.

One of the only upsides to these difficult times was that he became firm friends with Niall Walsh, a handsome young GP from County Offaly and one of several doctors he visited in this period. He and John would meet regularly in O'Neill's public house on Suffolk Street, and he became one of a very small cohort of people with whom John would correspond into later life. Ten years after their first meeting, Walsh would make a crucial intercession in John's writing career by lending him a quiet house on Achill to finish writing what would be his next novel, *The Leavetaking*. John returned the favour by dedicating the book to his doctor friend.

Whatever the reason for John's decision to tone down the sexually disturbing content of his work, *The Dark* was a startling and dramatic rejection of the narrow, corrupt theocracy in which he had been raised. He was being somewhat disingenuous in a 1987 interview when asked how he felt at the time of the ban: 'I didn't really care for myself because it was something of the time. If you were a writer, you half expected it; there actually would be no shock or surprise. It was something that you lived with. You wrote the way you wanted to anyhow.' In fact, John more than half expected *The Dark* to be banned in Ireland. The novel had been rejected for publication, after all, in the severest of terms by the American publishers of *The Barracks*. On 24 September 1964, Cecil Scott, editor-in-chief at Macmillan, New York wrote to Peter H. Matson, John's then American agent:

> I think it would be (and I say this in all sincerity) a great mistake to have the present manuscript published either in this country or in England for the sake of the young man's reputation. It is a most unpleasant book with details that make the skin creep, and I cannot believe from a purely commercial point of view that it has any possibilities of sales. This, of course, is secondary; we published THE BARRACKS because of its literary distinction and the promise that it held knowing that it

> probably would not sell. THE PIT has far less of these two qualities. John is young and no great harm would be done, if he did put this manuscript away, forgot it completely, and went on to his next book.

Scott's harsh opinion, though wounding, in no way deterred John from forging ahead with the work in spite of possible future trouble. Disappearing into Spain was all part of a preparation for the worst: John's decision to confront the censors stems from a courageous determination to depict the realities of Irish life but also from lessons he had learnt when writing *The Barracks*.

That the use of the F-word in *The Barracks* stirred such discomfort and anger in Ireland could only leave what was on show in *The Dark* as an altogether more serious matter. *Lady Chatterley's Lover* constitutes an exploration of the joy of sex, a book in which Lawrence places open and honest sexual relations above any other human ends. *The Dark*, as its title suggests, is a much blacker and more painful consideration of the sexual instinct, of how this drive develops in a young man as he comes to maturity in an abusive, cruel and censorious world.

John decided, with *The Dark*, to be absolutely candid from the opening scene:

> 'Say what you said because I know.'
>
> 'I didn't say anything.'
>
> 'Out with it I tell you.'
>
> 'I don't know I said anything.'
>
> 'F-U-C-K is what you said, isn't it? That profane and ugly word. Now do you think you can bluff your way out of it?'
>
> 'I didn't mean, it just came out.'
>
> 'The filth that's in your head came out, you mean. And I'm going to teach you a lesson for once. You'd think there'd be some respect for your dead mother left in the house. And trying to sing dumb – as if butter wouldn't melt. But I'll teach you.'
>
> He took the heavy leather strap he used for sharpening his razor from its nail on the side of the press.

What follows is a frighteningly vivid account where the boy's father forces his son – who is never named – to strip in front of his sister and bend over a leather armchair, which he beats with the belt, terrifying the boy so completely that he wets himself and feels utterly degraded and robbed of his humanity.

Knopf, the American publishers who had taken on the manuscript in the wake of Macmillan's rejection, were so nervous about the opening scene and the language used that they persuaded John to change 'F-U-C-K' to something more veiled, which he reluctantly accepts:

> Change the fuck so. It is spelled. And I think what you say is right. There's only one danger I see – of making the same violence in the opposite direction and creating fuzziness; and perhaps the comma is too weak. 'Eff-u-c-kay' What do you think? Will you write and tell me! I'm very grateful; it does enforce the terror more in the real.

John knew that *The Dark* might be banned, but what hurt him was that the book had been essentially labelled as pornography and lumped in with other restricted titles in 1965, many of them designed for cheap titillation. Far from seeing *The Dark* as sexually inappropriate, he considered his second novel, as he told Michael McLaverty, spiritual in its deepest inclination: 'What disturbs me very much is that the book's a religious work if it's anything at all.'

Despite all its sexual explicitness – maybe even because of this factor – 'religious' does seem like an entirely appropriate word to use of *The Dark*. At its core is the confusion in a sensitive adolescent boy's mind between whether he should choose a life in God, as a priest, or a life in pursuit of self-discovery and worldly pleasure. Attempting to make up his mind, he goes to stay with his cousin, Fr Gerald, who gets into the boy's bed and caresses him on his first night in the house:

> 'You find it hard to sleep? I often do. It's the worst of all, I often think, to be sleepless at night,' he said, and you stiffened when his arm went about your shoulder, was this to be another of the midnight horrors

> with your father. His hand closed on your arm. You wanted to curse or wrench yourself free but you had to lie stiff as a board, stare straight ahead at the wall, afraid before anything of meeting the eyes you knew were searching your face.

Fr Gerald, besides this initial shocking introduction to a casual abuse of clerical power, is actually drawn sensitively and seems to understand very well the nature of the boy's turmoil; he speaks openly with him to such a degree that the boy feels able to ask the priest if he ever struggled with the sin of masturbation. Fr Gerald answers the query obliquely – but tellingly:

> 'The only thing I see wrong with you is that you take things far too serious, and bottle them up, and brood,' he completely ignored the question. 'Most of those in my youth who became priests were gay. They kicked football, they went to dances in the holidays, flirted with girls, even sometimes saw them home from the dances. They made good normal priests.'

'Gay' as a synonym for 'homosexual' was still not common currency in Ireland at this point, though the term had been widely used in certain quarters since at least the 1930s and was regularly used in bohemian London's Soho, where John had formulated significant portions of the novel. The presence of 'gay' is likely to have seemed entirely innocuous to the Irish Censorship Board and to most Irish readers. Earlier drafts had been even clearer in the use of the word, hinting at a predatory instinct among priests, with Fr Gerald telling Young Mahoney: 'Most of the lads who became priests from my class were gay sharks.'

The Dark is the first work of Irish fiction that held to the light clerical sexual abuse. This blight became a national obsession and disgrace as its ubiquity was increasingly exposed from the 1990s onwards. But John was not anticlerical. Like Young Mahoney of the novel, he thought seriously as a boy that he might have a religious vocation, a path leading him to a life in the Church. It seems likely that he made promises to his dying mother, as described in *The Leavetaking* and in *Memoir*, about a future in the priesthood. Her passing when he was nine forced him, at a very young age, to think about the shortness of life, about death, about the meaning of it all. As the nameless narrator of 'Doorways' puts it: 'the religious life had seemed for long the one way out'. Were John to become a priest, he could honour his mother's memory and attempt to conquer death. Yet to enter the priesthood for this reason, as his characters realise again and again throughout the fiction, never quite works.

Everywhere, John's characters seek consolation, try to cheat time, escape their inevitable fate. Except occasionally through love, they always fail. Among the most common means of failure is a flight to the priesthood. The best example of this pattern comes in 'The Wine Breath', which follows a day in the life of a country priest who recalls his reasons for entering the Church. Though prompted in large part by a sense of love and duty towards his devout mother, he cannot escape a realisation: 'it was out of fear of death he became a priest, which became in time the fear of life'. The story ends with a familiar turn to the sexual, to life:

> Somewhere, outside this room that was an end, he knew that a young man, not unlike he had once been, stood on a granite step and listened to the doorbell ring, smiled as he heard a woman's footsteps come down the hallway, ran his fingers through his hair, and turned the bottle of white wine he held in his hands completely around as he prepared to enter a pleasant and uncomplicated evening, feeling himself immersed in time without end.

But reading 'The Wine Breath' as an endorsement of the world of sensuous pleasure over the world of religious contemplation would be a mistake. John is reluctant to permit simple escape or consolation in the flesh, his fictions peopled by restless, dissatisfied, lonesome lovers. There is no sense in which we are invited to despise or to dislike the doubting priest of 'The Wine Breath'. He faces the same dilemma we all face and has gone about attempting a solution in his own ordered way. For all the power wielded by the priests of John's youth, he frequently argues that the ordinary people of the Irish countryside paid them little heed, that these people 'went about their sensible pagan lives as they had done for centuries'.

Patrick Moran of *The Leavetaking*, while still a young boy, promises his devout mother that he will one day become a priest and say Masses for her. Much of that novel is about how he copes with the guilt of not keeping that promise after his mother's early death. In a key passage, he reflects on the choice and on the possibly sacramental nature of sexual instinct:

> The true life was death in life. The sexual life was destruction; the sweet mouth, ruin. In my end was my beginning. One day I would say Mass for her.
>
> Could not the small acts of love performed with care, each normal, mysterious day, be a continual celebration, as much as the surrender of the dream of woman would allow the dubious power of the laying on of anointed hands?

Though framing the statement as a question leaves us in doubt as to the narrator's commitment, his decision to marry and stay with Isobel, his American lover, and thus to lose his teaching post, is one of the best examples in John's work of the religious, even priestly, nature of romantic love:

> My love waits for me in a room at Howth. The table will have bread and meat and cheap wine and flowers. Tomorrow we will go on the boat to London. It will be neither a return nor a departure but a continuing. We will be true to another and to our separate selves, and each day we will renew it again and again and again. It is the only communion left to us now.

For John, that stark religious need is sated by the transcendent, ceremonial power of sexual intimacy and of writing.

John's continuing admiration for aspects of Catholicism and his many friendships with priests over the course of his life are all the more remarkable given the unhappy times he experienced in the shadow of Church power. He describes, as we have seen, his time in a Catholic teacher-training college in stark terms, with physical violence always near at hand and surveillance an ever-present obstacle to freedom. The subordinate role played by teacher to priest is brought to terrifying life in his short story 'The Recruiting Officer', when the teacher–narrator, a former Christian Brother, witnesses the savage beating of a boy by the school manager Canon Reilly with a length of electric cable:

> In a half-circle the beating moves, the boy trying to sink to the floor to escape the whistle and thud of the wire wrapping round his bare legs but held up by the arm, the boy's screaming and the heavy breathing of the priest filling the silence of the faces watching from the long benches in frightened fascination.

John, for the majority of his life, did not believe in God or practise the Roman Catholic faith into which he was born. Yet his fiction, in spite of that biographical context, stands among the most interesting and the most lucid engagements with religion generally, and with Catholicism specifically, provided by an Irish writer. Far from having 'no religious feeling', as Seamus Deane writes of John's first four novels, those books, as well as his short stories and later novels, are drenched in religion. John was insistent on the religious nature of *The Barracks*. Writing to the trustees of the Macaulay Fellowship while still composing the book, he attempts to describe his aims and motivations: 'As it is not a novel, but an attempt to break that form down into a religious poem, I can only hope to indicate some of its tones as it moves to its end.'

In one of his earliest published interviews, John describes his work as 'a religious activity which is keeping faith to the sources of one's own being and it is, in the pure sense of the words, a form of praise and of prayer.' John's final published essay, 'God and Me', is the clearest of his pronouncements on Catholicism. Again he remembers the immense power of the Church in his youth:

> I grew up in what was a theocracy in all but name. Hell and heaven and purgatory were places real and certain we would go to after death, dependent on the Judgement. Churches in my part of Ireland were so crowded that children and old people who were fasting to receive Communion would regularly pass out in the bad air and have to be carried outside. Not to attend Sunday Mass was to court social ostracism, to be seen as mad or consorting with the devil, or, at best, to be seriously eccentric.

In such a world, the varieties of afterlife were as real to him as England or America. But this intense, unquestioning belief slipped away during adolescence. As John memorably puts it, 'Gradually, belief in these sacred stories and mysteries fell away without my noticing, until one day I awoke, like a character in a Gaelic poem, and realized I was no longer dreaming.'

When trying to come to grips with an Ireland that was rushing to secularism, John feared that the more worthwhile aspects of Catholicism would be lost in the race to cosmopolitan modernity. These fears are evident in the concluding paragraphs to his short story 'Oldfashioned', when the Irish Church of the late twentieth century is described in unflattering, depressing terms: 'As in other churches, the priest now faces the people, acknowledging that they are the mystery. He is a young priest and tells them that God is on their side and wants them to want children, bungalow bliss, a car, and colour television.'

Marcel Proust, a hundred years earlier, had witnessed and regretted similar trends towards disregarding the traditions and the lifestyles that the French Church had created over centuries, noting his worries in a letter quoted by John:

> I can tell you at Illiers, the small community where two days ago my father presided at the awarding of the school prizes, the curé is no longer invited to the distribution of the prizes since the passage of the Ferry laws. The pupils are trained to consider the people who associate with him as socially undesirable, and, in their way, quite as much as the other, they are working to split France in two.

Proust laments the separation of the religious sphere from the secular spheres of commerce, education and medicine. He believes that the mystery underlying the religious impulse should not obscure this impulse's centrality and importance. Access to a sense of transcendence, local and universal in equal measure, continued to matter to a central Irish writer, a hundred years later, every bit as much as access had mattered to a French master. 'I never found the church ceremonies tedious', wrote John. 'They always gave me pleasure, and I miss them still. The movement of focus from the home and school to the church brought with it a certain lightness, a lifting of oppression, a going outwards, even a joy.'

Despite the long-standing sustenance that John got from the Church and its ceremonies, with the publication of *The Dark* he had drawn a line of battle with powerful enemies and would have to be seen to be punished. In Garrucha, as he enjoyed the sea and the sun, tried to write, and passed the time by reading Primo Levi and Henri de Montherlant, he wondered if he would be 'allowed back to the school because of the censorship trouble'.

On 10 June, Monteith wrote to say that the book was selling well in Britain and that it would doubtless do likewise in Ireland were the ban to be lifted. Those hopes capsized the following month when the Appeals Board rejected Faber's pleas for the unbanning of *The Dark*. John was disappointed but unsurprised. As he wrote in immediate response to a Monteith letter of 20 July:

> The appeal failure is bad, the whole business, but it doesn't surprise me, it got very much publicity, and, with the Irish system, from the Customs up, once any move becomes public, to revoke something amounts to one part of the machinery betraying another part of it in public and that's never done.

This bad news rounded off a difficult month for John and Annikki, after July had begun with them crashing the Vespa they used to go back and forth along the dirt road between their house and the village, with Annikki needing several stitches to a facial wound. As so often over the course of John's life, however, misfortune was ultimately spun as fiction. The long short story 'Peaches' is set around Garrucha and features the unhappy, squabbling marriage between a writer and a Finnish theatre translator, who are referred to simply as 'the man' and 'the woman'. Their relationship swings from threats of divorce to lovemaking and back, with the woman drawn as an intense neurotic, keen to salvage the marriage through therapy and analysis, while the man is passive, even paralysed, by what seems its inevitable failure. The man reflects at one point, 'It had not seemed as hopeless as this once though there had always been trouble, and there'd been less talk of rights and positions, less talk of the fashionable psychologists in paperback on the floor by her side of the bed.' The story ends with the couple having to flee their Spanish coastal retreat to escape the clutches of a lecherous Francoist magistrate.

How true 'Peaches' is to life we cannot say, though certainly the Vespa crash features as it happened, and the marriage was troubled almost from the outset. The crackling intensity that had initially attracted John to Annikki in that hot Parisian summer a year earlier had quickly become overwhelming. That said, and despite the misfortune of the moped crash, John's letters hint that the couple enjoyed certain aspects of Spain and entertained John's Knopf editor, Patrick Gregory, for several days through late June.

At the end of July, John received the unsolicited offer of the use of a County Donegal cottage from Brian Friel – then best known for his *New Yorker* short stories but soon to gain fame on the Dublin stage with his examination of small-town Irish life, *Philadelphia, Here I Come!* Friel wrote in sympathy at the banning. At that point, the two men had not met, though they would come to know each other well over subsequent years. Although John was not in a position to take up the offer, he wrote warmly in thanks, trying to predict future events:

> What I plan to do is to go back to my place in early October in Dublin. I am on leave of absence. The Appeal Board have now rejected the Faber plea to revoke the ban. So I may get sacked. I intend to return

as if nothing had happened and I have no other plans. I am anxious to live in Dublin for some more years if I can. If that's not possible I think I'll go to London.

All of this inference was to prove prescient. On 9 August, John and Annikki left Garrucha, slowly making their way home via Almeria, Granada, Madrid, Zaragoza, Barcelona and Paris. On 5 September, they arrived back in Leytonstone.

John had informed the authorities at Belgrove that he would be unable to return to his teaching duties on 20 September, the day on which his Macaulay Fellowship leave of absence expired, since he was not fully recovered from his motor accident. In fact, he was fit and well after the crash. His no-show resulted from attendance at the Cheltenham Literary Festival from 4 to 9 October, at the invitation of an up-and-coming young poet and editor, Ian Hamilton. This figure was to become one of John's most important English champions in the years that followed.

Back in his sisters' house, John had begun work, in collaboration with Annikki, on a translation of the Finnish writer Veijo Meri's comic novel of the Russo-Finnish War, *The Manila Rope*, a project cooked up with Patrick Gregory in Spain earlier that summer. Annikki left for Paris, working towards a translation of Chekhov's early play *Platonov*, and John was increasingly anxious about the return to teaching. 'Much rumbles of dismissal', he wrote to Gregory. 'It won't be easy on the nerves going back.'

Three weeks after the school reopened, John notified the manager that he would be returning within a week. On the morning of the day he was due to travel back to Dublin from London, he received a telegram from his principal, Mícheál Kelleher, asking him not to come without telephoning first. This shadowboxing was a game that John felt unwilling to play. He asked Roger McHugh, his former UCD lecturer and friend, to ring Kelleher and ascertain the reasons for the difficulty. Kelleher refused to disclose anything.

On Monday, 11 October, uncowed by Belgrove's stonewalling, John reported for work. 'I saw that the only way to effect anything was to turn up physically and report to the headmaster. On the day I was supposed to go back, I just got the bus out as normal and turned up at the school.' The result was quiet consternation: 'Everybody was in a state of absolute dismay – including myself. Everybody was absolutely frightened. We must have drank gallons of tea in the teachers' room.' John was told by the headmaster that he would have to speak to the school manager, Fr Carton, who was away on holidays.

Before returning to London, John wrote to Patrick Gregory, bringing him up to speed on the whole sorry mess:

> The headmaster read me a note that I was suspended until the priest interviewed me, this would have to be after the 6th of November, end of his holidays. I then saw the Union: they were willing to fight sacking on the grounds of DARK; but not on a civil marriage.
>
> I do not think I could go through the farce of a ceremony, cage Anu here, bow my head, work humbly for them; and live with myself, and work with myself.
>
> Anu doesn't want to go through with it either, and she doesn't want to live in Dublin, which I want, but it seems impossible, it seems it must be the woman's land of London.
>
> So I meet Anu in London tomorrow. We'll decide over the days what to do. I'll then go to see the priest after November the 6th and probably get sacked.

Two things become clear from this letter. First, John's marriage in a civil ceremony genuinely seems to have been as much a stumbling block to returning to work in Belgrove as was the publication and the banning of *The Dark*. Second, Annikki's dislike of Dublin was such that a return to work and living there as a married couple may simply have proved unviable, ban or no ban. A week later, John wrote again to Gregory, making Annikki's feelings about a possible life in Ireland even clearer:

> What the priest may present us with is the choice of getting married in the church or getting sacked. I doubt if I am able to go through with it. Also whether it'd be as possible in the school as before the Dark (a protest is already organised and waiting). Anu couldn't ever hope for any work beyond translations in Dublin. She didn't like it either. On the other side the Dublin I love, the scarcity of sufficient money for very few hours. We mull and mull but it seems it must be London.

By the time 6 November, and John's showdown with Fr Carton, came around, his mind was made up about the impracticability of a life with his wife in Dublin. The couple's springtime trip to Grevisk had been a painful failure, tilting Annikki definitively away from any thoughts she may have harboured of an Irish sojourn. Knowing how she felt about Dublin likely made John's final encounter with the avuncular Fr Carton a fairly painless one. With a week to go to the meeting, John was clear about his losing position, come what may:

> And I'm almost fatalistic, that it hardly matters what way the priest or myself hop.
>
> The question doesn't even depend on my ability to teach. It's the civil marriage. And the thing finishes on this: that I do not think I am able to go through with a religious ceremony. Even if I did, it would not be the same to teach there again, because of the DARK, and Anu – that was clear when I went back. I'll miss Dublin, a few friends.

It remained important to John that there be honesty about the reasons for the dismissal, and he was more determined than ever not to let the authorities off the hook.

The meeting with the school manager took place on 11 November. John had no personal dislike of the elderly priest, a man who had originally appointed him almost ten years before. It was not the civil marriage but the publication of *The Dark* that was primarily on Fr Carton's mind. Almost the first words he uttered related to the novel: 'What entered your head to write that book? Such a terrible shemozzle you caused. I couldn't take you back after that. There would be an uproar if I did.'

Many years later, while discussing the controversy on RTÉ television, John had come to think of Fr Carton's role as essentially innocent:

> And the old parish priest was very sort of charming about it. He made a kind of tactical slip, which is to his credit, which he probably shouldn't have done. He actually told me that the Archbishop of Dublin, John Charles, had ordered my dismissal and there was absolutely nothing he could do about it.

Asked if he felt bitter about the whole affair, John answered with characteristic grace: 'I've always thought it's a dangerous activity to be a writer anyhow, and you have to be prepared for that sort of thing.'

The *Irish Times* drew a similar blank in its efforts to have John blame the Church, despite Fr Carton's unintentional slip that the intervention of Dublin's rigidly conservative archbishop had made dismissal inevitable: 'My own belief is that the Catholic Church in its origins is such a beautiful and great vision of truth that it is big enough to contain us all, and more along with us.'

Because it was banned and therefore unavailable for purchase in the Irish Republic, *The Dark* was not as widely reviewed on publication as would ordinarily have been the case. The *Irish Times* was embarrassed by the whole affair, and even the traditionally more conservative and Catholic *Irish Independent* felt that banning, whatever one thought about the book's merits, was excessive. And this was in spite of the fact that the newspaper features in the novel as an aid to Young Mahoney's masturbatory fantasies via an advertisement promoting hair removal for women. 'The net result of what has been done', argues a June editorial, 'seems likely to confer on Mr. McGahern the reputation of being a major novelist, which he may not deserve, or of being a pornographer, which he scarcely merits.'

The British reviews were unperturbed by the controversy the book had caused in its author's homeland and were, for the most part, positive. These accounts tended to dwell on the novel's depressing portrait of modern Ireland. Christopher Wordsworth wrote in the *Guardian*: 'This is that stone-breaker's Ireland, prison of prejudice and modified poverty, the underside of the shamrock.' Most enthusiastic was Julian Jebb's one, which John had excitedly read from a street stall in Barcelona. Jebb's only reservation came in relation to the regular switching of the narrator's voice from first to second to third person, which he found 'distracting and unnecessary'. The reviewer in *Catholic World* was even more discomfited by this unusual modulation of voice and may well have been on to something when writing of John that 'he simply could not bring himself to write in the first-person singular' such was the traumatic nature of the plot. 'It is indeed a bleak and pitiless little book', concludes the review, 'so secret, so deeply personal that its author apparently could not even bear to reread it.'

The least favourable review of *The Dark* came in the *TLS*. This periodical's practice at the time was anonymous publication. But John quickly discovered that its author was the Irish poet and editor Anthony Cronin, a man he knew well through both Irish and London literary circles, a man whom he dismisses in a letter to Michael McLaverty as 'a Dublin public house oracle'. Titled 'Swotting Out of the Farm', Cronin's assessment lays out a number of charges. For him, the novel is 'slightly too repetitive about everything'. The central character, argues the review, never truly develops: 'remains a bit of a suffering machine – the swotting is also too repetitive'.

Angry about what he considered a betrayal by someone who was, however tangentially, part of his circle, John saw the piece as a product of the small and bitter world of the Dublin literary pub. Likely what hurt most of all about the review was that it gnawed away at some of John's own misgivings about *The Dark* and, in a more existential sense, about writing and publishing fiction at all, a subject on which the unnamed writer of 'Peaches' ruminates as he reads the reviews sent to him in Spain by his London publisher:

> It was never easy to read reviews, and he read through them quickly when the beer came. It was much like listening to talk about yourself from another room, and the listener cares little about the quality of the talk as long as it is praise. Always the poor reviews rankled and remained, they were probably nearer the truth in the long run.

Despite the supportive reception given to his second novel, Cronin's opinion lingered longest in the memory. Twenty years later, John would have his revenge via 'Parachutes', where the characters of Paddy and Claire Mulvey, based on Cronin and his first wife Thérèse Campbell, are depicted as a neglectful, bohemian couple, more interested in the next drink's source than in caring for their young daughter.

While John was unenthusiastic about apportioning blame over the whole banning affair and had little interest in a protest letter being drummed up by Peter Lennon in Paris, he remained doggedly committed to transparency. His immediate instinct as he left Clontarf for the last time was to let the whole thing drop. A subsequent meeting with the Irish National Teachers' Organisation (INTO) saw John indicate that he had experienced more than his fill of publicity. He was congratulated for his pragmatism.

This mood did not hold. On returning to London, he changed his mind. The union sought to get off the hook by pointing to John's lapsed membership while on sabbatical, despite the fact that he had paid his dues for the previous eight years. Shortly afterwards, Treasa MacManus, who was being hired at Belgrove's girls' school, had to visit INTO head office to sort out her own membership. The general secretary got agitated when he heard where she was headed, talking about the disgrace that John had brought upon the profession and asking her if she had read any of his books. He anticipated her reply: 'Well, if you haven't, DON'T. *The Dark* especially is pure filth.'

Ultimately, the union agreed to contact Fr Carton, seeking the reason, in writing, for John's dismissal. 'The whole business', wrote John to Michael McLaverty, 'reminds me of the more savage pieces of Carleton.'

After much prompting, a reply came from the school manager: 'Mr McGahern is quite well aware of the valid reason which would render his resumption of duties here inadvisable.' The response drew a wry smile, the fight was over, and John could joke about the priest's parting shot in a letter to Jimmy Swift: 'The Union spent 2 months pressing the priest for an answer, he produced a jewel though, well worth the long wait.' 'I did not believe my case was very important', he would reflect long after the events had passed. 'On a relative scale, consider a great writer like Isaac Babel who was forced into silence for years, then put in a concentration camp, where he was shot or died of typhus.'

There were practical and uncomfortable results from the whole affair: John was missing Dublin, the Friday evenings in the Stag's Head, the long walks along the bay, the bookstores and the barrows. London's East End now seemed pallid in comparison. As he memorably sketched to Jimmy Swift:

> Remorseless fog, blue where it can't be penetrated, utterly depressing. In Dublin there's always an expectation of some change or there'll be some crack in the sky, to little virtue certainly, but not here.
>
> I always want to laugh when I see a sun or moon over London, it seems always they've come to the wrong place.

For those figures who censored his work and effectively banished him from Ireland, he was coldly dismissive: 'I didn't think that they were, in the strict sense of the word, *serious*.' John was open to Patrick Gregory in his doubts about the permanent move to England: 'physically and financially it cannot be as easy in London as it was'. And yet he was more committed than ever to fulfilling his artistic mission: 'Nothing now can affect my work, it grows only more clear, this journey into my changing self, in search of style.'

With the American edition of *The Dark* due out from Knopf early in 1966, Gregory urged John to travel to New York to promote the book, something he was loath to do, always disliking the whole circus around publication. After much prompting, John and Annikki flew from

Heathrow to JFK on 6 February, settled into their hotel and then went for a meal with Gregory and his dinner date, Madeline Green. John was not to know it, but this event would prove one of the most important of his life. Though Knopf's promotional tour was something of a flop, John would never, had he not undertaken this trip, have met Madeline, who, over the following years, became his closest friend, his wife and his most astute adviser.

Because both of them grew up in painful family circumstances, John found himself able to commune openly and honestly with Madeline. And it was not just on this profound emotional level that the two connected. 'Not only did she type, and help edit my work', he writes towards the end of his life, 'but she was the reader I trusted most. When anything was wrong with the work she was always the first to see it.'

The four diners met by arrangement in the Russian Tea Room at 150 West 57th Street, a Manhattan restaurant frequented by artists, actors, politicians and writers. Located in proximity to Carnegie Hall, this venue was a particular favourite of concertgoers and a place well known to Madeline. She had been invited to attend by Gregory, a friend of her youth whom she knew from her early years in Snedens Landing, then a community of artists and intellectuals on the banks of the Hudson. In later childhood, when she was not away in various boarding schools, Manhattan became home, with the Russian Tea Room a short walk from the apartment on West 56th Street where she and her father, Niels Gron, took up residence in 1943. For many years, her concert-pianist father also kept a studio in the Carnegie Hall building. These lively Midtown blocks were about as close to home as Madeline knew.

At dinner that evening, Madeline was drawn to John's melancholy separateness, finding him thoughtful and interesting company. Annikki was full of vitality, despite the effects of creeping jetlag. This occasion was the only time these two women would meet, with Annikki going onward to Canada within days. While Gregory knew his date from the days the two had been childhood neighbours, they were not close. Madeline, John and Gregory would meet three more times during John's three-week

New York sojourn. On the last such occasion John gave Madeline his London contact details, suggesting she look him up if ever in England.

Madeline Gron – or 'Bambi' as she was affectionately known in childhood – was born on 29 October 1934, twelve days before John, in New York City. That coincidence of a birth year and a shared experience of an unhappy childhood (they joked in later years over the idea of their fathers meeting in Hell) was about all they had in common.

Both of Madeline's parents were born into privilege. Her mother, Katherine 'Kate' Delafield, met and fell in love with Niels Gron when they were nineteen. They married shortly after. By the time Madeline was four, the marriage had ended, with her father gaining custody of his daughter. Kate Delafield went on to live a peripatetic life, marrying a further seven times, including to Tom Carnegie of the Carnegie line, and only seeing her daughter occasionally.

After 1951, Madeline and her mother lost touch almost entirely, besides one visit by Madeline to see her mother in Alamosa, Colorado in the late 1950s and a visit in January 1972 to Atascadero, California, where Kate remained for the rest of her life, ending her days in sheltered housing, a ward of the state of California, and dying in September 1995. Madeline and John managed one more visit to California before Kate's end, with John writing to his French translator and friend, Alain Delahaye, of his impressions:

> I liked California. San Francisco is a wonderful city. The hills everywhere drop into the sky. I spoke in Berkeley and we were very lucky in our hosts. Then we drove south to visit Madeline's mother, a small town Atascadero, the prison for the criminally insane, child molesters etc. She lived alone with an aged cat, feeding birds, and wild animals. She's a terrible person, almost worse than Madeline's father. It may be luck that we have no children.

As much as John disliked Kate, however, he insisted that he and Madeline travel from Ireland for her 1995 funeral, a gesture that meant a great deal to his wife.

Madeline's father, Niels Gron, was born in Norway in 1913, the year in which his entrepreneurial father, Niels Jensen Laurids Grøn, ran unsuccessfully for the Danish parliament. Niels junior was a tall, handsome, charismatic man with ambitions to become a concert pianist and harpsichordist under the tutelage of Polish virtuoso Wanda Landowska. Like Frank McGahern, he could be charming, but he was also deeply troubled, with an insatiable and pathological libidinal drive that would see him take dozens of lovers over the years, both women and men.

He would come to dominate his daughter's life in various unwelcome ways in the years before she and John came together, using her as a token and attempting to control her in whatever self-promoting way he saw fit. Reflective of his manipulative charm and penchant for taking on a variety of personae, he was known by several surnames: Masters and Masters Stone were two of them. When he married Kate Delafield on 31 May 1933, he used the name Edgar Lee Stone. He reverted to Gron when aged about forty, for a piano recital, and then retained the name. Madeline McGahern's birth certificate gives 'Gron' as her surname, which she legally changed to 'Green' in 1964 as an assertion of independence from her father.

Madeline was sent to boarding schools from early childhood, ultimately graduating from Windsor Mountain in Lenox, Massachusetts in the summer of 1951, with hopes perhaps to go on to college in Bennington. Alas, her father had other ideas. Unbeknown to Madeline, he had, in characteristic fashion, seduced a seventeen-year-old classmate of hers. Using his daughter as an alibi in an act of double betrayal, he arranged for them all to travel to Europe in the summer after graduation.

Madeline would spend most of the next two years variously in France, Italy and England. She and her father spent the summers of 1951, 1952 and 1953 in Siena, where they both studied at the Accademia Musicale Chigiana founded by Count Guido Chigi Saracini in 1932. Madeline and Gron stayed in the Siena villa of the Vivante family, whose son Paolo would go on to be a noted classicist, writing *The Homeric Imagination: A Study of Homer's Poetic Perception of Reality*.

This book became much admired by John in later years, helping to form his thinking about the significance of the day as a discrete and sacred unit of time.

In 1953, Gron came up with a self-aggrandising solution to the problem of what to do with his daughter: an arranged marriage into wealth and privilege. In August of that year, aged eighteen, Madeline was married to someone she barely knew, the twenty-one-year-old Armar Archbold Strauss, a young man whose great-grandfather on his mother's side, John Dustin Archbold, had been one of the key figures, along with John D. Rockefeller, in the establishment and rapid growth of Standard Oil.

Armar Archbold, Armar's uncle, was Madeline's godfather and someone of whom she was particularly fond. He had been Gron's schoolmate at the elite Choate preparatory school for boys in Wallingford, Connecticut. Soon after Uncle Armar's death in July 1957, aged forty-eight, Gron took up with his late friend's fiancée, Nina, the Countess Seafield, one of Britain's wealthiest women. The countess was someone who would become, indirectly, an important figure in the lives of John and Madeline. She is fictionalised in *The Leavetaking* as 'Caroline'.

Madeline's first marriage lasted five years, ending in spring 1958. At the break-up, Gron concluded that his daughter was insane and began making arrangements to confine her in a Swiss sanatorium. That Madeline was mad became, for many years, an idée fixe for Gron. When she and John first started to see each other, Gron, convinced that John was a fortune hunter, was quick to tell him of Madeline's supposed instability. A document written by John in later years describing his early encounters with Gron is instructive:

> I met Niels Groen in 1967. My first impression was that of a persuasive, charming, cultivated man. This was to prove superficial. Once he saw that my relationship with his daughter was serious it brought out extraordinary reactions. For instance, he called on literary friends of mine, saying he suspected me of being a fortune hunter, that his daughter was a rich woman, and that it was his duty to protect

> that fortune. These people were so dumbfounded by the visit that they wrote me at once. I had never reason, then or now, to believe my wife had any fortune. Next he tried to persuade me to leave his daughter, on the grounds that she was crazy, hated him, and that she would come to hate me in the same way. In the many years of our marriage I've never had the slightest evidence of this.

The document continues, summing up in unsentimental terms what John understood to be at the root of this sad relationship between father and daughter:

> In regard to her feelings for her father, I believe them to be the very contrary to this statement. As an only child, mostly brought up by her father, I believe that she loved and trusted him to excess, and that all normal desire for a natural relationship had to be abandoned because of the impossibility of his character. To this day she holds no rancour, only a very deep regret.

Given the various and many cruelties inflicted on them as children and youths, it is remarkable that Madeline and John had emerged unembittered into mature adulthood. When the fateful Russian Tea Room dinner of February 1966 took place, Madeline was single, adrift and increasingly unhappy. She left New York in September 1966, taking the SS *France* to Le Havre, setting up in Paris to work for her father at his recording studio on rue de Seine.

Gron was capitalising on his love affair with the Countess Seafield, fulfilling a long-standing dream of living an opulent, rentier life, and acquiring properties all over Paris on the strength of her generosity. These acquisitions included a large, six-storey townhouse on rue Guisarde that he made his home, where one was expected to dress for dinner and where he lived a life of lavish excess. When Madeline first arrived in Paris, she lived in a hotel on rue de l'Université, before her father moved her into a duplex apartment at 1 rue Christine, purchased in her name in order to allow him to accumulate yet more property.

The deal was that rue Christine would be Madeline's inheritance, though this arrangement later led to a stand-off when Gron tried to seize the property during the early years of John and Madeline's courtship. John insisted that Madeline needed to hire a lawyer and find out the exact situation. Ultimately, Gron sold downstairs, and Madeline was able to establish via a solicitor that the top floor was hers.

The apartment at 1 rue Christine would become an important base for the couple, generating a crucial source of income in the lean decades of the 1970s and 1980s. Most importantly, it offered a place of refuge from the world, where John wrote or completed many of the stories that would form his first collection, *Nightlines*. Located in the sixth arrondissement and named for a daughter of King Henri IV, the narrow rue Christine was developed in the early seventeenth century and was a short walk from the Pont Neuf. The top-floor, one-bedroomed flat at number 1, which acted intermittently as a home for John and Madeline, is small but beautifully formed, with views from the windows of the living area across the rooftops of the city, the dome of the Panthéon prominent on the southern skyline.

A charming apartment and beautiful vistas did little to help Madeline Green towards any sort of inner peace. By the summer of 1967, she had reached an impasse. She was not to know that by year's end all would be utterly changed.

6
Ferocious Silence
1966–68

I would prefer not to.

HERMAN MELVILLE,
'Bartleby, the Scrivener'

Friday morning, 24 November 1967. John's mouth is dry, he is jittery and has a pounding headache as he paces over and back across the stage of Belfast's Whitla Hall. Seamus Heaney, five years John's junior, introduces him as 'a writer of courage and honesty'. It is a year since *Death of a Naturalist*, Heaney's debut collection with Faber, was published to critical acclaim. The two men cannot know that morning that they will tower over Irish literature for decades to come.

John speaks slowly, deliberately, thinking as he walks. His opening comment sets the tone not just for this lecture but for his writing life: 'I am only interested in poetry, which occurs more often in verse than in prose.' The crowd of some two hundred people is mesmerised. Among them are Charles Monteith, Ian Jack, Marie Heaney and Richard Murphy. Also present is Madeline Green, who has rapidly gone from being an incidental dinner companion to the most important person in John's life.

This hour is an experience that one journalist present will not soon forget. McGahern, Ray Rosenfield writes, 'had the gift and technique of the Ancient Mariner for holding and enthralling an audience'. The lecture, on the subject of Herman Melville, is titled 'I Would Prefer Not To'. John's talk bears some magical quality that will stay with the audience while other events of Belfast's Festival 67 fade from the memory. Marie Heaney recalls being 'transfixed'.

The best account we have of the feelings summoned up in the Whitla that day was published the following morning in the *Irish Times*:

> It may be that not a few of the 200 people who went yesterday morning to hear John McGahern at Festival 67 went more out of curiosity to see a writer whose second work has been censored than to hear him talk about Herman Melville.
>
> There could, however, have been very few at the end of one of the most illuminating talks at the festival who were not as curious and excited about Melville and his lesser-known work as they ever had been about Mr. McGahern.
>
> Mr. McGahern clearly has a profound love for the art and the thought of Melville and he revealed this so movingly that even the totally ignorant would have been drawn into an equal absorption. He chose to concentrate on the one work – a longish short story, 'Bartleby', which has a recurrent phrase, 'I prefer not to'; this he took as the title for his lecture. With a poetic insight and delicacy he explored what he called 'the extraordinary intellectual vision of comedy' of the story.
>
> He took sequence after sequence from the story, reading in a voice of rare beauty. He subjected them to an analysis so acute and so detailed that with any other critic it could have damaged the fabric, but with him it only revealed the quality of the work.

Ian Jack, then aged twenty-two, knew John's work thanks to his Irish girlfriend, Carolyn Robb. But he had never heard of 'Bartleby, the Scrivener'. Nor had he attended any event in which a writer addressed a public audience – a far rarer occurrence then than now. The couple had caught the overnight boat from Glasgow, warmed by a welcome coal fire in the first-class bar. They arrived in the city on a cold morning, with frost on the streets and mist rising off the river. Jack had not been to Belfast before, and he was struck by the red-brick terraces, which gave it a surprisingly English look: 'Glasgow was then a city of blackened tenements – and of course the policemen with guns added to its strangeness.

The pubs served "hots" – or were they called "warms"? Anyway measures of spirits that had been diluted with hot water – just the thing for a cold morning.' Jack would champion John's work many years later in his editorship of *Granta* magazine.

A year before his own death in 2022, he could still vividly summon up the event:

> I recall a brightly lit hall on a darkening day, and John standing on a stage – pink-faced, animated and completely informal. I can't recall a lectern, though there may have been one. Nearly 40 years later I mentioned to John that I was present in the audience that day and he said something like 'Oh goodness, were you now, I was terribly hungover and don't know how I got through it.' He was laughing.

Richard Murphy, the County Mayo-born Anglo-Irish poet, was in Belfast that day to discuss plans with his editor, Charles Monteith. Their discussion concerned the publication of Murphy's long historical poem about Ireland's riven past, *The Battle of Aughrim*, alongside *The God Who Eats Corn*, his poetic critique of British imperialism in Africa. Murphy had read English at Magdalen College, Oxford with Monteith, in the years after the Second World War. Monteith was six years older than Murphy, but his studies had been interrupted by his service in India and Burma with the Royal Inniskilling Fusiliers, where he rose to the rank of major and received a leg wound that would leave him with a lifelong limp.

Monteith had encouraged Murphy to contact John in late 1962. The two became friends, despite John's doubts about Murphy's work. As the young novelist wrote to Monteith in May 1963: 'I admired it very much, its formal exactness above all, but it is not the personal poetry that excites me most.' John's Whitla Hall lecture, as for Ian Jack and for the *Irish Times* correspondent, left its mark on Murphy. As the poet recounted in his memoir of 2002:

> he made an oral poem out of his love for the story, the style and the vision. The rhythm and sound of his Leitrim voice uttering the

> refrain, 'I'd prefer not to,' the clarity of his obscure thought, the trembling of the piece of paper he was holding in his hand, kept me on tenterhooks, not to miss a word, hoping he'd not break down. Of course he didn't, and went on to talk about Proust's *Contre Sainte-Beuve* and to quote Bergson on laughter and Kafka's story *The Metamorphosis* about a man who turned into an insect.

More than three decades later, Murphy could still recall in precise terms how John concluded that evening in Belfast: 'We write to please ourselves. It's amazing that someone should want to publish what we write. That is not our concern, our concern is to write well, to write as well as we can.' Just days before his own death some fifty years after the event, Murphy could still clearly remember the performance, with John entrancing the crowd: 'Sitting on the edge of their seats. He was wonderful.' For Monteith, too, the experience was unforgettable: 'The lecture was – by common consent – the outstanding literary contribution of the entire Festival. It was an extraordinarily moving, stimulating and utterly sincere exposition of one artist's reaction to the work of another.'

'Bartleby, the Scrivener: A Story of Wall Street' is a long short story first serialised anonymously in two parts in November and December 1853 and reprinted with minor revisions in Melville's *The Piazza Tales* in 1856. In the story, a Wall Street lawyer hires a new clerk who decides, after an initial bout of hard work, not to make copies or do any other task required of him, refusing with the polite but firm words: 'I would prefer not to.'

In his lecture, John repeats this phrase over and over again like an incantation. These words are, he reckons, 'as powerful as the great opening of Kafka's "Metamorphosis." As Gregor Samsa awoke one morning from uneasy dreams he found himself transformed into a gigantic insect.' For him, both stories are 'very similar allegories'. For him, both stories 'are developed with ruthless realistic logic'. John argues for an equivalence: as the insect is to Gregor Samsa, so the refrain 'I would prefer not to' is to Bartleby.

John then argues for a further equivalence: so are both to their society – and so, finally, is their poetry to life itself. John is explicit about what he discerns as the underlying dynamic of social implication in both Kafka and Melville:

> Using this imaginative basis a world is created in the logic of the imagination, almost the logic of a dream, but not at the caprice of fantasy, since the whole of society is involved in it, and so it is dream dreamed by the whole of society, lighting up the dressage about its temporarily animated clay.

John lays out early why he thinks 'Bartleby' decisively succeeds as a work of art. For him, the story ultimately consists of universalised experience, a quality that transcends its deceptive singularities:

> so that its movement and images animate our memories, draws our lives into it, so that there exists a harmony between it and us, so that our dead or half forgotten life assumes in the work a harmony or vision it does not have outside the animated imagination. For in the sense we can only love what we know, what it allows us to put into it of ourselves.

John identified strongly with the recalcitrant but courteous clerk at the heart of the story who uses aggressive good manners to keep the world at arm's length. His demeanour was premised on the principle that politeness is a social virtue, a civil graciousness; he also appreciated its utilitarian value. 'Politeness is a protection', he pronounced to one university colleague in later years. When expulsion from his teaching post was all the news in Ireland, John would play no role during the public scandal. Good breeding, equanimity, cautious reserve: he used these qualities as a shield against political and religious controversies that took the form of attacks on his work and character. Confronted with a rude accusation, he simply bowed; manners were entrenched.

As early as 1962, John was recommending to friends that they read Melville's short fiction and was disappointed when Michael McLaverty could not see the true value of 'Bartleby', writing to say that he preferred 'Billy Budd' and thought that 'Bartleby', though fascinating, might not repay rereading 'since it leans too much on the element of curiosity'. John writes back in the story's defence: 'it seems to me a beautiful and shocking vision of all-is-vanity, and the last passage a pure poem'.

In Belfast that morning, he urged his audience to see in the character of Bartleby a kind of heroic teller of truths. In his thinking on the writer who gave birth to this vision, he points to a letter written by Melville around the time of the story's composition to Nathaniel Hawthorne: 'For all men who say yes, lie; and all men who say no – why they are in the happy condition of judicious unencumbered travellers in Europe; they cross the frontiers into eternity with nothing but a carpetbag – that is to say, the Ego.'

What John was keenest to stress throughout, and what Seamus Heaney recalled when reviewing *The Leavetaking*, was that prose of the type on display in 'Bartleby' contains more poetry than most verse. In this sense, John always thought of his own writing as a form of poetry: 'I call Melville a poet . . . a distinct voice speaking out of a world of the imagination shaped in its own logic.'

Besides the poetic nature of John's prose, there remain other, more defined traces of Melville in his fiction. One of the earliest stories, 'Christmas', tells the tale of a nameless boy sent out from an industrial school to work for Moran, a churlish country man who makes his living selling firewood. When asked by Mrs Grey, a well-to-do customer, what he would like for Christmas, the boy replies, '"Whatever you'd prefer to give me." I thought *prefer* was well put for a homeboy.'

'Oldfashioned' sees a description of the garda sergeant modelled on Frank McGahern that points at 'Bartleby', when Brother Benedict, principal of the local boys' secondary school, tells Colonel Sinclair not to underestimate the man: '"He's a survivor and far from being without guile. Like the rest of the country he has a great store of negative capability. He'd much prefer not to."' And in 'Doorways', the narrator names the two tramps of the story Barnaby and Bartleby, both of them like Melville's eccentric clerk in mannerism:

> They never answer strangers who ask about the times of the buses out of Abbey Street. They have their different ways, too, of not answering. Bartleby, the younger and smaller, just moves his boots and averts his face sideways and down but Barnaby stares steadily over his steel-rimmed spectacles into his interlocutor's eyes. Otherwise, they seem to take a calm and level interest in everything that goes on outside their doorway.

Melville's Bartleby can be read as a model for the kind of writer John admired and wished to be himself. Independent to the point of obstinacy, he would write only what he wished to write and at the pace he wished to write it. 'Bartleby, the Scrivener' can be read, like Kafka's 'Metamorphosis', as a prophecy and as a warning. While working hard and with purposeful integrity at worthwhile tasks should be admired, the world of the office is dehumanising and needs to be treated with caution. As John tells his sister Dympna in a revealing letter on the subject of work from the early 1960s:

> You should try to come to terms with the people about you and with your work: if you can't endure them find devices to avoid them or to see as little of them as possible or to get clear of them altogether; if you dislike your work set about getting another kind of work. To do any of these things you'll have to discipline yourself and work. There is no such thing in life as freedom, only the freedom to choose and that not always. And our choices impose their own tyrannies on us, but only a person who fails, who gives everything up as hopeless can become wooden.

Here John is thinking of another literary exposition of the drudgery of office life, Charles Lamb's 'The Superannuated Man': 'Lamb didn't let the wood get into his soul – how could one piece of wood say that an office makes people into other pieces of wood? Only a thinking person could recognise such a thing.'

A 1979 preface to a James Joyce Exhibition Catalogue at Colgate University has John's preference for seeing the writer as clerk on show.

He recalls a piece Joyce wrote about Thomas Hardy for a special number of *La Revue nouvelle* in 1928, a piece in which the author of *Ulysses* pairs himself with Hardy and the writers he admires: 'we other clerks'. John remarks: 'I find the statement not only moving but useful. They were uttered by a great clerk. They are even more needed now than then.'

Writing, then, is a job like any other one, not some mystical vocation; the activity is a question of slow, patient work rather than of sudden, flashing brilliance. The practice is never easy. As John reflects in one 1990 interview: 'It often takes me two hours with several pots of tea to lead into the two hours of writing . . . It's the most intense form of life that I know, which is part of its attractiveness. While you hate having to do it, you'd never experience such intensity otherwise.' For all its difficulty, writing fiction permits a degree of independence and purpose unavailable to Bartleby or to Gregor Samsa. This insight was one John first realised as a boy taking the barracks boat out on the lakes and the rivers of north Roscommon, understanding that the world of the imagination permitted many and varied lives.

John, repeating the phrase 'I would prefer not to' on that Belfast stage, was speaking as a writer who had gone his own way, who had refused to bend in the face of censorship. He would continue in that vein for the rest of his writing life, working uncompromisingly at the steady pace needed, writing the novels and stories that grew slowly in his imagination, never thinking about commercial gain, audience desires or literary fashion. Perhaps that is why the lecture was so successful, so memorable: the speaker was a writer with something at stake, not just sharing his views about Herman Melville but about himself at a critical juncture in his emotional life.

* * *

The atmosphere had been so different on 6 February 1966 in the Russian Tea Room. Since then, Patrick Gregory had struggled to find speaking engagements for his newly acquired Irish writer. *The Barracks*, received well by the critics, had not sold in any great numbers. Macmillan, the book's publisher, had abandoned John after taking fright at the sexually graphic nature of 'The Pit'.

Gregory called in a favour with Professor Teddy Shedlovsky – a neighbour of his parents in Snedens Landing – to set up a public lecture for John at the Rockefeller Institute on Manhattan's Upper East Side. Born in St Petersburg, Russia, Shedlovsky came to the USA in 1908, was a star student at the Massachusetts Institute of Technology and in later years worked as a scientist at the Rockefeller Institute. A lover of music, he founded the Rockefeller University Concerts in 1958 and was happy to respond positively to Gregory's approach to set up an event promoting this visiting Irish writer's work.

As part of the planned event, Gregory encouraged John to compose a short lecture, a task John found difficult despite his years as a teacher. Fortunately, a tape survives from the Rockefeller that day – the earliest known recording of John's voice. What he delivers is 'The Image', the closest he ever came to composing an artistic manifesto. He begins by reading so quietly that an audience member has to ask for greater volume. Occasionally extemporising, he sticks largely to the script as it eventually appears in the *Honest Ulsterman* for December 1968.

The reading of 'The Image' ends at 7.16 on the tape in hesitant fashion: 'If you like I'll read that to you again. I said it was full of doubts. It's something that I possibly believe.' And that is what he does, first reading Chapter 20 of *The Dark*, in which Young Mahoney and his father have one of their many showdowns, this time about whether prayer ought to be used to ask for direct divine intercession. Once John finishes this extract, he returns again to 'The Image', this time reading it out more firmly and with greater volume, as though he has begun to convince himself of something. That said, he prefaces this second effort with a series of caveats:

> One thing that privately obsesses me, I think more than anything else, in aesthetic language is 'The Image'. When I went to university I never knew what it was. I still don't know what it is, more than it's

a direction, and these are just a few scribbles and as I said, as you can guess from the maybes and the possiblys and the probablys, full of doubts, and I'll simply present them to you, and if you find any little stimulation or pleasure from them I'd be delighted.

After reading the piece for the second time, he takes a few questions from the audience. One asks that he recite something of his own choosing. John responds, after some thought, with the opening stanza of W. B. Yeats's 'The Wild Old Wicked Man'. That John should choose Yeats is not surprising, given his great reverence for his countryman's poetry and plays. And yet the choice takes on added significance in the context of the first public airing of 'The Image', working almost as a Freudian slip through which John allows us to speculate on the conception of the ideas contained therein.

He had developed a fixed and unshakeable devotion for Yeats at least as early as his schooldays. An inference that his interest in the image as the central building block of artistic creation comes primarily from Yeats is confirmed in later years by his work alongside, and great admiration for, D. J. Gordon. A Yeats scholar, Gordon was professor of English literature at the University of Reading, where John took up a visiting fellowship with the help of Richard Murphy in the autumn of 1968. For Yeats, 'nature and experience were a book of images. Places and persons that had most deeply moved him took on a further dimension of meaning.' And here we get one of John's favourite definitions of what art ought to achieve: 'art that abolishes time and establishes memory'.

While Yeats's poetry is certainly replete with thoughts and representations of the role of the image in the creation of artifice, Gordon, in using the phrase 'a book of images', is thinking specifically about Yeats's introduction to a volume of the same name. *A Book of Images*, published in London in 1898 by the Unicorn Press, consists of a series of line drawings by W. T. Horton, Yeats's friend and fellow member of the Order of the Golden Dawn, with Yeats's introduction speculating on the magical nature of art:

> All Art that is not mere story-telling, or mere portraiture, is symbolic, and has the purpose of those symbolic talismans which mediaeval magicians made with complex colours and forms, and bade their patients ponder over daily, and guard with holy secrecy; for it entangles, in complex colours and forms, a part of the Divine Essence.

We are getting close now to John's thinking on artistic value. Like Yeats, he shares a suspicion of writing that is 'mere story-telling' and is always in search of deeper, more permanent significance. For this reason, John infrequently fixes his work in an identifiable time. This avoidance is condemned by some critics as an unacceptable failure to engage with the political, a lack particularly notable, supposedly, since he was writing at a time when Ireland was in a state of turmoil. But John, like Yeats, is unafraid of equating art with a kind of sorcery: 'Most good writing, and all great writing, has a spiritual quality that we can recognize but never quite define.' This piece concludes in emphatic terms: 'Call it moral fragrance or style or that older, healing word – magic.'

Yeats concludes his introduction by declaring of Horton that his 'art is immature, but it is more interesting than the mature art of our magazines, for it is the reverie of a lonely and profound temperament'. And that is the last we hear of Horton in Yeats's work until the publication, more than twenty-five years later, of 'All Souls' Night', the haunting poem that works as an epilogue to his mystical meditation on history and time, *A Vision*, the 1961 Macmillan edition of which formed part of John's library.

Over the course of the poem, Yeats summons up the ghosts of three friends:

> Horton's the first I call. He loved strange thought
> And knew that sweet extremity of pride
> That's called platonic love.

Yeats envies the dead who can 'drink from the wine-breath / While our gross palates drink from the whole wine.' John borrows this image to write one of his finest short stories, 'The Wine Breath', a reflection on involuntary memory and the priestly vocation, published by the *New Yorker* in April 1977.

This usage is but one of many moments when John draws down from Yeats's unrivalled artistic storehouse, and one sees the hand of the great poet in much that is argued for in 'The Image':

> Image after image flows involuntarily now, and still we are not at peace, rejecting, altering, shaping, straining towards the one image that will never come, the lost image that gave our lives expression, the image that would completely express it again in this bewilderment between our beginning and our end.

In this description of the imaginative process, one is reminded immediately of Yeats's 'Ego Dominus Tuus':

> Because I seek an image, not a book.
> Those men that in their writings are most wise
> Own nothing but their blind, stupefied hearts.

This poem, one of John's favourites, prefaces Yeats's intriguing essay 'Per Amica Silentia Lunae', which acts in part as a consideration of the workings of imagination and its constituent parts: 'If you suspend the critical faculty, I have discovered, either as the result of training, or, if you have the gift, by passing into a slight trance, images pass rapidly before you.' John's urgent search for 'the lost image' as explicated at the Rockefeller Institute certainly resembles this effort of Yeats to tap into 'a Great Memory' or Anima Mundi. An artistic process of this type is difficult to describe. We can hardly be surprised that John is so hesitant on first airing a conviction that he feels instinctively but has not, as yet, fully rationalised in intellectual terms.

In the question-and-answer session that followed the reading, he tried again to define the nature of his quest: 'Some single, magical image that would simply absolve and reveal our state. I don't think it's possible – that's why I describe it as a false God – to reveal our state in language . . .

We can only ask questions, they cannot be answered. Religion simply states that this image is God.'

John spent his writing life pursuing solidity. We see this right through, from 'The Image' to the final masterpieces of *That They May Face the Rising Sun* and *Memoir*. One 1992 interview sees him at perhaps his clearest on how that one, clear image might work in the composition of literary art:

> I see the whole function of writing as circling on the image. The shape comes last; it is the intellectual quality in the work. Part of writing is technique, but it is only a part. You have to try to pick the image that's sharp, that can dramatise or bring into the light what is happening, be it a wedding ring, or a Coca-Cola bottle, or someone rolling an orange across the floor. As well as having technique, you have to be able to feel and to think clearly in order to find the right words.

For the 1966 talk at the Rockefeller Institute, John focused in his conclusion on 'a yard of lead piping'. Why he should choose this one image is unclear, though he considered its retention in the published version of the talk crucial, as a letter of October 1971 to his French publisher reveals:

> I am very disturbed to learn that the last paragraph was cut out of my The Image in the preface to Lignes de Fond.
>
> As the last paragraph brings together all the threads of the argument, and reveals the image as possibly something concrete – a yard of lead piping – the piece as a whole is nonsense without it, and while I dislike interfering with a publishing house I admire as much as the Mercure de France, I have to insist in this instance that the paragraph be restored.

The reason behind John's insistent choice of that lead piping must remain obscure. What is certain is the very solidity of the image.

We get that same aesthetic proclivity in the section of *The Dark* read in New York. The chosen passage, the twentieth chapter of the book, revolves around an argument between the novel's central protagonist, Young Mahoney, and his irascible father about the rights and the wrongs of praying for God's help while sitting exams. The father objects rather churlishly to his son's prayers, they argue, and Young Mahoney is left alone in the kitchen of the family home while his father retires to bed:

> Stupid vanity had caused it all. The house had gone to bed. You were alone in the kitchen. You wanted to say to him you were sorry but you weren't able.
>
> His boots, wet from grass, stood drying by the raked fire. They started to take on horrible fascination.
>
> They were your father's boots, close to the raked fire. They'd been put there to dry for morning. Their toes touched where the ashes spilled out from the fire on the concrete, boots wet from the grass. Your father's feet had been laced in their black leather, leather over walking flesh. They'd walk in his hopes, be carried over the ground, till they grew worn, past mending, and were discarded for the new pair from Curley's, on and on, over the habitual fields, lightly to the football matches in Reegan's field on Sundays, till the feet themselves wore, boots taken off his dying feet.

And so the emphasis goes on, this meditation on the image of the boots, for a further eighteen lines. While the yard of lead piping in 'The Image' is seen 'in terror', these boots, considered anew in the light of yet another bitter falling-out with his father, 'take on horrible fascination' for Young Mahoney.

John's artistic technique of bestowing near-human powers on inanimate household objects might also be seen as communion with another of his masters, Rainer Maria Rilke. Having read through 'The Image' twice, in addition to giving the audience Chapter 20 of *The Dark*, John takes a number of questions from the floor. Attempting to answer one about why he insists on just a single image, he refers the audience to Rilke's *The Notebooks of Malte Laurids Brigge* and specifically to the moment in the novel when Malte's mother appeals to him that he must never forget to make a wish for himself. Moving from Malte's wishes to think of his own, John returns to the image: 'Things I have wished for myself that I'll never find is this one image from which I think my life in some form or other took its full expression, its most complete expression.'

Rilke, like Yeats, was devoted to the centrality of the image. Four years after Yeats's introduction to Horton's *A Book of Images* appears Rilke's *Das Buch der Bilder* (or *The Book of Images*). How or when Rilke entered John's orbit is difficult to say. The first letter to mention him comes from spring 1964, and through the earlier 1960s he made generous gifts of both *Letters to a Young Poet* and *The Notebooks of Malte Laurids Brigge* to a variety of friends.

John's favourite Rilke essay was 'Some Reflections on Dolls'. This piece is the oeuvre's most searching treatment of its focus on the strange power of the inanimate:

> I pass over the intimate, the touching, the deserted, thoughtful aspect of many things, which, as I passed them, moved me deeply by their beautiful participation in human living; I will only cite in passing quite simple things: a sewing clamp, a spinning-wheel, a domestic loom, a bridal glove, a cup, the binding and the leaves of a Bible; not to speak of the mighty will of a hammer, the self-surrender of a violin, the friendly eagerness of horn spectacles, – indeed, only throw that pack of cards on the table, with which patience has been played so often, and it forms at once the centre of melancholy hopes, which have long since been realized in ways not hoped for.

Mahoney's boots of *The Dark* are viewed with the same sort of sympathy and human solidarity for which Rilke argues in the case of dolls, once loved and now abandoned. And so go these linkages throughout John's work.

On his return to London from New York in March 1966, John was in poor spirits, exhausted from the whirl of socialising and networking. 'Hardly able to wag', he writes to one friend. 'It was fairly terrible. It'd not take much more to cause an undying hatred of the human grimace and handshake, my own included. The book, it's too soon to say, started well, with the exception of a lead attack in the N.Y. Times.'

The review in question, penned by the Irish academic Vivian Mercier, then working as a professor in the English department at the University of Colorado, is not as bad as all that – a puzzling mix of opening hostility and closing praise that ends by comparing the novel favourably with Joyce's *A Portrait of the Artist as a Young Man*. This account begins, on the other hand, with a decidedly downbeat note: 'Oh Lord, here we go again – yet another novel of Irish adolescence.'

Though now being reviewed in all the best places and having acquired an element of fame via the banning of *The Dark*, John was flat broke and had to take the first job he could find, that of a supply teacher in Whitehall Primary School, Chingford. This position involved a commute of over three hours a day from his and Annikki's newly acquired flat in Notting Hill, which they had found through the good offices of Richard Murphy, one of many valuable intercessions the poet would make on John's behalf in these years.

The new place, in Powis Square, was sublet by Tony White, Murphy's great friend. Once a Cambridge undergraduate acting star, White increasingly wished to spend more time in Connemara, County Galway, away from the world. He specifically wanted to live in Cleggan, the coastal village from which one sailed to Inishbofin and where Murphy himself now lived for large parts of the year.

Though inconvenient for work, the apartment was in a pleasant neighbourhood, as John describes to Patrick Gregory on 6 March:

> We've installed ourselves in the flat, it's small but adequate, 20 yards from the Portobello Road, the end of it, the fruit and vegetable part, the antiques at the Notting Hill Gate end. Westbourne Park is behind. The lower part of Kensington Gdns, the Round Pond, is 10 minutes or 15 walk away, Queensway; another 10 the fountains at Lancaster Gate, the Pan, the Serpentine, the great plane trees, and at the direct end the Victoria and Albert.

These surroundings, so close to the Serpentine, feel briefly like a place where the couple might at last begin to settle:

> On the water the boisterous boys and girls in the boats, not so much people as giggling cunts and penises tottering on the edges of their fulfilment, drunk with the imagined glimpses of their joy. We had two pints of Watney's best bitter in the Archeries. We put the world in false order there. We were very happy. We wished you could be with us.

That married happiness would be short-lived. The situation was not helped by the couple working together on a translation of Veijo Meri's 1957 novel *The Manila Rope*, a project over which they squabbled before eventually having their work published in the following year thanks to Gregory's support at Knopf. By July, with Annikki away working in Helsinki, John was applying the finishing touches with little enthusiasm. He complains to Gregory: 'Nothing seems to be able to leaven the first chapters: but it's improved generally: but often I get sick that I'm not able to see or hear it anymore, as if it's outside my grip and senses.'

The drudgery of translation was representative of a wider malaise in John's efforts at writing in this period. He was making slow progress on two short stories, 'Christmas' and 'Why We're Here', with both items requiring multiple revisions and long hours of labour. The former title, first drafted in 1962, was rejected by the *New Yorker* the following year. On most days, John told Gregory, there was nothing to show, and the act of writing was like 'deliberately putting one's head under the yoke and then hoping to get the rest of one's person miraculously through in some way'.

In spite of Annikki's absence, there were constant unwelcome distractions. 'Persecuted with people', John told Gregory: 'the telephone a menace'. He let Gregory's nephew – on a last holiday before being shipped out to fight in Vietnam – stay with him for a few days and immediately regretted the decision. He found most members of the London literary circles in which he was moving tiresome and phoney. Partly in apology for failing to provide a better welcome to the nephew, as well as expressing frustration with the publisher Tom Rosenthal, John writes to Gregory: 'What I find disturbing about Rosenthal, your nephew too, is the ferocious silence of the work they're fiddling about with without knowing.'

Among those writers, editors and critics John socialised with at this time, there were a handful of exceptions. Most of these he met through Richard Murphy, others via Ian Hamilton. He had particular affection for the playwright David Halliwell. The same point held for John's attitude to Julian Jebb, who had reviewed *The Dark* so favourably in the *Sunday Times*, and for J. R. 'Joe' Ackerley, editor of the BBC's magazine, *The Listener*.

John developed many editorial relationships over the years and established one of the more fruitful instances with Ian Hamilton. Four years John's junior, Hamilton was a Norfolk grammar-school boy who went up to Keble College, Oxford to read English after completing his national service in Mönchengladbach. From his earliest schooldays, Hamilton had a fascination with literary magazines and their influence. As a secondary-school student, he established a magazine named the *Scorpion* that survived for two issues. Then, at Keble, towards the end of his first year, he founded *Tomorrow*, which lasted for four issues, and published an early Harold Pinter play.

These youthful, short-lived efforts proved useful practice for what would become one of the most successful post-war British poetry periodicals, *The Review*. Established by Hamilton in 1962, this title survived till 1974 and ran to a total of thirty issues. In its early years, *The Review* survived on a minimal budget, edited from Hamilton's Beechcroft Road accommodation in North Oxford. The magazine had enough about it to endure and to relocate to London. Later issues were published from 11 Greek Street in Soho, where the magazine's offices were next door to a strip club in what was then a decidedly seedy part of the city. Prior to receiving Arts Council funding, Hamilton had to be imaginative in keeping himself afloat, taking a three-day-a-week job at the *TLS* in 1965. This appointment soon grew into the position of poetry and fiction editor, a post he held until 1973.

John's sole appearance in *The Review* came in the April 1968 number. His short story 'Why We're Here', the piece in question, would be adapted by him, three years later, into the radio play *Sinclair*. That this story is John's only work published in a magazine given over almost exclusively to poetry and poetry reviews is not surprising. Hamilton had greater editorial ambitions, which were realised in April 1974 with the launch of a larger format, the *New Review*, a magazine that would go on to play a much greater part in John's growing reputation.

Having managed little writing of worth through the summer of 1966, by August, John was becoming depressed by the prospect of a return to teaching in Chingford. On the 17th of that month, Annikki writes from Finland, offering to shoulder any money problems should John decide to resign. Shortly afterwards, he travels to Helsinki to spend time with his wife and get to know her social circle a little better. 'Anu always complained I never would meet her friends', he tells Gregory. 'In the last ten days I met droves. A hangover a permanent fixture after the first four days. The sky blue, the girls blonde and beautiful, not forgetting Anu, the prices exorbitant.'

Then it was back to the dreaded teaching, the long commute allowing far less free time than he had enjoyed in Clontarf: 'I teach every day. I get home at five. I don't generally answer the telephone now. I leave at 7.40 in the morning. I used leave at 8.30 in Dublin and get home at 2.30. It makes much difference. Now if I have a marvellous run I get a half a page in reasonable first competence for the day.' And yet, despite the bellyaching about work, John remained a committed teacher. His school was in a deprived area, and many of the children he taught came from straitened circumstances. Rather than teaching the intricacies of the Gaelic conditional tense as in Belgrove, he frequently found himself instructing in basic literacy, as he recalled in one essay:

> Where you have the father and mother interested in education, as most of the people in Clontarf were, it makes teaching much easier, but in the East End of London they couldn't care less. I remember

> teaching a class that couldn't read, but the beginning of teaching was to get them to believe in their lives. You didn't teach them formal English, you got the *Evening Standard* and taught them about football. I had about fourteen kids in that class and I think I taught about twelve of them to read. I remember getting a marvellous sentence from one of the kids: 'My grandad used to roll barrels at Whitbread's Brewery at London Bridge, but now he's puffed when he comes up the hill for his dinner from the betting shop.' I thought 'puffed' was a marvellous word.

Richard Murphy, who met regularly with John in these London years, recalled another of his friend's teaching strategies:

> I was to learn of John McGahern's success in teaching at a school in the East End of London a boy who was thought incapable of learning to read or write. The boy could not recognise the same group of letters if he saw them in a different position. For six months, according to John, he gave the boy special care in class. He threw him a bottle to catch – the bottle fell and broke. John said 'B for Bottle, B for break, B for Bits,' making the boy feel the letters in the broken bits of bottle as he picked them up. Because the pupil never looked at the page but always at the teacher, John made him cut out a cardboard mask, which he put on his face, and then made the boy stick letters on the mask, and read out a word – B A T. After six months the boy read the headlines of the evening paper at home to his father, who came to the school and thanked John with tears in his eyes.

Not surprisingly, with having to deal with the daily trip across London, John had little or no time for a Chingford social life. He did make friends with one fellow Irishman, Tom Davey, a Belfast dentist, whom he met in the King's Head pub one lunchtime and with whom he stayed in touch over many years.

Knowing that Tony White would need his Powis Square flat back in January, John and Annikki spent a good deal of time through the autumn of 1966 in search of a more permanent property solution. This quest put further strain on the marriage. John confided to Gregory in October: 'Things going rapidly from bad to worse here.' By February 1967, the couple had moved to Walthamstow, close to John's sisters in Leytonstone and now just a twenty-five-minute bus ride from John's school. This property was a much larger flat and a more suitable location, although John regretted that they had narrowly missed out on securing the purchase of a large, dilapidated house in Notting Hill. As he wrote to Gregory:

> We almost bought a house with three decaying tenants, two flunkies on the ground floor, two floors free, in Portland Road, Simone Weil lived there once; it was opposite the Victorian pub T. White brought you to once, where you can walk from one street to the next only through the pub, but we couldn't get enough money from the Council, because of its condition, they'd only loan ½ the price, the price was £6,000.

Through spring 1967, John continued to flounder despite having been successful late in 1966 in securing a grant of £800 from the British Arts Council, alongside, among others, his old friend Elizabeth Smart. He hated the two stories he had been working on for months: 'I got into unholy despair reading through them again, they seemed so THIN.' When *The Manila Rope* was published by Knopf in March, even though he liked how the book looked, he despaired at the quality of the writing.

He read voraciously in an effort to break the deadlock, making his way through Hermann Hesse, liking *Steppenwolf* but unable to enjoy *The Glass Bead Game*; Saul Bellow's *The Victim*, which he considered 'honest work'; George Eliot's *Felix Holt, the Radical*, which had 'good bits'; George Borrow's 'charming' *Lavengro*; and Proust's unfinished novel *Jean Santeuil*, which he loved: 'extraordinary, the few themes over and over, the terrible pound the individual imagination must circle and circle'.

By early summer 1967, John and Annikki were once again on the move, this time to a pretty Bethnal Green flat overlooking Victoria Park. This Gore Road property was much more to John's liking, and by mid-July he was well settled and had purchased a beautiful oak writing desk in the hope that this acquisition might help break his writing torpor:

> We're about settled here. Long red curtains up: a big solid beech table: 6 black bentwood chairs with cane seats: a bed: an oaken writing desk with drawers down to the floor and brass handles, that I bought in the market: and much empty space, the best of all: and books along the wall in two rooms, candlesticks, one of them brass with an electric bulb, the small green chestnuts showing in the leaves across the road.

John was relieved to be on vacation, reading and enjoying Herman Melville's *Pierre; or, The Ambiguities*: 'The one thing always clear about Melville is that he's a poet.' But the pleasant new surrounds did nothing to help the faltering marriage, with barbs of irritation increasingly visible in John's letters: 'Anu spends most of her time with a friend at a sociological conference, to end the system of oppression and being oppressed.' On 11 August, Annikki left once more to work in Helsinki.

A fortnight after Annikki's departure, John's life suddenly and unexpectedly changed when he was contacted by Madeline Green, whom he had not heard from since New York, eighteen months previously. When her father had suggested that she leave Paris and accompany him to England to help promote his orchestra, Philomusica of London, she agreed, and Gron booked them into an extravagant hotel suite in the Carlton Tower, Mayfair.

John arranged to meet Madeline for a drink in Henekeys of The Strand. They enjoyed each other's company, and Madeline suggested as a next date a trip to see a play. John demurred, wondering if she was interested in sport. They agreed to go to a football match rather than to the theatre. A couple of days prior to the game, Madeline invited John to see the hotel suite. Taking this as a signal that he was meant to make a pass at her, he did – and was rejected.

Despite the faux pas, they agreed to keep the football date, at which Manchester United beat West Ham 3–1. On their long walk afterwards to Greenwich, John and Madeline were completely honest with one another, concealing nothing. By nightfall, after a simple meal in a burger bar near the *Cutty Sark*, the pair were falling in love. John was once again in that dangerous, heightened state he both desired and feared most.

The immediate aftermath of that London day saw Madeline moving into John and Annikki's Gore Road flat for two blissful weeks. But a furious showdown with her father ensued when she went to the Carlton Tower to pick up her things. He told her that she was 'like a dead bird' around his neck. This encounter would be far from the last fight, and Gron was not the only obstacle to a happy future. John was a married man, and his wife was away in Finland. In John's mind, his marriage was over in all but name. Madeline accepted this account and the inevitable furtiveness of the love affair that followed.

She returned to Paris later in September, with John visiting as often as he could. Madeline was living in rue Christine and working occasionally as a receptionist at Gron's Studio Acousti on rue de Seine. The large building that housed the recording studios also held a bar, Le Temps Perdu, and the Countess Seafield's main Paris residence. John and Madeline grew friendly with the countess's housekeeper, Sophie, and butler, Marcel, who could see all too well the subterfuge that was going on with Gron.

When not with Madeline in Paris, John relied on letters and phone calls. Sophie would arrange for the coast to be clear in rue de Seine for long chats between the lovers. John's intense fear that every moment with Madeline might prove the last – a feeling which first began with losing his mother and which was stoked by the failure of his love affair with the dark-haired girl in 1962 – was more powerful than ever. As he writes to Madeline on 18 October 1967:

> I am conscious almost always of your absence, of putting hands out, and finding them empty, of re-enacting in my mind the simple and terrible things we seem to do ordinarily well together.
>
> To walk in some eternal market full of meat and vegetables and eggs and cheese and wine, or the soles of our feet together, or to talk about your father, or when you winked at me Sunday over coffee and

> it was to tell me this particular confusion was a generality you were aware of. Will you sometimes remember me?

Much as he suffered in those early months, John need not have worried; Madeline felt equally in love, seeing this turn as a stroke of extraordinary luck that they should have met as and when they did.

Like all lovers in the first flush of an affair, there was an insatiable desire to know and possess everything that was possible of one another, and those autumn days of 1967 passed in a whirl of excitement. Plans were made for the couple to have a weekend away together on neutral ground, helped by John having been invited to speak at the Belfast Festival. Writing to Paris in the week before this event, John speaks to Madeline of his dreams, his fears and his desires:

> Write to me all you can, as much as you are able, all I care is that it is about you in some way, that's the only way you spare me.
>
> I only mean slight in the sense of our lives, there are no Importances, as the moon in a bucket of water is more real than in the sky, as if suddenly it's frail as our own flesh.
>
> Why do you threaten me? – 'For these days at least'?
>
> I do not know how to tell you of the torment of these last days.
>
> There are many things more now I want to ask you about your own life.
>
> I dreamt last night I climbed the stairs of the Rue Christine, with an empty milk bottle, and the bed was unmade, and no light except the streetlight, and I sat down to wait, and nobody came, only the mockery of drunks singing on their way home outside.

All of these anxieties were swept away by the long weekend in Belfast, the success of his lecture, the introductions among friends and colleagues, and the unfettered, unrushed time together in a hotel room bearing an unforgettable and unheeded notice: 'No Bedroom Entertaining'.

Just a week earlier, John had appeared on the popular television programme hosted by Gay Byrne, *The Late Late Show*, from Belfast's King's

Hall, where he was asked to talk primarily about the banning of *The Dark*. John recalls the event as 'an amusing experience' that showed him how the South was viewed from the North:

> I was invited to attack the Catholic Church, and when I declined, separating the Church spiritual, which was the emotional weather of my early life and for which I had nothing but gratitude, from the Church politic, its priests and bishops, the live studio audience would have none of it, seeing it as Jesuitical casuistry, or worse. A man rose, pointing at me, and said: 'There's a fellow whose book has been banned in Dublin and he's been sacked from his job by the Archbishop and he gets up here on his hind legs and praises the Catholic Church. Now, could Moscow do a better job of brainwashing than that?'

Among the other guests were the American harmonica virtuoso Larry Adler and the poet Thomas Kinsella.

The Sergeant wrote a supportive letter to John about his performance and how it was received in the newspapers:

> In the Irish Times of 23rd Ken Gray in a review of the Late Late Show insinuated you had no grievance in regard to you leaving your teaching job in Dublin. I am sure you saw it. I would like to have written about it but you never told me the reason you were dismissed. If my memory serves me right the P. P. would say nothing only that you were well aware of the reason you were removed. Had I known I'd have written the I. T. Editor – a letter for publication. At the time Sheehy Skeffington fought a great battle on your behalf.

John can only have been amused at his father's sudden advocacy. From John's point of view, this appearance on *The Late Late Show* was nearly insufferable. As he tells Jimmy Swift in a letter seeking greater detail on Patrick Kavanagh's death: 'It was gruesome sitting there, drinking water, feeling you should have learned to dance or play the French fiddle, hearing the spontaneous conversation you heard a ½ hour before in the dressingroom, and then the embarrassment of being expected to talk.'

That the Sergeant had kept up to date with Senator Owen Sheehy-Skeffington's support of his son in the depths of *The Dark* controversy is remarkable. The best contemporary account of the affair was published by Sheehy-Skeffington in *Censorship* magazine, between pieces on state repression in East Germany and in Hungary. He had tried, unsuccessfully, to fight John's case in the Senate and now, resigned to defeat, wished to set out the final position:

> The most striking thing about the victimization of John McGahern for the crime of writing a book that was banned by the Irish Censorship Board, is the closed-circuit clerical machine which wielded its absolute power to cut off his right to earn his living in Ireland as a primary school teacher.

Frank McGahern's support of this openly anticlerical stance is notable: closing family ranks was always his instinct, even before church loyalty. For his efforts, Sheehy-Skeffington was rewarded with silence, stonewalling and rebuke. One anonymous letter-writer put him straight: 'McGahern offended God by his "marriage" and by his immoral book. God comes first.'

Attempts to escape Chingford continued apace. Early in spring 1968, John got word from Western Washington University that he had been unsuccessful in a job application despite a stellar reference from Charles Monteith describing the power of the Belfast lecture. Stranmillis College in Belfast, a teacher-training institution, also proved a bust. John writes in despair to Madeline: 'It looks more and more to get out it'll have to be for a time Paris.' Fortunately, his modest success as a writer shortly afterwards came to the rescue. As he tells Patrick Gregory:

> I have signed a contract with Faber. They'll pay me £500 over the next two years and the Arts Council may pay me a similar sum, I dislike it, but I owe them no money, and it is necessary that I leave this school. I know that I am able now to write better than I've ever been, in my own style, if I am granted grace.

In June, it was fully confirmed that he had secured an £800 Arts Council bursary. His agreement with Faber for the next novel meant four tranches of £100 between April 1968 and October 1969, before a final £100 on delivery of the manuscript, which did not take place until 1974. By any measure, these payments are small sums of money, even taking inflation into account. But they were enough, alongside the untaxing teaching fellowship at the University of Reading fixed up for autumn 1968 by Richard Murphy and D. J. Gordon, to release John from the cursed Chingford.

Not everything was working out. If leaving schoolwork behind him was the solution to one problem, there were other, more pressing issues closer to home. Immersed in a secret love affair with Madeline, John found that relations with Annikki became more and more angry and confrontational. Writing to Gregory, he asks for subterfuge: 'Can you write two letters, one with no hint of disturbance to 43B Gore Road; and the other to the school.' His next letter explains further: 'The reason for the school as address is, among others, that if the letters appear personal, or to me, that Anu uses them against me; and she almost always gets and opens letters first. Neutral letters to here are alright.' John's pain is evident: 'I don't want to go into it here, it seems close to illness, the whole business.'

For Annikki, ignorant of John's affair, the root of their troubles as a couple lay in John's traumatic childhood and particularly in the overbearing figure of the Sergeant. She writes in one letter from this period of her feelings of suffocation, the sense that John's father is an ever-present weight on her chest, an invisible yet powerful presence in their life that will need to be excised if they are to flourish as a couple. Annikki may not have been far off the mark in her analysis. But the marriage, whatever the case, was beyond saving.

Early in May 1968, Madeline introduced John to her father at a dinner party in his house on rue Guisarde. Not surprisingly, the two men disliked each other while managing to retain an air of civility: 'the dinner seemed mean, and in a way competitive, how children try to be first to the lavatory'. There were bigger problems than stilted dinner parties to be faced in the Paris of May 1968. By the time John was back in London, the city was engulfed by civil unrest, with Sorbonne students at the core of protests against the Vietnam War and, more generally, their own authoritarian government. The Latin Quarter became a battlefield, with streets barricaded and cars overturned. Even staunch conservatives were shocked by the ensuing official reaction. Madeline experienced the violence at first hand: on one occasion, as she walked around L'Odéon, she was caught up in a protest and witnessed police brutality. One officer spat in her face, before a stranger pulled her into a doorway to save her from worse.

Saying yes was easy when Gron once again offered her the chance to leave Paris and return to London to work for him. By the end of May, Madeline had moved into the flat of the lead violinist in her father's orchestra, the Philomusica of London. This flat was on Cromwell Road, Kensington, where she would live until the following January. The orchestra had its London offices on Russell Square, where Madeline spent her time as a receptionist, reading books, answering the phone, kicking back.

Annikki left for Finland early in the summer, and John and Madeline could luxuriate in real, unhindered time for each other. They were now in a position to do a good deal of socialising, and John felt able to introduce Madeline both to his sisters in Leytonstone and to his closer London circle. Richard Murphy, a great believer in John's talent as well as an adept fixer, was among the first she met. They also saw Ian Hamilton and his wife Gisela regularly, going to football matches together (primarily to White Hart Lane, where Hamilton could indulge his fanatical support for Tottenham Hotspur, though Fulham and West Ham were also on the menu), dining in restaurants such as the Good Friend in Stratford or lunching in the Old Bell Tavern on Fleet Street.

A letter written a few years later by John to a friend planning to visit London gives us a firm sense of the places he liked most in the city. He suggests travelling by Tube to Bank station and walking up Cornhill to Leadenhall Market:

> Stroll back towards the Monument – 4 or 5 minutes – toward Billingsgate, the streets around it are charming, and there's a marvellous knife shop across from the Market House. Beside it there is The Olde Wine Shades on Martins Lane between Cannon St and Uppr Thames St. curved by Arthur St. This is one of the loveliest wine bars as well as one of the best. It's probably worth it to take a taxi across the river to The George, the old coaching inn, probably busloads of Germans there for 2 minutes. At the back is Guys Hospital, some of it beautiful. 4 or 5 doors from the George is The Boot, the entrance is easily missed, black and small; the tourists do.

He suggests a walk, after lunch in The Boot and Flogger on Borough High Street, by the Borough Market down Clink Street to the river so as to see the house in which Christopher Wren lived when overseeing construction of St Paul's Cathedral. And so the counsel continues, giving us a nice sense of the entertainments John most enjoyed:

> Bethnal Green St, very interesting branch of the V&A beside station: Furniture, Materials, odds and ends, 17th C. Shoes, dolls etc. Brocades.
>
> Up Bethnal Green Road under railway br. away from Wren Ch. Balls Bros, a lovely old pub, which serves good lunches very cheaply, and they only charge you corkage on wine.
>
> Etoile in Gerard Street is expensive but worth it. Rely for everything but the main course on the trolleys. I like especially the marinated herring but you can't go wrong with anything there except your wallet. Choose from 3 or 4 cheapest wines.
>
> Everywhere round Greenwich is worth it but you probably show it with the children.
>
> Courtaulds Gallery have a small marvellous collection. Woburn Sq. shared by the Warburg Inst N.W. Corner.
>
> Wards Pic Circus corner of Shaftesbury Ave. Wheelers Fish Old Compton Street. Very good house Chablis and sole.
>
> York Minster, Dean St, good bloodsport at lunch, lots of artistes loving one another.

This map of one part of London is all reflective of an ease and an admiration that John developed in the city over his years both as an exile and as a returning visitor.

Through spring and summer 1968, John and Madeline also spent time with Matthew Evans, then an up-and-coming editor at Faber, and his wife Elizabeth, with long lunches in a favourite Greek restaurant on Charlotte Street a feature. They occasionally saw Charles Monteith at L'Étoile or Wheeler's in the same area. For a short, exhilarating period, the two couples helped themselves to a case of 1922 Grand Champagne Cognac secreted by Gron in Madeline's flat. An especially raucous party at this time was hosted for a visiting Norman Mailer in the home of Tony and Fay Godwin. Tony was then Penguin's chief editor, and Fay would go on to take a series of photographs of John for the *New Review*, where she was photography editor in the mid-1970s.

One of the only accounts of John in London of the later 1960s is left by Melvyn Bragg. Along with Tristram Powell, and prompted by their friend Julian Jebb, he made a 1966 BBC2 documentary on this controversial, censored writer. 'He was far and away the most confident young writer I had met', recalls Bragg, 'and, as time has gone by, I can add – have ever met.'

There was doubt in some quarters about the wisdom of a documentary on a writer merely in his early thirties. But Bragg was certain of his subject: 'It was because there was that about him which, from me, called up reverence. Perhaps it was the all but visible sense of vocation that clung to him. Perhaps it was that awe-inspiring certainty of his.' The professional relationship led, for a time, to something more informal, with football and beer, as usual, acting as lubricants:

> Save for outbursts of almost violent cheerfulness – at or after a football match (we used to watch Fulham at Craven Cottage after a few drinks in the pub at the north side of Putney Bridge) – or outrage when some ignorant or crass remark had inflamed his sensibility, there was almost an incantatory tone to his speech. It was even a

> little 'sung' from time to time, like a chant, and more often than not streaming with quotations from his several cherished writers – Proust, Flaubert, Joyce, Beckett, Yeats . . . They and so many others embellished all his conversation. Often they were his conversation. It all went back to the primary intention to be a priest and, however fully he had shaken off the skin of the observances and ceremonies of the Catholic Church, there was little doubt that he was still dyed in the spiritual mystery of things.

Those who knew John in these often-frustrating London years realised that they were dealing with someone of unusual and fixed character. Bragg is warm and emphatic in conclusion: 'Apart from all that, he was charming company, a singular man with a lovely smile, a bard of what can seem ordinary, a writer who alchemised much of his life into fiction.'

7
Lost in Translation
1968–70

> I am happy, which induces more panic than gratitude, since I find it an extraordinarily perilous way to be.
>
> JOHN McGAHERN

Ever since being introduced to each other in Dublin by Charles Monteith in the summer of 1963, John's and Richard Murphy's lives had intersected in various fruitful ways. Murphy was fond of John, even if his friend 'could be hurtful'. Murphy told me in our one conversation at the end of his life, 'John was pretty dismissive of all other writers.' When I asked him if he could locate the source of this confidence, there followed a long pause before a brief answer: 'From his soul.' Murphy, despite their occasional disagreements, had gone out of his way to set up John with a new opportunity via a university visiting fellowship in the autumn of 1968. As *Memoir* recounts:

> I was given a research fellowship at Reading University that entailed a little teaching but in fact was designed to allow me to write. 'What will I teach?' I asked deferentially after I'd been given the job. 'Teach them anything you like, my dear,' the brilliant Donald Gordon, the Professor of English, told me gaily as he poured us both another gin-and-tonic. 'I've been teaching them for the last twenty-eight years, and they have never understood one word *I* have taught them; and you can take my word, my dear, that they will not understand one word you say to them either: so teach them anything you like, my dear.'

Gordon's answer was typical of the man for whom John would develop a great fondness. The weekly train journeys down to Reading were a time of ease, and the writer's block that had afflicted John for much of the previous year began to abate.

Towards the end of that autumn term, Murphy would once again decisively change John's destiny. He had been approached by a man named Bruce Berlind to consider taking up the visiting Olive B. O'Connor Chair at Colgate University in Hamilton, New York for the spring semester, teaching creative writing and modern British and Irish literature. Having just days before accepted the Compton Lectureship in Poetry at the University of Hull, thanks to the good offices of Philip Larkin and Cecil Day Lewis, Murphy felt he had to turn down Colgate despite much better remuneration than Hull was offering. He suggested to Berlind that he contact his friend. Short of cash and having no concrete plans in place for 1969, John took the job, thus beginning what would prove an enduring relationship with this beautiful university set on 575 rolling acres in the Chenango Valley of mid New York state.

Colgate was not as cushy a number as Reading, and John had to immediately get down to work with thoughts towards a curriculum, timetables, a work permit and accommodation. An outline letter on the first of these issues, written to the librarians in Colgate in the days after Christmas 1968, stands as a valuable document in revealing how John saw the Irish canon, such as it was. The books he asked to be ordered were as follows: William Carleton, *Traits and Stories of the Irish Peasantry* ('or in fact any Carleton'); Somerville and Ross, *The Real Charlotte* and *The Big House at Inver*; Cecil Woodham Smith, *The Great Hunger* ('as social background to the 19th century'); Tomás Ó Criomhthain's *The Islandman*, translated by Robin Flower; Stanislaus Joyce, *Dublin Diary* and *My Brother's Keeper*; Richard Ellmann (ed.), *Letters of James Joyce*; W. B. Yeats, *Autobiographies*; Samuel Beckett, *Murphy* or *Malone Dies* and *All That Fall*; Patrick Kavanagh, *Tarry Flynn* and *Collected Poems*.

One could write a thesis on these eclectic choices alone: two books by Stanislaus Joyce but none by James beyond his *Letters*? Yeats's *Autobiographies* but no poems or plays? It would be misleading to think that these requests indicate any suspicion about books such as *Dubliners*, which John admired unstintingly (though less so the later Joyce, particularly *Finnegans Wake*). Or any doubt about the Yeatsian canon. But he found in less obvious material a useful angle from which to approach the better-known works, and he always considered *My Brother's Keeper* a classic book in its own right.

Several Yeats poems, particularly those from his 1928 collection *The Tower*, were soon being taught via *Autobiographies*. Carleton he knew but was not especially drawn to his writing. Still, like many lecturers before and since he had to figure out some way to fill the Irish nineteenth century. Somerville and Ross were the clearest examples he could find of an Irish novel tradition, a strand he believed barely existed and that he tended to think, in later years, was best represented by Kate O'Brien. And he was interested in eras and cultures as they come to an end – the Anglo-Irish Big House in this case.

For similar reasons, he chose *The Islandman* and continued to teach this book all his life, even going to the trouble of making his own translation from the original Irish. In its Homeric stoicism, *An tOileánach* was one of his sacred books: 'I believe it to be a true work. Such books always cast their own light, reflecting outwards. Besides, more than any single work in English it reflected the reality of the lives of the people I grew up among and who brought me up.'

As for the final two authors on his list, he writes to Colgate, 'I include Beckett and Kavanagh because of two different traditions in their continuance.' Beckett he saw as being close to Ó Criomhthain since the former figure had 'reached an elemental spareness that was equally shorn of local characteristics'. For John, there is in *The Islandman* none of Patrick Kavanagh's myth-making: 'There are no "turf banks stripped for victory," as in Kavanagh, no scattering, footing, clamping.' John was consistent in seeing Beckett and Kavanagh as the two most important living Irish writers of his youth.

John flew out from Heathrow on 31 January 1969 for the first of what would be many periods spent in Colgate over the years, the last teaching visit being autumn 2001. He was followed four weeks later by Madeline.

At first, he had feared the appearance of an unmarried partner might not be permitted, but he was able to fix up a place for her in the Faculty Club with the help of his enlightened boss. Bruce Berlind, eight years John's senior, was professor of English specialising in modern American poetry. Beginning his teaching career at Colgate in 1954, he founded the English department's visiting writers' series in the 1960s, when he began hosting readings by American and British poets on campus, and he devoted long service as department chair. A native of Brooklyn, he had attended Princeton and Johns Hopkins and served in US Army intelligence, being stationed in Germany after VE Day and then in Japan during the Korean War. A charismatic fixer and popular teacher, he quickly became known to John and friends as 'Brucey Baby'.

The move to Colgate was an eye-opener, a whole new world of campus comfort and privilege, a long way indeed from East End penny-pinching, as John tells Charles Monteith in a February letter: 'It's beautiful here, a village of Greek Revival Houses in the valley and the University on one of the surrounding hills; old avenues of trees from the village, the gold of the chapel tower against pine forest and snow.' But the teaching load that required him to be in class three mornings a week was heavier than the one with which he had been spoiled in Reading. Though he was managing to write a little, the demands of an academic schedule did not sit well with the solitude and silence required to compose fiction:

> I finished the first draft of the new story this weekend. Three days I have to teach in the morning, and they are finished. After Yeats' Tower Poems I had headaches all day.
>
> When I was an infant teacher I had to learn how to withhold all egotism in order to write afterwards, but at this level the students' demands and awareness make it impossible, it's no place for long for a writer.

He was able to break up his time with a guest lecture in Boston for the Irish Society at the end of February, where he also met up with an arriving Madeline and Patrick Gregory, who was now working in the city for Atlantic Monthly Press. Such a meeting was still potentially tricky since it represented the first time that John and Madeline would be out in the open as a couple in front of this man who knew both her father and Annikki well. John took it in his stride, Gron having visited Gregory's parents in Snedens Landing to warn them about this Irish writer who was trying to muscle in on his daughter's inheritance: 'we've got the benediction of laughter, in its way it makes things easier or less initially tense'.

For spring break, John and Madeline got driven to Maine by Bruce and Mary Berlind, where they spent time in Gron's Bar Harbour mansion, the Black House, surrounded by stunning pinewood and lakeside vistas. Madeline stayed on alone after John returned to Hamilton and remembers those days as among the happiest in her life, secure in the knowledge that she had a decent future to which she could look forward with a man whom she loved and admired.

Before the end of the academic year, Madeline flew back to Paris to take up residence in rue Christine, while John set about the wearisome task of marking end-of-semester papers. This arrangement was a pattern to which the couple tended to stick in future Colgate years, with Madeline setting up things for them wherever home was at that time. For John, probably the most valuable addition to his life from this trip, apart from the welcome money, were the friends he made: in the English department, people such as Neill Joy (who became John's loyal handball partner), Linck Johnson and Joe Slater; John Fitchen, Professor of Fine Art, whose study on the construction of Gothic cathedrals John found fascinating; John Head, a firebrand Texan historian whose book on the years leading into the American Revolution, *A Time to Rend*, John admired; and Wil Albrecht, a specialist in Romantic and Victorian literature to whom John would one day dedicate *The Pornographer*. These colleagues and their partners would remain important supports to him on future American trips, providing intellectual and social stimulation over many years.

Marking behind him, John flew back to London, into what he knew would be a maelstrom as he moved towards the final break with Annikki, who knew nothing of Madeline but could see all too clearly the growing chasm between her and her husband. A series of Annikki's letters survive from this time, which reveal increasing frustration with her distant partner. Through these letters, we witness a rapid unravelling – and behind all of this emotional turmoil, Annikki saw, again, perhaps at least in part correctly, the long, dark shadow of the Sergeant. When John eventually got back to Gore Road there was a series of showdowns, culminating with a final break on 17 July.

Mary Kelleher, the female character in 'Bank Holiday', asks Patrick McDonough, her lover, a question:

> 'Were you upset when your marriage failed?' she changed.
>
> 'Naturally. In the end, there was no choice. We couldn't be in the same room together for more than a couple of minutes without fighting. I could never figure out how the fights started, but they always did.'

The end of the marriage, though inevitable for some time, was something about which John felt acute pain and regret. 'Those who believe the availability of divorce makes it too easy to end marriages have no understanding of divorce', he writes in *Memoir*, some thirty-five years after the events of that summer. 'A divorce is like a death, but instead of that inevitable end, the person that we have loved stands there as a living reproach of deep failure.' After the final argument, John left to stay in Connemara with Richard Murphy for a few days as Annikki packed up in London and prepared to return to Finland, sending her husband a note, making it clear that she did not wish to see him again and that she would shortly return any monies owing. On his eventual return to the largely empty Gore Road flat to take the last of his things, John was stricken by painful childhood tremors:

> As the apartment emptied, those hours in the poor rose garden when the furniture was taken from the rooms in Aughawillan and stacked with the brown hens in the crates of the red lorry while my mother

was dying came back with such vividness that I started to shiver in the summer's heat.

His marriage over, John now moved to rue Christine, living in Paris until October 1970. Those twenty or so months proved tremendously productive, with the finishing touches put to many of the stories that were becoming his first collection, *Nightlines*. Writing to Patrick Gregory at the end of July to congratulate him on his marriage, he is positive about the present and optimistic about the future: 'I was never more certain of my work and it goes past the finishing of the stories which I can do in a few weeks once I start. I do not intend to begin until Anu is all right.'

In another letter to Gregory, with the dust still settling on his marital break-up, we see him bringing his story 'Peaches', about the unhappy marriage between an unnamed writer and his Finnish wife, to some sort of conclusion: 'I work every day here, it was impossible to work at all in the continual emotional violence of London. I'll have to go back to see about abandoning the lease, I'll put it off as long as possible, and try to finish the first draft of the Spain story.' The longest story by some distance in the collection, John was never fully sure of 'Peaches', with its painfully autobiographical narrative, and dropped it from the French translation, *Lignes de fond*, in favour of his short essay 'The Image'. Though it reappears in his *Collected Stories* of 1992, it is absent from his final adjudication of his best stories, the posthumously published *Creatures of the Earth*.

With money he made from selling 'Korea' to the *Atlantic* magazine, John regretfully paid off the last of his lease on Gore Road, which formed part of the Crown estate. He quickly got back the money with another *Atlantic* success, this time for 'The Recruiting Officer', the story with which he ultimately closed *Nightlines* and which the magazine ran in its July 1970 issue. By this time, Patrick Gregory had moved from Knopf to Atlantic Monthly Press and had taken John with him. 'Two stories by a single author represents a real investment of interest by the "Atlantic"', wrote Gregory, 'and I'm naturally pleased that the magazine is supporting the Press's enthusiasm in such a tangible fashion.'

Looking back several years later, John could see that the move, motivated by personal loyalty, had probably been unwise. This decision meant that he would have three American-published books by 1971 with three different publishing houses, a pattern that continued up until his late, fruitful return to Knopf with his *Collected Stories*, final novel and subsequent *Memoir*, published in the USA as *All Will Be Well*.

By mid-September, 'My Love, My Umbrella' was taking shape. Annikki had begun divorce proceedings. 'I am tired', John writes to Gregory, 'but it's good to wake up in the morning without the certitude of some violence before night.' By early October, Annikki, living again in Helsinki, was getting fed up with John's inaction and wrote sternly, asking why he was dragging his feet on signing the papers needed to process their divorce. The final, formal end to the marriage did not occur until 1972, with any other intervening relations brief but cordial. In February 1970, for instance, Annikki writes to John seeking his help in getting permissions to translate and broadcast James Plunkett's play *Big Jim* and concludes the letter by saying that she hopes to marry again.

The collection was almost complete to John's satisfaction by early November 1969. On the 6th, he wrote to Charles Monteith that he had sent 'Peaches' to Gregory along with 'a story that was not planned' (almost certainly 'Lavin'). John added, 'I have to butcher an early weak story (3/4 days) and then it is for worse or better finished.' This last refers to 'Strandhill, the Sea'. Later in the month, he asked Monteith if he may dedicate *Nightlines* to him, an honour deeply coveted by D. J. Gordon, who wrote to Monteith of his admiration for John's developing work:

> I cannot tell you how much I envy you the dedication of Nightlines. I've spoken to John on the telephone about it; but haven't yet written to him. So I won't go into detail. Except to say that I don't know whether to be more impressed by the – now – total mastery of the material – signified by the really remarkable change in his prose; or more alarmed. Because of course the epigraph should have been – though too banal to use – Cast a cold eye . . . For so many years I've

met – or known intimately – so many writers, including some great masters. Never in the last 20 years have I encountered a young writer (he's still young to me) with a more formidable literary intelligence.

The book was now almost over the line, though Gregory hated 'Lavin'. Strongly reminiscent of Joyce's 'An Encounter', the story follows two boys coming to sexual awakening in a rural Irish setting. At its centre is the eponymous Lavin, a once-handsome, hard-working local who has ruined himself with a Gypsy girl and fallen to seed, now fulfilling his sexual needs through predatory meetings with children. The story divided opinion, with Monteith enthusiastic and Gregory disliking it so much he wondered if it would damage the collection: 'Lavin still baffles me a bit, but I haven't reread it carefully yet and will have to do that before I can talk to you about it.' Again, ten days later, he argues vociferously for the exclusion of 'Lavin' from the collection: 'The piece strikes me as tight and true at every turning: there isn't a false note in it, and the writing maintains a concentration and intensity throughout. And yet John, I don't feel that it works at all as a short story.' John went ahead with it anyway, trusting his own intuition, as he always did. The story turned what was an already troubling collection a shade darker.

The book, before even being printed, ran into legal flak. 'Bomb Box' had been published in *The Listener* in December 1969 and soon after came to the Sergeant's attention. He threatened legal action against his son and his publishers. The story is about a hypochondriacal policeman who, believing he is fatally ill, takes his eldest son aside to leave him responsible for a metal chest – the box of the title – in which are kept £100 and all his important documents. Before leaving home for hospital, the Sergeant tells his son, 'You have a key and I have a key. When news of the death comes you'll go first thing and open the box with your key. Is that clear?' Of course, there is nothing the matter with the Sergeant, and he returns home embarrassed and defeated, his son at story's end throwing the key into the river, glad to be freed of responsibility for his siblings. (The story's title was later changed to 'The Key'.)

Frank McGahern, inevitably, and rightly, saw himself as the foundation for the ludicrous central character and rang his daughters in Leytonstone to garner their support for a legal case. John discussed his concerns with Monteith, who, after consulting with his Faber colleague Peter du Sautoy, waved the story through. Nothing came of the Sergeant's threats, and 'Bomb Box' appeared in the middle of *Nightlines* later that year with Guard Cannon's name changed to 'Bannon' and Doctor Vesey's to 'Neary'.

It was not just John's father who was causing trouble: Gron, after a few months of relative quiet, had begun to make unreasonable requests of his daughter, demanding, in particular, that she vacate rue Christine and return ownership to him. On John's advice, Madeline hired a solicitor and was able to prove ownership of the upstairs rooms of what had originally been a much grander duplex. But the whole experience was unpleasant, with Gron coming around with heavies to try and intimidate John, whom he saw as a carpetbagger.

As John tells Charles Monteith, 'The lawyer secured the upstairs for her after he tried to seize it. He wants us to stay here but it's apparent now he wants to involve M. in the Seafield case and to use the apartment as bargaining & we may leave Paris altogether. Last week was quite horrible.' A week later, John writes again to accept an advance of £350 for *Nightlines* and describes Gron's characteristic attempts to move from threat to seduction: 'We moved upstairs today. It was very dirty and disturbing and now we are being courted with invitations to the Ritz etc., which is the final pornography.'

John's account to Patrick Gregory, who had known Gron since childhood, was frank:

> Madeline owns a very small flat in this house, which he tried to seize, I think to have her in his imaginary power in the case, perhaps too the obsession with property, but she got a lawyer. Howls. In the fracas she mentioned that she knew all about his visit to your parents. Came around with 2 bodyguards to call me a liar and troublemaker. I told

him to calm down and we ended with handshakes (all an unfortunate misunderstanding). Then advised me, man to man, that M. was crazy, though I was the last person he should tell.

The Seafield case mentioned by John involved various legal wranglings over the estate of Nina, the Countess of Seafield, after her death on 30 September 1969. The countess had, for many years, been Gron's mistress and meal ticket, and after her death he had to scramble to retain as much of his ill-gotten property as possible before her children could cut him out. John and Madeline were caught in the crossfire and considered leaving Paris altogether. The situation gradually calmed. Madeline, for a period, refused to see her father, and John began to see the whole affair as 'in the most sordid way profoundly comic'.

By early March, it felt like the couple could remain in France for the time being. 'We moved upstairs today', John tells Gregory, 'out of Gron's world; it is small but very beautiful and with the roof glass windows – it is snowing now – I often feel I'm in a ship.' After a short trip to London in late March, when John stayed with his sisters and had dinner with Monteith and Seamus and Marie Heaney, he happened to run into Gron at Victoria Station, and they travelled back to Paris together by train and ferry. 'I was sufficiently ablaze', he tells Monteith, 'to give him a stiff talking to and to later set him imbecilely drunk on his own good Glenlivet in mid-channel: I was going into the nature of morality; and he trying to make a couplet in which BEER and QUEER rhymed.'

John was in high good humour when he got to rue Christine: 'You'll never guess who I ran into on the nightboat', he announced to Madeline. The Victoria Station encounter with Gron was one that John would later fictionalise in *The Leavetaking*, switching the crossing to the night boat from Liverpool to Dublin. The lifestyle of Madeline's father continued to stand as a singular example of John's dictum: 'Among its many other obligations, fiction always has to be believable. Life does not have to suffer such constraint, and much of what takes place is believable only because it happens.'

Of that 1969–70 period in Paris, despite the lack of society, Madeline recalls fondly: 'We had a ball.' She remembers a special time: 'Magical . . . We walked and ate . . . It was very cheap . . . All fun . . . Terrific gaiety.' Christmas 1969 saw Paris under snow, with John turning down an invitation from the recently appointed Nobel laureate Samuel Beckett – a man he admired unreservedly but never met – to spend the day with him. As John recalled in 2004, 'I knew Beckett was harassed by lots of people. I was appalled when I was in Paris with a writers' group and some of them were going to see Beckett when he was dying, in fact. I thought that was . . . well it wasn't my style anyhow.'

In the midst of all these personal difficulties, John's first collection of short stories was moving towards publication. In Britain, as ever, Faber was on board, but in the USA there was another stutter when Patrick Gregory left Atlantic Monthly Press in April for Gambit. John turned to Monteith for counsel and was advised to stay with Atlantic, where he would fall under the care of Peter Davison, long the *Atlantic* magazine's poetry editor and a major player in American publishing.

John had left Knopf for Atlantic originally out of personal loyalty to Gregory, but he felt it better to stay put now, albeit reluctantly. He writes to Gregory, inviting him to Paris and thanking him for their work together:

> Madeline is well and looking forward to your coming. Her beauty seems to me to have grown calmer and richer. In odd moments it causes me to catch my breath. I am happy, which induces more panic than gratitude, since I find it an extraordinarily perilous way to be. My feelings over Atl/Ga is of great gratitude to you for the much Nightlines owes you, and regret out of a depth of waters . . .

The friendship did not long survive these professional changes, and letters between John and Gregory soon peter out. But John was never quite comfortable with Davison as editor, and he would soon again be on the lookout for a new American publisher.

8

The Temple of the Holy Ghost 1970–71

I shall fight my fight quietly in this way & no
other – by calmly looking through my little window
at natural things & drawing them faithfully and with love.

VINCENT VAN GOGH

With Gron out of their lives for the time being, John and Madeline spent the summer of 1970 happily living in their small, and sometimes stiflingly hot, rue Christine flat. At first, they had to continue going downstairs to Gron's empty apartment to use the toilet or shower. John used most of his Colgate money getting a bathroom installed: 'Nothing but dust and work.'

He had begun work on a new novel, a transition he never found easy. He told one French journalist many years later that one of the reasons he relished the city was because there were so many distractions: 'That is why I like to write in Paris, because writing is always painful and everything easily becomes an excuse to escape that pain.' That said, there were few callers. The mornings tended to be given to writing, with John working in longhand before passing on manuscripts to Madeline, who would type them on an Olivetti 22. In the afternoons, the couple would walk the city, go to favourite bistros, play badminton in the Jardin du Luxembourg, watch puppet shows. While Madeline was comfortable speaking French, John never mastered the language.

One morning, John was disturbed from his work by the doorbell. Below on the street stood a young Irishman, Fran O'Rourke, seeking to talk. O'Rourke, then an arts undergraduate at UCG and someone who subsequently went on to a successful academic career and a chair in philosophy at UCD, was hitching across Europe that summer and had been given John's address by Richard Murphy. After some time, John opened the door, having descended the four dark flights of stone and oak stairs.

O'Rourke explained that he was auditor of the UCG Arts Society and wondered if John would be willing to make an appearance. (Seamus Heaney had given a memorable reading a couple of months before, his first in Galway.) John suggested that O'Rourke come back later and join himself and Madeline for lunch. 'I did so', remembers O'Rourke, 'and recall a very pleasant meal of delicious steak, salad and wine. Both John and Madeline were very warm and courteous. I had just read *El Arco y la Lira* by Octavio Paz and was discoursing on it with naive enthusiasm.'

By the time lunch was over, John had agreed to return to the campus he had abandoned some eighteen years previously. This appearance would be the first such event south of the border since the banning of *The Dark*, and he was well aware of the difficulties such an evening might provoke. On 11 August 1970, the Irish ban on *The Dark* was lifted, and the novel was permitted to be sold in unexpurgated form. The whole mess seemed so long ago that John found it hard to care, though he did comment to Charles Monteith about the Panther paperback cover of a cartoonish priest hovering lasciviously over a scantily clad young woman that the edition 'deserves banning'.

Media interest was not of so level a cast. A moment of renewed pressure for John arrived, which he negotiated with characteristic aplomb:

> Years later when *The Dark* was unbanned and Carmen Callil sent me a telegram from Panther books – THE DARK UNBANNED STOP PRESS TV RADIO WANT YOU STOP – I remained where I was. To have anything to do with the unbanning, for the sake of a few sales, would have been even worse than protesting about the banning in the first place: 'The minute the writer takes up a pen he accuses himself of unanswerable egotism and all he can do with any decency after that is to bow.' Chekhov's words were one of our early texts in the 'good manners' of the mind.

Like so many of their fellow Parisians, John and Madeline were keen to bail out of the city for some of August, and on the 17th they headed south to visit the dramatist and screenwriter Claude Duneton, whom they had befriended through David Halliwell and his theatre circles. After a week in Corrèze, they carried on for Barcelona, where the *London Magazine* proofs of 'My Love, My Umbrella' were waiting for John, with the story appearing there in the October 1970 number.

From Barcelona, they caught a train to Madrid in early September, where more publishing work was awaiting John's approval. This time, it was for the American edition of *Nightlines* and involved the proposed book cover, which depicted a predominantly green painting of a beshawled old woman, with a thatched cottage in the background. The stereotype enraged John, and he sat down to write an uncharacteristically heated letter to Peter Davison:

> My heart fell at the sight of the cover.
>
> Impression: a schoolgirl's book (11–15)
>
> A chocolate green or green chocolate of the pig in the kitchen.
>
> My prose stands against everything the cover says. Surely Yeats, Joyce and Beckett gave Irish letters some universal dignity.
>
> I might let it pass if I thought it would find its readers.
>
> My experience is that people likely to buy a book are people who enjoy the language. A cover like that is the same as selling cheese under a sugar label.
>
> MacMillan published The Barracks with an Irish cover. It got sensitive Irish reviews. It sold 750 copies.
>
> Knopf published The Dark in typographical cover. It got tough wide reviews as literature. It sold 3,500 copies and with a little luck could have done much better. Irish except Joyce/Beckett wasn't mentioned in the reviews.
>
> That hankering after the little old homestead is played out. Grove have no need of it. The cover is lazy, unimaginative and it stereotypes, since whoever designed it thought it a cliché, a long dead one at that.

Why can't it just get decent type and red and black, if nothing can be better thought of.

Though John won this argument, with the book being published in the USA under a plain black cover bearing the title in quadruplicate in varying shades of purple, his angry response to the initial proposal cannot have endeared him to Davison.

Returning to Paris in early October, Richard Murphy once again played a decisive part in their lives. Having lived on and off in Cleggan, County Galway since the early 1950s, sailing a Galway hooker in and out of Inishbofin, Murphy encouraged friends not just to come and visit him but to live nearby. Tony White fell in love with the place and began to live the life of a hermit. Charles Monteith and Rosemary Goad came to stay, as did Philip Larkin. For a short period in September 1962, Ted Hughes lived there with Sylvia Plath.

John, wanting to see what it might be like to live in Ireland again and keen to show Madeline his homeland, discussed with Monteith the idea of moving back to Dublin, an idea nixed by his editor, who saw the city as too in thrall to 'The Racket', a place that could give the false impression both of friendship and of anonymity. And so, Murphy's offer to find cheap accommodation on the Atlantic seaboard was taken up.

Travelling through London, John spent a few days in Leytonstone, enjoying time with his sisters, drinking bitter in the Three Blackbirds on Leyton High Road and seeing some old friends before being joined by Madeline and driven to Cleggan by Murphy. Madeline's first-ever night in Ireland was spent in the pub, where Murphy got into a row with a Clifden bank manager who had been drinking and playing the piano. She recalls a character coming out of the gents and declaring: 'Mind the fucking language: there are ladies present.' All of this hubbub she remembers fondly: 'It was a very novel and exciting time for me . . . Being with John – that was the first adventure.'

After a short stay in Murphy's, they took up November residence in what was known locally as Mrs Browne's house. Murphy enjoyed having the companionship and remembers these months as a life-enhancing time, though John had lost none of his acerbity:

> When I showed John a poem that had been through far too many drafts and still had a weak last line, he said 'You've given it a rose at the end – I'd give the knife another twist' . . . when he spoke of ordinary things, people or events, reality was intensified by his imagination and his style of darkness clarified.

The house that became home for the winter of 1970–71 had been a residence of the wealthy Twining tea-merchant family for the second half of the nineteenth century, which explains John's otherwise baffling paragraph at the end of the first half of *The Leavetaking*: 'The shadow had fallen on the life and would shape it as the salt and wind shaped the trees the tea lord had planted as shelter against the sea.' The house was inherited by Julia Holberton in 1902 and had since passed into the hands of Mrs James Browne. She now rented out the property – it was here that Ted and Sylvia stayed – and owned a wonderful collection of books. Madeline still has a copy of *Love's Labour's Lost* in Foxfield, 'borrowed' from the collection.

Cleggan and its environs was becoming an eclectic community, attracting literary people from Dublin and beyond, an aspect of life there that Madeline, especially, was keen to avoid. But there was much else, even if an emerging bohemianism was not to John's and Madeline's tastes, to enjoy and appreciate. 'Except for the impossibility of heating a place with high ceilings', remembers Madeline, 'it was a marvellous place to live':

> There was a large kitchen. Off it was a smaller room that was also a living room, where John worked and friends were received in front of a turf fire that was always lit. In spring, a magnificent wisteria vine framed the door that was the main entrance to the house that led immediately into the kitchen.

John, along with surveying reviews of the just-released *Nightlines*, was beginning to make serious inroads into *The Leavetaking*. He dabbled as well in radio plays, converting 'Why We're Here' into *Sinclair* for the BBC and preparing for the reading he had agreed to do in Galway.

On 30 November, the *Irish Press* ran a story that threatened for a period to capsize the pleasant life that John and Madeline were building for themselves. Titled 'McGahern Takes a Cottage in Connemara' and written as part of Mary Kenny's weekly column, the piece described McGahern's move:

> He has hired a cottage there with his Anglo-American wife, Madeleine, and leads a quiet, industrious life in the area. He meets his old friend the poet Richard Murphy in the Pier Bar almost daily, and next Saturday he'll be going in to Galway University to speak at a literary society there, but otherwise he seems content to be far away from people generally. Cleggan people recall his being there nine years ago when he wrote his first novel 'The Barracks' so he is well integrated in that spot.

The article, besides being inaccurate, was problematic for McGahern in several ways, not least for the fact that his father knew nothing at this point of the existence of Madeline. Writing to Rosemary Goad at Faber three days later, John is fed up:

> The roof leaks. The cows in the surrounding stables moo us awake. Eileen O'Malley gave headline gossip about us to the Irish Press (I have paranoiac visions of relatives descending from Roscommon) and now journalists have started to pursue Richard's phone. If I stay certainly O'Malley's will get the boycott treatment. Never worked so easily but I don't know how long we can stay now.

Before figuring out what to do about his father, who, inevitably, would have found out almost immediately about the *Irish Press* article, John had to face into his first public reading in the Irish Republic since the banning of *The Dark*. The event, held in front of a packed audience at the Aula Maxima in the university's old quadrangle, was the penultimate event of a campus week of merriment, as reported in the local press:

> College Week, an annual event and now in its fourth year, opened last Saturday with the election of 'Miss College Week '70' and will terminate on Friday night with a Tramps Ball. The 'rag' atmosphere, synonymous with such an event, has been slightly subdued with a festival aura . . . Literary giants Richard Murphy and John McGahern with organist Gerald Gillen bring culture into the week while the pram-pushing, egg-eating, bonny babies still participate to fill up the 'krak' side.

Originally Ted Hughes was meant to open the festivities but had to withdraw, his place taken by Murphy. John was intensely nervous. Having been introduced by the chair of English, Professor Lorna Reynolds, he decided to take the audience head-on by reading 'My Love, My Umbrella' in its entirety. Prudes or crawthumpers in attendance were in for a rude awakening through this strange tale of al-fresco sex on the rain-sodden streets of Dublin:

> Our lips moved on the saliva of our mouths as I slowly undid the coat button. I tried to control the trembling so as not to tear the small white buttons of the blouse. Coat, blouse, brassière, as names of places on a road. I globed the warm soft breasts in hands. I leaned across the cold metal above the imitation leather she held in her hands to take the small nipples gently in teeth, the steady beat on the umbrella broken by irregular splashes from the branches.

One lady in the crowd stood up during the question-and-answer session that followed to point out to John that he did not seem to realise that the human body was the temple of the Holy Ghost, a comment that John mulled over carefully before replying that he agreed. From that point onward, he relaxed and enjoyed what was an almost entirely enthusiastic reception. The whole event was a triumph, topped off by copious pints in the back room of the Skeffington Arms Hotel with students and faculty.

Galway conquered, John now had to turn his thoughts to the much trickier Roscommon campaign. Fortunately, he had befriended a young priest named Mick Gibbons through going to Oliver Coyne's bar in Cleggan. The pub was busy the night of their first meeting, and John suggested Gibbons drop by next day for lunch. The priest had read and admired *The Barracks* and *The Dark*, and he still had a sense of outrage at the way John had been treated by his school manager and union. John was interested – perhaps as much in this uncollared and casually dressed young clergyman as in anything he had to say for his church. Gibbons' abiding memory of this lunch was his first meeting with Madeline:

> Tall, statuesque, Nordic, pleasant, yet reserved – and with vivid blue eyes, full of perception and alive with attention. She eased in and out of the conversation and left much of the talking to John. Later when we met on our Renvyle Hotel visits she would engage energetically in our 'ping-pong' games while John headed for his shower and sauna.

The conversation with John was general, with Gibbons trying to convey to him how ashamed he felt at the narrow-minded abuse of power by the Church in sacking him from his school, and how natural it would be for him to feel insulted and belittled. John made his pause. 'Ah well', he said. 'The Church has been around a long time. It's the weather of my life.' Gibbons recalled almost fifty years later, 'I had never heard this phrase before now. I have never forgotten it. I was quietly taken over by the simple, profound, benevolent meanings of the expression.'

Over several subsequent months, the two men continued to meet and chat and go for a few drinks some evenings. John would read from work in progress and talked of his mother and her passing. In the course of these conversations, he spoke frequently of the Catholic Church's liturgies, especially of the 'Requiem', with which he was intimately familiar and which he knew to be the final context of his mother's life and death. Gibbons mentioned to him that he was strongly involved in the Maynooth college choir and knew these liturgies well. John was solemnly interested in this information, and it was obvious that he had thought much about the formative influence of the architectural, theatrical and visual aspects of the Church on the lives of its people.

However, remembers Gibbons, not all was scholarly discussion: 'the next I would hear reference to liturgy would be on our homeward journey from our Renvyle revels in the early hours and late in our cups!'

> John would ask me to sing some of the plain chant Requiem Mass liturgy. I sang Kyries and Dies iraes. I told him of less familiar pieces – In Paradisum dedicant te angeli and Libera me domine for the graveside. They are very beautiful pieces, and he loved them and listened rapt. Madeline meanwhile sat and listened courteously. What must this lovely lady have thought as she was borne along the narrow roadways of north Connemara with a partner in dark ecstasy and a young priest – both inebriated – to the strains of 'may the angels lead you into paradise' and 'quando coeli movendi sunt' – when the heavens are to be moved and the earth . . . She, of course, was not aware that she was now in the land of the 'Cóiste Bodhar' – the driverless coach which appeared to people as harbinger of imminent personal doom! What indeed would my own bishop have thought of my liturgical extravaganzas or the Irish Liturgical Commission itself?

This warm friendship with a man of the cloth, genuine and mutually enriching, would prove useful to John in his efforts at placating the Sergeant.

John had spoken a lot about his father – using words such as 'watchful', 'clever', 'manipulative' – and would recall the Sergeant's involvement in the Troubles with General Seán Mac Eoin. Gibbons had agreed readily to oblige John and Madeline with a lift to and from Grevisk in the wake of the Mary Kenny article. 'Be sure to wear your priest's clothes and your Roman collar!' John injuncted. Not to do so would have handed his father an irretrievable advantage: 'And he'll regard us as fools!'

Gibbons was apprised of the likely dynamic: 'He'll ignore me entirely. He won't even acknowledge Madeline's existence because as an ex-divorcee she is legally a non-person. He'll focus full attention on you because you're a priest. He'll measure every word you say.' And that is exactly what happened on the day. Agnes talked on as she set table.

The only piece Gibbons could remember of the Sergeant's talk was a query: 'And what d'ye think of Bishop Browne?' The question, which today means little, was then a real tester. Michael Browne, Bishop of Galway, counted as a notorious arch-conservative, an outspoken Church commentator on all topics: immorality in dance halls, young women's dress code in church, public drunkenness (especially during the Galway Races). He was highly regarded for his ability as a canon lawyer and former professor of moral theology at Maynooth.

Gibbons did not share the lofty opinion and played safe by saying he thought the bishop a very able man, a man of his time. Then he absented himself for a few hours and on his return found John and Madeline exhausted, notably tense and relieved to be over the ordeal. They drove into Boyle and had a drink and something to eat, John quoting an old neighbour in Cootehall who would say: 'Some day, we'll dhress up, the two of us and go into Boyle and have our dinner in the Royal Hotel.'

Madeline's memories of the visit are of 'beautiful flagstones, the cool of the house, tea, cake'. The priest had been a good idea. When the Sergeant was left alone with Madeline, he went out to the toilet and on his return glowered at her. She glowered back. Afterwards, John told her she had done well and that his father liked tall, good-looking women. The next time they met, some years later in the house in Foxfield, he was charming and shared with her a recipe for jugged hare.

All things considered, John and Madeline got off pretty light that day. Other callers had not been so fortunate, Tristram Powell being one: 'A Mr Powell favoured us with a visit but we were not very well disposed towards strangers . . . we have decided we don't want strangers. I now understand that Mr Powell may have been genuine.' An unannounced Benedict Kiely fared even worse: 'A Mr Kiley blew in one day last week. I think he was on the "razzle". Should you see him tell him I heard he was a decent fellow and that I'll attend his funeral if I hear of it.'

Back in Cleggan, through the spring and summer of 1971, the couple's remaining months passed in blessed calm, with John writing well and Madeline blooming: 'It was absolute happiness', she thinks of those times. 'My life was beginning.' They enjoyed spending time with Eoin and Eleanor Goff. Eoin was a fine sailor and a staunch Republican who had thrown over the legal profession and a life at the Bar for Cleggan, where he bought a boat and earned a living as a fisherman, supplying hotels and restaurants in Connemara.

When a larger, more modern house – the property of Dorothea and Conrad Ormond – came up for rental in Emlough, John and Madeline decided to move. As a bonus, their new home came with a fourteen-foot boat, and John loved to go fishing with another local man, Patrick O'Malley, who became a close friend. They soon bought the boat between them and would go fishing in the evenings with Patrick's teenage son, Thomas, at first looking for pollock and mackerel, later for white trout. Thomas recalls one magical occasion when John appeared with a bag in which he had netted a 28-pound salmon: 'I'll never forget it as long as I live.'

John and Madeline declined the offer of a house for sale that Patrick had found for them close to the village, a decision about which John felt torn. To live by the sea, to fish with Patrick, to have chats over pints, to visit him and his wife Bernie in their living room or collecting letters from the post office, Bernie at the helm, juggling the switchboard, groceries, ongoing crises, while Patrick extracted or spilled post out of large canvas sacks onto the floor to begin sorting.

When Christy Day arrived with the mail from Inishbofin, the banter was choice. 'No matter what was or wasn't happening in that post office room, there was always something undefinable', remembers Madeline. 'Affection and sincerity probably. The opposing view was that there were too many incidents of invasions from Dublin. John did admit that one gets too used to the smell of the sea, for that matter, but not to freshly cut grass or saved hay because it comes around rarely.'

There were many visitors, among them John's beloved uncle Pat, who came down from Ballinamore, a man who in later Leitrim years would become their dearest caller. D. J. Gordon visited from Reading and proved, as ever, wonderful company: smart, witty, vulnerable. Madeline enjoyed listening to him talk about the Vivante family of Siena, with whom she had stayed for several summers as a younger woman just out of high school. The friendship with D. J. would endure until his early death in 1977, aged just sixty-two, including several occasions in London: at an exhibition of Chinese sculpture; at Wheeler's restaurant; in Little Venice.

Charles Monteith had been a regular visitor to Cleggan over many years, and Madeline recalls him at Richard's house on a summer's day reading William Dunbar aloud in a manner she 'could not forget'. Mary Hutchinson, whose patronage had been so important for *X*, John's first publisher, came for a week in August, gifting John and Madeline a splendid copy of Vincent van Gogh's *Letters* and a bottle of champagne to celebrate their purchase of a tumbledown property in Leitrim.

She and John disagreed on the merits of Nabokov's *Ada*, which she had sent to him in the spring, a book she admired for its 'elaborate style' and which John unsurprisingly disliked for just that reason. They were able to agree, however, on their admiration for Chekhov and on some Henri Hayden watercolours that they and Madeline had seen on a day out in London before the Cleggan move. On her way back home, she visited Dublin for a few days, staying in the Central Hotel and dining in the Stag's Head, a main meal at lunch and cheese and biscuits in the evening, accompanied by a glass of Guinness: 'I always get the corner table by the door.'

Having decided against purchasing the Cleggan house Patrick O'Malley had shown them, John and Madeline began in earnest to think about living back on John's home patch of Leitrim. Helped by John's cousin Emmet McGarry, they managed to locate a couple of possible properties and travelled north for viewings. There was a general feeling that they would not be able to afford a house near water. So, when the local Ballinamore auctioneer and publican John Joe McGirl showed them the house in Foxfield that they eventually bought, with lakes both in front of and behind the land, Madeline was so thrilled that John had to signal to her to stop talking and veil her excitement.

John was a tactician, always cautious, a brilliant draughts player. His uncle Pat had a name as the best player of solo whist in that part of Leitrim. Unlike Madeline, who was entirely new to the intricate dance of Irish country manners, John knew this language as well as anyone. He liked the property too but was careful not to show his hand. His cousin urged him to strike: 'The land offers a wide variety of exciting prospects for a house location and I think it would be a shame not to take advantage.' And so, using Arts Council money and Faber advances, John and Madeline bought their first and only home in the summer of 1971.

Joe Kennedy, John's journalist friend, drove him up to inspect the house and start considering how the place might be renovated:

> After a stop-over in Sligo we crossed into Leitrim to visit his father and step-mother and although this chauffeur was unexpected, they were hospitable; lamb chops were served, his taciturn father remarking on the unexpected arrival of another newspaper person the previous week, the author Benedict Kiely who at that time was writing a column as Patrick Lagan in the 'Irish Press'.
>
> We soon headed off on a trail of exploration of by-roads and country lanes which eventually took us to a place of dust and decay. Of that day in Fenagh I recall a feathered jackdaw skeleton on the ground before a fireplace and an adjustable date calendar in the kitchen set a year in the past.

Kennedy concludes his reminiscence with a haunting aside: 'On a bed, the covers appeared to have remained as when they had been pulled aside to remove the last encumbent to hospital or undertaker. I did not ask.'

The new home purchased by John and Madeline was a classic three-room cottage, now in poor shape after the death of its last inhabitant, having stood atop a rushy drumlin for the best part of a hundred years. As John explained to an English journalist: 'one room for the old ones, another for the young marrieds, and the middle room for the kitchen and the pigs.' Yet the McGaherns saw, in all of this decline, great potential. Though it would take some thorough refurbishment and the digging of a well to make the house habitable, the move back to Leitrim was now possible, and this ramshackle cottage on forty poor acres would become John and Madeline's home for the rest of their lives.

Trying to find the house more than thirty years later, Michel Déon recounts a problem:

> the most disturbing thing of all was that Foxfield didn't exist. Before leaving, I looked for it on the most recent Michelin map of Ireland, and it was nowhere to be seen. On a map dating from thirty years earlier you can find Foxfield between Fenagh and Keshcarrigan: just eight tiny letters, without even a spot to indicate a hamlet. On all the other maps Foxfield has disappeared. What must it feel like to live in a place that no longer exists, which has only existed perhaps in the imagination of a cartographer or in a story of fairies and witches?

Déon might have been on to something: the address is given as Aughaboniel in all of John's and Madeline's early correspondence. But whether Foxfield existed or not, several summers were spent there in preparation for the full move, which eventually came to pass in May 1976.

Work had gone well in Cleggan, and it was with a certain regret that they packed up in late September and left for London, where they had been offered the use of Barbara Ghika's large and beautiful house in Little Venice through the good offices of her mother, Mary Hutchinson. Cleggan, as well as fostering warm friendships and vivid memories of the Atlantic coast in all its splendour, would always be the place that saw the appearance of *Nightlines* and established John as one of the best short-story writers of his generation. Yet he hated, believing this designation a twee national stereotype, Bernard Share's description of him in the *Irish Times* as 'in the great tradition of Irish short-story writers'. Just as he had furiously rejected the old-lady-with-country-cottage cover for the American edition of the book, John always bristled when corralled by reviewers into an Irish pen. Charles Monteith and Faber were urged to think harder about their marketing:

> I saw the Fuller ad in the S.T. today. Do Faber think respectable/dull quotes sell books? Obviously the same person is picking the quotes. If it's like Dubliners then the sensible thing to do is read Dubliners (same way of dull thinking as 'great tradition'). The end of Fuller is the obvious quote.

The Roy Fuller review to which he refers appeared in *The Listener*: 'Reviewers confronted suddenly by an author of this quality are apt to make wild and perhaps unhelpful comparisons, but it is worth saying that for me the present book constantly recalled *Dubliners*.' The closing sentence, preferred by John, describes a virtuoso talent: 'An exciting blend of penetrating realism and sad lyricism, and a sympathy with and understanding of great stretches of human life extraordinary in a young writer.' John quickly felt bad about his grumpiness, writing to Monteith in the New Year to apologise for being 'a garrulous old bastard' while continuing to insist that Faber use a more thrusting and imaginative range of quotations from reviews to market the book.

Overall, *Nightlines* could hardly have asked for a more enthusiastic critical reception, the only consistently discordant note pointing towards a proclivity for unremitting bleakness. 'Is there no escape?' wondered Derek Mahon in *The Times*. The literary editor of the *Irish Times* fired an early shot across the bows, one that would rise to something altogether more aggressive when he came to review John's next book, four years later: 'if one critic is to stick out his neck it is to say that his work is vitiated by sexual obsession. As if to revenge us against the censor, our more gifted scribes seem to bring all their powers to bear on this area of life.'

Ultimately, John had proved himself a master in two forms, and what mattered to him most were the reactions of those small few he truly respected. In this regard, he treasured a letter received from Horace Gregory, father of Patrick, whose translations of Ovid had sustained him on those lonely commutes to and from Chingford as the stories that became *Nightlines* were conceived:

The real purpose of this note is to tell you how deeply I enjoyed reading 'Hearts of Oak', 'My Love, My Umbrella', and 'Peaches' in your Nightlines – in these, so I think, the fine and high regard for words has created your own kind of beauty, something that no one will ever be able to take away from you – and this also something you can hold onto whether you're Irish or Greek, English or Hottentot. It is what Henry James called 'the real thing'. It's the kind of writing that demands the same attention that Synge gave to his. And poetry is in the background of it. The trouble is having the strength, the 'character', to sustain it. That's your responsibility.

Do give my warmest regards to Bambi – and Mrs Gregory's very best wishes to both of you: I still remember Bambi as a little girl in a sailor blouse stepping into a large room in a ruined old house after midnight where an all-night drinking party was taking place. It was I think the first time I met her. The time must have been 1942.

9
Dark and Inland
1971–75

I shuddered as I felt already that the journey would
be dark and inland through sex and death.

JOHN McGAHERN, *The Leavetaking*

The house that John and Madeline purchased in the late summer of 1971, and where John spent much of the second half of his life, is not easy to find. Perched on a hill between two lakes in south Leitrim drumlin country, it is located down a boreen in the parish of Foxfield, its nearest village Fenagh, on the road between Mohill and Ballinamore. The most notable landmark on that road as you drive north is a statue on Selton Hill, where, atop a concrete plinth, stands an IRA man in limestone, rifle in hand, head turned to look over his left shoulder towards the high ground of Sliabh an Iarainn.

The memorial, erected in 1936 to mark the twentieth anniversary of the Easter Rising with funds raised among Leitrim exiles in the USA, marks the death of six IRA volunteers: M. E. Baxter, Joseph Beirne, Seán Connolly, Séamus Wrynn and two men named John Joe O'Reilly (born six months apart in 1899). They were ambushed nearby on the afternoon of 11 March 1921 by a combined force of Black and Tans, Auxiliaries and troops from the Bedfordshire and Hertfordshire Regiment. A week before Selton Hill, the Bedfordshires had suffered casualties at Sheemore, near Carrick-on-Shannon. Lieutenant Wilson was killed, and four of his men were wounded alongside two RIC constables. Black and Tans later undertook reprisals in Carrick, including the burning of the Temperance Hall in nearby Gowel and of the creamery stores in Kiltoghert.

The volunteers killed at Selton Hill are named on a plaque, alongside a passage in Irish outlining the nature of their sacrifice. This tribute ends with the words of Seán Mac Diarmada:

> *Geobhaimid-ne bás ionnós go mairfidh an*
> *Náisiún Gaedhealach. Déanfaidh ár gcuid fola*
> *an sean tír a áit-bhairteadh agus áit-bheodhadh.*
>
> We will die so that the Irish Nation
> may live. Our blood will
> revitalise and re-awaken the old land.

Mac Diarmada, the chief organiser of the 1916 Rising and second signatory of the Proclamation of the Irish Republic, grew up in the mountains of north Leitrim above the village of Kiltyclogher. Executed by firing squad just before dawn on 12 May 1916, his last letter home spoke of a deep peace: 'feeling a happiness the like of which I never experienced in my life before'.

On the Friday afternoon of the ambush, two local boys, Frank McGrail and his brother John, were planting seed potatoes near their home in Coldermin, Foxfield, when they heard a lone gunshot coming from the Gorvagh direction a little to the south. Normally, such a break in the peace of a spring day might have disturbed them. But these were unusual times. Leitrim was at war, IRA flying columns were on the move throughout the country, and the hated Black and Tans and Auxiliaries were billeted in nearby Mohill, their patrols along the roads a regular, and unwelcome, occurrence.

The boys returned to their house for tea, but no sooner had they arrived than a sustained volley of shots was heard from nearby. Climbing a hill by their home to get a better sense of what was happening, they came upon a scene that they would never forget and that would scar the collective memory of this small Leitrim community for generations to come:

> We could see the men falling where they got shot. We seen one fellow get a long distance away from them by running through cattle. He

was wounded, got as far as a ditch, crept across it and into shelter the other side. An officer gave a command. Two or three soldiers searched around, passed by him, but didn't see him. Then two Tans were sent away to the same place. They seen where the man was lying in a gripe the far side of the ditch and shot him dead. It was Joe Beirne. He was dragged up, with the others, by the heels to the lorries on the road. There was another fellow wounded. Hurt. He must not have been too bad. He got out of it, I don't know how.

Then there were two or three other fellows in McCullaghs. They weren't all in Flynns. They got out and escaped, McDermott from Ballinamore, Guckian from near Drumsna. Andy McPartland made his escape, the best of the lot of them. He didn't go for the open. He crawled along a ditch, got around it and into a gripe. They didn't see him at all, because he stayed under cover. He got on to the back of Murphy's and away. The other fellows (in Flynns), when they were surprised, went out into a pure open face. Baxter was the first killed. He was from Cavan. He had a job in Leitrim and that's how he came to be with the Leitrim brigade. Three were shot in a little bit of a drain, where they had taken cover. John Joe Reilly [*sic*] was also killed in a drain with no cover, out on a bottom.

Bernie Sweeney from Ballinamore survived by hiding in a drain, where the cold water prevented his death and slaked his terrible thirst. He was rescued and hidden from enemy forces by locals, before spending a month being nursed in Quill's house on Sliabh an Iarainn. Sweeney deposited a detailed account of his IRA service with the Bureau of Military History in 1955, including a memorable description of the events at Selton Hill and their aftermath:

I looked through the shrubs where I had taken up position and could see the enemy with machine guns set in position. Enemy machine guns immediately opened up a barrage of fire on our position. Each of our sections concentrated on the direction from where the machine gun fire was coming from and opened fire in that direction. The

> enemy were well informed of the position of the place and they had a force of military on the south side of us also and they opened up with rifle fire and we had not a chance from the start. This section of the enemy was most destructive to us. Five of our men were killed almost immediately. Connolly was wounded and captured and died that night in Carrick-on-Shannon Military Barracks. As I tried to change my position I was hit by one bullet in the groin and another in the leg and toppled into a drain with my rifle beside me. The water covered my body and a bunch of rushes concealed my head.

IRA flying columns, dependent for success on stealth and local support, were unaccustomed to open exchange of fire of the type encountered that day at Selton Hill, and the sound of the Lewis guns must have been terrifying. Capable of firing up to 600 .303 rounds a minute over an effective range of more than 800 yards, this weapon was a resource the British, many of whom were veterans of the Great War, had come to treasure.

One of the Bedfordshires left an account of the engagement: 'The frontal attack was pushed hard and the Lewis guns opened fire, demoralising the rebels completely, and giving excellent cover fire from the flanks. Bombs were thrown by two rebels, but exploded harmlessly. These two were immediately shot dead.' The Lewis guns' dreadful percussive tattoo meant, for Seán Connolly and his men, near-certain death. 'It was very evident', concluded Sweeney's account of the Selton Hill engagement, 'that someone had reported and pin-pointed our location to the enemy.'

Consequences for the perceived informants were swift and severe:

> Some short time after the affair a Mr. Lattimer – a Protestant who lived in the neighbourhood – was shot dead by the Volunteers and a Dr. Pringle, who had a dispensary in the area, cleared out of the country. This Dr. Pringle was killed in London by being crushed against a wall by a lorry. Some people believe that this was done designedly, but it may have been just an accident.

William Latimer was indeed a local Methodist farmer and someone who was assumed to have given away the flying column's position to a fellow Protestant, Dr Pentland (not Pringle), who had served with the British Army in the Great War and who ran a practice in Mohill. Sweeney is right in thinking that the doctor was later killed by a lorry in London, but there is no evidence to suggest that this tragedy was anything other than an accident.

Selton Hill and its monument feature twice in John's fiction, first in passing in *The Pornographer* and next, at greater length, through the eyes of Jamesie in *That They May Face the Rising Sun*, where the site is renamed Glasdrum. His boyhood memory of the episode has the local Protestant man Sinclair shot for no other reason than his religion: 'They shot him like a dog beneath the cows and said he had confessed before he was shot. Oh, we are a beautiful people, Kate. They shot him because somebody had to be made to pay and poor Sinclair was a Protestant and the nearest to hand.'

John's retelling of Selton Hill is largely historically accurate except in one respect. He renames Bernie Sweeney 'Big Bernie Reynolds' and has him saved from the watery ditch by a young Jamesie Murphy and his father and kept safe in their house till he is fit to be moved. After the war, he becomes successful in business but never returns to thank the Murphys, as Jamesie explains to Ruttledge: 'He was on every committee in the county. As he got old he used often sit outside his shop on a warm day. Do you think he'd ever recognize us as we passed?' Not surprisingly, Bernie Sweeney's descendants – some of whom were friends of the McGaherns – were wounded by the portrayal, and it took some time for the breach to heal.

The tale of the executed – and innocent – Protestant is revealing of the long-held sympathy and interest that John had for the dwindling numbers of the faith in Leitrim and Roscommon. When John and Madeline got into the habit of driving across the border to Enniskillen after their move to Foxfield, he would point out a particular field where he said a man had been shot just because he was Protestant; this sectarian side of Irish history he always deplored.

Because of the proximity of Cootehall to the country seat of the King-Harmon family in Rockingham, John was conscious of having grown up around the final days of Anglo-Irish gentility, a world brilliantly captured by David Thomson in *Woodbrook*, his account of days spent as a tutor to the Kirkwood family in their home near Carrick-on-Shannon. 'They were a separate society from the society whose only moral values were from the Catholic Church', said John in one television interview, 'and naturally that's interesting for its dramatic quality . . . The Protestants seemed to have a much more cultivated life. That was from the distance of the other side of the demesne wall . . . They certainly had a freedom we didn't have.'

Born into that larger society just thirteen years after the establishment of the Free State, with a father and uncles who had seen active service in the IRA throughout the Tan War, John could not but have been exposed to accounts of the conflict, despite the reticence of many of its participants about retelling the parts they played. Writing to his youngest sister Dympna in the early 1960s, he is strident in his dismissal of Republican tall tales. 'I always found I. R. A. narratives boring in the extreme. But then I never found these external dramas exciting. What Curiosity I have is what impact they made on the individual concerned.' He goes on to draw a distinction between the life of external action and the more sacred interior life:

> The real drama of life doesn't go on in war, the drama of all our lives under God, but how our consciences weigh the triumphs and disasters of each day. It does not matter what way our lives pass, somebody could make a walk through the woods as passionately vivid as an ambush, provided he loved it, that is all that matters.

While a tendency to revere the everyday would persist throughout John's life, his complete rejection of IRA narratives did not endure.

Ernie O'Malley's memoir of his part in the revolution, *On Another Man's Wound*, became, in later years, one of John's favourite books and one that he wrote about with marked enthusiasm. O'Malley was the one exceptional guerrilla fighter who managed to merge the outer life of war and conflict with the inner world of stillness and contemplation. The account of his middle-class youth in Castlebar and his eventual epiphanic turn to Republican commitment via the 1916 Easter Rising and subsequent years of fighting, imprisonment and escape was published in the same year as the erection of the Selton Hill monument and stood out from the mass of such memoirs so sharply dismissed by John in his letter to Dympna. 'What is so extraordinary is not the material itself', writes John in a passionate essay about the book, 'but that most of it is so well written. For far too long its right to a permanent and honoured place in our literature has been denied.' O'Malley's memoir of the war is, he concludes, 'the one classic work to have emerged directly from the violence that led to the founding of the Irish Free State.'

Though O'Malley did not take part in the Selton Hill engagement, he saw active service in Leitrim, Longford and Roscommon. He describes the fire fight at some length in his posthumously published biography of the Longford IRA commander Seán Connolly, the most senior volunteer to be killed in the ambush. Connolly was a man well known to Frank McGahern, who was awarded, in 1952, an IRA Service Medal without Bar in recognition of time he spent in the field with D Company, 6 Battalion of the Longford Brigade between 1918 and 1922.

In O'Malley's prose, there is a stylishness and a care for accurate description of landscape lacking from most such accounts. Here, for instance, is Bernie Sweeney as he lies in the cold water of the ditch, awaiting his fate:

> They would probably come back again to search he thought, but his only hope now was the covering cloak which was creeping over the western sky. Birds low flying and calling to each other in the now hushed indifference of evening mist swung across the lake and back over the tufted grass.

Unsurprisingly, in O'Malley's accounts the IRA tend to be portrayed as acting from noble motives, while the British and their Irish allies are generally cruel and brutish, as in his description of the treatment of the captured Connolly:

> When the lorry reached Mohill Barracks, Connolly asked for a drink of water, but no one would offer him a drink. 'Piss in his mouth, that's good enough for him,' said an RIC man as he leaned over the side of the lorry. Then as they set out for Carrick, the soldiers shouted 'Fresh meat, fresh meat,' in imitation of a huxter's cry, while the District Inspector's parting shout was: 'We'll salt them down.'

As much as John admired Ernie O'Malley the writer and intellectual, he did not sympathise with his unswerving brand of separatist Republicanism. And this dislike became more marked when thinking about the rise of the Provisional IRA in the years after 1968 and the explosion of the Troubles in Ulster. 'I am not a pacifist', he explained in one interview. 'I can imagine situations when one would be forced to take up arms, but I dislike all forms of violence, which include lies and sentimentality as well as physical force. For me, life is precious.'

Jamesie's retelling of the ambush in *That They May Face the Rising Sun* is prompted by the annual Easter march of Republican sympathisers from the statue at Glasdrum to the cemetery in Shruhaun, where several volunteers are buried. We know from a few prompts – the TV show *Blind Date*, the Enniskillen Remembrance Day bomb of 1987, the coming of telephone poles and wires – that the novel is set mainly in the late 1980s and that the Troubles are at their height. The march, seen through the eyes of Ruttledge, is a tawdry affair:

> They wore black shoes and pants, white shirts, black ties and gloves, black berets and dark glasses. Out in front a lone marcher bore the tricolour. In threes the others marched. They carried placards with slogans and photos of Pearse, McDermott and Sands on green, white and gold backgrounds. The effect was somehow sinister and cheap. A small crowd followed the band. A few were local activists but most were from the North. In the middle of the crowd, Jimmy Joe

> McKiernan walked quietly, the head of the Provisionals, North and South, with power over all who marched.

Jamesie, who wears the Easter lily in his lapel in remembrance of the 1916 Rising, has a grudging respect for McKiernan, a regard entirely lacking from the peace-loving moderate, Ruttledge:

> 'One thing you can say about Jimmy Joe is that he never pushes himself out in front,' Jamesie said with approval.
>
> 'They'll probably be putting up another statue to him one of these years,' Ruttledge said.

John knew, of course, that such a monument already existed: John Joe McGirl, the man on whom Jimmy Joe McKiernan is based, does indeed have a large memorial dedicated to his memory in his home town of Ballinamore today. On an imposing black-marble obelisk in raised lettering are his name, his dates of 1921–88 and the inscription 'An Unbroken and Unbreakable Fenian'.

McGirl had brokered the sale of the Foxfield property to John and Madeline, who, while not agreeing with his politics, found him a charming and agreeable character. Devoted to the unification of Ireland and overthrow of British rule on the island, he was for many decades a leading figure in Irish Republicanism and someone elected to the Dáil in 1957 on a Sinn Féin abstentionist ticket and who spent periods imprisoned in Mountjoy, the Curragh and, in later years, Long Kesh.

The McGaherns' new home in Foxfield was situated a twenty-five-minute drive from the border just beyond Swanlinbar, and they would often shop in Enniskillen, with Blake's pub on Church Street becoming a particular favourite. So familiar did John become with the place and its proprietors that he used Blake's as his address for incoming correspondence during postal strikes south of the border.

The Troubles rarely spilled over into Leitrim, with one notable exception being the events that surrounded the IRA kidnapping of businessman Don Tidey in late 1983, when John and Madeline were away in

Colgate. Tidey was eventually rescued from a forest bunker after a search operation and a shoot-out between IRA volunteers, the Irish Army and members of An Garda Síochána at Derrada Wood, a short distance from John's mother's homeplace. A soldier, Private Patrick Kelly, and a garda, Gary Sheehan, were killed.

John wrote to Charles Monteith – a regular visitor to his brother in Castlederg, County Tyrone throughout the Troubles – to tell him the news:

> Did you see about the kidnapping and shooting in sleepy Foxfield? May from across the lake said it was a pity I wasn't there – I'd have had lots to write about. The boy from the post office was shot by mistake at a checkpoint. Some of the Irish soldiers are supposed to have thrown their arms away at the very sound of firing.

This somewhat jaundiced view of Irish military efficiency is repeated in an oft-revised essay about County Leitrim in which John recounts the story of one border-crossing. 'Generally, the Irish will glance out of the window and wave each car through, especially if it is raining', he writes about the Swanlinbar crossing. The atmosphere is notably more serious as he enters Fermanagh:

> At the British Army checkpoint it is very different. People have been killed here. There are ramps and screens and barriers and a tall camouflaged lookout tower. A line of cars waits behind a red light. A quick change to green signals each single car forward. In the middle of this maze armed soldiers call out the motor vehicle number and driver's identification to a hidden computer.

On one such shopping trip, the commanding officer at the British checkpoint asks the McGaherns to bring back two wheaten loaves from Enniskillen. On their return, they hand over the bread, turning down the officer's payment:

> When the money was refused – 'with the compliments of the country' – he looked at a loss for a moment, before coming to attention

Frank McGahern, back row, third from right, and his Garda Síochána class, *c.*1922.

Sergeant Frank McGahern and his children, with Aunt Maggie (their late mother's sister) on far right, *c.*1945.

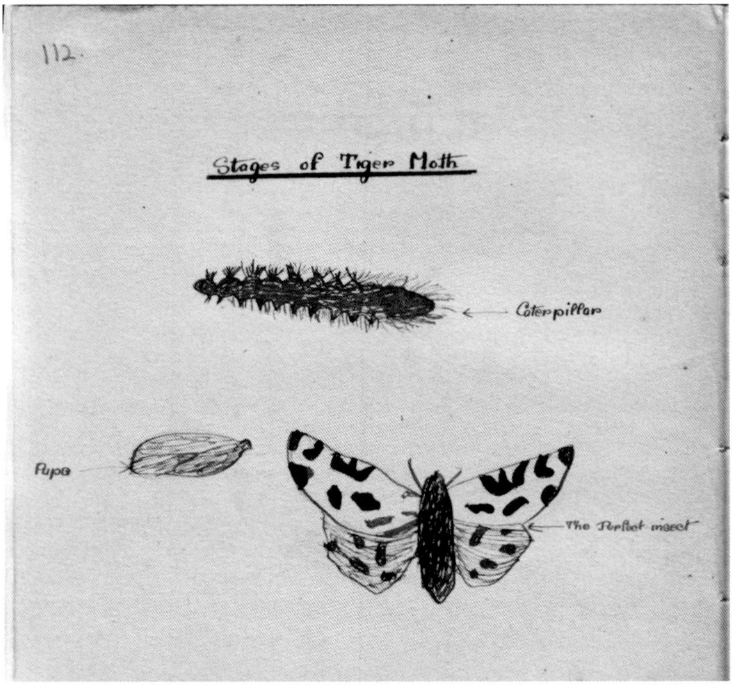

Top: Illustrations drawn by Susan McManus in her 'Nature Study Record Book', *c.*1918–20.

Left: Susan McGahern (back right) with friends.

Above: Annikki Laaksi and John McGahern, *c.*1964–65.

Portrait of John, *c.*1963.

Top left: Portrait of Madeline Green, Paris, *c.*1967.

Top right: Photo-booth images with Madeline Green, Paris, *c.*1968.

Left: John at work in 1 rue Christine, Paris, *c.*1969–70.

Top: Peter Woods and Francie McGarty saving hay in the McGaherns' Foxfield shed.

Right: John's uncle Pat McManus at work in his Ballinamore garage.

Bottom: The McGahern home in Foxfield, 1980s.

Patrick O'Malley, Cleggan.

Francie McGarty and John, the McGarty kitchen in the 1980s.

John and Jimmy Swift, the International Bar, Dublin, *c.*1990.

Above: Tom Jordan.

Right: Neill Joy.

John with his boat at the lakeside, Foxfield, 1980s.

John in his Foxfield home, mid-1990s.

> and honouring us with one of the sharpest salutes I have ever seen, out there beneath the mountains, in the middle of the wilderness. I wish the whole commerce of Northern Ireland could be as simple as that human request.

Sadly, things were rarely quite that straightforward.

John's reluctance to comment on the national question was not untypical for many of his generation. The most interesting of his thoughts on Irish history – stemming from an interview he did in Foxfield with the American politician and writer Tom Hayden in January 1996 – lie buried in his archive. Hayden was working on a book about the Great Hunger that would be published the following year. John, after speaking with unusual candour, subsequently had a change of mind about allowing publication, feeling that the American's political slant was too monochrome and anti-British.

John speaks about his father's membership of the IRA along with both his uncles on his mother's side, one of whom went on to become a Blueshirt. None of them talked about their experiences, forming part of 'a whole culture of silence'. John diagnoses the formative energies within this dynamic: 'It's got to do with a cult of masculinity where there was god the father on top, the catholic church, the head of the household, and masculinity, which was strong silence, which was somehow feminine and degenerate and endangering to talk too much.' It was not just the men with whom John grew up who buried the past deep. He comments that he knew both his grandmothers but never heard a single mention of the Famine. 'It was considered unmanly to speak too much. I've often wondered at the fact that some of the people who survived the Famine would certainly have done so at the expense of others. It would have been shameful to account . . . deprive other people of bread.'

As a result of this repression and silence, there developed a neurotic fear of poverty that he saw running very powerfully through his father: 'There is a mentality in the Irish countryside I can only define as a blind grasping after all advantages, even useless advantages. This comes from the Famine. It was very common in the generation around here, the generation that just died.'

At a Galway reading John gave in 1985, Colm Tóibín witnessed him muse on these facets of his country's character:

> Both sides of the family had been involved in the War of Independence and there was always talk, hushed talk, of what had happened. If you asked a question you would be told nothing, but if you sat and waited and listened you would hear them talk of ambushes, of men followed to Australia and murdered there, of men dumped over the side of boats.

Several years later, this dark viewpoint reappeared when John introduced his edition of John Butler Yeats's letters. He writes in this piece that to believe in 'the goodness and kindness of people' remains 'a very un-Irish quality'.

Certainly, all around south Leitrim, if one cares to read the signs, both hidden and open, lies a history of ruin and loss. The dispossession of Catholic land in the county was all but complete by the later seventeenth century, with rebels taking to the woods and mountainsides keen to be avenged. The Lord Lieutenant wrote at the end of February 1667 that the 'little rebels known here by the name of Tories, do grow as fast as they are cut off, and have upon the matter, rendered the whole county of Leitrim unuseful to the King and uninhabitable by any English'. When, at the end of the following century, General Humbert's army marched through the county after success in Killala, Castlebar and elsewhere in Mayo, they were joined by enthusiastic Leitrim Catholics, among them Philip Meehan, John's distant relation, cut down at Ballinamuck.

Gorvagh, one of the McGaherns' neighbouring townlands, went from a population of 204 in 1841 to 122 a decade later. By 1911, this number had fallen to thirty-four. In 2021, it had dropped to just eleven. The bleeding-dry of the Famine years led to an unsurprising politicisation in the late nineteenth and early twentieth centuries, with Sinn Féin's emergence onto the national electoral stage in 1908. That year, Charles

J. Dolan, who had resigned from the Irish Parliamentary Party in frustration at its Westminster impotence, ran for Sinn Féin in the North Leitrim by-election, with Seán Mac Diarmada as his election agent. Though Dolan lost, he gained a far more important tribute. Arthur Griffith, a subsequent leader of the party and later first president of the Irish Free State, wrote: 'Ireland's resurrection would be dated from the day when 1,200 Irishmen in the poorest and most remote county in Ireland voted for Sinn Féin.'

* * *

The book that coincides with John and Madeline's gradual move to Leitrim is *The Leavetaking*. This novel, while problematic, holds many treasures for a biographer. Nobody was more conscious of the work's fault lines than its author – so aware of these difficulties that he even took two shots at writing the book, a decade apart: '*The Leavetaking* had to do with a young man's idea. I think that the idea was erroneous to begin with. But it was an experiment that I had to do. A writer learns by mistakes. The only objection I have to it is that they shouldn't be made in public.' In his preface to the revised 1984 edition, prompted by questions from Alain Delahaye, his French translator, John reflects on the problems that drove him to rewrite: 'the work lacked that distance, that inner formality or calm, that all writing, no matter what it is attempting, must possess.'

The book's narrator, Patrick Moran, shares a name with a local hero from John's youth, hanged with five other men in Mountjoy jail in March 1921 for his part in the events of Bloody Sunday the previous November. The novel is only obliquely political, reflecting on an Ireland that has squandered the fruits of Independence and marshalled its native language for purposes of coercion. Split into two parts, the narrative centres around Moran, a teacher, fleeing to London to escape an unhappy love affair, only to find himself falling for an American divorcee. They marry in a register office; he returns to Ireland with her and is dismissed from his post because of marriage outside the Catholic Church.

Part One sees Moran in his final day on the schoolyard before dismissal, thinking of his beloved mother's last illness, death and funeral. The school is portrayed as an ugly and brutal place, where discipline is strict and the Irish language is used as the lexicon of control. Moran uses the language to speak to his 'Old fanatical peasant' headmaster. He tells us, 'I prefer to thank him in the patriotic and official idiom since in it I am unable to betray shades of feeling.' And there will be no feeling or solidarity for the boys in his charge either:

> 'Anybody moving after the bell goes straight to the office,' the headmaster is outside the swing door, shouting into the voracious shrieking of the gulls. The second bell drowns his voice. They run to their lines. 'No talking after the bell,' I hear him shout as some murmur rises into the gull shriek.
>
> '*Lamha suas*,' I say and the lines stretch out as they put hands on each other's shoulders. '*Lamha sios*,' their hands slap their sides.

There is a monotonous and wearying militarism about all of this routine that will be familiar to any Irish reader born before 1980, and we are left in no doubt that this school, this place, is the product of a failed state: 'The lavatories and schoolrooms are flatroofed and concrete, the single arm of the assembly hall alone v-roofed. Ragged rose bushes hang limp under its windows, a strip of black earth in concrete, the concrete beginning to crack after ten years, half-arsed modern as the rest of the country.'

All of the teachers described are recognisable fictionalised versions of those men with whom John taught: Joe Joyce, Diarmuid Harrington, Desmond Millett, Colm Mullen, Seán O'Boyle, Frank O'Dea and Fergus O'Kennedy. Mr James, who is given the most sympathetic portrait, is drawn from John's closest friend and confidant at the school, Tom Jordan:

> James takes up to try to concentrate the life he feels haemorrhaging under the headmaster's eye until he can get to the quiet of his

classroom, where he'll try to restore his loss of self with a silent curse before making the class stand for prayer before work, the work he'll do scrupulously and well.

The book inevitably became, when published, a source of mirth in the staffroom around attempting accurate identification of characters. This game was easy to win. In addition to Part One being about individual teachers, the novel also reflected on the act of teaching itself by considering the narrator's mother and her entrance into the profession. The sense of the transcendental power of good writing is given voice by the character of this woman, a teacher who is being sounded out by the Mother Superior of her school for a possible life in the Church:

> 'Doesn't poetry remain always in some way the unknown, Mother?' she ventured after thought. 'It can be felt, but not known, as we can never know our own life or another's in the great mystery of life itself.'
>
> 'I'm afraid, Kate, I don't quite follow.'

Such spiritual profundity is beyond the nun's grasp, as it is beyond that of most of her fellow teachers: 'She'd learned too that most teachers read little, had even an instinctive hatred of the essential mystery and magic in all real poetry, reducing it to the factual or sentimental and preferably both, four ducks on a pond and a grassbank beyond.'

Part Two sees Moran escape his native land to the exciting anonymity of London. The very size of where he has left rises bitterness and regret: 'What a small country Ireland is, where everybody who is not related knows someone who knows someone else you share an enemy or friend with.' Much to his relief, he finds in England the answer to such claustrophobia: 'The thronged vastness of London was the natural element of my need to be alone and slowly I was seeing that for the first time in my life I was free.'

He gets a job as a barman with a landlord named Mr Plowman – a kind of decent English everyman – and there meets Isobel, the American woman with whom he falls in love. One of the revised version's notable additions is greater expansiveness in descriptions of this landlord. The 1984 text supplements the 1974 text, offering a fresh gloss: 'He arranged a meeting with the manager, a tall, courteous Englishman who had served in the R.A.F., Mr. Plowman.'

Both this figure and his wife are kind in their treatment of Patrick and Isobel, a generosity of spirit that is markedly lacking in Patrick's Irish employers when the couple move back to Dublin. Patrick recalls with shame the obsequiousness that marks the Irish teacher's life: 'I blush still as I hear the slavish caution of my whole forever overmastered race in my voice.' England would again become a place of refuge and escape in both *The Pornographer* and *Amongst Women*, though by the closing years of his writing life John has come close to some sort of rapprochement with his homeland.

The Leavetaking began its public life in England in May 1974, when a rather jumbled series of extracts appeared in the second issue of the *New Review*. This work appeared between a characteristically swashbuckling editorial, attacking everything from the New York chattering classes to the portentousness of Jorge Luis Borges and an admiring profile of Roland Barthes. The new magazine quickly became *the* place to be seen as a serious writer in 1970s Britain. Funded generously by the Arts Council and succeeding from its more modest predecessor, *The Review*, also edited by Ian Hamilton, the magazine survived for fifty issues. Published from the same Soho offices, the *New Review* became synonymous with names such as Clive James, Jonathan Raban and Robert Lowell, Hamilton's friend. Ten of Lowell's new poems appeared in the first ninety-six-page issue.

Hamilton's opening editorial was typically combative, taking aim variously at an edition of F. R. Leavis's letters and the practice of publishing anonymous reviews in the *TLS* (a practice, incidentally, under which John received his only shaky notice for *The Dark*). Hamilton was keen to get John more closely involved and invited him to join an editorial board. But John, with the exception of his late involvement with the Irish Arts Council, was never a joiner of clubs. Though happy to be published in the magazine, he ducked getting in any deeper. Meetings between the two men generally took place in the Pillars of Hercules public house or in nearby Soho restaurants, where Hamilton chain-smoked, pushed his food around the plate and doled out generally strident, exacting and well-informed editorial advice.

Al Alvarez recalled Hamilton as 'a hard man to please and almost impossible to fool', with 'a beady eye for whatever is phoney or sentimental'. John had a similar disdain for sentimentality, as per the tough-minded, dark stories he published in the *New Review*. 'Faith, Hope and Charity' revolves around the death of Joe Cunningham, a Derrada navvy, killed on a London building site. 'Doorways' and 'Along the Edges' are stories of painfully stunted love. 'The Beginning of an Idea' counts as one of John's rare attempts to look back on his failed marriage to Annikki. 'It is plain that this author will never be surprised out of his own sadness', wrote the *TLS* reviewer when the stories were published in book form as *Getting Through* in 1978.

John's closer-than-usual engagement with the London literary scene was facilitated by two separate periods spent in the city during *The Leavetaking*'s composition: the first in Barbara Ghika's large Little Venice home in the autumn months of 1971 after leaving Cleggan; and the second through autumn 1973 and spring 1974, when John and Madeline lived happily for a time with his brother Frankie and family in Highams Park on the edge of Epping Forest. In between these periods, the couple kept up their familiar itinerant lifestyle, returning to Colgate for the spring semester of 1972, before another nine months spent in rue Christine and seven months on Achill Island from March to October 1973. The move away from Cleggan had come about because the house they were renting was becoming unavailable; coupled with Mary Hutchinson's offer of her daughter's London house, the decision was not a hard one to take.

For that autumn in Little Venice, John resumed his light teaching duties at the University of Reading and made final arrangements to have *Nightlines* published by Mercure de France in Paris under the title *Lignes de fond*, translated and introduced by Pierre Leyris, the prominent

French poet and translator. The publication was largely engineered by Mary Hutchinson, who was friendly with Leyris. This connection provided a fortunate beginning to what would prove a fruitful relationship with the French reading public.

One of the most celebrated French translators of the twentieth century, Leyris translated, among others, Shakespeare, Milton, Melville and Jean Rhys. His four-volume translation of the works of William Blake earned him the 1974 Prix Valery Larbaud. By the time of translating *Nightlines*, he had begun to bring out Yeats's *Autobiographies* and was an admirer of Irish literature in general. His introduction to *Lignes de fond* – which reserves special praise for 'Lavin', 'Korea' and 'My Love, My Umbrella' – points to the progress John makes between *The Barracks* and *The Dark* but feels that *Nightlines* marks a huge step forward, creating what Leyris calls '*une comédie humaine irlandaise*'.

John continued to work on *The Leavetaking* and on some radio and television ideas, writing that had begun in Cleggan after being contacted by Susanna Capon, a commissioning editor at BBC Radio 3. She had acted on the recommendation of P. H. Newby, inaugural winner of the Booker Prize, McGahern fan and controller of the station. John's conversion of 'Why We're Here' into a play called *Sinclair* was broadcast by Radio 3 on 16 November while he was living in London, with Cyril Cusack playing Boles and Norman Rodway as Gillespie.

The experiment was judged sufficiently successful for more BBC commissions to come his way, including a long radio version of Tolstoy's melodrama of peasant grasping and infanticide, *The Power of Darkness*. This work had been rejected by the Abbey Theatre on the grounds that 'the ignorance and superstition does not at all translate to Ireland at any time' and that 'the excesses – the murder of the child especially – here as depicted, would cause laughter even if well done'. Capon quite rightly assured John that the Abbey response was 'really stupid and the comments totally invalid'. When, more than a decade later, modern Ireland's most infamous case of infanticide – the so-called Kerry babies case – filled the headlines, John must have permitted himself a wry smile before returning to the script and preparing it anew for the Abbey stage.

While he was happy enough with the radio adaptation of Tolstoy, John was much less pleased with some of his other attempts to work with the BBC in these early years of the 1970s. Most notably, he considered his television adaptation of Joyce's 'The Sisters' an unmitigated failure, despite finding the director Stephen Frears 'very good to work with'. This assessment came in a letter of October 1972. Interviewed in October 2004, John had not changed his mind: 'Stephen Frears and I were friends. He told me he didn't know what he was doing, and I said I didn't know what I was doing. I was horrified when I saw what I had done.'

Other television work included adaptations of his short story 'Swallows' and parts of *The Leavetaking*. Although none of these projects quite came off to John's satisfaction, they did lead to one particularly warm friendship, with Susanna Capon's husband, the producer Barry Hanson. Later to find fame with a classic gangster film, *The Long Good Friday*, Hanson produced 'Swallows', a mess about which John could eventually laugh:

> When I saw the actors they had got in the BBC in Birmingham I knew we were ruined, because you can tell that. So I said to Barry Hanson, who was the producer, I said we haven't a chance with this script and those actors. I said the whole idea of 'Swallows' is a kind of elusive poetry. And the actors were all policemen from *Z-Cars*, which was a popular series at the time, and he said, 'If you think you'll get poetry out of these guys you'd better start thinking about transmigration of souls fast. We're going to shoot in an hour's time.'

Not until a 1990s BBC adaptation of *Amongst Women* did John's work appear successfully on television. By that point, having had enough, he chose not to watch the show.

Having bought the house in Foxfield, using up his advance for *The Leavetaking* and whatever remained of his Arts Council grants, John was badly in need of money, and so in early January 1972, he headed back out to Colgate for his second semester as a visiting professor. He was shortly joined by Madeline, who had flown ahead to California to see her mother for the first time in sixteen years.

As would usually happen, John's teaching commitments, coupled with the inevitable round of socialising, proved detrimental to his writing. 'It depresses me already', he told his doctor friend Niall Walsh, with whom he had reconnected in Cleggan, 'even more than the last time, this morality of success, bright hopefuls of all ages or bewildered hopefuls of later age searching for the absent next move'. Later that spring, he restated his case to Walsh:

> It's not that the work is too hard but with it and trying to put names on faces and the social demands it's almost impossible to get enough calm to do my own work. It's as if one's real life was put away with camphor balls in boxes like summer clothes until May. Even the huge monthly pay checks increase the unreality though they are the only reason to be here.

Unable to write much of substance, John turned his mind to putting himself in a stronger position with American publishers and spent parts of the spring unsuccessfully trying to move from Atlantic to Random House, including having dinner with Jason Epstein, then a vice president with the firm, in New York on 7 April. He would just have to continue with paltry advances and honour his commitments. *The Leavetaking* was eventually published by Atlantic, Little, Brown early in 1975.

Back in Paris, that summer and autumn of 1972, John worked away slowly on the novel. With the divorce from Annikki now finalised, he and Madeline were at last free to marry. On Christmas Eve, John wrote to Niall Walsh in Ballinasloe to invite him and his wife Phil to Paris for the wedding on either the last Saturday of January or the first Saturday of February. The Walshes could not come, and the date was fixed for 3 February at La Mairie in the Place Saint-Sulpice. The occasion was the simplest of affairs, with just one witness, their friend Paddy Hogan, who worked for the Irish Fisheries Board in Paris.

John had been making plans around Madeline's wedding ring for some time. He had taken advice from Giles de la Mare at Faber on some wording from Milton's *Paradise Lost*, from the passage in Book 4 where Eve has become aware of her own reflection in the Garden of Eden before hearing an intercessionary voice. John had engraved on the inside of the narrow silver band, 'And I will bring thee where no shadow staies thy coming.' The second time around for both husband and wife, this marriage would prove an enduring and mutually enriching bond interrupted only by death.

If Niall and Phil Walsh could not be there in person, they were generous in their treatment of the newly wedded couple, offering them use of their Achill Island holiday home as a place to live while John tried to complete work on the novel. And so, in March, they packed once again and picked up, with a fish lorry borrowed through Paddy Hogan, possessions stored in the twins' Leytonstone home, before having them deposited at the Walshes' house in Ballinasloe. They subsequently arranged for their delivery onward from Ballinasloe and arrived to live in Achill on St Patrick's Day 1973, a small parade winding along the roads as though to welcome them. The house was located in Dooagh, halfway between Keel and Keem, with a view across the road of the sea and adjacent to Lourdie's pub, which soon became a favourite haunt.

It was immediately clear that Achill Island would become a place of productivity and happy memories. Within three days of arriving, John is writing to Niall about pollock fishing, Mrs English's hens, scraping a gate for painting and, most importantly, writing fluently. 'Both of us are incredibly happy and grateful', he tells his friend, someone to whom he regularly sent drafts of work and who would eventually become the dedicatee of *The Leavetaking* on its appearance in the early days of January 1975.

Charles Monteith, who had visited the island many years previously, was delighted to know that this new home would see *The Leavetaking* to completion. John had written to him enthusiastically in April:

> It is very lovely here and I was able to work almost at once.
>
> The cottage is in the village and looks out over the bay. Sometimes I walk to the other village of Keel, which is two miles away; and Keem Bay is as beautiful as you described it. They started to shark and salmon fish with nets there last week. The people are obviously used to tourists for generations, which makes it much easier than Cleggan.

Monteith could not resist John's descriptions of Achill's charms and came to stay for a rainy week in July, enjoying meals centred around the cheap and plentiful local lobster and taking the 210-page manuscript of the almost-finished novel away with him when he left to stay for a few days with his brother in Castlederg.

On 19 July, he writes with his impressions: a mixture of high praise and aesthetic concern.

> With one reservation – which I'll mention in a moment – I think the book is stunningly good, easily the best you have ever written, and I'm quite bowled over by it. It's a splendidly controlled and sustained piece of narrative – and I thought marvellously well structured. My very warmest and sincerest congratulations on it. I'm very much looking forward to publishing it.
>
> My reservation is this, and I thought I'd write to you about it quite frankly and of course you may not agree at all with what I'm going to say: the question is really one of what I might pretentiously call 'tonality'. The whole narrative of the girl's past life – though of course I know what it's based on and how closely it's modelled on what really happened – does somehow, being so bizarre, fail to fit into the book as a whole. The prevailing tone or pitch of the book up 'til then is a fairly sombre and low-keyed one – and suddenly to introduce this narrative and to highlight it as you do seems in some strange way off-pitch or out of key. In fact, I think many readers might simply dismiss it as an unsuccessful piece of over-melodramatic invention – and there might be a total failure to induce that essential 'willing suspension of disbelief'.

> What I'd suggest is that the real facts should be rather muted and toned down, and some of the more extraordinary touches eliminated. For example, I would suggest that the Duchess – and again I know who she was in real life – should become simply a widow or divorcee of a multi-millionaire.

Monteith then cautiously raises his other chief concern, clearly worried that he might offend his author:

> The other thing – and again you may disagree completely – is that I wasn't entirely happy about the general tone – to use that word again – of the girl's dialogue. I know that by reproducing all these Americanisms with their almost brutal directness and frankness you probably meant to show how she was a clean and honest wind, as it were, blowing through all the fog that had hung over the narrator's life; but to cram so much and so many of them into short or shortish speeches seems to me not to ring entirely true, and to produce a quite unintended effect of something like coarseness.

'I do hope', concludes Monteith, 'you won't be cross with me for passing on all these criticisms – but I felt that you would prefer me to be completely frank with you at this stage.'

If these criticisms hurt John, he did a good job at concealing emotion, quickly writing back his thanks for what he agrees are cogent points:

> Thank you for such praise and for such a useful letter. All of the reservations are to my mind justified. The 'Duchess' has become ridiculous already, as has the woman's language in the working – it is 30 pages on, and in about another week I will have left London completely – grown quieter. It is strange that when one is unsure of tone there seems always exaggeration. Rather than any 'crossness' I am indebted and grateful.

He concludes with warm personal memories of their time together on Achill:

> It was a great pleasure for Madeline and myself to have you in Achill and we miss you. The next day was fine and we walked again on Keel Strand. A strong wind was blowing from the golf links and fine sand was moving like smoke across the strand into the curl back of the spent waves. The Menawn cliffs were clear and beautiful and you were very much in our thoughts.

And yet, despite all the changes John makes to the book in light of Monteith's suggestions, there is still too much of the truth, of 'real life', about Part Two, a truth that, ironically, but typically, becomes unbelievable. As much as he tried to convince himself otherwise, John was able to see in retrospect that the experiment was a failure.

In general, the reviewers saw the same flaws that had been raised by Monteith. John Mellors in *The Listener*, while admiring Part One for its lyricism, gets lost in Part Two. For him, there is an odd and ironic dislocation to note: 'the poetry fades, and the novel teeters between the flat and the fantastic. It is as if the author is fully nourished only among the bleak hypocrisies of the country from which his narrator is determined to break free.' Jonathan Raban wrote what is the most perceptive review in *Encounter*, seeing much to praise in the book's first half, comparing McGahern favourably with Joyce:

> It is written with extraordinary purity and exactitude and it makes the desolation which it records at once fiercely unique to the child in the novel and universal. It would be barbarous to give a quotation from it, but it should be said that its rhythm is as stately as that of a requiem, its vocabulary has a dignified simplicity, yet it is always miraculously alert to the particular. A wren flitting among the branches of a laurel interweaves with the mourners and altar boys, bringing the general tragedy of everybody's dying into sudden unbearable sharp focus. McGahern has a genius – and that word does not overstate what he does – for mediating between the deep currents of feeling which belong to myth and history and the exact texture of the moment, seen so freshly that it comes off the page in a vivid

> cluster of sensations. As long as *The Leavetaking* stays in Ireland, it reads like a masterpiece.

As with so many other readers, however, Raban saw the novel's second half as a failure:

> McGahern, so brilliant on the familiar, turns out to be surprisingly clumsy when it comes to dealing with strangers. He simply has very little gift for making people talk outside the phatic code of the family. And Ireland in his work is a vast extended family of dull relations who know too much about each other for their own comfort. England, a neutral territory, is a place of long creaking sentences and incomprehensible characters.

Ultimately, the review argues that the characterisation in the book's second half fails to hit the mark:

> The girl's father, who gets too much space to himself in the crucial middle of the book, is a ramshackle creation out of cultural science fiction, a bug-eyed monster. The girl herself is too beautiful, too tender, too evanescent to be real; a dream or a muse rather than a person.

Other readers were more forgiving. On the book's US release, Peter Prescott in *Newsweek* wondered if 'there is another practicing writer of fiction in English as good as John McGahern who is so little noticed in this country'. Julian Jebb in the *TLS* discerned no lowering in standard: '*The Leavetaking* represents an achievement of a very high order and substantiates the belief that its author is among the half-dozen practising writers of English prose most worthy of attention.' Seamus Heaney in the *Sunday Independent* was confident that his compatriot and friend had lost none of his mastery: 'McGahern's imagination is ruminant. It chews the cud of the past, digests and re-digests it, interrogates it for its meaning, savours it for its bittersweet recurrence. This is the way to understand the compulsive return to certain landscapes and themes in his work.' For readers with concerns about John's progress as a writer, Heaney concludes by offering further evidence of excellence: 'And those "worried" about his development, by the way, should look up his masterly story "The Beginning of an Idea", in last August's issue of the *New Review*, and think again.'

That Heaney's closing remark is meant as a shot at Terence de Vere White's tough *Irish Times* review of the book, three weeks earlier, is clear. In what frequently feels like a personalised attack, the piece accuses John of resting on his censored laurels: 'The making of martyrs in Ireland has always advantaged the cause of the victim. John McGahern was dismissed from a teaching post because of his novel, "The Dark." This gave him international fame and an opportunity to escape from servitude.' From there, the review takes on a decidedly prissy tone: 'We are to believe that the heroine is attractive, and are quite prepared to find her sophisticated: to me the use of excretory expletives would not be aphrodisiacal; that is a matter of taste.' Overall, the book is written off as a notable failure, with de Vere White's doubts about the quality of *Nightlines* confirmed in John's third novel: 'When Mr. McGahern is not consciously polishing his prose, he lets a good deal that is slipshod pass through the critical net.' Not content with having given the book just one kicking, de Vere White took the unusual step of returning a year later to pick over the bones:

> If this was the first novel by an Irish country boy about his experiences in a wicked city, it would be understandable; but Mr. McGahern is within a few years of the age at which Balzac died. I was disappointed, because I had hoped from 'The Dark' Mr. McGahern would advance.

While Heaney went public with his rejection of the *Irish Times* critique, another of John's countrymen preferred to do so in private, with Brian Friel, having just read the novel, writing him a supportive letter:

> It was very right for you to return to the territory you staked out & claimed in the earlier books; because it is your territory where your

> unique memory-imagination becomes quickest. And the deliberation of that return is important to all of us. The only review I saw was in the I. Times & any poor bastard who is apparently immune to the image & experience you offer is to be pitied. I think it's your best book & this note is a gauche congratulations & thank-you.

Though Friel and McGahern would not always see eye to eye over the coming years, John was moved to reply in gratitude: 'A writer can only hope for such a letter from another writer he respects once or twice in a lifetime.'

10

Geordieland
1974–76

> Manchester, Leeds, Newcastle-upon-Tyne, Glasgow – they were like cards spread out on a green table.
>
> JOHN McGAHERN, 'Eddie Mac'

From early autumn 1974 to late spring 1976, John spent some of the happiest and most productive months of his life in Newcastle upon Tyne. Many of the stories that came together to form his acclaimed second collection, *Getting Through*, were written or germinated in this singular northern city, and his experimental fourth novel, *The Pornographer*, started to take shape there. John loved the Geordie spirit, the city's many well-stocked markets, its characterful pubs, its fine restaurants and the North Sea air. 'It's very hard to describe', he writes to Niall Walsh. 'I've never seen anything quite like it. Almost exotic in a harsh way.' A later letter confirms these positive early first impressions of England's north-east:

> We were at the sea yesterday, a stark North Sea beach, but somehow very English and cosy, plump horses galloping, leisurely golf swings, dogs and flasks of tea. Some of the stone villages are incredibly calm and beautiful. Everywhere is the Norman influence. The land is very rich. Durham is said to be the finest Norman cathedral.

When, towards the end of his time there, John was commissioned by an Irish newspaper to write an essay on Newcastle's charms, he came as close to reverie as he ever would:

> The pale blue half-circle of the Tyne Bridge meets you coming into Newcastle. The blue star of the Scottish and Newcastle breweries

> shines above the bars in the evenings. The same half-circles of glass and riveted blue steel roof of the great covered market, where deer and hare, their heads in little plastic caps, hang beside cheap tennis rackets. There is the red and gold of the first Marks and Spencers bazaar among hundreds of stalls, and the blue Weigh House, where you can see the overcoated Tynesiders get tickets with their weight and porters in their bloodstained aprons weighing their trays of kidneys and of hearts.

This sojourn was a two-year fling, a perfect, anonymous love affair with a place that owed him nothing and where he could have as much or as little solitude as he pleased. John had been recommended for the Northern Arts Literary Fellowship, held primarily at Newcastle University, with certain responsibilities in nearby Durham University, by his predecessor in the post, the English novelist Paul Bailey. An admirer of John's work, Bailey put the Irishman's name forward without much expectation that he would say yes if offered the fellowship. Local writers Basil Bunting and Tony Harrison had previously held the position, and the fellowship board was keen to branch out.

Though Bailey left behind a greeting card of the Marx Brothers in the fellow's office, a picture that John would keep in his Leitrim study to the end of his days, the two men did not meet until years later, when Bailey interviewed John in Foxfield for a BBC Radio 4 *Kaleidoscope* programme to coincide with the publication of *Amongst Women*, travelling to Leitrim with his producer, where the arrangement was made for John to meet them in Luke Early's bar, in Mohill. In the hour that they waited they drank a round of Guinness, watched locals buy groceries and witnessed a funeral leave the premises, a coffin carried gingerly down the stairs.

If Bailey was the instigator, John's key patron while at Newcastle would prove to be Robert Woof, to whom he eventually dedicated *Getting Through*. Three years John's senior, Woof had begun teaching in the School of English in 1971 and became best known over the years for his work with the Wordsworth Trust around the poet's former home at

Dove Cottage, Grasmere, in the Lake District. Woof is almost certainly the source from whom John extracted a formula of words held dear by the unnamed narrator of *The Pornographer*. Josephine, the pornographer's by-now-unwanted lover, retains a desire for orthodox romance that pitches him into ever-deepening sloughs of despond:

> Troubled by my own confusions in meeting her at the idiotically beribboned almond tree, I started to take down books in the room, unconsciously searching for some general light, as I'd gone out for allies at the first news. It was an ungenerous attitude, but my position was hardly aristocratic. I eventually found a sentence which brought me to a sudden stop: 'Everybody must feel that a man who hates any person hates that person the more for troubling him with expressions of love; or, at least, it adds to hatred the sting of disgust.' I wrote it down, and kept it about my person like a scapular, as if the general expressions of the confused and covered feelings could licence and control them.

The quotation that soothes the pornographer's soul and which he chooses to carry on his person is drawn from Thomas de Quincey's *The Lake Poets*, an account of the author's friendships with the leading Romantic poets of the day, William Wordsworth, Samuel Taylor Coleridge and Robert Southey.

The Northern Arts Fellowship was meant, primarily, to give authors time and space to write. This position was as close to a sinecure as John would ever hold, far less onerous than the work he had undertaken, and would continue to undertake, at Colgate over the years. While doing so was not a requirement under the terms of the award, John chose to hold one-to-one creative-writing tutorials on the ground floor of the Percy Building in Newcastle's Quad, where he occupied a small office – 'like a monk's cell', as one former student recalls the space – with a chair for himself behind a desk facing the door and a couple of chairs for casual or committed callers. He undertook to be there for two-hour spells on two designated days every week. He took the job seriously and would, apart from talking with students, sometimes join academic seminars and tutorials at the invitation of lecturers.

John also occasionally held an adult-education evening class in the city. There he discovered only one writer he thought could be good: a short, feisty and possibly shell-shocked Second World War veteran named John Chandler. At the time, he was writing long romantic poems about dusky maidens in the South Seas, but John counselled him to cease that emphasis and instead write about his experiences in the war, which he did, publishing a memorable 'War Diary' in an ephemeral student magazine called *Soft Lob* in May 1978.

In early October 1974, shortly after John took up his duties, two young undergraduates, Richard Taylor and Anthony Allan, plucked up the courage to make an unannounced social call on the new fellow. 'It was', remarks Taylor, 'the start of a literary camaraderie that marked me profoundly.' Knocking on the office door, the pair were summoned in by a West of Ireland accent and explained that theirs was a 'Welcome to Geordieland' visit, with no other specific purpose or ulterior motive. John opened up, spoke about the essential loneliness of the writer's vocation and mentioned a letter he had received from Samuel Beckett one Parisian Christmas, offering hospitality and participation to an Irish exile in France. John wrote back, expressing gratitude for the thoughtful offer but politely declining. 'I never did meet the great man', he told them, 'but I have always been wary of meeting one's heroes; it can so easily lead to disappointment.'

Taylor and Allan were then in their second year. While sharing a floor in Henderson hall of residence as freshers, they had read *Endgame* aloud in Taylor's room, and Allan had found it hard to take the play seriously. Perhaps this experience prompted his tactless intervention: 'Such Dickensian conviviality on Beckett's part suggests that his dramatic voice is a strategic pose, a bankable vision he enjoys exploiting, in every sense of the word.' John's body tensed, recalls Taylor, and his eyes blazed with a cold anger: 'I happen to share that vision, but it doesn't mean you can't have good manners does it?!'

Taylor confessed that Beckett, apart from *Endgame* and *Waiting for Godot*, was yet to be explored. John recommended *Murphy* and the trilogy as fictions not to be imitated but impossible to surpass: 'Beckett has a quietly subversive sense of humour and his works are full of good jokes.' Taylor agreed and offered a favourite one: 'Let's hang ourselves – mmm it would give us an erection!' John jumped in eagerly to cap his quotation: 'Sexual intercourse is a mug's game and it's tiring into the bargain.'

Before the students left that day, John had a question: 'Does either of you write yourself?' Allan brushed off the query as too embarrassing to contemplate. 'I try to write', pleaded Taylor. 'None of us does more than that!' countered John. 'If I can be of any help with your work, you know where I am.' He held up a blank sheet of paper: 'We'll have to say goodbye for now. I've got to write a speech for my official inauguration, and you two likely boys don't need me to tell you what the authorities are like when it comes to getting your work in on time!'

This encounter was the beginning of a happy relationship that would see Taylor blossom first as a student and subsequently as a teacher of creative writing. In later years, after university, he and John corresponded for a while, Taylor never forgetting John's introductory remarks to the university's 1975–76 short-story competition: 'This has been a painful process for me. For the Writer there is only the one writer; that is one's self!'

And yet John, while that dictum was held sincerely, is remembered fondly from those days as being gregarious and sociable. He was a figure who could be seen at literary gatherings in Newcastle, particularly at Morden Tower, a thirteenth-century structure in the old city walls that had been a major centre for poetry readings in the north-east since 1964. John himself read there on at least one occasion, and during his time as fellow, he invited several Irish writers to appear. Seamus Heaney, Paul Muldoon and Michael Longley all travelled to Newcastle, while Derek Mahon wrote back to say he had given up public appearances for the time being.

The visit of his old friend Richard Murphy, who had played such a central role in landing John previous university positions in both Reading and Colgate, caused him considerable anxiety. Murphy had been married for a period to Patricia Avis, who had herself at one time been wife of the head of philosophy at Newcastle, Colin Strang. He had subsequently married Barbara Carr, then professor of English language and general linguistics. This rather complex Venn diagram left John in a tricky position. As he recounted to Niall Walsh:

> The Murphy saga grows even here. 'His wife with the emotional problems' was first married to the now Professor of Philosophy here, who is in turn married to the lady above. As the Newcastle version is that Mr M. filched the Prof's former wife there is a certain frost on all things Irish – Murphy's story is that she, hearing of his homosexual fame, set her cap at him and stormed his defences.

When, towards the end of the fellowship, Murphy did eventually read at John's invitation, he lived up to expectations: 'The Poet Murphy was here and surpassed even himself in a kind of shamelessness.'

At the heart of much that happened in Newcastle literary life in this period was the poet and editor of *Stand* magazine, Jon Silkin. One former student recalls his amusement at meeting John in Silkin's Jesmond home: 'he told me he had submitted one of his short stories to Silkin's magazine and Jon had offered him "a tenner" for it.' The low fee irked John, but his desire to support Newcastle's only established little magazine saw him publish 'A Slip-up' there in the summer of 1975.

Among friends and in private letters John took to calling the magazine's editor 'Shit' Silkin. When Silkin insisted that *Stand* would have to be acknowledged in *Getting Through*, where 'A Slip-up' appeared as the second story, John was furious. *Nightlines* had been published minus acknowledgements, and John's preference was that his books be set up with as few fussy appendages as possible. When Faber published *Getting Through* in 1978, and in all subsequent editions, Silkin's journal is misnamed *Strand*. This is not a misprint but a deliberate piece of roguery, a black joke and John's waspish way of getting his own back.

One can imagine a hapless copy-editor's assiduous and unavailing query, the intervention failing to move John to correction. *The Strand*, birthplace of Sherlock Holmes, was one of the most successful periodicals in British publishing history but had folded in 1950 after an almost sixty-year run. John had relented to Silkin but took his revenge in his own inimitable way, with *Strand* evoking a piece of limp, unattached string.

This minor piece of jousting aside, John's warm feelings for Newcastle were undisturbed. As with other beloved cities such as Dublin and London, John liked to explore the pubs: his favourite in Newcastle became the Bee Hive in the Bigg Market. He was fascinated by the underground public toilet across from the pub, which had a glass roof in the shape of a beehive. These features were the sorts of things he noticed and treasured as he walked around the city, charmed by the Victorian splendour of Central Station and the neighbouring Lit & Phil Library.

More than anything, he loved the city's markets, having a particular affection for the Grainger, taking in the smells and atmosphere of the stalls and the sounds of the traders. His favourite local writer was the proletarian essayist and novelist Jack Common, who had died in 1968, and he was sufficiently impressed by the posthumous reissue of the two novels *Kiddar's Luck* and *The Ampersand* to review them for the *TLS*. John commented favourably on the 'shrewd, hurtful, ironic, humorous, seedily elegant' prose, written in a register he found 'as slow and sure as the Tyne itself'. But as much as he could admire Common's style, he ultimately found his vision of life flawed:

> The writer, naturally egotistic, if he cannot choose silence and is forced to go on, must hold life in his vision and reflect it in the light of the idea, not in its own light. Deprived of this tension, much of *The Ampersand* dwindles to something all too like life.

Here is a common McGahern complaint: the writer mistaking life for art, failing to achieve sufficient distance for the aesthetic to flourish. One image of Newcastle life that John himself wanted to get into a story was of an old couple shambling round Grainger Market together, the man holding the shopping bag as his wife dragged him about the place. Though he ultimately chose to set 'A Slip-up', his story that fictionalises this couple, in London's East End, it was born in the markets of Newcastle.

Another *Getting Through* story directly inspired by Newcastle's streets is 'Doorways', John's most openly Beckettian piece of fiction. A characteristic attempt to understand love's failure, the story sees its narrator develop a fascination for a pair of tramps, whom he names – with a nod towards Herman Melville – Barnaby and Bartleby. The pair habitually move in and out of the title's doorways on Dublin's Abbey Street, where the fastidious pointlessness of their lives fascinates the unnamed narrator: 'I have never seen them leave. They seem to be there one moment and gone the next. I have never watched them go.' As so often in John's work, the particularities of this strange scene quickly expand into a reflection on life more generally: 'Often I want to ask them why have they picked on this way to get through life, but outside the certainty of not being answered I soon see it as an idle question and turn away.'

An earlier draft of the story, when it carries the title 'Getting Through', locates the men not in Abbey Street but in Newcastle's Haymarket. By story's end, the narrator's own failed attempts to give his life some greater meaning via a love affair with an attractive American, Kate O'Mara, seem just as pointless and absurd as the tramps' quotidian shambling: 'everything seemed to be without shape. I understood nothing. Perhaps we had come to expect too much. Neither Barnaby nor Bartleby would tell. They didn't know. They just lived it.'

The men who prompted John to write the story mounted their daily sentinel close to the university, in doorways located between Lloyd's Bank, a high, nineteenth-century, red-brick building, and the Haymarket pub, a favourite watering hole with students and faculty alike (and one now, sadly, no more). Between the pub and the bank was a newsagent's where Madeline was once deputed to buy top-shelf magazines as raw material for the composition of what was beginning to take shape as *The Pornographer.* Also here, along Percy Street, was a disused building that is now the Crows Nest pub and restaurant: John was fascinated by the two tramps who stood bolt upright in adjoining doorways there, staring ahead all day and then disappearing after dark. When leaning on this strange image to write the story, he altered the scene by transporting the men to Dublin and changed the geography slightly. (The weighing machine described in 'Doorways' was down the road in Grainger Market.)

John had first been alerted to this odd couple in all their lonesome rigidity by a young Australian member of the faculty with whom he had become friendly because they joined the university at the same time in September 1974. Bob White had come straight from Oxford, where he completed his doctorate on Elizabethan literature at Balliol College. This area was one in which Newcastle's School of English had particular strengths. Its then head was Professor Ernst Honigmann, a leading Shakespearian scholar, someone who had arrived in England as a child in flight from Nazi Germany forty years before. As newcomers to the department, John and White naturally fell in with each other in exploring their new environment. They had much in common: White was a keen cricketer, having captained Balliol's first XI, and so the pair had an immediate shared interest beyond the literary. White recalls John being especially proud that Samuel Beckett's name made an appearance in *Wisden*, the esteemed cricket almanac.

Having been alerted by White to the strange rituals enacted by the Haymarket tramps, John became equally intrigued and would compare himself and his Aussie friend to Bartleby and Barnaby, as he quickly dubbed the vagrants. White's Shakespearian expertise came into play in providing John with an arresting phrase on the story's first page: 'nature, having started to lose interest in me'. White had, in turn, found this formulation in Michael Goldman's 1972 study, *Shakespeare and the Energies of Drama*.

John was never quite satisfied with 'Doorways'. For him, Barnaby and Bartleby, although the presiding spirits, obstinately refused to integrate or to engage with the rest of the story. For this reason, 'Doorways' failed to make the cut in *Creatures of the Earth*, John's valedictory judgement in 2005 on his short fiction. The magpie theft of White's Shakespearian jewel is entirely typical: whether it was some angle of light or an attractive formula of words, if John found a phrase from which he could draw sustenance, he was happy to introduce this element, usually unremarked, into his own work, as he would with the quotation from de Quincey in *The Pornographer*.

Another nice example of this facet at work in 'Doorways' comes via Proust's *On Reading*. In March 1976, White and John offered two informal seminars to students and staff: John 'On Reading' and White 'On Criticism'. The Proust essay was one with which John spent considerable time in the mid-1970s, his well-thumbed copy being a Souvenir Press 1971 volume published alone as a slim but rather beautiful book with parallel French and English pages. As had been the case more than a decade earlier with Rilke's *The Notebooks of Malte Laurids Brigge* and *Letters to a Young Poet*, John was generous when he particularly valued a book. He liked to gift a copy to friends. Bob White soon became the owner of *On Reading* as well as of Paolo Vivante's *The Homeric Imagination* and E. R. Dodds' *The Greeks and the Irrational*.

One particularly lyrical passage in 'Doorways' comes towards the end of the story, after Kate O'Mara puts the narrator to the test by asking him not to take the bus into Sligo from Strandhill to meet his friends but rather to spend the evening with her. The narrator decides that this request is too much ground to concede but is filled with regret as the bus climbs slowly out of the seaside village:

> I stirred uneasily, feeling that I had left some hurt behind. Yet what she had demanded had been unreasonable, but far more insistently than reason, or the grinding of the bus, came, 'If you had loved her you would have stayed'; but all of life turns away from its own eventual hopelessness, leaving insomnia and night to lovers and the dying.

That last elegant phrase is lifted almost directly from Proust, who remarks at the end of one of his long, rapturous passages about rooms and their splendour:

one has then the feeling of shutting in with oneself this secret life, when one goes, all trembling, to bolt the door; of pushing it in front of one into the bed and finally lying down with it under the large white sheets which come up over one's face, while close by the church rings for the whole town the hours of insomnia of the dying and of lovers.

The Irishman and the Australian walked endlessly together around the city, chiefly in the middle of the day, always talking. Other pubs that became Newcastle favourites, besides the Bee Hive, included the Trent House, immediately behind Morden Tower, and so a natural venue where everybody gathered before and after readings. This choice was a nondescript corner boozer but light and airy with attractive windows, and had an upstairs room if downstairs was crowded. The Hotspur on Percy Street was large and traditional, and never crowded except when Newcastle United played at home, when this spot was a preferred venue for the Toon Army both before and after the match.

The Side's magnificent Crown Posada on the way down to the Tyne was another haunt. Built over three storeys, and bearing two impressive Pre-Raphaelite-style stained-glass windows, one depicting a lady serving a drink and the other a Tudor gent about to imbibe it, the pub, with its darkened wood surrounds and many nooks and crannies, was precisely the sort of premises preferred by John. If the space was free, his favoured perch was in the snug immediately to the left on entry, a room, recalls White, that was 'very beautiful and atmospheric and quiet enough for talking'.

Besides pub life, John and Madeline enjoyed visiting the city's theatres and Miller's, its marvellous auction house. The Black Gate, with its simple black and white elegance, became their favourite restaurant. John and Madeline enjoyed jugged hare (a house speciality), tasty tripe and the plentiful supply of fresh fish from South Shields. Its pease pudding and saveloy butty was a special lunchtime delicacy. Though modest in its exterior and interior decor, this eatery had more pretensions to fine dining, with crisp white tablecloths and equally crisp (elderly male) waiters wearing black aprons and white shirts.

The McGaherns also liked to entertain at home in their generously proportioned Marris House flat, set over one floor of the university chancellor's grand former residence. John's New Zealand Film Studies colleague Bruce Babington recalls one dinner party with rare lamb, fine wine and much conviviality, amidst which, handing out plates, John gave the advice to the company to enjoy themselves since they could all be dead of cancer in a year.

Marris House was a pleasant walk across campus both for John and for Madeline, who quickly found work as a secretary in the School of Economics, undertaking untaxing tasks that she thoroughly enjoyed, mixing happily with a wider team of Geordie administrators. One fond memory is of attendance at the wedding of one of these canasta-playing colleagues, with John and a visiting Seamus Heaney. The ensuing boozy weekend saw John apologising for flawed hosting: 'I'm sorry not to have seen you off – Excess suddenly caught up with me on the railway platform.' Heaney reassures by return of post that the fault, if he 'left shaken by excess', was his own and thanks John for 'a delightful intense couple of days'.

John discovered in Stowell Street, Chinatown an eccentric vintner who sold good wholesale French wine. White and John would take their bottles along, and the proprietor, who lived upstairs, filled them from barrels for fifty pence a vessel. Every now and then the vintner's amiable mother would toddle down a ladder, and they would all try a glass of his latest wine together, sitting on empty barrels and chatting.

Of all Newcastle's hospitality venues, the one that made the greatest impression on John and Madeline was Balmbra's, a pub by day and a music hall by night that they visited repeatedly, enthralled by its elderly performers, its tap dancers, clowns and acrobats. Situated near the bottom of the Cloth Market, the venue is now defunct, but the place is immortalised in Tyneside's anthemic 'The Blaydon Races':

Aa went to Blaydon Races, 'twas on the ninth of Joon,
Eiteen hundred an' sixty-two, on a summer's efternoon;
Aa tyuk the 'bus frae Balmbra's, an' she wis heavy laden,
Away we went 'lang Collin'wood Street, that's on the road to Blaydon.

Speaking in letters to friends of Newcastle's 'exotic' nature, John has places such as Balmbra's foremost in his mind. He writes in a 1976 *Sunday World* piece:

> By way of Nun Street you enter the Cloth Market, fruit and vegetable stalls pitched on the cobbles, Indians selling coloured bales, a china stall that sells factory seconds cheaply, some little flaw in the glaze or print; and at the very bottom of the street you come to the last music hall in England: Balmbras.

This piece likewise strives to capture the charms of English music-hall life just at the point that this attraction fades from existence. Balmbra's, John comments, 'must be one of the most beautiful rooms in Newcastle'. Then he elaborates in terms that again recall reverie: 'It is like the inside of an enormous gilded barrel, the same half-circle of the bridges and market. Ironware of oriental design in shapes of six by four break the regular curve of the ceiling into arches, the empty spaces in the ironwork glowing a velvet-blue above the lamps.'

The place became even more intriguing to John when he learnt that the master of ceremonies was a fellow Irishman, Pat Healy from Monasterevin, and his article turns into a series of reminiscences, a particular slice of disappearing emigrant life. Having grown up poor, one of fourteen children, Pat took the boat and got his first break in the Pride of Eireann Dancehall in London's Tottenham Court Road. He went on, he tells John in the article, to play every music hall in Britain:

> I was 'Boots' Healy in the City Variety of Leeds, Canada's Singing Cowboy. There was this old horse we had there that we used to have to walk around the streets before we went on, but once didn't he open

> up on the stage. 'You see what the horse thinks of the act,' someone shouted. I played in so many halls.

In Pat's litany of locations, one hears echoes of the concluding paragraphs to 'Eddie Mac' and the title character's dreams of British escape in the wake of stealing and selling his employer's cattle and doing a bunk with the ill-gotten gains:

> Manchester, Leeds, Newcastle-upon-Tyne, Glasgow – they were like cards spread out on a green table. His only regret was that he hadn't hit out for one of them years before. He would miss nothing. If he missed anything, it would probably be the tongued boards of the ceiling he had never managed to count. In those cities a man could stay lost forever and victory could still be found.

For Pat Healy, too, the far-flung corners of the island held the possibility of adventure: 'The Empire in Woolwich; The Queens in Dundee; Collins Theatre in Islington; The Hippodrome in Aberdeen; The Shakespeare in Liverpool; The Empire in Newcastle.' This lively, unorthodox Irishman brought John back into that wistful migrant world of which, in England's north-east, he was once again part and to which he would return in both fiction and journalism over the years to come.

The world of the cattle boat to Birkenhead was the one in which John had grown to manhood. They were tough, uncompromising times, as he remembers towards the end of his life, when Ireland has become a much more prosperous, if coarser, place:

> Between 1951 and 1961 well over four hundred thousand people emigrated, far more than in any other decade in the entire century, nearly all of them to Britain. They were young, poorly educated for the most part, ill prepared. Names like Holyhead, Chester, Crewe were burned into the national consciousness; but this was a silent generation, and it disappeared in silence.

Many of the emigrants who had taken the boat in those years come back to populate John's fiction in all their vivid loneliness, from the elderly couple of 'A Slip-up' to Johnny Murphy of *That They May Face the Rising Sun*, making his annual summer pilgrimage from the factories of Dagenham to the lakeshore where he was born.

For John, as an Irish migrant in England of the 1970s, there were new complications: the Troubles exploding on the streets of Derry and Belfast in 1969; the coming of British troops to those streets; the bombing of English cities by the IRA. Early in their Newcastle sojourn, John and Madeline experienced the fallout from the Birmingham pub bombings of November 1974. By the mid-1970s, anti-Irish sentiment had reached new levels, and miscarriages of justice had become all too common.

In Durham, where John regularly taught and read from his work, sisters Ann and Eileen Gillespie from Bunbeg, County Donegal were serving time in the maximum-security prison, convicted in connection with an explosion at a house in Manchester in 1974. Presenting a packaged gift to Madeline in the vicinity of the prison one day, John was questioned by a policeman as to its contents and whether it might present a danger. 'Some would say so', he answered. Within the wrapping, when opened, the constable discovered a copy of David Sylvester's interviews with Francis Bacon, a book still in Madeline's possession today.

A more uncomfortable brush with fractious Anglo-Irish relations came for John in Durham at a reading of some stories that were beginning to come together as the book that would eventually be published in 1978 as *Getting Through* – still under the working title, at that point, of 'Doorways'. He had, as always, taken the short train journey from Newcastle and was accompanied by Bob White and an undergraduate student with writerly ambitions named Sam Milne.

'When you were with John', remembers Milne, 'you felt you had his full attention, that he had your best interests at heart, even though he could be harsh in his criticisms.' Unsparingly honest critiques were something to which everyone who ever shared work with John had to get used. But Milne was a strong enough character and believed sufficiently in John's good intentions to survive such feedback:

> Personally he taught me to throw away everything that sounded a wrong chord, and listening to his advice, I waited four years before I sent off my first poem for publication. It was immediately accepted by the *New Statesman*. Needless to say, I was thrilled. If I had sent in work earlier I am sure I would have been greatly discouraged by rejection. Another recollection is that I cannot ever remember him recommending any reading outside the curriculum I was studying. He was a typical teacher in that he didn't want the students to be led astray. I now feel that was very responsible of him, as he clearly felt a writer should be disciplined and well educated, that there was more to life than 'creative writing.'

I was lucky enough to track down Milne after a letter of his appeared in the *TLS* of January 2022, which he was prompted to write by a review of *The Letters of John McGahern* that commented on its subject's 'harsh teaching style'. The review brought back to Milne an amusing encounter:

> As an undergraduate at Newcastle University in 1974, I showed him a play I had written (he was the Northern Arts Literary Fellow at the time). He told me politely that 'it was the worst play I have ever read', and that I'd be better off considering a career in business management. We then retired to The Haymarket pub for a pint. There he asked me what I was reading, and I told him *The Brothers Karamazov*. This did not impress him one bit. 'Far too hysterical for me,' he said. I didn't feel too bad about my play at that point. Later, I accompanied him to Durham University, where he was reading some of his short stories. I then went out and bought *The Dark*, *The Barracks* and *Nightlines*, and became one of his fans. His bark was definitely worse than his bite.

In subsequent correspondence with Milne, he shared further, moving remembrances with me about that Durham event:

> At one point in the reading I noticed John becoming very uncomfortable and somewhat red in the face. Clearly something was wrong, and when he finished the story he said he had to leave, very abruptly. We were all surprised, of course, but as I was travelling with him I asked him on the train if he was alright. 'I'm fine,' he said, 'but I apologise I had to leave early. A student sitting behind me,' he continued, 'whispered "Fuck off you Irish cunt" in my ear. I didn't want to make a scene. Better just to leave.' I was dumbfounded, and utterly shocked. 'Why didn't you do something?' I asked. 'I didn't want to hurt him,' he said. The anger was visible in his voice and eyes, and he shook. It was then I realised what being Irish meant, being Irish and living in England. Prejudice all around, even among the so-called educated classes, and the patience, humanity and resilience needed to counter it.

Bob White was also conscious during the reading that something was amiss, that his Irish friend seemed more than usually nervous. As they left to go home to Newcastle, he noticed that John had drawn blood from his palms, so tightly had he bunched his fists.

'There was more to him than just the work', writes Milne, 'there was a grand and kind personality that shone through everything he did.' Having become acquainted with McGahern, Milne decided to make a Christmas gift of *The Dark* to his mother:

> After a week or so she said, 'I loved that book' (this from a woman who only read Agatha Christie!), 'it reminded me of life, full of joy and sadness, the light and the dark.' Like any pretentious literary youth I was amazed. The seeming simplicity of her comment summed up my own feelings (although mine were now all tied up with supernumerary critical tags). I saw that although he worked in the academy, he was not of it. He wrote for everyone, and there lay his greatness. His spirit was of the people, not the scholars.

For all that grace and generosity, however, John could also be fierce, as Milne recounts in his favourite undergraduate anecdote:

John read one of his stories to an audience at the university and at the end asked if anyone had any questions. Ernst Honigmann said he didn't have a question but he did have a comment. John said, 'And what would that comment be?' Ernst replied, 'I find the story broken-backed.' John said, 'I'll break your fucking back,' and the whole room went quiet.

Despite the impact that the Troubles were having on John's life and the life of his country, one would be hard put to guess from his work that any such violence had ever occurred around him. The Enniskillen Remembrance Day bomb of 1987, mentioned in passing in *That They May Face the Rising Sun*, is one of the few distinct markers of the conflict to be found across his books. In that period, when he was being baited by an anti-Irish student at a reading of his work or hassled by police in front of HMP Durham, he was composing the stories of *Getting Through* and working away on *The Pornographer*, with not a whiff of cordite in either book.

The issue of the *Sunday World* for 25 April 1976 that carried the essay on Balmbra's stands as an interesting historical document in any effort to come to a sense of how the Troubles were impacting the popular mind. The front page, as well as promising 'A famous author writes about the old-time music hall' under a picture of John, points to a three-page spread by Eamonn McCann on the dramatic story of Derry IRA volunteer Marion Coyle:

> There was nothing furtive about the IRA in Derry at that time and nothing murky about the territory in which it moved. 'Free Derry' was a living reality, a barricaded patch of triumph for the resurgent forces of republicanism. To the young and urgent, membership of that force was a status to aspire to.
>
> 'It felt like the greatest thing that ever happened,' recalls a girl who joined at the same time as Marion. 'We were actually in the IRA! It was days before we could believe it.'

Elsewhere, in between Popeye comic strips and full-page advertisements for Ford Capris and Afton Mild cigarettes, the paper is peppered with a scarifying array of news stories about a country descending into bloody civil war. Page 2 alone carries stories about three British soldiers remanded in military custody for raping a girl in Holywood, County Down; the shooting of three men in a bar in Dunloy, County Antrim; and the jailing of two men in New York for their involvement in a shipment of twelve semi-automatic rifles to Ireland.

These were difficult, violent times that could not but have had their effect on John's imagination. If there is no sign of political soul-searching or commitment in stories from the period such as 'The Wine Breath' or 'Swallows', one does see, more obliquely, the effect of the Troubles on John in later work. Specifically, one might read *Amongst Women*, in its thinking about a guerrilla-war veteran and the disappointment of post-revolutionary Ireland, as reflecting light on more contemporary conflict.

By Christmas 1975, John was in serious conversation with Charles Monteith about collecting the stories with which he had been making such progress in Newcastle into a book. The *New Review* had taken 'The Beginning of an Idea' and 'Faith, Hope and Charity'; 'Swallows' had been published by Alan Ross in the *London Magazine*; 'The Stoat' in *Vogue*, thanks to John's friendship with Derek Mahon, who was then working at the magazine; 'All Sorts of Impossible Things' in *Encounter*; and 'A Slip-up' in Jon Silkin's *Stand*. John writes to Monteith on 6 December to say that he has just completed another story, 'Along the Edges', and is working on a further three pieces (presumably 'Doorways', 'The Wine Breath' and the story with which he eventually chooses to close the collection, 'Sierra Leone'). These last two items are the strongest stories in *Getting Through*, a fact reflected by John's success in having them both placed in the *New Yorker* in 1977, a triumph that would lead indirectly in the same year to a memorable Harvard reading.

Having finished the tenure of his Northern Arts Fellowship in May 1976, John packed up in Newcastle and was accompanied back to Foxfield by his English department Victorianist colleague Kelsey Thornton and his wife, Val, who stayed for a few days in Leitrim. Madeline remained behind in Newcastle with the Woof family to complete university entrance exams, before joining John the following month. The exams were duly passed, Madeline proving something to herself that she had been forced to leave behind many years previously by her controlling father.

Writing to Madeline on 8 June, John is happy and relaxed about his homecoming but seized with a kind of sadness as what he knows is a new book comes to its natural conclusion: 'After Val and Kelsey left I just worked at getting seeds down. Niall came late on Thursday – he found me in the back garden as the light was beginning to fail – and we had two drinks in Mohill, and afterwards sat by the fire for an hour or more.' He continues into the latest news about his uncle, Pat McManus, and a neighbouring farmer, Jerome Donnelly:

> I went into see Pat that evening, he hadn't heard I was home, and he left me out to the house. He was a delight, and abrim with prejudice. He is coming out with the man 'about the wood' this Thursday: 'we can throw him the odd lock of petrol.' Jerome comes daily.

But truest news concerns the burgeoning short-story collection: 'Even to me the book of stories are finished, once I counterpoint Along the Edges with the story of the day. So another private act is becoming public, another nail visible in the wood.'

A fortnight later, John and Madeline were reunited. As the couple began their new life together in Foxfield, the weather was settling down into what was to become the warmest and sunniest summer anyone could recall. Leitrim beat Mayo in the Connacht Championship, and all was well with the world. Bob White, John's Aussie pal, visited for a few days, writing home to his parents about this little slice of heaven:

> It must be the quietest place in the world and it's perfect for restoring city-jangled nerves. I spent today just walking, lying in the sun,

> reading and then a spot of log-chopping. A week ago I wouldn't have thought I'd be here so it's a bit dream-like. The Irish are a strange race . . . You ask them a direct simple question, and they seem deliberately to misunderstand it in a perverse way, and you never get a straight answer. But if I approach them indirectly in a gradual slow way they are helpful, friendly and fun.

Today, twenty years after John's death, White sums up what the friendship meant to him: 'I think what I value most about John's presence in my life was his clear-eyed and curt debunking of anything false or pretentious in both people and books – a lesson once learned never forgotten, and somehow he never let me get away with anything time-wasting.'

At last, the couple had a home. The day was one for which they had been longing: 'Madeline, as well as I, is tired of climbing other people's stairs', John wrote to a friend. 'It's eleven years of having no place now. We'll not move until we go to Colgate the following January. I find as I get older I can only afford violence or excitement like holidays. Otherwise there's no energy of calm left for the work, only surfaces.'

11
Getting Through
1976–78

But McGahern lures us in, and we think.

NUALA O'FAOLAIN

Charles Monteith called with the McGaherns in Foxfield on 30 September 1976, taking away with him the completed typescript of *Getting Through*. This occasion would be the first of many such visits over the years, with Monteith enjoying the conviviality, excellent food and long solitary walks around the lake, slowed, inevitably, by his wartime limp. He was a tall, imposing, elegantly dressed man of impeccable manners, a man who liked to dine always with a large linen napkin and silver service, liked very much by both John and Madeline and given the best part of nine pages – the single most sustained cameo – in *That They May Face the Rising Sun* as the Ruttledges' annual London visitor:

> Robert Booth came from humble origins in the North of Ireland, a small draper's brilliant son. Scholarships took him all the way to Oxford, where his studies were interrupted by the war. After the war he returned to take a double-first in history and classics and then entered the law to discover that it wasn't acceptable to practise at the Bar with a thick regional accent; so he took himself to acting school where he acquired the accent that would serve him for the rest of his life, its only flaw being that it outdistanced what it sought to emulate.

This account is an almost precise description of Monteith, even down to the veiling of the Ulster accent. He spoke, as another one of his Irish authors told me, 'like an English bishop'. John always affectionately broke his first name into two – Char-les – and was steadfastly loyal to him despite occasional differences, usually around money. On one occasion, while dining at L'Étoile on Charlotte Street to celebrate the publication of a new book, John suggested that he would have preferred a bigger advance over an expensive luncheon. To which comment Monteith replied, 'That's not the point!' When Monteith retired as chairman of the firm in 1980, his exit began a period of doubt and restlessness in John's mind as to his own publishing future.

Coincident with Monteith's visit was a turn in John's American publishing fortunes. Days before, he had received a letter from the *New Yorker* that would prove to be the beginning of a happy professional relationship. By the time Frances Kiernan wrote this letter, canvassing for new stories, John had all but given up on the magazine, writing to Kiernan:

> I'd be glad to publish at The New Yorker and some time ago sent Sierra Leone, a story, to Miss Kierstead there. I've had no decision on it yet. It is the last story, and maybe the most perfect, in the collection; and I'm afraid if it goes down I can have very little hope of luck with The New Yorker.

John had had bad experiences in the past: despite early success in having 'Summer at Strandhill' (later 'Strandhill, the Sea') accepted for publication, he complained to Monteith that the story was 'much spoiled by editors'. In subsequent years, the magazine had rejected several stories, among them 'Christmas' (*c.*1962), 'Bomb Box' (1969) and 'The Beginning of an Idea' (1974).

Between 1977 and 1984, the *New Yorker* accepted six of his stories for publication in what would prove to be his most successful run with any periodical, both in terms of writing quality and in terms of remuneration. For the first of the stories to be published, 'The Wine Breath' in April 1977, John was paid $2,700, more than half of what he had paid for his Foxfield house and land. One can assume that he was paid at least as much for each of those stories that followed: 'Gold Watch' (March 1980), 'High Ground' (March 1982), 'Crossing the Line' (August 1983) and

'Eddie Mac' (November 1984). Not everything turned to gold: among the stories to be rejected during Kiernan's tenure were 'The Conversion of William Kirkwood', 'Bank Holiday' and 'Oldfashioned'.

As John began the spring 1977 semester in Colgate, then, the knowledge that he was about to become a good deal more public in the USA made knuckling down to the teaching duties that so often adversely affected his writing somewhat easier. 'I've had one easy month', he tells Niall Walsh on 18 February, 'and I got real work done on the novel – it's the first time I've worked here – but now the grind has started.' For most students, John was just another professor, a hurdle to be jumped, a term paper to be written. As he tells Walsh of such students, 'Self expression is OUT. Explanatory writing is in. All are worried about grades, about law and medical schools. And heaven has provided the usual quota of clowns.'

For some, he made a life-changing impression. One such figure was Shep Ranbom, whose freshman year at Colgate coincided with John's 1977 sojourn. 'From the moment I read his first book of stories, *Nightlines*, in the field behind my dorm', remembers Ranbom, 'I wanted to learn what I could from him, and understand his way of looking at the world, how the artist turns the poor and sordid facts of life into something more precious.' John's learning and nimbleness of mind made both an immediate and a lasting impression:

> He particularly loved expressions that crossed the boundaries of what they were trying to say: 'True tragedy ends in triumph and is a great kick at suffering' (DH Lawrence). 'Who would have too much technique would be a monster; who do without, would be a fool' (Baudelaire). He also didn't care if the authors he taught didn't fit the course title. I once asked him how he could teach Willa Cather's My Ántonia in a course on 'The Contemporary Novel'. 'There's nothing more contemporary than good writing,' he told me.

John oversaw Ranbom's independent study, which he named 'Studies in Memory and Imagination'. That young man never forgot this experience:

'I knew John to be kind, sly, solicitous, learned, and – when he felt like it – wickedly funny, with the emphasis on wicked. Most of all he was high-minded and private.'

While there were still some similarities with his original curriculum of spring 1969, there had clearly been a good deal of expansion. Another Colgate student, Rob White, who took John's 1977 Irish literature class as part of his final year, remembers the reading list and the teacherly emphases:

> what I recall from the syllabus were poetry and plays – the grand, unavoidable exception being Joyce's 'The Dead' (which a group of us in Williamstown read aloud each December). Plays included Shaw's *Man and Superman*, O'Casey's *Juno and the Paycock* and *The Plough and the Stars*, and one by Synge that I'm pretty sure wasn't *Playboy of the Western World*, though I can't figure out which non-*Playboy* play it might have been. And Beckett, of course: both *Waiting* and *Endgame* . . . really the only poet I remember is Patrick Kavanagh, whose 'Shancoduff' John read aloud to us on the very first day of class.

Given that the very reason John was standing before that classroom was to pay the bills and keep his writing life afloat, White found the final lines particularly poignant:

> The sleety winds fondle the rushy beards of Shancoduff
> While the cattle-drovers sheltering in the Featherna Bush
> Look up and say: 'Who owns them hungry hills
> That the water-hen and snipe must have forsaken?
> A poet? Then by heavens he must be poor.'
> I hear and is my heart not badly shaken?

The performative aspect, from the start, proved crucial: 'I can clearly hear John pronouncing the penultimate line "A poet?" – making that designation sound like the saddest thing you'd ever heard of.' White elaborates:

> Like most writers he was less interested in critical analysis than in making sure his students appreciated what various authors, particularly those who came not long before John himself, had accomplished in terms of illuminated small snippets of the human condition. He talked a lot about rhythm and vision as essential components of 'lasting' literature, and he made sure we understood what that meant by reading long passages aloud.

White concludes by emphasising their teacher's keen sense of context:

> John's gift for dramatic sharing was on spectacular display when my classmate Coleman deKay and I performed the first act of *Waiting for Godot* in lieu of a final exam. We'd put a fair amount of work into it and had big plans to present a presumptuous analysis after taking our bow, but John preempted the analytical part by gently shooing us off 'the stage' in front of the classroom and acting out the rest of the play himself.

George Rockwood was another of Shep Ranbom's classmates. Someone who went on to be a Navy pilot, he has a pithier recollection of his Irish professor: 'The only instruction I remember from John was, "Jarge, yer writen da same ting agin wit difernt werds." One thing I got out of McGahern was the certainty that although I can usually identify really good writing, I cannot usually produce it.'

For Ranbom, the memories are more solemn, forming a crucial part of his coming to consciousness as a young man:

> He had a kind of nobility in the class. All he wanted to do was share what he could tell, and not everyone was interested in knowing everything, but I hung on every word. I had a window into how he saw the world through books, how he pushed himself to use what he knew.

John's influence became a lasting one:

> I can't read a book the same because of what he showed me about how to think about writing. I read slowly and I read the same books I love

> over and over. But knowing that I am carrying forth his views and have had that rare gift of being his student who took in his knowledge has always been something of a burden to me.

Courtesy and modesty ran together. As Shep summarises:

> He would never point to his own work, except one or two lines that he'd written that he was enamoured with that day. He was in the midst of writing *The Pornographer* and I remember him mentioning in class one day an image that he liked of his own: the line about 'the rude good health of crows.' It was so rare that he would do this, I remember it distinctly.

W. B. Yeats, unsurprisingly, continued to be perhaps John's most important touchstone, as, increasingly, did J. B. Yeats's letters to his son, an edition of which John would edit for Faber twenty years later. The letter that made the greatest impact on Ranbom from those upon which John dwelt sees father writing to son about dreamland. This epistle summarised John's view of reality and fiction, creating a world that was vaster and more sumptuous than any human habitation, that was built 'all out of our spiritual pain – for if the bricks be not mortised by actual suffering, they will not hold together'.

Ranbom remembers being stunned, when John taught Yeats's *Autobiographies*, by how the language used at the conclusion of 'Reveries over Childhood and Youth' – 'all life weighed in the scales of my own life seems to me a preparation for something that never happens' – was so close to the end of 'Wheels': 'all the vivid sections of the wheel we watched so slowly turn, impatient for the rich whole that never came but that all the preparations promised'. Underlined in Ranbom's old Colgate copy of *Autobiographies* is what he thinks of as the key to an understanding of John's writing life:

> As life goes on we discover that certain thoughts sustain us in defeat, or give us victory, whether over ourselves or others, and it is these thoughts, tested by passions, that we call convictions. Among

> subjective men (in all those that must spin a web out of their own bowels) the victory is an intellectual daily re-creation of all that exterior fate snatches away, and so that fate's antithesis; while what I have called 'the Mask' is an emotional antithesis to all that comes out of their internal nature. We begin to live as we discover life as tragedy.

* * *

'The Wine Breath', John's story of involuntary memory in the day of an Irish country priest, reminiscent of Proust in theme and drawing its title from Yeats's 'All Souls' Night', appeared in the *New Yorker* on 27 March. John was determined to make the best of this increased American visibility, entering into correspondence with DeWitt Henry, editor of *Ploughshares*. He offered the magazine 'A Slip-up', which they published in their spring number (a third publication for this story, it having appeared in *Stand* in England and in *Man Alive*, a short-lived soft-porn magazine, in Ireland).

Though paying nothing remotely like *New Yorker* sums, the *Ploughshares* connection proved profitable, quickly leading to the highest-profile reading of John's life. Initially founded and run from the basement of a Cambridge public house, the Plough & Stars on Massachusetts Avenue, *Ploughshares* was keen to champion orthodox realist stories by writers such as Andre Dubus and Raymond Carver, and John's work was an immediately attractive find. By a lucky break of circumstance, Peter O'Malley, the Irish founder of the magazine and proprietor of the Plough & Stars, had been helping to arrange a *Ploughshares* fundraising benefit in Harvard, where Robert Lowell had agreed to read alongside John Montague. The idea was to have a Town and Gown-style event, with Montague representing the city's large Irish cohort and Lowell standing as the ultimate Boston Brahmin. When Montague had to withdraw late, John was approached as a possible substitute. Since John liked Boston as a city and lived four and a half hours west, saying yes was easy, though his anxiety, as the Saturday 30 April date approached, began to build.

Arriving in Boston on Thursday, John stayed with his old Colgate friend John Head, who had visited John and Madeline in Newcastle and had changed employer to Boston University, trying and failing to get John employment there too. On Friday, John went for an oyster lunch with the *Ploughshares* people. Rather than calming him down, the meal, as he told Madeline, who did not attend, 'brought this horrible excitement'. As John further explains to her:

> Their energy is O'Malley, 32, ex Clongowes, a lawyer, who owns bars and hotels in Boston, tall and enormously handsome, who'll either wind up in jail or rich and powerful. He is married to Richard Wilbur's daughter, who was lovely in every way.
>
> He outlooked, outdrank, outtalked, outcharmed Head, which was a terrible trauma for Head, who was drunk all the time.

On the Saturday morning of the reading, John went shopping to Filene's Basement with Head's wife, Alberta, where he bought shirts and underwear for the prize fight with Lowell that night. After doing another timed check on his material (thirty-six minutes), he went for a walk and took Alberta to Jake Worth's for a beer. This occasion was, he recounts to Madeline, 'one of the worst days' of his life:

> Suddenly there was 6 hours to go to the reading, and then 5, and 4, and 3½, and 3, and next 2.
>
> I was put in a back room, crowds milling round in the hall, with a dirty glass jug, and one dirty glass. I washed them and got talking to the janitor and started to drink water. There was an enormous hall one side of the room, an examination hall and where people sometimes now give blood, dusty too, with at least a hundred marble heads of dead worthies along the walls. You could play football in it, it was so large.
>
> Lowell was late. I read first, having to walk across a whole bloody long stage. I think I won the audience over, after beginning nervously, an old story.

Lowell began strangely, saying there should be no competition between the speakers, which immediately introduced precisely that. Somehow he bungled it all, which didn't displease me.

Neill Joy, who had travelled from Colgate with John, sat with him in the green room and remembers his friend 'never before or since' displaying himself 'in such a high pitched nervous and agitated state'. Most of those who turned up on the night had come to hear what would prove to be Lowell's last public reading, the poet dying suddenly in a New York taxi cab the following September, aged just sixty.

But there were audience members there to hear John too. One was the Irish-American writer Anthony Glavin, for whom the night took on a magical quality:

I have the treasured memory of the 42-year-old, Leitrim-based McGahern, standing like an abashed schoolboy on the stage in Memorial Hall, still holding his story at his side, and listening as the rapturous applause swells to nothing short of acclimation [*sic*] in the very chamber where Matthew Arnold, Teddy Roosevelt, Winston Churchill and Martin Luther King Jr had also spoken from the very same podium.

John read from the closing paragraphs of 'Wheels' and the end of *The Leavetaking*, as well as choosing to read all of 'A Slip-up' and 'Korea'. Over a thousand people paid to attend the event, which proved a great success for *Ploughshares*, raising over $4,000 for the magazine. Despite all of the anxiety, the whole thing proved a singular triumph for John and a perfect springboard for the publication of *Getting Through* the following spring by Faber, though the collection did not appear in the USA (with the addition of one extra story, 'Gold Watch') until three years later.

The American delay was a hangover from the many switches in publisher. John had disliked working with Peter Davison and Atlantic. After the company published *The Leavetaking*, they rejected *Getting Through*, and John was on the hunt for a new American home. In the wake of his Harvard success, he wisely reached out to the literary agent Tim Seldes, then working for Russell & Volkening in New York, a company he would soon purchase and direct:

> Faber has always published me in England. Charles Monteith is my editor. While he is there I would not wish to leave. They have acted as part agents, but I have told them I feel I need an agent, and wrote into the book of stories – GETTING THROUGH – that unsold rights would become the domain of an agent, should I acquire one. Panther used to publish me in paperback, but Quartet bought THE LEAVETAKING, and are bringing out the early novels later in the year. Many of the literary magazines are anxious for my work, but – as I am sure you know – they do not pay very well.

By the following spring, Harper & Row had bought the American rights to *Getting Through*, with the agreement that they would also get the as-yet-unnamed next novel.

Autumn in Foxfield was quiet, with John finding it difficult to get back into the flow of the novel. He travelled up and down to Dublin once a week to teach a master's course at UCD, thanks to his old friend Professor Roger McHugh. The students were excited at the prospect of having John, now very much in the higher echelons of living Irish writers, as their tutor. At the first meeting of the seminar, he gave them a short reading list that several of the students found rather incongruous and disappointing: it included a couple of Yeats plays, a couple of Beckett plays, and Somerville and Ross's novel *The Real Charlotte*. This list included no recent or contemporary writers. One of those students, Tom O'Grady, a native of Price Edward Island who went on to a successful academic career in the USA, was able to recall the opening session for me:

> Me and my classmates were briefly heartened when McGahern invited us to propose other writers we might engage with together in the seminar. Someone suggested Benedict Kiely (I believe his novella

Proxopera was hot off the press). McGahern responded: 'I despise Benedict Kiely.' Someone else suggested Flann O'Brien. McGahern's response: 'Pseudo Joyce.' I don't recall any further suggestions.

On 21 November, Monteith sent a telegram to Foxfield telling John that he had been awarded a £3,000 Arts Council grant, news that helped bolster work on the novel, of which John was in a position to send Seldes 30,000 words in the spring of 1978. On the weekend before the students of University College Cork (UCC) broke up for their Christmas vacation, John attended a reading on campus. 'He looks an unlikely person to weave a spell', thought Mary Leland, 'with his hair in conservative curls, the tweed jacket, plain tie, and the round face of a satisfied cleric. Yet as John McGahern read "The Slip-Up" to one of the best audiences the English Literature Society at UCC has seen for a long time, his hold on the young listeners was absolute.' He batted away a question on the restrictive cultural climate of Ireland, dismissing the significance of country or nationality, using one of his favourite lines: 'We do as badly in Ireland as everywhere else.' The final question of the night – 'What does it mean to write?' – gave him pause for thought: 'I suppose I'd have to ask what does it mean to live. I don't think that question can be answered . . . It does seem that the human being needs an idea; I don't think there is any serious work that is not religious.'

June 1978 saw the publication of *Getting Through* by Faber. Monteith had counselled John to open and close the collection with what he considered the two strongest stories, 'The Beginning of an Idea' and 'Sierra Leone'. The former piece begins and ends with images of Anton Chekhov's funeral. For Monteith, its qualities are decisive: 'Quite apart from being a superb story in its own right, it's got the odd "merit" of not being an Irish story – and to make it your "lead" would, I think, startle reviewers into realizing that these stories have got to be judged as stories, not as "Irish stories".' Monteith had learnt the lesson of *Nightlines* and knew better than to market John's work as part of an 'Irish tradition'.

This facet of the fiction was picked up on by Ciaran Carty when he visited Foxfield for the *Sunday Independent*. The paper ran with the provocative headline 'John McGahern: "It Would Be an Insult to Be Called an Irish Writer"'. The article works as a kind of welcome home for an author who is becoming internationally famous, who has been signed by Harper & Row in the USA for his new stories and next novel and whose *Getting Through* is the summer choice of the New Fiction Society in London. Carty writes, 'Obviously his work is finding its true readers.' For him, this author has found his métier:

> He has a deceptive manner. He can seem vulnerable in the city, a shy man trembling in a handshake. But here by the lake, the weather in his face, he conveys a sense of calm, undisturbed even by the ordeal of submitting to an interview, something he dislikes and, over the years, has been adept at avoiding.

A young Neil Jordan, writing for the *Irish Times*, also felt that the new collection marked an important moment in moving Irish writing away from introspection and into a more international arena:

> one can see something changing and not only in McGahern, in the whole of Irish writing. The Sligo boarding-house could be on America's east coast, the Leitrim farms could be set in provincial France. The weight of association that has too often crippled these familiar landscapes has fallen off for good. Perhaps this is what the Getting Through of the title refers to.

Not everyone agreed. If Monteith, Carty and Jordan were determined to see John break free of 'Irish' shackles, the *Sunday Telegraph* was having none of it. Reviewed under the headline 'Real Irish Flavour', the paper found that all 'the familiar attributes of the Irish short story are to be found in John McGahern's work: melancholy, nostalgia, regret, elegiac lyricism'.

John Fowles, in the *Irish Press*, while deeply admiring the stories, also worries about a peculiar Irish addiction to melancholy: 'John McGahern is a new writer to me, and an impressive one; I haven't admired a short story collection so much for a long time.' Fowles summarises this addiction's core difficulty: 'The heart of the problem seems to lie in a violent distaste, part aesthetic and part emotional, for the notion of any reasonably happy and lasting relationship between the sexes.' Tom Paulin in *Encounter* also remarks on the ever-present darkness: 'Running through McGahern's work is a fusion of sex, death and hopelessness. They are the presiding trinity of his imagination.' But he sees this facet as in no way damaging to the stories, written 'in a prose that always possesses an astringent purity and delicacy'.

In fact, the British reviews were unanimous in their praise, with Anthony Thwaite seeing in the book a rare quality: 'a flavour so subtle and hauntingly pervasive that to try to make a synopsis of what actually happens in them is not only off the point but damaging'. And Thwaite's review is more alert than others to the governing principle of John's prose style: 'McGahern's tactics have more to do with poetry than with the procedures of most short stories.'

As usual, John would find his Irish detractors. Ulick O'Connor found the book a poor relation to the earlier work: 'McGahern appears to be trying to create a feeling of hopelessness as he remembers it from the past. That doesn't quite work.' But these are relatively mild criticisms compared to those summoned up by a dismissive Bruce Arnold in the *Irish Independent*, who thought the whole book a resounding failure: 'They could as well not have been written, and some of them – "Faith, Hope and Charity" for example – should not have been written. They do not matter.' These negative remarks, while no doubt hurtful, were easy for John to ignore, such was the near-universal praise from other, more thoughtful quarters.

The smartest, fairest and most eloquent review of the book was written by Nuala O'Faolain in *Hibernia*:

> Even if McGahern had repeated himself and was still young, still conducting his icy struggle with the Laocoon of mother, febrile,

> unplaced love, and the savagery of small Irish power – even then he would matter. But with this collection he has broken through all his limitations. He more than appeals to adultness – he assists it. 'Getting Through' leaves a residue of concern with McGahern's own philosophical or existential concerns, a continuing response which is the rare but infallible sign of being in the presence, now, of a writer who is sometimes great.

That O'Faolain is willing to reach for such an arresting summation of John's body of work is all the more remarkable given her concerns about some of his prose:

> McGahern can fall into a careless floridness. In 'Doorways' he is explaining that a certain hostess is a bore:
>
> 'But we still went to her parties, knowing we were being used as butcher's grass or chopped-down rhododendron branches to cover up the dusty margins of the processional ways in June.'
>
> But that kind of overkill is rare. Overwhelmingly, the pull in McGahern is towards a bareness that verges even on nothing.

The review is among the two or three most intelligent written about John's work over the course of his writing life, and O'Faolain's concluding remark gets to the heart of the matter in a way that perhaps no other reviewer ever quite managed: 'Without his skill we'd prefer not to ponder the checked gush of love, the mistakes that bring on living death. But McGahern lures us in, and we think.'

The birth of *Getting Through*, as ever for John when completing a book, brought both satisfaction and anxiety. Though critically acclaimed by those whom John cared about, the collection sold just 520 hardback copies. Writing to his friends Neill and Mary Joy in Colgate, he sees only hard times ahead: 'now I have to go back to the novel, horrible work, and I don't intend to move for the next few months'.

* * *

On 12 May 1977, less than a fortnight after John's triumphant Harvard reading, Frank McGahern died at home in Grevisk after a short illness. He had been poorly for a couple of weeks prior to his passing, but there had been so many false alarms in the past that when he eventually did enter his final days, the development took John by surprise, and he had to make last-minute arrangements to leave Colgate and get home. He did not make it in time. Madeline, who had gone home ahead of John to reopen the house, had visited the Sergeant towards the end, with him commenting to her that he never knew it was so hard to die, a thought that John would later give to Moran of *Amongst Women* on his deathbed.

John's surviving letters show few signs of this momentous event. He comments to his *New Yorker* editor in early June that he is 'a bit depressed', and of life in Foxfield writes that everything is 'upside-down here yet'. He is more interested in getting the last paragraph of 'Sierra Leone' into shape than in reflecting on his father's death. A month later, he writes to Niall Walsh in an otherwise newsy letter about tree-planting and the purchase of four in-calf cows: 'It was the heart my father died from, but he sank slowly, fighting each inch.'

But to think that Frank's death did not affect John deeply would be a mistake. Among the many artefacts in the Garda Museum at Dublin Castle is a copy of *Getting Through* signed by John in memory of the Sergeant. He would spend the rest of his life trying to understand this tough, mercurial man, a quest that would eventually lead to his final book, *Memoir*.

12
The Silkworm
1978–80

Art is art because it is not nature!

W. B. YEATS

With its dust jacket bearing a sepia-tinted, back-to-front Rathmines streetscape, the dome of Mary Immaculate, Refuge of Sinners jutting skyward at the end of a curving terrace, *The Pornographer* is John's most determinedly urban novel. Its provocative title dares the reader towards strong opinions before the book is even opened. Sexual-thrill seekers will be quickly disillusioned. 'No member of the dirty mac brigade', wrote Anthony Thwaite in the *Observer*, 'is likely to get more than a few pages into John McGahern's *The Pornographer* without a strong sense of resentful disappointment.'

Charles Monteith felt that this might at last be the book that would bring John into the mainstream. The critics were starkly divided, some hating this tale of existential drift and moral decay, others just plain baffled by it. 'McGahern has adopted, or succumbed to, a narrow and unimpressive fictional mode, which the reader finds at first disturbing, later degrading, finally repulsive', argued one particularly severe reviewer. An *Irish Independent* review opened with a striking claim: 'John McGahern is probably the best novelist we have.' Then he got compared favourably with Mauriac and Camus, before an even more striking verdict about his standing in Ireland arrived: 'though praised, he is little liked'. Tom Kilroy thought that the book 'worked but was hard to place'. Like *Getting Through*, published just sixteen months earlier (though in the USA the novel pre-dates the short-story collection), the book was a popular flop, selling fewer than a thousand copies in Faber hardback.

How did it come to this artistic pass? What motivated John, up till this point seen as a sort of laureate of rural Ireland, to write a novel set largely in Dublin, in a world of bedsits and dreary bars, about a nameless man from the country, adrift, facing his thirties and making a living from writing absurd pornographic fantasies about Colonel Grimshaw and his trusty assistant, Mavis Carmichael? To answer these questions, we need to go back at least five years, to the period when he was still putting *The Leavetaking* to bed and was about to commence his visiting fellowship in Newcastle.

In the same month that John moved to Tyneside, his story 'The Stoat' got a reading on The Third Programme and appeared simultaneously in British *Vogue* and in *Man Alive*, 'Ireland's first magazine for men', as it liked to describe itself. Both publications seem a rather unlikely forum for this story that draws parallels between a stoat hunting and killing a rabbit on a Sligo golf course and a widower seeking a woman to replace his dead wife. But John was happy to get the money and was in no position to pick and choose. Both appearances came about through long-established connections: *Vogue* because of Derek Mahon's time there as a features editor; *Man Alive* through Joe Kennedy, John's old journalist friend from his Drogheda days twenty years before.

Man Alive came from the same stable as the *Sunday World*, both periodicals wishing to see if money could be made in the Irish market from colourful, sensationalised news reporting and from soft porn. John Coughlan, the Cork-born editor of *Man Alive*, had begun his professional life at the *Cork Examiner*, leaving in 1963 to establish *Spotlight*, which quickly became Ireland's most important show-business magazine. In the 1970s, he cooperated with Hugh McLaughlin's Creation Group and came up with the idea for an edgy tabloid to compete with the likes of the *News of the World* and the *Sunday People*, which he called the *Sunday World*, poaching Joe Kennedy from the *Evening Herald* as its first editor. Coughlan was publisher of *Man Alive* and the later, more successful travel magazine, *Holiday*. A larger-than-life character, he is in part an inspiration for aspects of Maloney in *The Pornographer*, as is

Joe Kennedy, though John denied the influence when asked by an upset Kennedy if this linkage was the case.

That there would emerge, after fifty years of rigorous censorship, a group of Irish journalists, entrepreneurs and writers who wished to see how far they might go with a journey into moral rule-breaking was perhaps inevitable. One can sense an air of relief mixed with swagger in the editorial for the fourth number of *Man Alive*, in which 'The Stoat' appears: 'believe me we're glad to be still alive. We were told it could not be done. If an Irish magazine attempted to feature pictures of naked female body, "dirty jokes" and risqué stories . . . it would certainly be "done in". Or so they said.' This tone then switches to libertarian high-mindedness:

> Freedom should be absolute . . . but we are still old fashioned enough to want to exercise a certain amount of self censorship. We deem it unnecessary to enter into the rat race of photographic 'pornography,' but we think the human female body a subject of such healthy interest to the average man, as to merit quite a lot of attention from us. Sexuality in all its forms is a subject much underdiscussed (publicly anyway) in our damp Irish climate. We intend to change that also.

John had no such exalted ambitions and was happy just to see the cheques for work submitted lodged in the Bank of Ireland, Westport, where he had opened an account while living in Achill. When, the following summer, *Man Alive* published a second story of his, 'A Slip-up', he wrote to Joe Kennedy that the magazine's illustrations were 'a good demonstration in how to crack an eggshell with a sledge hammer'.

Pornography and its place in Irish life continued to be discussed in the pages of the *Sunday World*. The 25 April 1976 edition of the paper, which carried John's paean to the Newcastle music hall Balmbra's, points on its front page to an article titled 'The Great Nude Debate', in which Kevin Marron curates a series of readers' letters on the subject of the newspaper's penchant for carrying photographs of partially dressed young women:

> Have you been in any bookshop recently? Have you studied the covers of the current crop of paperbacks? I direct this question to those who have been complaining that the pictures I use each week in 'my sort of TV column' have a corrupting and depraving influence on younger readers. The picture 'strip' at the top of this page is a sample of paperbacks on sale in Eason's, O'Connell Street, Dublin at the moment. Even they are rather mild in comparison to what can be found with a little more searching around city and country newsagent shops.

The strip Marron mentions features a selection of books with soft-porn covers and titles such as *Blondes Don't Have All the Fun!* and *House of Pleasure*. He then reproduces a series of letters on the issue of pornography and censorship sent to the *Sunday World*, running from principled defenders of freedom of expression to outraged upholders of moral decency. One letter-writer signs herself 'a woman in Cork':

> The girls on your page are not disgusting but WHY HAVE NEAR NAKED GIRLS . . . WHY WHY WHY. You menfolk think it a great CRACK. You make fun and sheer DIRT of the girls and there is no NEED WHATSOEVER for such publications. Dearest me, they do make a big change from the usual trash you write BUT WHY NAKED GIRLS . . . The women are the gombeens and I feel like telling your photographer where to stick his camera . . . For the sake of St. Peter, take those pictures off your page . . . You sicken me up to here, Sir.

This epistle's clichéd stridency has the whiff of forgery about its composition. But the contribution, real or fake, forms part of a debate in a widely bought and read Sunday newspaper as John is writing his fourth novel in a quiet campus apartment overlooking a Tyneside park.

Of course, the novel, though eventually called *The Pornographer*, is only passingly about pornography and its creation. John struggled terribly, and characteristically, to find a title. At one point he seriously suggested to Charles Monteith that the new novel be called 'This Isn't

Grenoble'. The inclination stemmed from a moment late in the book, when the narrator and his editor have gone to the countryside for the funeral of the pornographer's aunt:

> Maloney was at breakfast when I went into the Commercial. He probably had a hangover. He was in a sour mood.
>
> 'How did you find the local blooms?' I asked.
>
> 'This isn't Grenoble and I'm not Stendhal's uncle. Have some coffee? Tell me how you got your decoration.'

Not until very late in the day did John decide on the title by which we now know the book. While this false start in nomenclature comes from John's deep reading in French literature in translation, the narrator of *The Pornographer*, in his moral passivity, owes more to Camus's insouciant Meursault of *The Outsider* than to Stendhal's Julien Sorel of *The Red and the Black*. The youngster growing up in the provinces in the latter novel, struggling with a priestly vocation, guilt-ridden in the face of masturbatory fantasies, lies in strong part behind the creation of Young Mahoney in *The Dark*. In fact, of all John's novels, *The Pornographer* is the most intensely literary one. This quality derives both from its influences and from its preoccupations. This novel is consumed by the need to meditate on the creation of images – albeit on the creation of craven images.

By the later 1970s, when John was teaching at Colgate, Albert Camus's definition of art had become a cornerstone of his thinking: 'Art is the distance that time gives to suffering. It is man's transcendence in relation to himself.' In a meaningless, absurd world, art can help to make life bearable. As John himself put it in 'The Image':

> For art is, out of the failure of love, an attempt to create a world in which we can live: if not for long or forever, it is still a world of the imagination over which we can reign, and to reign is to purely reflect on our situation through this created world of ours, this Medusa's mirror, which allows us to celebrate even the totally intolerable.

Art, then, allows one to look at aspects of life that cannot be accurately examined or judged in their raw state. And it is crucial not to confuse life with art. One must feel confident in invention, as John repeatedly told his students: 'Art is not life. Life is less believable than fiction. Drawing too closely from the experience is deadly to the artist.' John stressed in his teaching the importance of creating a sense of distance and reshaping of the world by blending memory with imagination: 'Art is artifice. It is fabrication. But every lie is based on an element of truth.'

John liked Yeats's dictum, borrowed from Goethe: 'Art is art because it is not nature!' Yeats expands on the essence of art and puts us in mind immediately of the McGahern aesthetic: 'It brings us near to the archetypal ideas themselves, and away from nature, which is but their looking-glass.' There is an irony that John, so often admired for his realistic fidelity, and frequently placed alongside Patrick Kavanagh as a great Irish nature writer, should so determinedly see writing, like Yeats, as manufactured or 'unnatural'. So much did John like this Yeatsian phrase that he quotes it in *The Pornographer*. Maloney, the editor of the journal to which the nameless pornographer contributes, begins his professional life in a small Irish town working as a journalist on the *Echo*. He has his heart broken by a local beauty and subsequently gathers a group of people in a hotel to listen to his poetry and his thoughts on writing:

> He warned against the confusion between art and life. Art was art because it was not nature. Life was a series of accidents. Art was a vision of the law. Rarely did the accident conform to the Idea or Vision, so it had to be invented or made anew so that it conformed to the Vision.

One can see in *The Pornographer*, both in its construction and in its narrator's failure to create satisfying images, a meditation on the artist's job.

The Pornographer borrows a fascination in an instance of collage. This fascination is with the world of journalism and newspapers, a world that provides the overarching narrative scaffolding for John's novel. The borrowing, with little care for the covering of tracks, comes from Nathanael

West's 1933 novella set around a Great Depression-era agony column, *Miss Lonelyhearts*. Maloney takes the place of that work's cynical, jaded editor, Shrike, sharing similar views on art and its value:

> But before he had written a dozen words, Shrike leaned over his shoulder. 'The same old stuff,' Shrike said. 'Why don't you give them something new and hopeful? Tell them about art. Here, I'll dictate:
>
> 'Art Is a Way Out.
>
> 'Do not let life overwhelm you. When the old paths are choked with the debris of failure, look for newer and fresher paths. Art is just such a path. Art is distilled from suffering.'

While Miss Lonelyhearts slakes his thirst in Delehanty's speakeasy, listening to Shrike's unwanted, sententious speeches, John's pornographer takes refuge in the Elbow Inn, along with others who work for the same magazine. As with the pornographer, we never learn Miss Lonelyhearts' name, and both books revolve around a one-sided love affair. While the emotionally paralysed Miss Lonelyhearts and his lover Betty attempt a pastoral escape to an old farm in Connecticut, the pornographer and Josephine take a boat out on the Shannon, a trip subsequently adapted by the pornographer for one of his erotic stories.

In *The Pornographer*, Josephine becomes pregnant and decides to have the baby despite the pornographer's wishes. The inverse happens in West's novella, with Betty being talked out of a termination by Miss Lonelyhearts, who tries to convince himself of a happily married future, before being murdered by a jealous husband in the book's closing scene. All told, *Miss Lonelyhearts*, likely first read by John as preparation for his late-1970s Colgate classes on the novella, becomes a remarkably effective sounding board for *The Pornographer*.

This type of literary borrowing forms part of a pattern. As John developed as an artist – and particularly in this middle period of his writing life – he increasingly used moments and phrases from those artists he most admired to sustain his own work. So, just as he quotes from Yeats or borrows from West in *The Pornographer*, he draws directly from

'Dover Beach', Matthew Arnold's reflection on lost faith, at the end of *The Leavetaking*:

> The full tide surges against the wall and boats, withdraws, and surges back. 'Begin and cease and then again begin.' It was Matthew Arnold. And . . . 'it brought into his mind the turbid ebb and flow of human misery.' That bright girdle he spoke of had been long broken for me too before this last night.

While he would never again openly namecheck, John creates in *The Pornographer* a novel out of a dense collage of quotation and influence. The collage factor is evident if we turn back to Stendhal for a moment, to John's head-scratching suggestion that the novel be called 'This Isn't Grenoble'. While *The Red and the Black* acts as a kind of primer for *The Dark*, the great French master is harder to find in *The Pornographer*. Most instructive now are not his novels but his autobiography, for Stendhal's short, pugnacious *Memoirs of an Egotist* is on John's mind throughout.

One passage early in *The Pornographer* sees the narrator introduce us to his pornographic creations, work that, though ludicrous and comedic, allows us to see the emotional sustenance of the act of writing:

> I sat and typed frivolously, like dabbing toes above steaming water: '*There was a man and a woman. Their names were Mavis Carmichael and Colonel Grimshaw. They lived happily, if it could be said that they lived at all*,' and I x-ed it out and put a fresh page in the typewriter, and then started to work, the worm at last spinning its silken tent.
>
> Several hours and blackened pages later I got up from the typewriter for the day when the barely audible turning of a key sounded from one of the upstairs rooms after a loud banging of the front door. I thought it could be only two or three o'clock and yet it must have been close to six if one of the office girls had got home. It had just gone six. Seldom is it given, but when it is it is the greatest consolation of the spinning, time passing – sizeable portions of time –

> without being noticed. Is it a promise of a happy eternity or just another irony, the realization of the unawareness. We feel that we have been freed of the burden of time passing, and the happiness is in the feeling and not in the blind forgetful play among the words.

The image of the writer as silkworm is taken from two sources. The first is Stendhal; the second the Australian poet Douglas Stewart. Here is Stendhal:

> Have you ever seen, gentle reader, a silkworm that has eaten enough mulberry leaf? The comparison isn't very dignified, but it is so apposite! This ugly beast doesn't want to eat any more, it needs to climb up and spin its silk prison.
>
> Such is the animal known as a 'writer'. For anyone who has enjoyed the profound occupation of writing, reading is merely a secondary pleasure. So often I thought it was two o'clock; I looked at my clock: it was half-past six. This is only my excuse for having blackened so much paper.

The 'uncle' to whom Maloney refers in his conversation with the pornographer is the puckish Gagnon, Stendhal's favourite Grenoble relative, a man on whom Maloney himself is partially modelled. Stendhal describes him in notable terms: 'a charming man. His conversation, which struck men as being like a grandiloquent and elegant novel, struck women as being delightful. He was always droll, delicate, full of those turns of phrase that can mean anything if you let them.' When Stendhal, as a young man, is leaving Grenoble to attend the École Polytechnique in November 1799, he is taken aside by Gagnon and advised that it 'is possible to make progress in the world only through women'.

John came across, in 1974, a similar use of the silkworm image in Douglas Stewart's work. The discovery happened thanks to his friendship with Bob White and a scheme run by the enlightened Australian Whitlam administration to supply books promoting the country's culture to British universities. John knew immediately that he would lean on Stewart's 'The Silkworms' for sections of the novel he was beginning to write.

> And here is the tribe that they know, in their known place,
> They are gentle and kind together, they are safe for ever,
> And all shall be answered at last when they embrace.
> White moth moves closer to moth, lover to lover.
> There is that pang of joy on the edge of dying –
> Their soft wings whirr, they dream that they are flying.

One can see how, when coming to write *The Pornographer*, John might be drawn to Stewart as an exemplar, to his poem about life, death, sex and instinct. Yet he drops only one small clue as the pornographer surveys the dance floor, where he returns again and again in a vain quest to satisfy his sexual appetite and thereby salve the pain of his existence:

> All around us on the maple the old youngsters danced. The stained skin did not show in the blue light, but paunches did, bald heads, white hair, tiredness. People do not grow old. Age happens to us, like collisions, that is all. And usually we drive on. We do not feel old or ridiculous as we pursue what we have always pursued. Tonight, as any night, if we could anchor ourselves in the ideal greasy warm wetness of the human fork, we'd be more than happy. We'd dream that we were flying.

Knowing that it is to 'The Silkworms' John is turning underlines the sexual instinct's central role throughout *The Pornographer*. This instinct leads to the dramatic core of the novel via the pornographer's impregnation of his lover, Josephine, whom he has so casually conquered in the dance hall, and his subsequent desperation to escape what Patrick Kavanagh called, in another context, 'the curse that domesticity brings'. At all times in the novel, Philip Larkin, with his deep-seated fear of marriage and the settled life of the petty bourgeoisie, is also a pervasive presence.

For the silkworms of Stewart's poem, instinct is personified in the fifth stanza as 'the ancestral voice'. They know not why they spin but feel compelled to do so. And so too with the pornographer as we reach the final page of the novel: 'Not to have a reason is a greater reason still to follow the instinct for the true, to follow it with all the force we have, in all the seeing and the final blindness.' The first time the two central characters of the book have sex is especially germane to this discussion since we see several of Stewart's images and ideas coalesce:

> Within her there was this instant of rest, the glory and the awe, that one was as close as ever man could be to the presence of the mystery, and live, the caged bird in its moment of pure rest before it was about to be loosed into blinding light; and then the body was clamouring in the rough health of the instinct, 'This is what I needed. This-is-what-I-need-ed.'

Entrapment, blindness, ecstasy, instinct: these forces are all here as John tries to get to the root of what he believes about the sacred power of human sexuality, and here he links *The Leavetaking* with *The Pornographer*. The relationship is an oppositional one, romance versus anti-romance. The eponymous pornographer, a writer of sorts and incapable of love, is condemned to obey an instinctual drive in pointless affairs. Crucially, in a degrading translation, he uses an affair with a decent woman who loves him and will bear his child as raw material for a pornographic story. The pervasive secondary plot – illness, hospital ward, nurses and a funeral – underscores the protagonist's aberration: a sexually aggressive death wish. Only his non-sexual love for his dying aunt is allowable; her age ensures she is past conceiving.

Nothing in the text, including a sketched-in new liaison, supports his sudden intention to risk an adventure and propose marriage. This thought seems gratuitous coming late in the novel except that he concludes nothing really matters, but life must be lived. His employer, Maloney, ill-equipped morally, nonetheless administers a comic assessment of our anti-hero, a verbal assault paralleling the pornographer's earlier physical beating at the hands of Josephine's London-Irish landlord. Reason can take you only so far: Maloney, the jaunty entrepreneur of pornography, in the driver's seat, a careless chauffeur, with the pornographer seated next to him, sings out a nonsensical greeting to the road they travel together. Who sings 'Yoo-hoo' in the last sentence – Maloney or the protagonist or both chorusing – is unclear. This moment reads as a greeting or a madcap acceptance, not as a jeer.

These ambiguities offer a wide range of differing interpretations – of conflicting ones, even. Nevertheless, the anti-romance motif is a constant. The pornographers have the last word and share a concluding symbol, accenting human energy without meaning or purpose in life or art. The characterisation of a recognisably male type withholding sympathy and harmful to women avoids stereotyping, and, instead, a credible, proficient study of inhibited existence evident in conversation, actions and thought emerges.

The book gives the lie to any comfortable categorisation of John as a 'country writer'. He had lived in Dublin for the best part of a decade, knew the city well and was fond of it. In a revealing letter of 14 October 1975 to the young American editor Jonathan Coleman, whom John had first met when Coleman was working as an intern at the *New Review*, and who was at this point working at Knopf in New York, John gives a straightforward summation of *The Pornographer* as a novel that draws much of its motive force from setting up an opposition between country and city:

> On a level it's the City and the Country clashing in the Psyche. After the failed idyll – a bid for sexual order – he meets – the opening of the novel in Time Present – a journalist – 38 (he's 29) – she gets pregnant, refuses an abortion, puts pressure on him to marry. The chickens have come to roost. She's basically an eternal full of brightness, says he's sick.
>
> One of these terrible instincts without mind, all is black and white. She has the child in London while he attends the funeral in the country. He's just come from London, a last bid on his part to get rid of the child – adoption – and she to get him to assume responsibility. And he's beaten up by a protector. He's black and blue for a wedding as well as for a funeral.

John concludes his summary with typically mordant wit: 'What I haven't worked out is the resolution but you can see it's the usual hopeful brew.'

Elements of the plot are close to the details of John's 1962 love affair with Joan Kelly, and, in the way events are set out by the narrator, one might see an attempt to get off the hook on his part (and therefore on John's part). By coincidence, just as John completed the novel, he became reacquainted with Joan and met for the first time his son, Joseph, now living in Portsmouth, where Joan worked as an information officer for the Royal Navy. Formally based in Whitehall, her rank, when visiting naval bases across the country, equated with that of lieutenant commander.

It would be the first of several such meetings, the last taking place in Dublin in 1992. Tom Paulin, who knew nothing of the affair, reviewing *The Pornographer* for *Encounter*, is one of those readers made uncomfortable by the author's treatment of Josephine: 'I'm not at all sure that McGahern isn't committed to his narrator's point of view here.' For Paulin, this perceived allegiance undermines the reader's credulity: 'McGahern fails to render the woman's suffering and by portraying her through the narrator's eyes as a hearty scheming extrovert he exculpates his glum pornographer.'

John did not write the book as a means to clear his conscience – the pornographer, after all, is not a character it is easy to like, though Lucille Redmond, in her *Irish Times* review, had a grudging admiration:

> The writing is crisp and cruel. '"It's wonderful just to lie and bathe in another's body. You have a very beautiful body," I heard my own words hang like an advertisement in the peace of the firelight,' and McGahern has achieved the almost unachievable in producing a hero who's a complete bastard, yet likeable in his confusion.

John did not mean for his readers to identify with the pornographer any more than Nathanael West wanted people to sympathise with Miss Lonelyhearts. 'The reason that the main character is so uninteresting is that this obsession with sexuality is enervating', John says in one interview.

> He falls into that disease, which is a very Irish malaise, that since all things are meaningless, it makes no difference what you do, and best of all is to do nothing. In this way he causes as much trouble, to himself and to others, as if he had set out to deliberately do evil.

Camus's outsider, Meursault, who shoots an Arab for reasons unknown, is the model here. This strange new novel's existential roots particularly appealed to a younger Irish audience. On the day that John was laid to rest in 2006, among the many appreciations to appear in the national press was Colm Tóibín's *Irish Times* consideration. The book to which Tóibín turned first, the book to make the most immediate and lasting impact, was *The Pornographer*. He recalled a proof copy landing on his desk when he was working as a rookie journalist at the edgy *In Dublin*: 'The book was read in a short time by a number of us who wrote for the magazine. We were in our early 20s and not special fans of the work of McGahern and yet we were stunned by the book.' Some of those young journalists may have been fooled by John's previous work into thinking that he was another of those Irish writers wishing to capture a peculiarly rural, post-colonial malaise, what Tóibín calls 'the dull life of Ireland, full of rain and families and priests and early closing time'. But what the young gun journalists instead perceived was rather different. Far from seeing a novel about this sort of failed state, they discerned a narrative known in intimate terms: 'set in a Dublin we recognised but, in its relentless darkness, in its sombre dramatisation of sex and death, it could equally have been written by a French existential novelist'. Not just its urban setting and liberated subject matter ambushed Tóibín and his friends but even more its experiments with style: 'in the way the writer played with narrative, it could have been written by a modern anti-novelist'. For Tóibín and others of his generation, *The Pornographer* became an exciting way forward, leading them to look afresh at John's early work.

Paula Meehan, born like Tóibín in 1955, remembers John as someone who held a special place of honour and influence for her and her peers.

For their generation, he was a writer understood in particular terms: 'ground breaker, trail blazer, shibboleth shaker'. At about the same time as Tóibín and the Young Turks at *In Dublin* were marvelling at the achievement, Meehan was part of a writing workshop being directed by John at UCG. Her memories of that time are revealing of a writer at a cusp:

> In 1979 I was twenty-four; the other participants were mostly in their twenties and thirties; McGahern was forty-five. *The Pornographer* had just been published. He was defensive about it. Or maybe the word is defiant. And memory tells me that he felt the novel had been misunderstood. 'Judge yourself not by your successes but by the grandeur of your failures,' he said more than once during the workshop. In fact he said it each time the workshop convened. He said it enough times anyway, usually followed by snide remarks about the critics, for me to have formed the strong impression that there had been somewhere a negative or ignorant response to the book. Something said or written that had struck a nerve. 'That's like something a journalist would say,' was his response to particularly vacuous remarks. He warned us not to believe our own press, good or bad.
>
> And I have the strong impression – and it could only have been inscribed in my memory banks at that workshop – that he believed *The Pornographer* was one of those grand failures. He definitely believed there had been a grand failure on the part of the readership to 'get' the book.

John believed in 1979 that *The Pornographer* was his best book, a belief shared by Madeline, who would continue to have a particular and enduring admiration for the novel. For John Montague, the book represented 'a real advance'. John knew that *The Pornographer* marked, via daring experiments in style, a turning point. 'I don't think I could have gone on and written *Amongst Women* and the other books if I hadn't written *The Pornographer*', he told one interviewer. 'It was an important stage in my evolution.'

Tom Paulin may have been on to something when he wrote of John in the wake of his fourth novel: 'It's as though he has started to recognise that his nordic lyricism and bedroom existentialism are an imaginative dead-end.' Though that emphasis might sound like a put-down from Paulin, he finishes his review on a hopeful note:

> McGahern is saying that the mnemonic muse of his fiction is dried-up and repetitive – he is recognising that the saw mill, the woman dying of cancer, the merging of sex and death are predictably familiar. Thus *The Pornographer* is a terminal work which may promise a new beginning, a fresher inspiration.

Similarly, the *Irish Times* saw it as a necessary change in direction: '*The Pornographer* is without any question McGahern's fork on the road: he can now consolidate to step into a place in European literature, from the place he has held as one of Ireland's foremost writers.'

The Galway workshop of autumn 1979 had come after a full academic year at Colgate, something John did only twice, for the second time in the academic year 1983–84. With his books not selling, he was glad to accept money where he could get it. Interviewed by the *Colgate Scene* before *The Pornographer* is published, he reflects on the impossibility of teaching students how to write, saying that he does not expect masterpieces but that he will have succeeded if, by the end of term, they are 'able to write better love letters'. His reflections are level and clear:

> I don't think anyone can really be taught to write . . . My students usually have some talent, but I find they have to write so many factual essays that imaginative writing comes hard. The thing I must constantly emphasise is to use language afresh and get rid of the thundering clichés. Is there any point in saying 'this moment in time' when you can use the beautifully simple word 'now'? I've never complained about a student writing too simply.

But John certainly had enough in his locker, even if he believed that writing could not be taught, to inspire Paula Meehan and her ten Galway classmates later that year at the National Writers Workshop. Among those writers to speak were Nuala O'Faolain, Seamus Deane, Neil Jordan, Paul Muldoon and Frank McGuinness.

What Meehan remembers best is John's marked taste for aphorisms: 'John told us, too, that he wrote with his table to a blank wall so as not to be distracted by looking out of a window. Distraction was the enemy of writers, he proposed, and confided in us the many distractions the day in Fenagh, Co. Leitrim might hold.' A moral was constantly drawn: 'The world was full of distraction and settling to the desk was the hardest thing – so the blank wall was a refusal to be derailed from the work.' Varieties of distraction were not the sole foes. As Meehan recalls: '"The only sin is foolishness!" John would say to the assembled morning hangovers.' She likewise recalls being told in the toilet by another female participant of this woman's insecurity and nervousness, of how she could not get through the sessions without taking a Valium. Meehan returns to their room with an altered perspective: 'As if reading my mind John comes in with "The proper territory of the writer is doubt. Let doubt be your best friend. The moment you are sure of what you're doing is the moment of greatest danger. Complacency is the enemy of art."'

Part of doubt's creative power concerned the moment of publication. Their workshop director constantly emphasised this point:

> He especially warned us of premature publication, which he made sound very like a prescribed sin of the Catholic Church. Publishing before one had mastered the material was, in John's book, a mortaller. It wastes your own time as well as the reader's time. Publication, he said, was the burial of your dead. The material once published was dead to you and you could move on. A book might live in a reader, be resurrected again and again in each new consciousness, but it was stone dead to the maker, the material mastered, the life for the writer gone from it. Dead and buried.

This advice was absorbed as part of the Galway experience. But another aspect went still deeper. What struck Meehan most, more than all these commandments, and helped her both as a developing writer and as someone trying to make her way in the world, was John's personality as its force impacted the class: 'I will remember with deep gratitude his kindness to a young confused woman, his steadying steer on the road. I will remember most of all his voice. Rhythmic, in love with his own language, every crafted syllable, savouring the roll and whip of it on the tongue.'

The publication of *The Pornographer* in 1979 saw an end to what was the most prolific rate of output across John's career. In five years, he had produced two novels and a collection of short stories. He would never write at that pace again: it would be more than a decade until the appearance of his next novel, *Amongst Women*, and six years till *High Ground*, a slim volume of short stories. Now among the most widely admired Irish writers of fiction, he continued to live happily with Madeline in a quiet, three-roomed house without a phone, driving a clapped-out Volkswagen Beetle, with just enough money coming in – primarily via Colgate and rents from the rue Christine flat – to stay afloat.

More than ever he was certain of his vocation and fixed in his desires, as is made clear in a letter to Brian Friel from Tom Kilroy:

> And McGahern! Had few days with him last weekend and 'met' him for the first time. Well, we finally, I think, agreed to disagree about most things in the cosmos but I like him very much and, despite immense exhaustion, his company. He is unashamedly intolerant, a real black and white minstrel with a line dropping down through literature with a hell of a plumb weight at the end of it. Did you find that? Or as he'd say himself, do you know what I mean?

13
A Sort of Happiness
1979–85

A style is the outcome, not the cause, of a certain view of reality.

PAOLO VIVANTE

On the Feast of the Epiphany 1961, Frank McGahern sat down to wish his eldest child the compliments of the season. Beginning with the customary complaints about his health, the letter moves briskly to a somewhat baffling discussion on the subject of watches:

> I think and I have been assured the watch is a good one. For that reason it would be wrong for me to leave it thrown in a drawer especially when you are not a manual worker for 10 or 11 months of each year. I was going to send 24/- to Clearys last week for one I saw. I have not been able to save my pocket watch so I meant to chance a wrist one and see how it worked out. A very cheap one is the ideal for farm life.

The letter prompts John to send his father a belated Christmas gift, and we see the Sergeant writing again on 2 February: 'I hasten to thank you for the watch received today. I feel humiliated by your generosity. The watch is a beauty; the only fault I could find, is, it is far too expensive.' The key word here is 'humiliated'; this emphasis would lead John, many years later, to write one of his greatest stories.

'Gold Watch', for me and for many readers through the 1980s and 1990s, was the first exposure we had to John's work, when it was anthologised in the Benedict Kiely-edited *Penguin Book of Irish Short Stories* (1981) alongside classics such as James Joyce's 'Grace', Elizabeth Bowen's 'The Cat Jumps' and George Moore's 'Homesickness'. Though John was generally irritated by any easy lumping of his work into an 'Irish tradition', he had no issue with allowing what he knew to be one of his very best stories to form part of what would inevitably become an influential volume.

'Gold Watch' is perhaps the single most powerful portrait of John's father. That Kiely sought this story for his Penguin collection was no surprise. First published in the *New Yorker* of 9 March 1980 and then collected in the American Harper & Row edition of *Getting Through* later that year, the piece remained uncollected on the other side of the Atlantic until the publication of John's next book of stories, *High Ground*, in 1985. This publishing curiosity made 'Gold Watch' all the more attractive to Penguin, whose anthology became a canon-forming favourite of university curricula and school libraries through the closing decades of the twentieth century.

As with *The Pornographer*, the story is set between Dublin and an Irish countryside modelled generally on north Roscommon and specifically on Cootehall. In one scene, the narrator's father, in an effort to destroy the new wristwatch gifted to him by his son, sledges stones 'that had fallen from the archway where once the workmen's bell had hung'. As the story begins, the narrator runs into an old university classmate on Grafton Street, and they enter into a blissful relationship, quickly moving into a flat together off St Stephen's Green: 'There was extraordinary peace and loveliness in those first weeks together that I will always link with those high-ceilinged rooms.' There is much here that is reminiscent of the first thrilling days with Madeline in London in 1967, though John borrows from another recent encounter with the academic and critic Denis Sampson for details of this woman's life: 'That early summer we drove down one weekend to the small town in Kilkenny where she had grown up, and above her father's bakery we slept in separate rooms.' This description is recognisably drawn from Sampson's wife, Gay, who is the daughter of a Castlecomer baker. And Montreal, the Sampsons' home town, is chosen as the place where the narrator buys the expensive wristwatch with which he replaces the gold pocket watch, passed down from his grandfather, of the story's title.

The main action allows us to enter squarely into the world of Frank McGahern and his second wife, Agnes. That the story should have come to John in the wake of his father's death on 12 May 1977 is no coincidence. All his life he had tried to understand and to placate this man, and 'Gold Watch' becomes a haunting meditation on their difficult relationship. For the narrator's first (and last) trip home with his lover, John returns to the excruciating failures that marked his own attempted introduction of both Annikki and Madeline to the Sergeant:

> My father tried to be charming when we went in, but there was a false heartiness in the voice that made clear that it grew out of no well-meaning. He felt he'd lost ground, and was now trying to recover it far too quickly. Using silence and politeness like a single weapon, we refused to be drawn in; and when pressed to stay the next morning, we said unequivocally that we had to get back.

Despite repeated efforts over the years to have a calmer and more settled paternal relationship, the bond was never what John wished for. Even from beyond the grave, John's father continued to cause him difficulties.

As far back as the early 1960s, Frank McGahern had hoped to pass on his Grevisk house and lands to his youngest child, Frankie, leaving Agnes homeless. When Irish law was changed to make this sort of spousal disinheritance impossible, the move infuriated the Sergeant, forcing him into a rethink. As he tells John in one typically disgruntled letter, which is clear, though never naming Agnes, in its targeting,

> Too bad you saw fit to introduce a discordant and controversial note into an otherwise excellent letter. I have no wish to enter a controversy.
>
> When I bought here I knew & was told it was property and entailed having responsibilities I did not wish to saddle on you I made a will. All my responsibilities will in 1964 reach full age. Since last year an Act of parliament made my will useless and on my death all my property goes to one person. Reasonable provisions are already in existence by pension. Furthermore, I would much prefer spending

> my days left to me far removed from certain people as I suspect them rather expensive.

John did his best to point out to his father that Agnes had rights and had every reason to expect to be able to see out her days in Grevisk should she outlive him. All of this trouble came back into play on Frank McGahern's death, when John was made executor of a will that sought to leave house and lands to Frankie. While John and his younger brother had always been on friendly terms, the will introduced controversy, with Frankie determined to honour his father's wishes and John seeking compromise. The impasse eventually led to filial communication by solicitor's letter, with John receiving the following on 7 November 1980: 'Francis is extremely worried that the matter seems to be getting nowhere and to this end he has informed us that unless you either accept or reject the Probate within 14 days he will have to take such unilateral action as may be necessary to protect his interests.'

The case dragged on for a further four years, with Agnes being left the house, which was subsequently inherited by John's sister Margaret. Having spent the full 1983–84 academic year in Colgate, John writes to his faculty colleague and friend Linck Johnson on his return to Leitrim:

> I came back straight into the court case, which was settled in court, but only after the Judge had agreed to retire to see if a settlement could be found – in fact incurring the same expense as a trial. My brother had to take what he was offered 4 years ago. He had his daughter with him in court as, I suppose, a kind of shoulder padding. Then my aunt died in June. So much for families.
>
> We've had hot gorgeous weather. It broke only a week ago. The hay is saved, the fruit trees heavy, and Charlie frisks scatterbrained through onions and peas, imagining itself a lion among the pea stakes.

To have this troubling business over with was a relief, and that closing paragraph of the letter is typical of a growing tone of contentment in several of John's missives through the early 1980s. From May 1980 to

August 1983, John and Madeline lived an uninterrupted stretch in Foxfield, John taking a break from teaching in Colgate and fully settling into Leitrim life, trying to write for a couple of hours each morning before tending to his small number of sheep and cattle or working in his vegetable garden at the front of the house in the afternoon.

They kept a rowing boat from which John liked to fish on both front and back lakes. Setting nightlines for eels was a favourite pursuit, as he tells Neill Joy: 'I cut hedges, shoot pheasants, go on the lake, very seldom go to the pub; but the usuals are in amazing steam every time I go.' The two pubs in walking distance were Quinn's and Ellis's of Fenagh, of opposing political loyalties, one traditionally Fine Gael, the other Fianna Fáil, with the McGaherns careful to give their custom to both houses. 'Two bars watch one another across a road', John tells us. 'The site of the one public telephone was a major focus. For some years now it stands outside the Fianna Fáil bar, but once it used to move with every change of government, all of thirty yards to the other side of the road.'

Early's of Mohill was another favourite haunt, with that town tending in these years to be the place where John and Madeline would shop. 'In its plain way I think it is beautiful', he would write. 'I like the town best in winter, the outskirts glistening with frost, the excitement on the faces of people in from the countryside for the late Saturday-night shopping, children and parcels being dragged about under the street-lamps. When the shopping is done, they go to the bars to meet the people they know and to discover the news, each locality to its own bar . . . I think of Mohill as one of the happiest towns in the world.'

The shooting John refers to in his letter to Joy, which had been a hobby for several years prior, came to an end after the killing of a hare, which filled him with remorse. Madeline began to keep bees, with hives kept in a small orchard behind a corrugated metal shed where hay and logs were stored and where John parked his small red tractor and mower. The land was poor, but John cared for it well, not allowing the rushes to take over, as happens if Leitrim land is neglected, and in 1985, the McGaherns expanded their smallholding by purchasing the neighbouring Earleys' farm.

The construction of the shed, with the assistance of neighbour Peter Woods, was an ongoing saga that eventually became an intriguing subplot in John's final novel. Its erection over several years gives an insight into John's patience, showing that his farming was a hobby, a distraction and not his main occupation.

Not coming from a farming family, John had limited boyhood experience of tending to animals and was not particularly knowledgeable about husbandry or other matters relating to the land. But he worked well with his neighbours, and they would advise him about what to do, when to dose cattle, to treat sheep for maggots and other seasonal chores. John, in turn, was a good neighbour, helping friends around the lake to round up cattle to bring to the mart or mowing grass in summer.

The saving of the hay was an important annual part of the calendar, as is reflected across so much of John's fiction, from 'Faith, Hope and Charity' to *Amongst Women* and beyond. John's mowing machine was the old-type finger-bar mower – not one of the more modern rotary mowers that some farmers were using by then. These finger-bar mowers were suitable for meadows that were not fertilised – ones that did not have a thick crop of grass. Uncle Pat would be called upon for any repairs to machinery.

Going to the mart was a big occasion, a chance to meet the neighbours, catch up on the news and sell or buy an animal. John was friendly with a local vet, Iggy Feeney, and he came to the rescue whenever an animal was unwell. The cattle were pets and would come down to the back window of the house when they wanted something. John and Madeline became attached to them, and they were often kept too long because of this attachment. 'We're sick of the rain', he tells Brian Friel in one letter. 'The cattle come up to the house and boo when they want a change of pasture.' Farming, then, became an important part of John's life, and he loved the connection it gave him to the land, the seasons, the neighbours. Having animals was a problem when the McGaherns went on longer stays in Colgate and elsewhere. Sometimes John got a neighbour to look after them when he was away; at other times, he reluctantly sold them and bought others when he returned.

Farming chores gave John exercise, and he remained fit and active until sickness took over in the final years. Neighbours would often call unannounced (the McGaherns had no phone until late 1986), as was typical in rural Ireland, and every Sunday Uncle Pat would drive over from Ballinamore for dinner. Francie and May McGarty from across the lake became particularly warm and beloved friends, with May knowing everything about the McGaherns' Aughaboniel side, being a native of the lakeshore.

John was always delighted to have an excuse not to write. While beginning to toy with the idea of a new novel in the early 1980s, he entered into a more sustainable working rhythm that occasionally concerned him such was its slow pace. 'Nothing seems to run for me this weather', he tells a friend in the spring of 1982.

> Every sentence has to be fought for. And it is hard to stay indoors in this good heartbreaking weather. We let our few cattle out last week. Every Thursday now, outside Luke Early's in Mohill, they are selling bundles of Early York and Flat Dutch. For me, that's a sort of happiness.

During this period, John and Madeline, in partnership with John's sister Margaret, a successful Dublin-based civil servant, bought a small terraced house in Stoneybatter. Margaret soon became dissatisfied with the purchase, and John and Madeline bought out her half. This decision came at a time of stark economic depression and high unemployment, when the very idea of a Dublin property boom would have seemed laughable.

Being able to stay in the house on visits to the capital, as well as frequently lending the place to friends, was a convenience over the years that followed; they were not to know that the neighbourhood, forty years later, would be replete with hipsters and chai lattes, houses selling for north of half a million euros. Writing to Frances Kiernan in March 1982, John describes the new place and brings the news from Ireland:

> The government fell here, and there was an election, an indecisive one, and it looks as if we'll have a crowd of crooks in power.
>
> Nothing else much. Saw a delightful production of She Stoops to Conquer in The Abbey. A few solid Australian movies. Re-reading Turgenev (what a wonder he is) and digging odd bits of the garden, the style desultory. I grow sort of fond of Dublin. Where the house is suits me, in the unfashionable middle of the city, near the markets, and the river, the dirty Liffey, with the old churches and the brewery chimneys on the hill. On the other side stands the Zoo and the Main Lunatic Asylum – no nation needed it so much.

Related to the dire economic state of the country was a period of marked political instability, and we see in John's letters a consistent suspicion of the Fianna Fáil party under the leadership of Charles Haughey and a concomitant respect for Garret FitzGerald, leader of the opposition Fine Gael. Typical is a note to Neill and Mary Joy in Colgate from January 1982:

> The Government fell last night, the most decent Government I suspect the State ever had. I'm sure Haughey and his crooks will come running back. The election is on Feb. 18th. Margaret wasn't happy with the Dublin house. So we bought her share, and redid the whole house, which has put our finances more or less on par with the country's.

The government referred to here was led by Garret FitzGerald, with support from Labour and several Independents. At 252 days, this term represented the second-shortest government in the history of the state. This administration, failing to get its budget through parliament on the issue of tax on children's shoes, set an election for 18 February. Charles Haughey led another weak coalition after the election, with his government lasting just 279 days.

This was a changing Ireland of increasing secularisation and political patronage where power was slowly being shifted from priest to politician, with all that had been good about religious tradition – as John saw it – swept away. This change is described with regretful accuracy in 'Oldfashioned': 'No one beats a path to the presbytery. The young priest is seldom there and has no housekeeper. Nights, when he's not supervising church bingo, he plays the guitar and sings at local hotels where he is a hit with tourists. He seldom wears black or the Roman collar.' Then a sardonic moral is drawn: 'A politician lives outside the village, and the crowd that once flocked to the presbytery now go to him instead.'

The purchase and refurbishment in Stoneybatter could not have happened without John's winning streak at the *New Yorker*, with four stories published in the five years between 1980 and 1984. These stories would form the backbone of his 1985 collection, *High Ground*, a book that would not appear in the USA until 1987. Yet again, John's American publishing life had taken an unexpected and unwelcome turn. *The Pornographer* was published by Harper & Row in 1979 to coincide with the Faber release in London, with *Getting Through* appearing in 1980. John had quickly established a happy working relationship with his editor, Fran McCullough. In August 1978, the firm sent photographer Jim Kalett to do a photo shoot in Foxfield, and John writes to McCullough that Kalett 'was here and shot and shot and talked. His wife was quiet and lovely. Their son drank Pepsi and played in the bales of hay.'

A December meeting with McCullough in New York went well, with publication dates agreed. And John, when he saw the proposed cover for the American edition of *The Pornographer* in May 1979, was pleased with its plainness, bearing just the title of the novel in cursive script and the legend 'A Novel by John McGahern' over a teal background with orange trim.

But John's luck with US publishers was yet again about to run out. No sooner had *The Pornographer* been released to largely positive reviews, including a long, somewhat contrary piece by John Updike in the *New Yorker* that praises John for writing 'entrancingly, with a lively pace and constant melody' but dislikes the central character's 'deadly coldness', than McCullough was fired from her position. John dashed off a sanguine note to Charles Monteith:

> My editor at Harper and Row, Fran McCullough, was fired last week. She really fought to have The Pornographer noticed. And that was without any advertising, because before she was fired they started to direct advertising away from her books. And so far a bare dollar hasn't been spent on the Porno Man.

Before clearing her desk, McCullough wrote to John to say that she had enjoyed working with him and that she thought the Updike piece 'a priggish, grudging piece of work'. In the months after writing his review, Updike had second thoughts about the tone he had struck, writing an unsolicited April note to John:

> Just the other night I got to thinking about the brief scene where the pornographer is beaten up by a pious lout and wondered at your tact in describing it, and if that wasn't all the retribution a reader could want. Your short stories, which I read afterwards, are magical, and honest with a purity rare on all five continents.

While John was tied into a contract that meant *Getting Through* would come out with Harper & Row later that year, he was not interested in staying with a firm he felt had been unfair to McCullough and had failed to get behind him when support mattered. What all this happenstance meant ultimately for *High Ground* was that the collection came out two years later in the USA than in Britain and that John was onto his fifth American publisher, with Tim Seldes helping to strike a deal with Viking for a collection of short stories and a novel.

As unsatisfactory as his American book deals continued to be, John could be happier both with his *New Yorker* work and with another project to which he had unexpectedly turned his mind at this time: the revision of *The Leavetaking* in light of a French translation by Alain Delahaye. John and Delahaye had first been in contact in the spring of 1980, when the Frenchman was translating *The Dark*, which would appear later that year as *L'Obscur* with Éditions de la Sphère. John was happy to explain to him details in the book that would mean little to a French audience.

These details included the significance of Mountjoy gaol, why shoes could be purchased in a draper's shop and the reasons why a job with the Electricity Supply Board might be desirable ('a semi-state body. Quiet office job').

This exchange of letters soon led to a warm working relationship. Delahaye gifted the McGaherns two handsome collections of his poetry, *L'Être perdu* (1977) and *L'Éveil des traversées* (1971). At the same time that Delahaye and John were beginning to know each other, another French publishing house, Presses de la Renaissance, bought the rights to *The Pornographer*, and John arranged for Delahaye to be the translator. The working relationship continued to bloom, with Delahaye, his wife and daughter coming to stay in Foxfield for a few days in August 1980, the two men talking over translation issues and saving hay. A subsequent gift to Madeline of Eugène Delacroix's journals became treasured volumes that were read repeatedly over the years that followed.

Le Pornographe was published as a paperback in France in autumn 1981, selling far better than the Faber hardback had on its release in Britain and Ireland two years earlier. By Christmas, Delahaye was writing to say that the novel had sold 2,500 copies and that Tony Cartano of Presses de la Renaissance was interested in publishing another of John's books of his choosing. *The Leavetaking* seemed the best option to John, though he wrote to Delahaye in late January 1982 that he would 'like to go through it before you'd start to translate'.

So began the unusual process of not just considering points in the novel that might need careful explanation to a translator but the actual revision of whole sections in English. What emerged was sufficiently different from the original to be issued by Faber as a 1984 paperback with an explanatory preface by the author:

> That the second part of this edition of *The Leavetaking* came to be reformed is in part an accident. Several years after its first publication, I found myself working through it again with its French translator, the poet Alain Delahaye. The more I saw of it the more sure I was

> that it had to be changed. The crudity I was attempting to portray, the irredeemable imprisonment of the beloved in reportage, had itself become blatant. I had been too close to the 'Idea,' and the work lacked that distance, that inner formality or calm, that all writing, no matter what it is attempting, must possess.

John concludes this brief but important statement of his aesthetic doctrine with a characteristic note of caution and self-criticism: 'What is certain is that this luck of a second chance is undeserved. It should have been written right the first time. What is still uncertain is if it is right even now.'

There was the usual come-and-go between author and translator: among other things, Delahaye was puzzled by what a 'pioneer pin' represented and what the 'modh múinte' was. Delahaye also caught and changed an error from 1974, in which the narrator's mother tries to ease her son's fear of a thunderstorm: 'You won't die and it's moving away. You can count between the clap and the flash. It's a mile away for every second you count.' Delahaye points out in a letter that the counting ought to take place between the lightning and the thunder. John agrees and corrects the error for the reworked book, which was published in France as *Journée d'adieu*, slightly ahead of the new English-language version from Faber, and further adding to John's growing reputation in France.

Delahaye's careful work and the easy friendship that developed between the two men were important factors in this French popularity. John's books were enthusiastically reviewed over the years across a range of French newspapers, from *Le Monde* to *Libération* to *Le Canard enchaîné*. He appeared on the France 2 arts show *Le Cercle de minuit* and was eventually honoured with both the Prix de Littérature Étrangère du Salon du Livre de Bordeaux 1994 and the Chevalier de l'Ordre des Arts et des Lettres.

Alongside his revision of *The Leavetaking*, John was working with Frances Kiernan at the *New Yorker* on trying to get several of the stories into shape. For 'High Ground', Kiernan had concerns about possible libel, with John writing to reassure her: 'Master Leddy and Senator Reegan are mostly based on real people, though they have fictitious names, and Reegan was never a Senator, and they are both dead. The place names are real. What do you suggest I change?' Those names were retained, and the story appeared in the magazine for 22 March 1982.

Another of the stories that John had submitted to Kiernan for consideration could not be so easily fixed and was eventually rejected. 'Bank Holiday' went through a series of radical revisions from its beginning in 1980 under the title 'The Natural Process' to its ultimate publication in 1985 as the closing story of *High Ground*. For a period, John referred in shorthand to the work in progress as 'the razor story', including as it did a scene where the chief character is confronted by his lover holding a cut-throat razor beneath her bedsheets, ready to castrate the man. The piece, as eventually published, contains nothing so melodramatic and is, in fact, the closest John ever gets to writing a happy short story. Not even this factor alleviated the dislike of the reviewer in the *New York Times*: 'Mr McGahern is more persuasive in evoking the moon's dark side than in describing moonlight and roses.' John knew that 'Bank Holiday' had to be part of the collection; that he should make it the final story is indicative of his high regard. Named partly in homage to the Patrick Kavanagh poem of the same title that John admired, the story uses memories of Mary Keelan from the mid-1960s to enter into a meditation on the nature of time and its passing.

Central to John's thinking in this period on how time ought to work in fiction is Paolo Vivante's *The Homeric Imagination: A Study of Homer's Poetic Perception of Reality*. Vivante's subtitle offered John a key for his own work. Madeline had known Vivante and his family since as far back as the early 1950s, when she lived in their Siena villa with her father while they both studied music at the Accademia Musicale Chigiana. They were reacquainted in the spring of 1979, when the McGaherns visited McGill University in Montreal, where John read from his work, and Paolo, a professor of classics, gifted them a copy of his book.

Madeline vividly recalls the moment when John opened the book, reading in concentrated silence for several minutes. She had never before seen him respond so immediately to a volume. To read Vivante is to read McGahern. One is struck again and again across his study by lines that must have been strikingly useful to and redolent of John's own thought processes about artistic representation and the workings of the imagination.

'Can any story', wondered Vivante, 'be told as if its incidents took place entirely by themselves, in their own time, out of relation with any definite period?' In answering this question, he finds himself drawn to a Greek epic: 'Such is in Homer the time of nature. Its basic unit is the day.' John quotes from Vivante's study in early drafts of 'Bank Holiday', when he has the story's central character, the middle-aged, high-ranking civil servant Patrick McDonough, become obsessed with a particular line he returns to again and again, read in a Dublin bookshop: 'McDonough had come to Hannas to look at one book, a book on Homer's world and a phrase that had fascinated him for months.'

The phrase then quoted comes from Chapter 4 of *The Homeric Imagination*, titled 'Time and Life in Homer': 'What is he doing with his life, we say: and our judgement makes up for the failure to realize sympathetically the natural process of living.' Here Vivante expands on what he sees as Homer's particular way of treating time, and it is here that John and Vivante overlap most strikingly. 'Homeric poetry is concise, forcible. Its condensed power partly resides in the way it renders the lapse of time, of life', writes Vivante: 'what we mean by life and experience is integrated into the meaning of each verbal form, while for Homer the actual fact of living is nothing else but being alive, keeping alive, growing'.

Interestingly, in later drafts of 'Bank Holiday', and in the final published version, all mention of Homer is excised, as is the quote from Vivante. But the plot line of the book to which McDonough feels compelled to return, but not to buy, is retained in a scene where the bookstore manager offers a discount but is repelled:

> The manager moved away, flicking the feathers along a row of spines in a gesture of annoyance. The spell was ended, but it was fair enough; the shop had to sell books, and he knew that if he bought the book it was unlikely that he would ever give it the same attention again.

While Homer and Vivante are no longer named, their presence informs John's treatment of time in the story. That McDonough's basic unit of time is the day is made clear throughout. There is a telling gloss when the young American woman he woos in the story agrees to a date: 'A whole day was secured.' This supremacy of 'the day' is underlined further in McDonough's pained remembrance of a previous passionate affair's end: 'It was eerie to set down those days beside the days that had just gone by, call them by the same name. How slowly those days had moved, as if waiting for something to begin: now all the days were speeding, slipping silently by like air.'

John is open about his admiration for Vivante in 'What Is My Language?', his essay on *The Islandman*, Tomás Ó Criomhthain's account of life on the Blaskets:

> I have taken the original argument – that style itself must be the outcome of a view of reality – from Paolo Vivante's great work, *The Homeric Imagination*. Ó Criomhthain's style is such an outcome, and while it would be foolish to compare him to Homer, he did give vivid utterance to a society brought to refinement by the conditions of an unchanging reality over many days and generations.

If the basic unit of time for Homer is the day, the same is true in John's later work, with *High Ground* in general – and 'Bank Holiday' in particular – marking a turning point. His characters' reverence for the day and their fear of time-wasting is a constant, as it is for Ó Criomhthain's islandman. This structuring of time around individual worlds called days gives much of John's fiction, and particularly his late novels, a feeling of mythic timelessness. Consider, for instance, the opening lines of *That They May Face the Rising Sun*:

> The morning was clear. There was no wind on the lake. There was also a great stillness. When the bells rang out for Mass, the strokes trembling on the water, they had the entire world to themselves.
>
> The doors of the house were open. Jamesie entered without knocking and came in noiselessly until he stood in the doorway of the large room where the Ruttledges were sitting. He stood as still as if waiting under trees for returning wildfowl. He expected his discovery to be quick. There would be a cry of surprise and reproach; he would counter by accusing them of not being watchful enough. There would be welcome and laughter.

What sort of language is this? The opening paragraph has a numinous, transcendent calm to it, very far from straightforward realist storytelling – what Vivante calls 'a pervasive subjective craving for what is not'. And then the following lines are told almost entirely in the subjunctive mood, where everything is predictable because life in this small place among these dear friends has become so quiet and repetitive that it has a circular, ahistorical, mythic quality. Vivante argues that this approach to time is characteristic of the Homeric imagination:

> This strong feeling for the days and for the life which they enclose accounts for the perfect stillness and almost timeless atmosphere which we find in the poems whenever the moments of tension subside and people, or things, simply exist in themselves and by themselves. Men and women seem then immune from all hazard, as solid and whole in their natural life as a full-grown tree.

The subjunctive, which works so well to give this feeling of time that is no longer linear (or 'that did not have to run to any conclusion', as described in the final line of 'Gold Watch'), is a favourite mood of John's prose. Another paragraph-length passage driven by the subjunctive mood comes quickly after the opening of *That They May Face the Rising Sun*, with a description of how Jamesie's brother Johnny will be welcomed home for his annual summer trip from England: 'The holy pictures and the wedding photographs would be taken down, the glass wiped and polished. His bed would be made with crisp linen and draped with the red blanket.' And so on. That the paragraph ends with a notably epic sweep is not coincidental: 'The house couldn't have been prepared any better for a god coming home to his old place on earth.'

This temporally slanted facet of *High Ground* is picked up on in the *Sunday Times*: 'McGahern has an exceptionally acute sense of time in all its aspects, from time of day to human ageing, and perhaps his most distinctive quality is his remarkable quietism, an acceptance of transience that is not resignation.' The review is typical of critical reaction to the book, which was almost unanimously positive, one exception being, yet again, Terence de Vere White in the *Irish Times*: 'I must confess to an uneasiness about this writer; his preoccupation with grace-notes leads to preciousness.' Seamus Deane, on the other hand, praises John for 'writing with the accuracy of a man obsessed'. Seamus Heaney continues to understand the work as unique in its consistent quality and import:

> As always, the melody of the prose is in tune with the characteristic themes of loss or compromise or sadly pondered decision. As always, we visit the country of memory, not in order to savour its nostalgias but to map more accurately its network of byways and blocked-off roads.
>
> At such moments we realise that John McGahern writes poetry as it was defined by Wordsworth – a history of feeling and a science of feeling.

When Colm Tóibín attended a packed reading from the new work given by John in Galway's Nuns Island Arts Centre, he found a man comfortable in his skin and in command of his audience:

> Tonight he is funny. Tonight he does not select parts of his work which dwell on death, isolation, the loss of love. Tonight he is satirical, reading with enormous gusto, acting out the lines: the drunken teacher talking to the drunken locals in a pub; neighbours back-biting;

> the peculiarities of the gentry; a local politician . . . Standing there on the raised platform he has a teacher's command over his audience.

Now turned fifty, John had become one of Ireland's most respected living writers. But he was as unlikely to run a lap of honour as he was to sink into a midlife crisis. 'I'm interested in what I'm trying to write now and it has always been that way', he tells one interviewer. 'Assessing oneself fifty – or any other age for that matter – would seem ridiculous to me. That is for other people.' Nobody could have known as he batted away such questions – not least himself – that with his next book he would move from critical respect to popular stardom.

14
Plain Ordinary Work
1985–90

A writer knows that he is only as good as the next day's page.

JOHN McGAHERN

Over lunch with Charles Monteith in the Garrick Club on the afternoon of Thursday, 1 November 1979, John told his editor that he expected to finish and submit his next book by the end of 1980. The novel was to be 'a love story set in London'. And that certainly remained the intention for some time:

> When I came to write *Amongst Women* I thought I was writing a novel about that lost generation of the 1950s and 1960s, a lost generation that disappeared into England. They included most of my family and most of the people I went to school with. I worked in England myself as a young man and again after the banning and the dismissal. The first images of *Amongst Women* are a park near London and a couple in it. It was near the docks. Long-distance lorry drivers used to sleep opposite the park, and in the winter the leaves would disappear off the trees and you could see as far as an artificial lake, the swings and the deer. In the summertime it was a wall of green. All that English experience, which must have been about two hundred pages, got pushed out by that Irish family, the Morans, and the London scenes with which the novel began were completely marginalised.

Just as well Monteith knew by now to take John's more optimistic timetables with a pinch of salt, though at least Faber had become used to their man delivering near-perfect, if crucifyingly slow, copy. 'When he hands the book over, he has done all the editing that is necessary', commented the firm's Jon Riley, several years later. 'All one can do is read it, telephone him and say, "John, it was worth the wait."'

The Garrick conversation is our first archival tremor of what would become, a decade later, one of the best-loved, and most highly respected, books of the Irish twentieth century, *Amongst Women*. One year later, Monteith retired as chairman at Faber, with Matthew Evans taking over the role. While Monteith continued in an advisory capacity, the company was modernising quickly, and John would never again have quite the same close editorial bond as he did with the man who had discovered him back in the spring of 1961 and for whom he retained genuine affection up to his death in 1995. 'I owe you too many, and too deep, debts of gratitude and affection to want to name them here', writes John in a letter to mark the retirement. 'The dedication page in Nightlines tells more about the seriousness of my feelings than anything I can say here. And that you accepted it is a continuing source of pleasure for me.'

The next day, John writes to Frances Kiernan to tell her that he has finished another story, that he is working on a play but is distracted: 'I have ideas, maybe too many ideas, and I'd like to work in the theatre, but I keep putting it off.' An old problem re-emerges. 'There's another novel it seems I'll have to write', he confides. 'And that's dismaying. Some of the scenes I can't get away from, which is probably some of the troubles with the play.'

A full year on from his Garrick declaration, he seems to have made little progress, though the images that always sparked work for him were circling. While sometimes a novel appeared in his imagination near to complete – *The Dark* is the best (and possibly only) example – there were other occasions where the process took long fermentation. In this period of his writing life, one gets the sense that he is sometimes working towards other projects in order to avoid the grave responsibility of a new novel.

When asked once if he would like to be free of writing altogether, John responded 'yes', as 'one knows that it's only through suffering that anybody grows and only a fool would like to embrace suffering'. And so, to avoid the acute pain of more serious writing, a long-discussed project to edit a 'Faber Book of Irish Prose' came back into play. Originally floated by Monteith as far back as 1971 as an anthology of Irish short stories to replace the Valentin Iremonger-edited Faber collection of 1960, this project never crystallised. John waxed and waned in his enthusiasm over the years. Now that a new novel was intruding insistently into his imagination, he sought shelter in planning the anthology that never, however intriguing a prospect, came to pass.

Though stillborn, the outline John sends to Monteith is valuable as an indicator of the Irish prose writers he considered worth reading:

> It will be in two volumes: Volume 1, 1860–1920; Volume 2, 1920–1980. In the final arrangement the shape of the work would be more important than the dates. The first volume could stop short of 1920, or go some years over.
>
> I'd begin with Carleton, the first important writer working in English whose base was Gaelic. He is as obvious as Lawson would be to an Australian. It will not be a short story anthology, though it will probably have to lean heavily on that form, because of space, and its strength in the tradition.
>
> The book would claim its place as literature beside the Faber or Oxford Book of Verse, but it would stay outside their territory. It would include the novel, drama, autobiography, and even criticism, if such that looked permanent could be found. The one work of verse to be included is Yeats's <u>Purgatory</u>, since I see it as a key work, and whose rhythm is half prose anyhow. The immediate figures are Carleton (short story), Green (<u>Autobiography of a Landlord's Agent</u>), Somerville and Ross, George Moore, Yeats, Joyce, Forrest Reid (the novel), Beckett, Corkery, Kavanagh (the novel), O'Connor, O'Crohan (from <u>The Islandman</u>), O'Cadhain (if he can be translated), O'Casey, Synge, Behan (perhaps), McLaverty.
>
> I won't go into the 'moderns' at this stage, which may even include myself, and the problem will be that of exclusion. I will need to do a great deal of reading and re-reading, and names will be added to,

> maybe even taken away. Shaw and Wilde will be a real problem but I cannot see them being included now.

Monteith writes back enthusiastically, though somewhat dismayed by the inclusion of Yeats's late play in a prose anthology. But John is insistent:

> I'd include Purgatory even if it were pure verse, because it is so important that I couldn't afford to hold verse against it. As it is, it's ½ prose, verse crossed with a prose rhythm (see A General Introduction to my Work). Yeats himself began his Ox. B. of Mod. Verse with a very good piece of prose (Pater), much better than a lot of the verse that followed. There are other precedents. It's the only verse likely to be included.

One can share Monteith's discomfort. Despite John's defence, pleading Yeats's eccentric editing of *The Oxford Book of Modern Verse* as justification, to include *Purgatory* in a prose anthology feels needlessly contrarian. So why the insistence? This achievement was a play that had long fascinated him, a meditation on fathers and sons, genealogy and the fall of Anglo-Ireland. As John noted in the context of introducing letters by the playwright's father:

> In its starkness of symbol and setting it presages *Waiting for Godot*. Based on a Sligo ghost story, *Purgatory* contains many of Yeats's recurrent ideas. A play as powerful and rich will act as many mirrors, and it has always fascinated me that every line of *Purgatory* is filled with the drama of opposites.

'The Faber Book of Irish Prose' never did come to pass. One always gets the sense through John's letters that at one point he saw the proposal as a possible source of money but that his heart was never fully in it, and with Monteith slipping further into Faber's shadows the project was allowed to die a quiet death.

But the rhythms of *Purgatory* would not go away so easily: the preoccupation with shattered families, with the Big House, with Irish historical darkness started to make itself felt in John's thinking around a new novel, his tyrannical father and the rise and fall of a place that his imagination had begun to call Great Meadow. 'Monaghan Day', as John soon titled the new project, continued to take shape through the mid-1980s, if slowly, and by late 1986 he could write enthusiastically to Alain Delahaye that he had 'lately done real work on the novel'.

The year before, *High Ground* had been another critical success but popular failure. Fewer than a thousand copies were sold in hardback, granting John's third book in a row a quiet disappearance. This fate came despite stellar reviews and a growing reputation in France, where *The Barracks* was published in 1986, as *La Caserne*, to considerable success. This novel eventually formed part of the curriculum for the *agrégation*, a competitive examination to recruit senior secondary-school teachers, thus opening up John's work to an even wider French audience.

Offers of work continued to arrive, one such from the University of Victoria in British Columbia, where the McGaherns decided to spend the spring of 1987. The job was untaxing, consisting of one weekly seminar with twelve students. 'I took the bus out to the campus 8 miles from the city centre', John tells one friend, 'and never put foot there again until the following Wednesday. As a way to teach, I recommend it highly.'

John and Madeline enjoyed Victoria as a city, living in a hotel on the harbour, a two-bedroom suite with a kitchen and bathroom. This location could at times seem quiet and 'a bit depressing because of the crowds of old people escaping the prairie winters'. But the city was prosperous and well-mannered, with striking vistas wherever one looked:

> There was a great Victorian heap of a hotel, The Empress, sweeping views of the Pacific bristling with U. S. and Russian warships, the mountains of Washington State white on the other side of the strait of Juan de Fuca. The place was full of flowers and great trees and ½ magical islands.

The restaurants were cheap and varied, with excellent seafood and outstanding sushi. John especially enjoyed the local white wines 'with faint tastes of herbs or flowers'. Perhaps best of all, Victoria was where he first came upon the work of Alice Munro, a writer who would become a sustaining favourite and whose *The Moons of Jupiter* and *The Progress of Love* formed part of his reading at this time.

If the new novel had begun life in 1979 as a love story set in London, by the summer of 1987 its frame had moved some distance away from that conception and was edging towards the *Amongst Women* we know, a novel set in western Ireland, with an ageing Republican war veteran as its central character. The Canadian trip, as John acknowledges to Tim Seldes, injected some pace back into the writing and allowed him to see the developing narrative from a necessary distance: 'To justify the climate of violence in the novel I found I had to add an opening chapter which echoed the revolution of 1920/1921 and this affected subsequent chapters. This set me back too but I think it improves the novel greatly.'

And so the opening scene of *Amongst Women*, which circles around the failed Monaghan Day reunion of Moran and his old IRA colleague, the cattle dealer McQuaid, was now anchoring the book. John finishes his letter to Seldes by commenting on 'a rather handsome award' he is to receive in Galway. The cheque for £2,000, presented in the ballroom of the Great Southern Hotel as part of the Galway Arts Festival on 5 August, was another of those small sums which remained so crucial to keeping the show on the road in these otherwise lean years of slow sales and even slower productivity.

Another period spent away from Foxfield – this time in Trinity College Dublin in the spring of 1988 – allowed John to get close to the finishing line. 'Trinity is pleasant and easy', he tells Tom Kilroy.

> I have a beautiful room in Rubrics, with 6 light windows, 3 on the front entrance, 3 on the square behind. The work is light. Unfortunately I find it much better than Leitrim for getting my own work done. Madeline has been here a few times but it doesn't suit a couple and we don't like imposing too much on Francie with the animals.

John's humour flashes: 'The W.C. is downstairs and outside but it's all right if you hold your trousers.' Nicky Grene, John's Trinity host and a professor of English, whom he had not met prior to taking up the visiting position, recalls his embarrassment on realising the primitive lavatory arrangement. John quickly put him at his ease.

> I remember my first meeting with John when he came to us as Writer Fellow. I had never met him before, never even seen a photo of him that I could recall, and I imagined a difficult, saturnine figure, so I was astonished when this genial red-cheeked countryman turned up in my office only wanting to talk about the price of heifers in Wicklow – he had somehow learned I too was a part-time farmer.

With Charles Monteith having taken a step back from the Faber front line, John felt himself ever more detached from the company that now had Matthew Evans at the helm and a young Robert McCrum as editorial director. Faber's list expanded rapidly and successfully through the 1980s, new names including Kazuo Ishiguro, Wendy Cope, Peter Carey and Milan Kundera. In 1988 and 1989, the firm won back-to-back Bookers with Carey's *Oscar and Lucinda* and Ishiguro's *The Remains of the Day*.

A new publicity department was set up, moving away from the old model of just sending review copies to literary editors. While this tactic helped sell more books, the strategy could sometimes seem vulgar: a planned 1984 helicopter tour flying Craig Raine and Seamus Heaney between readings was nixed by Heaney after the story was reported in the *Sunday Times*.

John increasingly felt out of things, and when Robin Robertson, then editorial director at Secker & Warburg, asked in 1988 if he might see 'Monaghan Day' as the manuscript then stood, John was happy to oblige. John had first worked with Robertson in 1984, when the Scot was assistant fiction editor at Penguin and was commissioning new work for their *Firebird* series of anthologies. Robertson eventually purchased 'Like All Other Men' for £125 and included the story in *Firebird 4: New Writing from Britain and Ireland* (1985).

He and his then wife, Clare Reihill, who was from Irvinestown, County Fermanagh, subsequently visited Foxfield as part of a Secker & Warburg publishing project, *32 Counties: Photographs of Ireland by Donovan Wylie*, of which copies were signed by each of the thirty-two contributing authors. At this meeting, McGahern discussed his increasing unease at Faber and agreed to show Robertson the manuscript of his novel with a possible view to switching publishers.

By the summer of 1989, now aware of John's mounting dissatisfaction and not wanting to lose him from their list, Faber made an attractive offer. Robertson returned the manuscript, with John writing in thanks:

> I was a bit depressed taking it from its envelope. Obviously I would have liked for you to have seen it into print. I'll be grateful to you always. What happened was this. Faber doubled your offer and, depending on its acceptance agreed to make an offer for The Collected Stories within 3 months. Seldes thought it a very good offer and he felt that nobody wanted a bidding situation.

While Robertson was disappointed, the two men remained on good terms and would meet occasionally in the years that followed in Foxfield or in Blake's of Enniskillen.

The stage was now set. Faber would publish the novel in May 1990, cranking up their new publicity mechanisms in a way that had not been employed with any of John's previous seven books. It only remained now to agree on a title. As late as 24 October 1989, Faber wrote to Tim Seldes calling the book 'Monaghan Day', with 'The Morans' as another possible title. For a short period, John pondered titling his new work 'The Family'. But after a Galway dinner with Tom and Julia Kilroy, where Julia suggested the title 'Amongst Women', it was immediately clear that this choice was much the best possible one. Outside of Ireland, would anyone even know how to pronounce 'Monaghan' correctly? There is an arresting overlap between the novel's setting – a house dominated by women in the face of a tyrannical man – and the novel's frequent recourse to the 'Hail Mary'. That Moran uses the prayer as a kind of controlling punctuation mark on the day makes *Amongst Women* still more perfect as a title.

'I finished the novel', John writes to Alain Delahaye. 'It will be published next May. It is my best work but several times I thought I'd never have the strength to finish it.' The insistence that *Amongst Women* was a peculiarly difficult book to write comes through in much of John's correspondence from this period as he begins to get feedback from those people to whom he had arranged to have review copies sent.

Colm Tóibín, who had been so impressed by *The Pornographer* a decade earlier and who had got to know John better after meeting him at the Galway event around the publication of *High Ground*, knew immediately that what he was reading was a masterpiece. Tóibín saw that *Amongst Women* represented not just another admirable McGahern product but an important moment in the history of the Irish novel. John thanked him for his 'kindness and extraordinary generosity', going on to say that there 'were times when I thought it had me beaten and that I was finished as a writer'.

Two days later, he said the same thing to Seamus Heaney, who had written in praise of the novel: 'It is a work of heart-breaking purity and surety. Cello and honey, as Mandelstam said of bits of Dante. It wakened me and read me inside out.' John responded in a warm, gossipy letter, at ease now that the novel was off his hands: 'There's not much news. The bonesetter died, helicoptered to Dublin in the end. All the rest of us cling to the beds, some more shakily than others.' From there, he moved to a friend's new circumstances:

> The P.P. retired at 92. They gave him a wallet of notes and a colour tv. The housekeeper got an automatic washing machine, which was wheeled on stage. The P.P. said if he'd got the washing machine early on he mightn't have needed the housekeeper. I couldn't get your line about praising the homemade bread out of my head for days afterwards. I suppose it's that whole lost world. My poor uncle died in the town. I miss him.

John, as ever happy to switch between registers, concluded by wishing Heaney luck in his newly acquired role as Oxford Professor of Poetry. The letter is a telling snapshot of life in Foxfield at a time when John was, unknowingly, about to become a literary star, winning the popular acclaim for *Amongst Women* that had, up till now, evaded him. Not that such garlands mattered in the slightest other than that money inevitably made certain aspects of life smoother. John would never have to teach again, for instance, unless he chose to, and the remaining periods in Colgate – one in 1991, the other in 2001 – were done to fulfil previously agreed obligations or as a matter of courtesy.

The bonesetter mentioned in the letter was Boolie Woods, source of one of John's very favourite aphorisms: 'Life is a shaky venture . . . if you think about it.' The clergyman was Fr Frank McCabe, parish priest in Fenagh, with whom John, despite his failure to believe in God, got along very well and who made a point of coming to visit this writer of dirty books when he moved to the parish, without ever making any demands.

Though he lived to the good age of eighty-four, Uncle Pat's death was a hard blow. John and Pat had been close since John was a small boy: the earliest of his letters to survive sees him as an eight-year-old 'guggering' – or planting seed potatoes – with his uncle. Pat was a great help to his sister Sue when she lived in Aughawillan and other scattered south Leitrim locations through the early 1940s with her seven children, when the Sergeant was stationed in Cootehall. When John and Madeline returned to live in Leitrim from the mid-1970s, Pat came back into John's life as a support and a beloved friend.

The day of the funeral, 8 February 1988, was wintery and raw. After Mass in Ballinamore, the remains were brought to be buried by St Brigid's Church on the high ground around Corleehan, near the Cavan border, where he and Sue and all the McManus family had been born and reared. John retells the events to Neill Joy two days later:

> Uncle Pat died of cancer here in hospital last Saturday, February 6th. We took him home on the Sunday and buried him under the

> mountains this Monday. A light snow was swirling about the churchyard. The priest quoted from The Hound of Heaven. Many of the faces in the enormous crowd looked ½ wild. Few had any notion what the priest was talking about. I heard them say they thought he'd never stop. We gave a dinner afterwards in the restaurant where Pat had eaten for 40 years. For us a dear presence is gone. Mary and Theo may remember buying petrol at his garage. 'This dying is a cunt of a business,' he said to me in the last days. I fear that's more in my line than F. Thompson.

This day was one of only two occasions in their life together that Madeline saw John shed a tear.

* * *

Amongst Women was published by Faber on 8 May 1990. The novel immediately went to the top of the best-seller chart in Ireland, moving over 30,000 copies in hardback before the end of the year, followed by over 175,000 paperbacks the following year. In 1998, the work was made into a four-part television drama starring Tony Doyle as Moran and broadcast on the BBC. The novel continues to sell steadily to this day and is taught in Irish secondary schools and in universities around the world. John could not have predicted such a remarkable success. 'We had no idea how the novel would be received', he wrote to Nicky Grene, 'and are a bit taken aback by the reception.'

How can we account for this sudden change in fortunes? To acknowledge the book as obviously the work of a prose master is not sufficient. The same was equally true of the previous three books, which between them had sold fewer than 3,000 copies in hardback. *Amongst Women* was certainly marketed in a savvier and more focused fashion than any of John's previous books. While he may not have liked certain aspects of Faber's modernisation under Matthew Evans, there can be little doubt that advertising and smart behind-the-scenes promotion played an important role in putting the novel in the best possible position.

'There's a reading and reception in Trinity College and another in London', John wrote to Alain Delahaye, continuing:

> There will be no peace till it is over. Already journalists have been here and more are on the way. Francie won't come near the house without first making certain that all is clear. The one consolation is that many seem excited by the novel. And it is plain ordinary work. Not an elephant in sight.

John developed a good working relationship with Joanna Mackle of Faber's relatively recently created publicity department, after they first met in Dublin in 1987 at a dinner hosted by Seamus Heaney. The jacket image of the Irish tricolour was fixed upon early and to great effect, with John putting up no resistance despite previous squabbles with Charles Monteith about cover art. The cover worked as a kind of declaration that this novel was a state-of-the-nation book, whether that was John's intention or not: the Troubles were ongoing, and fraught Anglo-Irish relations were rarely out of the news. Some readers would misinterpret the semiotics, as John would discover on Booker Prize night.

Among those journalists courted by Faber in advance of publication was John Walsh, literary editor at the *Sunday Times*. Walsh liked the novel sufficiently to make a trip to Foxfield and interview John at home. 'His fifth novel, *Amongst Women* (from the line 'Blessed art thou amongst women' from the Hail Mary of the Catholic rosary), is published next week', wrote Walsh. 'Its emotional themes – of family love and hatred, escape, ritual, futility, rejection and moral hypocrisy – have all appeared in McGahern's work before, but never with such assured and stylised artistry.'

Those themes are all there for sure, and they are contained within a short book – fewer than 200 pages – that is more recognisably a novel than anything else John ever wrote. If he had insisted in the past that books such as *The Barracks* and *The Dark* were closer to poetry than to prose, then *Amongst Women* is more classically novelistic: a family saga replete with love affairs, where the characters are all named and differentiated, marriages take place, and death acts as a full stop.

That assessment is not in any way to criticise the book, merely to attempt an explanation for its success. Novel readers like reading novels. Walsh compares *Amongst Women* in his preview to its forebears in the Russian tradition, a comparison that would have been pleasing to John, given his reverence for Turgenev and Chekhov. 'The feeling that you are reading the lost work of some mid nineteenth century Russian master is strong, but so is the sense that only in Ireland could such a haunting amalgam of stark realism and romantic wistfulness as that of his best work, be found.'

Another important reason for the success of *Amongst Women* is that the novel was serialised on BBC Radio 4. In advance of that serialisation, the station sent the novelist Paul Bailey – the man who, coincidentally, had preceded John as Northern Arts Fellow in Newcastle some seventeen years earlier – to Leitrim to interview the author for its *Kaleidoscope* arts show. After arranging to meet in Luke Early's, the two men and the producer, Anthony Denselow, drove out to Foxfield, where whiskey was produced and conversation flowed. Bailey saw *Amongst Women* as John's 'most profound statement to date on the difficulties of loving, a theme he has explored in all his work'.

This comment is a judgement that John, in a rare lyrical flourish, seems to endorse towards the end of the interview when thinking about the centrality of place: 'The shape of that private world I carry around with me seems to be completely of Ireland. Place is incredibly important to me because I see place as where love happens. Place is the envelope in which we put love's letters.' But the relatively new, post-colonial Ireland that forms the backdrop for the novel seems a far cry from somewhere that values love:

> The whole family is a representation of a society and a country because the whole political emphasis of the time was of being enclosed and being an island. Of course it was a very young country. When this country was founded there was no member of the first cabinet older than 26 years . . . People like de Valera wanted . . . I mean it's very,

> very close to Fascism and the notion of the blue race, the blue blood . . . One of the reasons for learning gaelic was that if everybody knew gaelic it would keep all foreign corrupting influence out, which is practically the whole of civilisation.

John is rarely thought of as an especially political writer, and the above statement is about as close as he gets to admitting that his work – and this novel in particular – is tempered by a particular view of Irish history. That said, when Bailey tries to draw him on some kind of judgement of the tyrannical Moran, John is adamant in his refusal: 'I have no judgements to make on him and in fact I think it's only bad writers that make judgements.'

Bailey, like John Walsh, is interested in the novel's treatment of time and the difficulties in deciding on when *Amongst Women* is actually set. John's answer to this problem is revealing about the unusual ways in which he believed Ireland had developed over the course of his lifetime:

> Essentially I see it as a nineteenth century society that was kept in a mould until The Beatles and people like that came along. And then in the late 1960s we were in the twenty first century. We almost skipped a century. I find the country fascinating; it's almost a medieval society and it's also a high tech society . . . Of course sexual equality is quite rightly here as it is elsewhere.

The feeling that you could be in the nineteenth century is one shared by many readers. We are given almost no historical pointers beyond the fact that this is a world where cars exist but are still a luxury and great swathes of Ireland's young have moved to London to make their way, thus suggesting sometime in the 1950s.

Moran speaks about events that occurred in Irish history as if they were as straightforward as yesterday's news headlines. Driving from Great Meadow to Strandhill with Rose, in an attempt to make up for an ill-considered outburst a few nights previously he comments on a celebrated moment in the Nine Years' War of 350 years past: '"O'Neill and

O'Donnell crossed here with cannon and horses on the way to Kinsale in one night," he told her as the car was climbing into the low Curlews. "They were able to cross because the black frost made the ground hard as rock that night."'

History is fluid and alive. Indeed, at one point in the novel, John borrows a famous Yeats phrase from 'Easter, 1916' to describe historical process. Sheila and Mona, the young Moran sisters, are 'so poised on the edge of their own lives that they listened as if hearing about the living stream they were about to enter'. John was not to know that 1990 would mark a moment of profound change in Irish and world history: German reunification, the first Gulf War, the fall of Margaret Thatcher, the election of Mary Robinson to be Ireland's first female president and the invigoration of the tricolour in the stadia of Italy as the Irish football team went on an unlikely World Cup march, leaving the country at fever pitch through that high summer.

As well as selling in its tens of thousands, *Amongst Women* won the £10,000 *Irish Times*/Aer Lingus Prize, the £2,000 Hughes Prize and the £50,000 Guinness Peat Aviation Book Award, then the world's richest book prize. The last-named award saw John chosen by John Updike as the winner and presented with his cheque on Gay Byrne's *The Late Late Show* in December 1992. As with his previous 1967 appearance on the show, he hated the razzmatazz of it all, as he writes to some American friends: 'It was a horrible evening – except for the Award itself – and John Updike was stylish in a quiet attractive way and his words about the book were extraordinarily generous.' Updike's judgement was published in the *Irish Times* on 2 January 1993. Asked to choose his favourite from a shortlist of six widely differing Irish books, among them Eavan Boland's poetry collection *Outside History* and J. J. Lee's *Ireland, 1912–1985*, Updike had to make a subjective decision:

> In the end I had to select the book that gave me most pleasure, or can we say gratification, in the reading and in the reflective backward glance – the book that stirred the most sparks of recognition in me,

and that left the most embers of glowing afterthought, on issues both Irish and human.

In choosing *Amongst Women*, he found himself trying to explain Irish writing's startling success: 'The forked linguistic condition, it could be, of Ireland, echoing its forked political condition as a rebellious colony and now as a divided island, has helped give the voice of Irish writers urgency, that urgent *need to tell* which is the first condition for narrative or poetic art.'

His concluding thoughts about the novel supply a quotation that has appeared as blurb more often than any other on this work and on John's subsequent publications: 'McGahern brings us that tonic gift of the best fiction, the sense of truth – the sense of a transparency that permits us to see imaginary lives more clearly than we see our own, a sight that cleanses us even as it saddens and frightens.'

Updike's comment about *Amongst Women* being written 'without any apparent effort' is one that will resonate with many readers. Madeline remembers feeling the same as she was typing up the manuscript, that this writing had a different, more finished quality: 'As I was typing it I did feel that it was seamless, kind of perfect . . . it was as good as he could do.' For future generations of Irish writers, as well as being an inspiration, this masterpiece could prove a burden. As Donal Ryan recounts in one forthright essay:

> I read *Amongst Women* in 1995 or 1996. It almost finished me as an aspiring writer. How could a book be this good? Existence is inchoate and incoherent and senseless. How could this representation of existence feel so resolved, so correct, so like it hadn't been written at all but alchemised from flesh to paper and ink? How could this Moran character have seared his mark so indelibly on my consciousness?

The experience of reading the novel forced Ryan into making himself a promise:

I resolved there and then never to try to match John McGahern. To put him away. He was dangerous to my brittle sense of myself and my abilities. His bar was far too high. It took me years to shake off the sense that there was no point in trying; that McGahern had said already all that needed to be said, had created art of such clarity and pristine beauty that no paltry offering of mine could or should share the same shelves.

Amongst Women, of all John's novels, can at first glance appear the most straightforward. But its very simplicity is a trap, offering us few points of entry or of exit. 'McGahern brings all this off with extraordinary subtlety', writes John Boland in the *Evening Press*. 'The prose has a deceptive simplicity, so unadorned that it seems almost plain.' And in the *Observer* John Banville, comparing the book's economy of language to Beckett, warns the reader to be vigilant: 'Do not let the plain style or the quiet tone deceive you; this novel is the real thing.' Those obvious literary allusions and influences that characterised John's middle period have been ironed out alongside the libidinal drive that had so enervated and tormented his earlier narrators. To honestly engage with the book feels as much like living as reading.

'*Amongst Women* is much more than a good book', wrote Nicola Murphy in *The Times*, 'it is an overwhelming experience.' That sort of comment is not unusual, and the book got reviewed with near-breathless excitement on both sides of the Atlantic and further afield. When *Amongst Women* was published in France as *Entre toutes les femmes*, *Le Canard enchaîné* revelled in Moran's character despite conceding the attraction's paradox ('whom the reader is unable to completely dislike, even in his worst dictatorial moments'). This review continued: 'Moran is humanity's prehistory, going back to the Precambrian, his heart is a block of lava in fusion, his hair is wild vegetation, his thoughts echo in Plato's cave, and his three daughters are his philosophical stone . . . But what a bastard!' And yet the reviewer, Dominique Durand, cannot help but like him: 'And despite it all, on an afternoon in August, as he is harvesting the crops with his daughters and Rose, what a pleasure to be with him – and trust McGahern to describe the scene with a colourful, Renoir-like delight – his daughters love him absolutely on such days.'

The most perceptive review of the novel was written by Hilary Mantel in the *Sunday Telegraph*. She, ahead of any other British novelist of the era, had begun to realise that John was not just another Irish writer but was in fact one of the great prose masters of his age, or of any age. That this truth had not yet been recognised in her native land baffled her: 'His reputation in France, America and his native Ireland stands high and his neglect on this side of the water defies comprehension.' She continues: 'This is his eighth book. It can be read in two hours, but will linger in the mind for decades. It seems true; it is exact; it could not be done better.'

On and on came the plaudits: 'Before we go any further, it should be said that you are unlikely to read a finer novel than *Amongst Women* this year' (*Financial Times*); '*Amongst Women* is, quite simply, one of the best novels of this or any other year' (*Irish Times*); 'John McGahern is the quiet heavyweight of contemporary Irish literature' (*Listener*); 'A magical, suppressed emotion underlines the tension of his story. It never relaxes. It never falters' (*Irish Independent*); 'It deserves to last forever' (*Daily Telegraph*). There were few demurrals.

The only major jump *Amongst Women* failed to clear was the Booker Prize, narrowly losing out to A. S. Byatt's *Possession*. The night was the usual October black-tie affair in London's Guildhall. Before the winner was announced, the BBC producer Nigel Williams approached to let John know that he thought *Amongst Women* the finest Irish novel since *Ulysses*. 'You left out Beckett', replied John. The whole night was fun, with John particularly enjoying the company of Barry Hanson, his old cigar-smoking friend. Politics, as John recalls, only briefly reared its ugly head:

> The Guildhall itself was lovely to look at and, as well as the tension, there was plenty of fun and laughter, and only one unpleasantness in

the whole long Booker evening. Soon after the result was announced, Kenneth Baker, the Chairman of the Conservative Party, came over to our table and said how much he and his wife enjoyed *Amongst Women*. I saw it as a courtesy and kindness. The English critic A. N. Wilson, who was at the next table, got up at once and said, 'Do you realize, Mr Baker, that the novel glorifies the IRA?'

This unpleasant (and risible) moment at least prompted John into offering his own summary of the novel's outlook:

> *Amongst Women* glorifies nothing but life itself, and fairly humble life. All its violence is internalised within a family, is not public or political; but is not, therefore, a lesser evil. If the novel suggests anything, it is how difficult it is for people, especially women who until very recently had no real power at all in our society, to try to create space to live and love in the shadow of violence. How they manage to do that in the novel becomes their uncertain triumph.

This brief encounter was a minor discordant note on an otherwise enjoyable evening, and John took his defeat with characteristic stoicism. 'I'm secretly glad', he wrote to Alain Delahaye. 'It is bad enough as it is but it would be almost impossible if I had won. The novel has now sold 30,000 copies which is more than the sales of all my other books put together. I don't understand it. Does anybody?'

15
The Day of the Rabblement
1990–95

> No man, said the Nolan, can be a lover of the true or the good unless he abhors the multitude; and the artist, though he may employ the crowd, is very careful to isolate himself.
>
> JAMES JOYCE

'I'm apolitical', John told one journalist in 1985 on the publication of *High Ground*. He tried for long to stay that way – at least in public – but this statement, by the time he uttered those words, was already becoming less true. He mistrusted various Charles Haughey-led governments and was inclined towards a level of admiration for Garret FitzGerald. But by 1990, he had settled into a fixed dismay at the stasis of politics in the Republic. The two main parties, Fianna Fáil and Fine Gael, both products of the Civil War, 'haven't an idea between them', John declared in one interview.

Closer to home, he had been drawn into a public protest against the development of an offal-processing plant on the lakeside below his home. 'The lorries drawing in the offal inevitably must create a stink', John was quoted in the national press, 'and the soil is so thin that the raw material effluent would quickly flow into Laura Lake and cause pollution.' The Fianna Fáil politician who was behind the initiative assured the locals that they had nothing to worry about. 'Senator Ellis says there need have been no concern if the objectors had come to him in the first place', reported the *Irish Press*. 'He said that only the best and fresh offal – tripe, livers and lungs – will be used.' Ellis failed to get permission, with one supporter of the plant overheard reporting of John's role in rallying opposition among locals: 'The writer cunt has them all riz.'

Of the Troubles north of the nearby border, John had even less to say than of Southern politics. Far from being the IRA cheerleader that A. N. Wilson believed him to be, John was increasingly chary of nationalism in any form. Sounding a bit like Stephen Dedalus, he says in that same interview where he declares himself apolitical: 'Nationhood is not worth dying for, it's worth living for. I would like to see a united Europe and I see nationalism as almost an anachronism.' One can trawl through his entire surviving correspondence without finding a single mention of issues such as internment, the H Block hunger strikes or the Anglo-Irish Agreement. But he did feel that the twenty-six-county state was increasingly different from the six-county one, a difference that he believed, by 1991, stemmed largely from religious conservatism:

> The Catholic church's power has collapsed in the South. Not so much in the North – in fact I think the South has become a very different society than the North because of the opposition between the Catholics and Protestants which is more of a black and white issue than anything having to do with religion. Each is caught in a time warp and the Pope who is Polish, and involved in a similar time warp with Communism, is more friendly towards the kind of very conservative Catholicism in the North than that which exists in the more liberal South.

The belief that the two polities were drifting further apart did not make John any less fond of his Northern neighbours, and, through the spring and summer of 1992, in order to circumvent a postal strike in the Republic, he used Blake's pub in Enniskillen as his address. 'I have been going to Blake's of the Hollow for close to twenty years', he comments in one essay, 'and think of it as one of the happiest and most beautiful bars in the whole of Ireland.'

In one such missive from Blake's, he writes to Alain Delahaye in May of a scandal within the Catholic Church that would rapidly accelerate its collapse in Ireland. 'Did the story of the Bishop of Galway and his lady and their son reach Paris?' he asks, unable to resist his own bit of mischief: 'One woman near here burned her house down lighting candles to try to get the scandal to go away.'

The Bishop Eamonn Casey scandal was just one of several momentous breaches in the established social order to occur through the early 1990s, a decade that had begun with the almost unimaginable election of a woman, and a socialist, to the Republic of Ireland's highest office. John, fed up with the Tweedledum and Tweedledee of post-Civil War Irish politics, became an enthusiastic supporter of Mary Robinson's run for the presidency. As he had tried to show in *Amongst Women*, he felt that women in Ireland had, for far too long, been disempowered and disrespected, and he backed calls for the introduction of divorce and greater reproductive rights, including the legalisation of abortion. 'Ireland is changing very much', he proudly told the Colgate newspaper after Robinson's election.

> Mrs Robinson was a Professor at Trinity College and a constitutional lawyer. She was able to take the Irish government to court because we are part of the European Community and she won rights for women and for homosexuals in the Irish society against the Irish government . . . we felt that a start had to be made somewhere and she was a very good candidate . . . she really sort of appealed to the voices of Liberty, Decency and Fairness.

But John, if prepared to stick his head above the parapet south of the border, was less willing to engage with what was going on a few miles up the road. In choosing not to comment directly on the Troubles and their origin, John differed from many of the prevailing cultural orthodoxies of the period. While he had become, by the mid-1980s, arguably Ireland's most respected writer of fiction, Seamus Heaney had risen to the same status as poet and Brian Friel as playwright. These two writers, alongside four other Northerners, Seamus Deane, David Hammond, Tom Paulin and Stephen Rea, came together to form the Field Day Theatre Company. Tom Kilroy, the only member born in the Republic, joined the board in 1988. Asked to comment on his own apparent lack of interest, John said, simply, of Heaney and Friel that 'their experience is plainly different'.

And he could become irritated when prodded about his apparent lack of interest in the conflict, as Michel Déon recalls at a reading in Brittany:

> To be honest, when I first saw him at a conference at the 'Étonnants Voyageurs Festival' in Saint-Malo, I found him quite ordinary until he was annoyed by a perfectly stupid remark made by a member of the audience, who reprimanded him for ignoring the problem posed by the troubles in Northern Ireland between republicans and loyalists, and a burst of anger transformed his face in a way no one expected from such a quiet man. He pointed out, and quite rightly too, that a writer is above all free to make his own choices, and that what he thought about the bloody stages of this endless civil war was nobody's business, especially not a cretin who knew nothing about it at all.

Starting with the September 1980 premiere of *Translations* in Derry's Guildhall – an opening night attended by the McGaherns at the Friels' invitation – Field Day went on to become a dominant force in Irish theatre and culture over the following decade and more. John admired the play and had a good night, apart from a spat with Michael Longley that he recalls cheerfully in his annual Christmas card to Neill Joy in Colgate:

> I ran into Monsieur Longley on the opening night of a good Friel play Translations in Derry (It'll transfer to London in the spring). He seemed to want to recover some imagined loss of dignity, and sent a number of shots in my direction during the intervals, and at the party afterward. Anyhow I think he ran into a few late uppercuts. I seem to remember my own voice at the theatre bar: 'Heaney will get what he asked for, but you, Longley, will get who [*sic*] you deserve, which is the smallest of small measures.' At that stage, it was probably as rewarding as attempting to slow a swinging door.

If John's once-cordial relations with Longley (cordial enough, at least, to have him read in Newcastle's Morden Tower) were at an end, there would eventually be trouble too with Friel. John intended *Amongst Women* to be his final novel, as he told Alain Delahaye in late 1986. And so, in the aftermath of its publication, he faced into a new decade intent on turning his attention, at least for a time, to drama, a form in which he had been dabbling as long ago as the early 1970s and his conversion of the short story 'Why We're Here' to the radio play *Sinclair*.

Having put the finishing touches to *Amongst Women* in 1989, he returned to another project that had begun life as a radio play in the same period as *Sinclair*. This revived project was his adaptation of Leo Tolstoy's *The Power of Darkness*, a melodrama that circles around efforts to seize an elderly farmer's inheritance, even by foul means if needs be. John's appetite for playwriting had been rekindled in 1986 and 1987 by his work on the screenplay for the Kieran Hickey-directed *The Rockingham Shoot*, one of three plays by Irish writers on the subject of teaching and teachers commissioned by BBC2 alongside Anne Devlin's *The Venus De Milo Instead* and Frank McGuinness's *Scout*, all to be produced by Danny Boyle. After an initial offer of £3,500, John haggled up to £4,500 in what had become, by this time in his life, typical of his hard-nosed, and hard-learnt, negotiating skills. He had been paid £85 for *Sinclair* fifteen years earlier.

The Rockingham Shoot returns to all sorts of familiar McGahern themes in its examination of the relationship between a declining Anglo-Irish aristocracy and a rising Catholic peasant class in the years after Independence. At its centre is the schoolmaster Reilly, a fanatical nationalist, would-be politician and violent sadist. Furious that several of the children in his class choose to ignore his strictures against working for the annual Rockingham shoot held on the King-Harman estate with British Ambassador Massey as guest, he thrashes these absentees so brutally on their return to school the next day that he risks punishment from both parents and the law.

As in *The Leavetaking*, another of John's several reflections on life in the classroom, the Irish language is used as a weapon of control, with a spelling test of ten Irish words used as the pretext to terrorise the children in Reilly's care. It would be a mistake, however, to intuit from this facet of the work that John disliked his native language. He was fluent enough to enjoy Máirtín Ó Cadhain's stories, collected as *The Road to Brightcity*, in the original and to translate sections of Ó Criomhthain's *An tOileánach* for his own pleasure.

He includes one scene of linguistic confusion in the screenplay that is borrowed straight from Friel's *Translations* to show a softer side to the language, when Mary Armstrong, fiancée of Reilly's brother John, tells him in a tender moment, '*Tá mé i ngrá leat*.' He is unable to translate it to 'I love you', saying of Irish, 'I've forgotten every word of it except *tá* and *níl* and *anseo*.'

Working for television – hard graft in its own way – was a welcome distraction from the Sisyphean labours of *Amongst Women*: 'it was like learning a completely new discipline, much more a trade than novel writing'. John especially enjoyed the novelty of working on location at Lord Erne's Crom Castle estate near Enniskillen. 'During the shooting at night, real RUC [Royal Ulster Constabulary] with real guns were going around guarding Lord Erne while actors dressed up as gardai were doing the same for Massey. And Lady Erne came out in a silk raincoat with a glass of Beaujolais.'

The Rockingham Shoot was aired to widespread acclaim on BBC2 on 10 September 1987, wedged between Bruce Willis and Cybill Shepherd flirting with each other in *Moonlighting* – 'It's Maddie's first day as a detective, but where are the clients?' – and *Newsnight*, presented by Peter Snow. While John enjoyed complimenting *Translations* in that short love scene from *The Rockingham Shoot*, his subsequent efforts to write a Field Day play himself would not prove so happy. Having experimented with various versions of *The Power of Darkness* since the early 1970s, he was inspired to return to it by one of the great scandals of late-twentieth-century Ireland, the so-called 'Kerry babies case'. This story was recounted by John in a letter of May 1985 to Matthew Evans at Faber, to whom he was writing in an effort to get his friend Michael O'Regan's book on the subject published:

> One mutilated infant was found in a plastic bag washed up on a Kerry strand.
>
> A Hayes girl gave birth to a child in an outhouse and buried it in a field. It was illegitimate. She already had an illegitimate child by the same man, who was married, and worked with her in the local sports centre. They were poor, with a small dairy farm, dim-witted except for this girl, alcoholic.
>
> The police forced confessions from the family, and charged the girl with the murder of the baby washed up in the plastic bag, which plainly was not hers. There was an outcry when the facts were reported. The murder charges were dropped, a tribunal of enquiry was ordered, which has been running for the last 6 months, and is about to end.

Little wonder that John should have found the case so compelling, given that his adaptation of *The Power of Darkness* for a modern Ireland, replete with avarice, brutality and infanticide, had been rejected by the Abbey Theatre in 1972 in no uncertain terms on the grounds that it was wholly unbelievable.

Extracts from the two anonymous readers' reports can only have been bewildering to read: 'The grim and primitive life of the Russian peasant in the mid-nineteenth century, the ignorance and superstition does not at all translate to Ireland at any time'; 'the excesses – the murder of the child especially – here as depicted, would cause laughter even if well done. A great disappointment this from an established writer.'

When the play was ultimately published by Faber in 1991, John could not resist twisting the knife in his introduction:

> the sad lusting after respectability, sugar-coated with sanctimoniousness and held together by a thin binding of religious doctrine and ceremony, combined to form a very dark and explosive force that, generally, went inwards and hid. For anybody who might imagine this to be a description of a remote and dark age, I refer them to the findings of the Kerry Babies Tribunal in 1985.

In the wake of the scandal, John reworked the play and offered it to Field Day in early 1988. On 20 April, he received word from Brian Friel that the company had decided to reject it despite the fact that 'the response was very warm', as the letter notes, from the Field Day directors. Friel proceeds to give one director's specific take:

> Tom Paulin's comments would be representative; 'I heard John's earlier version of THE POWER OF DARKNESS on radio many years back and it made a great impact on me. This script is a brilliantly realised adaptation – the dialogue is perfectly cadenced, astringent, beautiful, the characterization and dramatic momentum exact and powerful.' But there is absolutely no possibility of Field Day doing any play with 13+ characters. The touring costs alone would absorb all our grants for five years. Only an institution – the Abbey, the British National Theatre, the Royal Shakespeare Company – can take on a project of this size but I'm sure you understand all this.

John, for right or for wrong, doubted the sincerity of this rejection, believing Friel to be the guiding hand in once more sinking the play. Not yet ready to give up, he turned to his friend Tom Kilroy for advice, with the playwright replying helpfully in an August letter:

> Have just finished reading the play and I think its central spine of action is the basis of a very powerful piece of theatre indeed. By that I mean – the death of old Peter, the amorous Paul, his mother and new wife and their machinations, the seduction of Maggie and the killing of the infant. All this and the dark world it inhabits must be preserved in any final final version. I think I'm talking about four or five big scenes. In terms of characters it means a reduction to: Peter, Eileen, Maggie, Paul, Oliver, Baby and possibly old Paddy.

Kilroy was also keen to make John consider the very different forms of writing involved in drama as opposed to fiction: 'does this material need "translation" for a contemporary audience? You know this world has a palpable existence. I know it does. But what form should it be presented in?'

John followed Kilroy's advice pretty much to the letter, cutting the dramatis personae down to just seven speaking characters from over twenty in the 1972 radio play. Despite Kilroy's misgivings, he felt he had to hold on to the character of the old soldier Paddy to act as the play's 'moral voice' – as his 'Introduction' to *The Power of Darkness* phrases the matter. 'Whether it ever goes on the Boards or not', he wrote to Kilroy a year after their early exchange, 'I needed to do it for my own peace.'

The next reader to see the script was Christopher Fitz-Simon, then the acting artistic director at the Abbey. He liked the play and invited John to visit his Dublin home to discuss ways of taking the project forward. To his surprise, John arrived with the English theatre director Pam Brighton, who had recently produced *Amongst Women* for the BBC's *Book at Bedtime* and whom John wanted to direct the play. Fitz-Simon recommended *The Power of Darkness* to the Abbey, where Garry Hynes had just been installed as artistic director after more than fifteen successful years with Druid in Galway. Hynes also admired the play and wanted to direct it herself, leading to a certain degree of tension over John's preference for Brighton.

At this time, Fintan O'Toole had taken a year's leave of absence from his position at the *Irish Times* to serve as literary adviser at the Abbey, where Hynes wanted him to work on programming. O'Toole, when sent *The Power of Darkness* by McGahern, was 'hugely impressed'. This enthusiasm, coupled with Hynes's admiration, brought about a decision to make the play a centrepiece of the 1991 Dublin Theatre Festival, to be performed on the Abbey's main stage.

Despite this turn in fortunes, John continued to feel wounded by the Field Day rejection, squarely apportioning blame for the decision to Brian Friel. On 29 May 1991, Friel wrote to John expressing his upset after Michael Colgan, then artistic director of the Gate Theatre and a leading light in Dublin theatre life, had reported to him that John had claimed twice that Friel had rejected the play. He sought to assure John that this was not the case, that the Field Day board had taken a collective decision and that he had, in fact, argued that 'we try to set up a reading of the play, a proposal that was overruled'. John replied to apologise if Friel was upset in any way and accepted that he had indeed made those remarks to Colgan, going on to explain why:

> Before I received your letter, Tom rang me to warn me of the decision. He said he was very distressed, especially since he felt that it was the kind of play the Field Day should be doing. He said nothing in detail about what had taken place; he was the soul of discretion. I just assumed that because you were the other playwright on the Board your weight must have come down against the play. This assumption was reinforced when Tom Paulin, around the time of the Booker, said much the same thing to me as Tom Kilroy. I also shared the popular belief that nothing went on at Field Day unless it was approved by you. When I made the remark to Michael Colgan, I thought I was just stating the facts.

He continued: 'I never took the rejection of the play in any way personally.' Then a final, telling remark: 'I knew the play wasn't political.'

One senses that John saw Field Day as something of a closed shop of Ulster writers interested primarily in responding to the Troubles in various ways that he felt were overdetermined and wrong-headed. As such, *The Power of Darkness*, speckled with western dialect words and replete with apolitical peasant grasping and melodramatic murder, did not fit the bill.

When the play was eventually staged, it proved a critical disaster and has, by and large, remained buried ever since, though John continued to tinker with *The Power of Darkness* right up to 2005. He recalls that it was 'met with such hostility by the first night audience that the actors found it difficult to act', and in his usual droll fashion goes on to tell an amusing anecdote about Mick Lally, who played the handsome but ultimately suicidal farmhand, Paul:

I didn't come into the Abbey until late the next evening, and was met by Mick Lally at the door.

'God, John, we thought you weren't turning up. Have you seen the reviews?'

'No,' I said. 'I suppose they were bad.'

'Oh, they were much worse than that,' Mick said.

'What are you worried about, so?'

'No matter what they say, that play is alive,' Mick said. 'Andy O'Mahony liked it at one of the previews and has a show going out at 7.30. A car is coming for you in half an hour. *That's* why I was worried. Get in the car and go out to RTÉ and talk about sex and sin and death – and especially Resurrection – to see if we can keep these swing doors open.'

The next day, John flew back to teach in Colgate, fearing that the play was doomed. 'Only the first Dublin notices had come in', he tells Alain Delahaye in a letter, 'and they were terrible.' Lally's alarm was well founded, and the Irish reviews were indeed as bad as John recalled. Gerry Colgan in the *Irish Times* blew the play out of the water: 'It was a debacle, a melodrama of crude simplicities that left one stunned and incredulous that lightning could strike again, and yet again.' Madeleine Keane in the *Sunday Independent* gave it a similar kicking: 'Maybe it's a blessing that some of the lines are lost in the hysterical screaming in which the actors feel bound to indulge.'

Paddy Woodworth wrote two years later of the play's 'ludicrous and hysterical incoherence under Hynes's direction'. He had been irritated at the time of the play's debut by Garry Hynes's decision to advertise it by quoting from favourable reviews in the English broadsheets. For example, Michael Coveney in the *Observer* had been deeply impressed:

> This sock-in-the-face of a play is given the most tremendous production by Garry Hynes, with a stark setting by Frank Conway and sickly green lighting by Rick Fisher. Here are no compensations of calming narrative prose, or indeed of Brian Friel's memorial

Lughnasa. Instead, we have a terrifying picture of poverty-stricken rural life shot through with Catholic guilt and oppression.

Woodworth objected to the Abbey's use of British critics to bolster the play in an odd piece that brought back memories of the long, controversial history of twentieth-century Irish theatre, from Synge's *The Playboy of the Western World* to O'Casey's *The Plough and the Stars*, and onward:

> This is a most curious tactic for the director of the Irish National Theatre to adopt. What is it supposed to prove? *The Observer*'s Michael Coveney may be right in praising the production, but it may also be that some British critics feel comfortable with a view of Ireland which seems embarrassingly stereotyped, if not altogether incoherent, to most of us. Besides, one eminent British critic – Irving Wardle in the *Independent on Sunday* – lambasted the production, while at least one Irish critic liked it. This is barren ground indeed for useful debate, but the Abbey has chosen it.

That Woodworth could hold such a view of Ireland in the wake of the Kerry babies scandal is hard to understand. For sure, *The Power of Darkness*, with its sexual incontinence, poisoning of an elderly man and disposal of a foetus in a drain, was melodramatic, but it was hardly unrealistic, as several letter-writers to the national broadsheets sought to point out. Typical was a short note published in the *Irish Times* of 7 November: 'Last night I was witness to fornication, misogyny, alcoholic abuse, greed, financial scandals, amorality, land grabbing, murder, hypocrisy and megalomania. No, I wasn't in the Dáil bar. I was at John McGahern's "Power of Darkness" in the Abbey Theatre. It should not be missed.'

One can only speculate as to the reasons for such a profound failure. Given that John had published the year before one of the best-loved Irish novels of the century, perhaps disappointment was inevitable about any follow-up from his pen. Some critics thought he had stayed too close to Tolstoy; others that he had stayed too distant. The public had begun to have a settled view of what might be considered McGahernesque: scrupulously realist, cautious, delicately crafted. And reading a novel, unlike attending a play, is a private affair.

John Mahony in the *Irish Press* might have been on to something when he wrote of McGahern's dramatic disaster that 'theatre in this country, and particularly in Dublin, is entirely populated by the middle classes, the very middle classes that McGahern has so little interest in'. John would have begged to differ here – he had just as much interest in the bourgeoisie as in anything else – but there was a growing perception afoot that his work stood apart from the enthusiasms of the chattering classes.

John knew that there was a sorry history of fiction writers failing to make the transition to drama. Writing to Brian Friel, clearing the air about the Field Day rejection, he comments, 'plays by ageing novelists are, historically, a disaster zone'. He might have done well to keep in mind the thoughts of a young Rilke, one of his most trusted exemplars:

> That is why drama is so degrading, because it *needs* the public. And drama's atmosphere, I believe, has infiltrated the other arts as well, so that it is as if a work of art were only there from the moment the crowd ogles and critiques it. On the contrary, there are few works of art that can survive this probing without internal damage.

John at least had the luxury, when *The Dark* had been banned a quarter of a century before, of suffering alone. But in the case of the flak taken for *The Power of Darkness* there were others involved, and he felt the pain and disappointment of criticism more keenly. 'It was very hard', he confesses to Alain Delahaye from the safety of upstate New York. 'With a book you only expose your poor self. With a play you expose a whole crowd of poor people. And it is instant and public and bloody awful.'

John was similarly frank in his response when Peter Fallon wrote to offer his support:

> I didn't mind the reaction all that much for myself, though I'd have preferred it otherwise. It was almost bracingly like old times. But in a

play you expose so many other people, especially the players who have to go on night after night, and that first night was so instant and public and brutal.

The whole thing had been a chastening experience. Though John did not lose interest in Tolstoy's play, he never got involved in another staging of it and left drama behind for the remainder of his life.

* * *

By January 1992, John was home in Foxfield, and *The Power of Darkness* mess was disappearing rapidly in the rear-view mirror. Fats, his favourite cat, was dying, affecting him more deeply than the critical failure of his play. 'Though we know it is foolish, it is distressing', he writes to Alain Delahaye. 'It is like watching a whole part of our life go.'

Now he was busying himself with knocking his shorter fictional pieces into shape for a 'Collected Stories' to be published later that year by Faber in London and Knopf in New York. *Amongst Women* under Viking had proved yet another American misfire. Responsibility for seeing the novel through to publication had passed on from Pat Mulcahy to Amanda Vaill after Mulcahy moved to Random House. Then Vaill left Viking, in yet another stroke of bad luck with American publishers, just as the novel was published.

John had failed in trying to change a dust jacket he hated, featuring a drawing of three young women sitting beneath a tree, giving entirely the wrong impression of the book, making its content seem more like young adult fiction than the austere portrait of a dying guerrilla fighter. Despairing of the image, he determined to break with Viking. And so 1992 saw him return to Knopf after twenty-six years away. This move would prove, at last, a happy partnership, in which John respected the editor-in-chief, Sonny Mehta, and he worked well with the firm till the end of his life.

Putting together a 'Collected Stories' meant combining his three collections – *Nightlines* (1970), *Getting Through* (1978) and *High Ground*

(1985) – with two new pieces, 'The Creamery Manager' and 'The Country Funeral'. The latter story – despite now being regularly touted as his finest-ever achievement in the form – John failed to place with a literary magazine. It was rejected in the USA by the *Atlantic* ('McGahern is good, but this seems to us a set-piece'), *New Yorker*, *Mother Jones*, *Harper's*, *Paris Review* and *Grand Street* ('Mr. McGahern writes with authority, but story's just nothing new').

In addition to the two new stories, he also permitted himself some minor revisions in stories with which he was never quite satisfied, such as 'The Stoat' and 'Peaches'. Of this process, he writes to Delahaye:

> I've been going through all the stories for The Collected Stories. I rewrote The Stoat and I enclose the worst pages from the others. They are mostly deletions. If they are too difficult ignore them. I hope it's not too much. Reading them again is a bit like listening to the 'stupid bastard' in Krapp's Last Tape.

But John was back, despite these difficulties, in the enclosure of the fiction writer, a cell in which he felt comfortable, far removed from the intrigues of the theatre world. His long-standing suspicion of what he called 'The Racket' – that group of opinion-forming journalists, writers and intellectuals that oils the wheels of every society's cultural machinery – had been confirmed in spades. He must have known that by bringing his work before the Abbey audience, he had broken one of his own rules of engagement: 'I think it is very dangerous for anybody to lose the anonymous quality. Writers shouldn't parade around as writers. Doctors don't parade around as doctors, teachers don't parade around as teachers: one goes around as a person.'

John returned from Colgate to Foxfield at Christmas 1991. Still feeling bad for those who had been caught up in *The Power of Darkness* fiasco, he invited Fintan O'Toole and his wife out for dinner. As O'Toole recalls, 'John, I think, was very hurt by the whole thing but also very philosophical and certainly not bitter about Garry or the production.' The author had wanted to meet on St Stephen's Day. Since the only place open was the Shelbourne Hotel, they dined there. O'Toole is clear in his recollection: 'He was very sweet about the whole thing, and I think anxious to make clear that he wasn't blaming anyone.'

But life in the period of his play's composition and staging was not all disappointment.

* * *

Most Irish people of a certain age can tell you where they were when Ray Houghton's headed ball hit the back of the English net in Stuttgart at the 1988 UEFA European Football Championships. Houghton, a small but tigerish Glaswegian, cannot have scored many goals with his head; this one came about in the sixth minute as the result of a defensive shambles, Kenny Sansom swinging his leg at a misdirected cross, skying the ball into the air above the English box, with Houghton in the right place at the right time to head the ball back across the stranded Peter Shilton in goal. But who cares how it was scored? It led to Ireland beating their old enemy 1–0, and the country went berserk, Houghton describing the eighty-four minutes that followed his score as the most difficult of his life.

The day before this historic match, John had teed the game up nicely in the sports pages of *Libération* in an article titled 'Souvenirs d'une Irlande en rouge et vert'. He recalled the ferocious parish rivalries of his boyhood that saw his local Cootehall club, St Michael's, fight it out on summer Sundays in the village field: 'The football practised in these wild parishes wasn't soccer but gaelic football.' The hyper-professional world of the Euros, with its television rights and corporate sponsorship, was born in childhood fields like those of John's Cootehall. Not until the 1960s, remembers John, did soccer become one of his fascinations: 'If soccer arrived in Ireland with the British garrisons, it belonged in England to the working classes.' He goes on to recount a favourite description of the English obsession with the sport: '"I see politics as a very simple thing," said Bill Shankly, the famous Liverpool FC manager. "The government, the police, the army only exist to ensure that the match takes place each Saturday at 3 o'clock."'

As he settled in London's East End after the banning of *The Dark* and his subsequent expulsion from Belgrove, John soon shared this English passion:

> There is an indescribable atmosphere around London's football grounds . . . more touching, in my opinion, outside the stadia: police on horseback, peanut sellers and badges in team colours, coaches carrying the supporters of Nottingham or Coventry, narrow streets around the stadium with their displays of fruit and vegetables, second hand clothes, washing powder, cheap cutlery shops adjacent to the pubs, proper Victorian palaces of glass and mahogany: The Red Lion, The Coach and Horses, The Jolly Butchers, all of which close at 3 o'clock on the dot until 5.30.

And now, the day before Ireland is to face England, the excitement builds as these two neighbouring countries, so intimately and fiercely linked for centuries, face each other in the still heat of a Stuttgart summer:

> The Irish team at the European championships has an English manager. Some players have as their only link with Ireland some Irish grandmother, long emigrated. Those born in Ireland all play in the British professional leagues. Without a doubt, the wild parishes would refuse with spite to support such mixed blood. But I will be there for the magic once seen at White Hart Lane, long ago, on that small pitch by the river, behind an abandoned barracks.

That John's only published thoughts on football should appear the day before the then greatest victory in the Irish team's history must have drawn a wry smile, maybe even a chuckle.

That *Libération* turned not to an Irish sports journalist or a former international but to the fiction writer John McGahern for an article on the European Championships is indicative of the increasingly strong position held by him in French cultural life at this time. His books had all been translated into French, with most of them selling in more than respectable numbers. John was fortunate in having *Nightlines*, his first book in French, translated by Pierre Leyris and then most of the later volumes by Alain Delahaye: both men were poets in sympathy with John's style.

In June 1989, John was named Chevalier de l'Ordre des Arts et des Lettres at the Ministère de la Culture, Place du Palais Royal. Delahaye joined John that day as they entered the hallowed hall, with its walls magnificently painted by Pierre Alechinsky. The minister for culture, Jack Lang, presented the medal after mentioning in his speech how important John's books had been to him in Nancy, where, as a law professor, he founded the university theatre. When he located John personally in the crowd, he sighed, 'Oh, *The Dark*, *The Dark*.' As John and friends walked to a favourite bistro at the end of the Île de la Cité, Delahaye pointed to the dome of the Institut de France to say that he had done all his translations there in the Bibliothèque Mazarine.

Five years after that memorable night in Paris, we see John writing once again to Delahaye with news of yet another French garland. The award in this case was the Prix de Littérature Étrangère 1994, presented as part of the Bordeaux Book Fair to recognise the achievement of a foreign writer and his translator. John and Madeline enjoyed their trip to Bordeaux, a city that John found 'Rich, extremely closed, formal'. 'There was an extraordinary dinner in the Gallery of Modern Art', he tells Jimmy Swift in one letter, 'once a workhouse for storing Barrels of wine for shipping on the harbour, the stone polished white. There must have been 300 red roses in the middle of the Mayor's table.'

Alongside word of the Bordeaux prize, John had yet more good news from France, where *La Caserne* had been placed on the curriculum for a nationwide state examination:

> They have put The Barracks on this year's C.A.P.E.S. et Aggregation. I refused to go on a tour of France when the Publishers asked but then Academics and the Embassy started to telephone and write. It appeared they'd consider it a discourtesy if I didn't go as I'm the only LIVE writer on the course, a lone lobster in a restaurant tank before dinner.

> Anyhow it seemed easier to go than to continue to refuse. So it is Poitiers, Bordeaux, Montpellier, Lyons, Caen, Lille, Rheims in January.

And so off he went in January for the kind of whistlestop tour he generally disliked, where hotel rooms began to merge into one indistinguishable and hazy memory. Returning to Ireland on 27 January, he wrote to a friend about another possible public event: 'I got back last night after a long round of France. I feel fairly battered. The last thing I want to think about is another audience but we can talk about it another time.'

Colm Tóibín recalled a Hiberno-French cultural tour two years later in which it became startlingly clear to him just how high John's cultural currency had risen in France: 'During *L'Irlandais Imaginaire* in the mid-1990s, there was a gathering at a literary festival in Saint Malo. All of us were on panels. No one spoke French, except Jennifer Johnston and Julia O'Faolain. But the panel John McGahern was on was about him, where French critics spoke about his work.' Tóibín concluded, 'I think it mattered enormously that he had been translated into French by a poet. He marvelled at Delahaye's poetry because it was so abstract and pure.'

* * *

Once he got *The Power of Darkness* debacle and the minor revisions to *The Collected Stories* behind him, John actually wrote less in the early 1990s than at any period in his writing life. His assertion to Delahaye that *Amongst Women* would be his last novel looked prescient.

In the spring of 1993, he took up a teaching post at UCG, which involved a few hours of relaxed work each Friday with two final-year undergraduate seminar groups. The books discussed were an interesting mix of some of his old favourites, such as *The Islandman* and *On Another Man's Wound*, and some newer discoveries, such as Richard Ford's *Rock Springs* and Alice Munro's *Friend of My Youth*. 'The teaching is fairly harmless but I find it tiring', he told Niall Walsh in a letter of 15 February:

> Tomorrow I go to New York and Washington for a week. I'm hoping to get a couple of days to myself to just walk around the

> place. Yesterday a fellow rang from the N. Y. Times. It's a disastrous medium for interviews. He went on and on as to why there was so little happiness in my work. I don't see large stacks of it around. I made the mistake of trying to explain so no doubt I'll appear as a complete asshole and then it'll be forgotten by the next Sunday.

Knocking about Manhattan later that month, he managed to lose himself briefly in one of his very favourite activities: 'The day I left I got away to the Oyster Bar in Grand Central and had a bowl of chowder, 12 oysters, a glass of Chardonnay and the whole passing show.'

John was a much-loved and admired figure in Galway. Always he seemed to wear a half-smile as he listened intently to whatever his students had to say in the dreary surrounds of the seminar room. The seriousness with which he took literature was unmistakeable and the mark he left on most indelible. Gearóid Ó Tuathaigh, the university's then professor of Irish history, delivered the citation the following June at the conferring of an honorary degree:

> The circle of McGahern's academic and other friends in the University was, in one sense, no more than the Summer School 'regulars,' in whose company John and Madeline would relax around a dining table after his day's teaching and mentoring was done. The charm of that company, for those of us who shared it from time to time, was the utter absence of formality or self-consciousness: opinions and anecdotes were exchanged, on politics (local scandals a *specialité*), sport, books, travel and the affairs of the day. There was no need to be guarded; nothing said was for quotation or assessment. They were nights of good talk and good faith, and they will live long in the memory of those who shared that company.

It was quite the encomium for a man who, forty years earlier in that very university, had fled his physics lecture in disgrace. 'One day, one day', thinks Young Mahoney as he leaves UCG for the last time, 'you'd come perhaps to more real authority than all this, an authority that had need of neither vast buildings nor professorial chairs nor robes nor solemn organ tones, an authority that was simply a state of mind, a calmness even in the face of the turmoil of your own passing.'

A month after the conferring, John writes in resignation to Delahaye of the impossibility of work: 'Good weather came. I went at the hay, but the tractor broke down, it is now in the garage, and the rain has returned.' John then confides a certain frustration:

> I haven't done a single thing with the play. I am working on a novel – but not in the last weeks . . . the hay . . . a degree in Galway . . . (The tinkers in Mohill told me I was a clever fucker as they saw I'll be taking blood pressures next) . . . too many visitors (Madeline calls this the silly season). I did finish a story that broke away from the novel.

In this letter, we hear the key turn in the ignition, the first slow grumbles of what would become over the next eight years John's story 'Love of the World' and its longer consequence, *That They May Face the Rising Sun*. He was back in his own country, facing the wall once again.

* * *

'What reason could there be to fear?' asks Paddy, the one character John insisted on retaining in the face of Tom Kilroy's welcome advice on revising *The Power of Darkness*. 'Aren't they all made of the same dirt as ourselves? They all have to die.' And it is only here, at the play's denouement, that we hear the voice we have come to know and trust, a voice that is at once dark but true and that would return to memorable effect in the fiction yet to be written:

> All the young women think the sun shines out of their arses and fellas like you, Paul, run around as if you had the meaning of life in your trousers. What does it add up to? It adds up to fuck all. What should you be afraid of them for? All they can make you do is die once, and then you're with the kings and county councillors. Tell the truth. Shame the devil. And tell them all to take running jumps.

16

An Intense Form of Life
1996–2003

> I believe that it is a great achievement for any man to state, even once, a measure of his experience truthfully.
>
> JOHN McGAHERN

'The evening was setting, and we had already drunk a few gulps of old whiskey', remembers Daniel Rondeau, the French man of letters, of his visit to Foxfield, 'when someone knocked at the door.' There follows a memorable encounter with one of John's regular visiting neighbours:

> A man in a flat cap dripping with water – it had been raining continuously – enters. The farmer dressed in a very wide jacket and plastic trousers. He limped and was using a cane. It was a farm worker with a strange story. A foundling, hired for decades by unscrupulous farmers, he barely knew the colour of money; it is possible he wasn't even rich enough to have a drink at Early's bar. He belonged to the dark people sung by Patrick Kavanagh: 'We are a dark people / Our eyes are ever turned / Inward . . .' He had only just opened the door and yet the full smell of the humid countryside had entered with him.

Pat Conway, the homeboy from the neighbouring Earley farm, having once more gone back into the rain, has his life narrated by John to Rondeau 'like he was one of his characters'. It was a painful story, and it remains so in its retelling as the character of Bill Evans in the author's final novel, *That They May Face the Rising Sun*. Bill is a so-called 'homeboy', a child sent out from one of Ireland's notorious network of industrial schools to work in conditions of near slavery on a Leitrim farm. Based on the man encountered by Rondeau as he sipped his whiskey in the

Foxfield dusk, he is one of the many unforgettable characters conjured up in this superb novel.

John was always interested in what Victor Hugo named *les misérables*: those people on the very bottom rung of society's ladder, condemned to spend their lives in the dirt, kept all but invisible from the busy world around them. One of John's first stories, 'Christmas', is told from the point of view of a nameless homeboy sent to work for a woodsman, Moran. Though young, the boy has already learnt to live on his wits:

> As well as a railway ticket they gave me a letter before I left the Home to work for Moran. They warned me to give the letter unopened to Moran, which was why I opened it on the train; it informed him that since I was a ward of state if I caused trouble or ran away he was to contact the guards at once. I tore it up, since it occurred to me that I might well cause trouble or run away, resolving to say I lost it if asked, but he did not ask for any letter.

In the local shop, the boy will not bend to the bullying of the congregating men: 'They used to trouble me at first', he recalls. 'They used to lob tomatoes at the back of my head in the hope of some reaction, but they left me mostly alone when they saw none was forthcoming. If I felt anything for them it was a contempt tempered by fear: I was here, and they were there.'

By the end of this very short story in which so much happens, the boy's consciousness has developed sufficiently for him to declare, in the manner of Bartleby, a quiet *non serviam* against his brutish master as he sets fire to a toy aeroplane gifted to him by a client in order to spite Moran, who had expected a share of some cash rather than a useless toy. 'By the light of the burning straw I put the blue and white toy against the wall and started to kick. With each kick I gave a new sweetness was injected into my blood.' And so, as in the concluding passages of *The Dark*, what might appear to be a defeat is actually a victory for the spirit: 'As I quietened, I was glad that I'd torn up the unopened letter in the train that I was supposed to have given to Moran. I felt a new life had already started to grow out of the ashes, out of the stupidity of human wishes.'

Rosie in *The Power of Darkness*, a barmaid in the American, is another of these victims of the state who is mentioned in passing but never seen. Now pregnant by the scheming Baby's son, Paul, Baby is keen to blacken and abandon her: 'There was this girl working in the bar they were said to have got out of some orphanage run by the nuns. You know the sort.' Baby's gossip will soon put paid to any talk of marriage between her son and the girl: 'Doesn't the whole of the country except himself know that she was the next best thing to the town bicycle.'

Bill Evans of *That They May Face the Rising Sun* is similarly tormented and bullied by his masters and by the community around the lake who turn a blind eye to his torture. That John should choose this portrait as the first extended character description in the book, running from pages 7 to 14, is telling since it works to explode any thoughts the alert reader might have that what they are reading is pastoral. As with Joyce's *Dubliners*, the author is writing 'a chapter of the moral history' of his country, and it is one that must leave every Irish reader of the generations that lived through these times flushed and ashamed:

> He would have known neither father nor mother. As a baby he would have been given into the care of nuns. When these boys reached seven, the age of reason, they were transferred to places run by priests or Brothers. When he reached fourteen, Bill Evans was sent out, like many others, to his first farmer.

Joe Ruttledge, the novel's primary subject and narrator, recalls a distressing encounter when he was in college with a homeboy who had been sent there as cheap labour for the priests:

> One morning a boy turned quickly away from a table and found the Dean unexpectedly in his path and went straight into him with a tray. Plates and bowls went flying. The soutane was splashed. Only the students who were seated close to the accident saw what happened next,

> and even they weren't certain. In the face of his fury it was thought that the boy broke the rule of silence to try to excuse the accident. The beating was sudden and savage. Nobody ate a morsel at any of the tables while it was taking place. Not a word was uttered. In the sobbing aftermath the silence was deep and accusing until the scrape of knife and fork on plate and the low hum of conversation resumed.

And then comes a devastating sentence that for many Irish readers will ring cruelly and irrefutably true: 'Many who had sat mutely at the tables during the beating were to feel all their lives that they had taken part in the beating through their self-protective silence.'

Ruttledge, who has spent a short period in a seminary training for the priesthood, is intrigued by Bill and tries to draw him out in conversation:

> 'Why are you asking me this, Joe?'
>
> 'Everybody comes from somewhere or other. None of us comes out of the blue air.'
>
> 'You'll be as bad as Jamesie soon,' he answered irritably.
>
> 'Weren't you in a place run by Brothers and priests before they sent you to the first farm?' Ruttledge ignored the rebuke. A troubled look passed across Bill Evans's face as swiftly as a shadow of a bird passing across window light and was replaced by a black truculence. 'Before the priests and Brothers weren't you with nuns in a convent with other small boys? Weren't you treated better when you were small and with the nuns?'
>
> This time there was no long pause. A look of rage and pain crossed his face. 'Stop torturing me,' he cried out.

Later in the novel, Ruttledge will work to have Bill Evans found a place to live in sheltered housing, just as John worked with his own parish priest, Frank McCabe, to find somewhere welcoming for Pat Conway to see out his days. Madeline recalls McCabe as 'very clever, sophisticated'. Seamus Heaney liked to tell a story that John had told him about McCabe playing poker one night in one of the Fenagh pubs. He was way ahead in the pot and then took his leave suddenly, declaring that he had Mass to say in the morning.

McCabe was a native of Aughavas, County Leitrim. He was ordained for the diocese of Ardagh and Clonmacnois in 1924 and was parish priest of Fenagh from 1957 until he retired. He was an active, sprightly and earthy man who was part-time priest and part-time farmer. Kind and practical, he was much loved by the locals and could be seen at fairs and markets selling his stock. John used to tell and retell with great gusto his first encounter with this priest:

> I was sitting here at the desk one day when I looked up and there was Fr McCabe sitting on a chair in the room beside me. He had let himself in quietly and seated himself without a word. His opening salvo was 'The man up in Longford [Bishop Cahal Daly, later to be Cardinal Daly] told me to call to see you. He likes your books. I don't read books myself, but if I did, from what I hear, yours wouldn't be the sort I would be reading!'

John took to him immediately, and they became good friends, cooperating in a number of instances – usually helping parishioners who were struggling. He is fictionalised in the novel as Father Conroy. 'Father Conroy is plain', says Patrick Ryan, the local handyman and builder. 'The priests had this country abulling with religion once. It's a good job it's easing off.'

Seamus Deane, reviewing *That They May Face the Rising Sun* for the *Guardian*, dwells on a tension. 'In one sense', thinks Deane, 'it could be crudely described as a relation between an older and an emergent way of life, between Ireland of the haemorrhaging emigrations and the new, more prosperous place where the returned emigrant is the crucial figure.' He glosses a challenge for McGahern's readers:

> Although he has indeed charted the internal history of a culture in which most of the old authoritarian systems have weakened or even collapsed, and has as such retained his status as an emblematic figure,

> the danger has always been that this view of him would govern the reception of his writing to the exclusion of all else. In the light of this work, such exclusion now becomes impossible.

Glancing at James Joyce, Deane concludes: 'At last an Irish author has awakened from the nightmare of history and given us a sense of liberation which is not dependent on flight or emigration or escape.' And certainly the novel straddles at least two distinct ages, looking back at a dark past of homeboys, marital rape, betrayal and casual cruelty while suggesting at the same time that some sort of salvation is possible, that one can – like Joe and Kate Ruttledge – be kind and decent, and still prosper.

Just as Ruttledge tortures Bill Evans, albeit clumsily and accidentally, in pursuit of some greater truth, John hurts himself into and through writing. 'I have said that literature is a deep pain', he tells Rondeau on parting that evening after their meeting with Pat Conway, 'but it is also an intense form of life. Any life would be small without literature.' John liked to say that the strangest thing about writing is that one never learns how to do it. The writer, Yeats tells us, 'is never the bundle of accident and incoherence that sits down to breakfast; he has been reborn as an idea, something intended, complete.' There has to be a period of reflection as the day begins again before a blank sheet, and John was never sure what would happen on that page as each new day dawned. He is always relieved when someone he trusts comments positively on work in progress, as Michel Gresset, the French William Faulkner scholar, does on reading the first extract of what is to become *That They May Face the Rising Sun*.

Gresset, whom John had first got to know when they were both visiting professors at Colgate in 1978, had come across the extract titled 'Easter', which eventually forms the opening pages of the novel, in the *TLS* of 30 April 1999:

> Michel, thanks for the fair, and generous words about the small piece of the novel. Even with the rarity of good writing there has to be true feeling and right thinking over the whole complicated form for it to be interesting. I have hopes I'm getting close but there is never certainty.

> 'Big Job. Not Easy,' my dear uncle used to say while clearing his throat like a huge chimney.

That he was writing a novel at all had taken John by surprise. *Amongst Women*, as we know, he had intended to be his last such effort in the genre. But a surprise commission from BBC Radio 4, first mooted in October 1994, got him thinking seriously once again about fiction. Frances Byrnes, a features producer at the station, had been deeply moved by *Amongst Women* and wrote to John with a proposal to write a piece that might fit into a new series called 'Spirit of Place'. Byrnes's idea was to record authors telling their stories in the place where they were set, evoking the sound of their world.

Over lunch in Dublin on 7 January 1995, John told Byrnes about a murder that had taken place on his home patch in 1982 and an image that had stayed with him: a local woman, shot by her husband, had died holding a handful of currants she had just pulled from a jar. Byrnes was gripped by this story and encouraged John to write it up as his contribution to the series. John was hesitant, fearing that the narrative was too close to actual local events of the not-too-distant past: 'In my opinion, no real people or even places could be used. The events are too recent and too shocking and compromise too many people – take the Mart Manager, for one – too deeply.'

But Byrnes was persuasive, and in early January 1996, John sent her the completed story:

> I have written a prologue and epilogue to frame the story. You'll notice that they belong to silence.
>
> My own feeling is that all sounds should be muted, and kept to a minimum, to be effective. The voice will carry most of it, but certain sounds – the auctioneers in the cattle mart is an obvious instance, and it should be ritualised rather than realistic – can replace the voice.

'Love of the World' was recorded in Bristol on 18 March 1996. Byrnes subsequently went with McGahern to Foxfield to record the 'real' version, and all its atmosphere, later that week, with sound man Iain Hunter. A cat answered back to John's voice as he read, causing many retakes. The piece was broadcast on BBC Radio 4 on 29 October 1996 and published in *Granta* magazine on 13 March 1997, an appearance over which John hesitated, knowing that the story was closely related to the novel on which he was at this point working well.

'Thanks for the kind words about the story', he tells Neill Joy:

> As it was broadcast in a truncated version while I was in Colgate, and it is the locale (not the theme) of the novel I wasn't anxious to publish it but the agent felt otherwise and sold it to GRANTA. I'll not write any more stories until I finish the novel.

In fact, John would never write another story, and all his efforts now went into completing *That They May Face the Rising Sun*.

Through writing 'Love of the World', John had found a character, Kate Ruttledge, and a tempo with which he felt comfortable and which one might characterise in style as 'late McGahern': 'It is very quiet here. Nothing much ever happens. We have learned to tell the cries of the birds and the animals, the wing-beats of the swans crossing the house, the noises of the different motors that batter about on the roads.' In attempting to describe a world devoid of action, John was getting as close as possible to Gustave Flaubert's dream:

> what I would like to create is a book about nothing, a book without external attachments held aloft by the internal force of its style, as the earth stays aloft on its own, a book that would have almost no subject or at least in which the subject would, if possible, evaporate. The most beautiful works are those that have the least matter; the closer expression hugs thought, the more words cleave to it and disappear, the more beautiful it is.

That said, while there are long passages in both 'Love of the World' and *That They May Face the Rising Sun* where the undramatic pace of nature is permitted to dictate prose rhythm, things do happen. Kate Ruttledge of 'Love of the World', like John's mother, has the bad luck to fall in love with an outsider, a handsome guard. For her, the infatuation will prove fatal, with Guard Harkin eventually gunning her down in a fit of jealousy before committing suicide in custody:

> A silence came down around all that happened. Nobody complained about the normal quiet. Bird cries were sweet. The wing-beat of the swan crossing the house gave strength. The long light of day crossing the lake steeped us in privilege and mystery and infinite reflections that nobody wanted to break or question.

The lake, birdsong, reflection: this was the world of John's final novel, a world it is likely he would not have entered had it not been for this story but one that would come to define him in his last years and that now became his primary focus.

Between periods spent facing the wall, searching for the right words, life carried on. In December 1993, Madeline's father died in Paris and was cremated on Christmas Eve. September 1995 saw the death of her mother in Atascadero, California. She and John travelled together for the funeral. *Amongst Women* was adapted for television, with Tony Doyle as Moran. Generally considered a success, the series was never watched by John. Spring of 1996 was packed with travel: Paris, Bristol, Aix-en-Provence, Berlin, Saint-Malo, Palermo.

That autumn, John and Madeline were back in Colgate, with John hitting the road again, this time for Dallas, Chicago and Fayetteville, Arkansas. Through spring 1997, Madeline was much in Paris trying to settle her father's inevitably complex estate. By March, John had had enough of the Leitrim rain and decided to take up the *New York Times Magazine*'s offer to hit out for the sun:

> We both go to Morocco for 2 weeks in April. I have to write a piece. When the offer came in January I said NO and felt virtuous for a few days. After 5 days of foddering cattle here in the rain and looking for myself I said to hell with virtue and telephoned to see if the offer was

> still open. I also persuaded them it was necessary for me to stop in Paris on the way in order to check out a Moroccan restaurant I used to go to early in the 1970's. Our itinerary is Rabat, Fez, Marrakesh, Taroudant, Paris.

Other than a brief reflection on Camus's essays and on his *Exile and the Kingdom*, the piece that John ends up writing on Morocco is standard travel-supplement fare. A spin-off article about the Parisian restaurant mentioned in his letter to Neill Joy, which appeared in the *Irish Independent* the following year, is far more interesting and revealing. 'Dreaming at Julien's' is the best account that John has left us of Paris, a place in which he spent several formative years of his life.

During periods of his and Madeline's life together in the early 1970s, as John recalls, they 'used to frequent a restaurant called Julien near the Arc in Strasbourg Saint-Denis. The long rectangular room was an art nouveau palace fallen on hard times, and it was the cheapest and most colourful place to eat in the whole of Paris.' Long walks were something John enjoyed, as Madeline had experienced from their early date at Upton Park, and the couple habitually strolled from rue Christine to Julien's: 'crossing the Pont Neuf to the Quai de la Mégisserie, passing the pet and garden shops that stayed open late along the quay and the many cafés around the Châtelet before reaching the Rue Saint-Denis'.

Now, with the *New York Times* footing the bill, John was anxious to return to Paris for reasons other than business. Always enchanted by the city, he recalls his 1996 appearance on the late-night television show *Le Cercle de minuit* on France 2, where he was interviewed by Laure Adler, who becomes increasingly, if charmingly, exasperated by John's sly evasions as a translator whispers her questions into his ear.

Surrounded by champagne buckets and a cigarette-smoking audience, Adler wonders if England had given to the Irish people and to Irish writers the language they needed so they could write literature. It is easy to imagine from that point on that John knew how to play ball: 'I write in English and the laws of language are English, but the spoken language is full of Irish rhythm. So it's almost as though the ghost of the dead language is living in English.' And he then, as many times before, becomes insistent on breaking Irish shackles:

> One belongs to the human race first, which is much more important than French or English but the language that I love is English. When I was young I was attracted more to French and to Italian literature . . . Because of the influence of the Catholic Church I think. In English literature it's bad taste to deal with mystery, to deal with origins – the proper study of mankind is man.

He mentions his admiration for the Italian writers Eugenio Montale and Leonardo Sciascia, before the interviewer returns with a comment that Ireland is a country of superstition and mythology, which in turn leads to another bout of jousting, John clearly beginning to enjoy himself: 'I think that poetry and religion and superstition are very close.'

Adler, now becoming a little irritated with what she thinks is obfuscation, asks simply, 'Why? *Pourquoi?*' Her subject is rapid in reply: 'I think they try to ask questions that cannot be answered.' Again asked to expand, John, with a smile on his face but in deadly earnest, says: 'I think that one can't answer any good questions. All one can do is to state the question well. Prayers that cannot be answered need to be more completely said since they are their own beginning and their end.' Adler, fed up with the riddling, asks if Ireland is a cruel country. To which the answer is given: 'I think that every country is a country of cruelty, that civilization is very frail.' It was quite the performance. 'To me', thinks Madeline, 'it looked like a fuck off for the whole enterprise he was part of.'

The show had had to be filmed much later than originally scheduled due to a technicians' strike. By the time the work had all been wrapped up in the studio just off the Champs-Élysées and the participants had dined in a late-night brasserie, the time was well after midnight. John turned down the offer of a taxi, wanting to make the long walk back to his hotel in Montparnasse. 'I crossed the river at the Pont des Invalides', he recalls. 'There was hardly any traffic, the city was almost silent. I could hear the hours and the half-hours being struck. I have never seen anything as beautiful as this silent, naked city. The walk took over two hours and I wished it had been longer.'

It had been a memorable night. One often finds a revelatory turn, despite Adler's frustration, in John's French interviews that is frequently absent when dealing with British or Irish journalists. One thinks of Jamesie's advice to Kate in the final novel's opening scene: 'Enter lightly, Kate, and leave on tiptoe. Put the hand across but never press. Ask why not but never why. Always lie so that you speak the truth and God save all poor sinners.'

John's thinking on the ghostly presence of the Irish language in the English of contemporary Ireland had been building for some time, and this facet bubbles up again in *That They May Face the Rising Sun* via a subplot that sees Joe and Kate Ruttledge's best friends around the lake, Jamesie and Mary, faced with the unwanted possibility of Jamesie's brother Johnny returning from London to live with them after being made redundant by the Ford factory in Dagenham. Jamesie approaches Joe for help, not knowing how to respond directly without breaking the tacit rules of family and society:

> The timid, gentle manners, based on a fragile interdependence, dealt in avoidances and obfuscations. Edges were softened, ways found round harsh realities. What was unspoken was often far more important than the words that were said. Confrontation was avoided whenever possible. These manners, open to exploitation by ruthless people, held all kinds of traps for the ignorant or unwary and could lead into entanglements that a more confident, forthright manner would have seen off at the very beginning.

This crucial paragraph concludes that such people's form of communication, like Irish, lacks an aspect: 'It was a language that hadn't any simple way of saying no.'

Ruttledge agrees to write a letter that Jamesie can copy as his own, 'explaining the situation clearly but softening it enough to give Johnny room, suggesting when he thought about the idea more he'd see how hopeless it was from his own point of view'. Johnny takes the bait, and the idea is forgotten. John's 'magnificently courteous attention to English as it is spoken in Ireland', as Penelope Fitzgerald put it while reviewing *The Collected Stories*, stood as an enduring strength in his prose.

* * *

As always when John was writing seriously, he was more than happy to be distracted away from his work. In late September 1997, he and Madeline made another trip to France, where John was conferred with an honorary degree by the University of Poitiers. Despite the sweltering heat, they enjoyed themselves, and John's love of the country and its way of life remained constant.

> On a Sunday we went to a small town and bought oysters, sardines, bread, cheese, lettuce, tomato, artichokes and went back to a 5 hour lunch under linden trees in a big garden. A couple of 22, both handsome, sat through the 5 hours without a flicker of boredom, and discussed the food and wine as knowledgably as if they were 2 centuries old.

In the same period, John was in discussion with the French publisher José Corti to produce a new edition, with introduction, of the letters of John Butler Yeats, a run of correspondence he had long admired, first edited by Joseph Hone in 1944. The copy John was working from through that autumn and winter had been gifted to him by Mary Hutchinson many years previously. By February 1998, the Yeats letters were ready, to be published simultaneously in Paris and in London the following year.

The novel, John thought, was also nearing completion, with him going through what he estimated to Frances Byrnes that same February would be 'the last or second last writing' of the manuscript. This statement would prove, as usual, hopelessly optimistic. In January 2000, he was writing to another friend: 'I'm working on nothing but the novel. The end is a good way off still, but it's in sight.'

He worried to Byrnes about the alarmingly early appearance of plants he would not normally notice for another month, sensing something was askew with the world: 'The daffodils are out here as well, and crocuses, and the primroses on the banks. I find it strange, too, disturbing.' In March, he read from his work in Newfoundland:

> It was very beautiful and stark, and incredible spaces. I liked the people very much. Waterford and Cork can be heard in some of the accents. The houses were like white boats on the edge of the sea. There's a writer from Nova Scotia, Alistair MacLeod, whose work I like very much.

MacLeod proved one of those rare and sustaining finds for John. A list of such finds, usually of a short-story writer, would also include names such as Richard Ford, Mavis Gallant, Eleanor Gilchrist and Alice Munro. When John taught a series of seminars at UCD through the spring of 1999, he insisted on gifting each of his students a copy of MacLeod's 1986 collection *As Birds Bring Forth the Sun*. Later that year, he found MacLeod's best-selling debut novel, *No Great Mischief*, disappointing. 'It seems art is almost as unpredictable as life', he comments to Neill Joy in his annual Christmas missive.

John's later comments on the difference between the short story and the novel as genres, when introducing a 2001 Jonathan Cape edition of MacLeod's *Collected Stories*, is more informative about McGahern's Ireland than it is about MacLeod's Newfoundland:

> I think of the novel as the most social of all the art forms, the most closely linked to an idea of society, a shared leisure and a system of manners. The short story does not generally flourish in such a society but comes into its own like song or prayer or superstition in poorer more fragmented communities where individualism and tradition and family and localities and chance or luck are dominant.

That Irish society was somehow more suited to the production of short stories than of novels was a theory that had originally been floated by

Seán Ó Faoláin as far back as the 1940s; that John had managed to succeed in both forms made him unusual. But not all long-form fiction fails, as he excitedly reported to Neill Joy: 'I read a marvellous novel set in a University', perhaps the best such campus novel he has ever read. And so we have the first mention of what would become one of the more rewarding tangents of John's later years, the rediscovery of the Texan writer John Williams and his 1965 novel *Stoner*.

Stoner, a novel about a Midwestern farm boy who becomes a successful university English lecturer before falling foul of his emotionally immature wife and an ambitious departmental rival, was first recommended to John by Skip Hays, who taught in the creative-writing department at the University of Arkansas, Fayetteville for twenty-five years and is best known for his 1984 baseball novel, *The Dixie Association*. Hays had come to know John when he taught each summer at the month-long Arkansas summer writing programme held at UCG. During the last week of each session, John tended to be the visiting writer. He would give a lecture to the class and, later, a public reading from his work. During those visits, John and Skip – over lunch, dinner, drinks – got to know each other and exchanged recommendations about books. Skip introduced him to the work of John Williams by mailing him a copy of *Stoner*, a novel he was sure John would love. He was right.

John was quickly telling anyone who would listen about *Stoner* and proselytised on the book's behalf in a way that he had only ever done once previously, and that was for Forrest Reid's 1934 novel *Brian Westby*, which he had urged Charles Monteith and Faber to reissue. Crucially, he sent Caroline Michel at Vintage a copy of *Stoner*: she loved it and bought it, together with Williams' epistolary novel of ancient Rome, *Augustus*. Michel asked John to write introductions for both novels. Though reticent, he agreed 'in the hope it might get them attention'. Both novels dealt brilliantly, in John's view, with issues of power. Of Williams' rendering of the Emperor Augustus, he says, 'Amidst his family, friends and enemies, he deals with the exactitudes that the use and retention of power imposes, and all is brought to such immediate life that it feels as present as Washington today.' In recapturing the vicissitudes of imperial Roman life, John argues, Williams has managed to achieve something extraordinary: 'the world of *Augustus* is so various in the brilliant play of lights the different epistles become that selective quotes seem to diminish the richness the whole lights reveal'.

As much as John admired *Augustus*, he saw the earlier novel as even better, a near-perfect masterpiece. 'When writing about *Stoner*', he declared, 'I found that the material was next to impossible to paraphrase, since the prose had already been so distilled.' He had never spoken so enthusiastically about another's work before, and his introduction helped the reissued *Stoner* to become a sensational international best-seller, first with Vintage in 2003 and then in 2006 with the New York Review Books edition. The book passed John's most important test, it being hugely enjoyable: 'There is entertainment of a very high order to be found in *Stoner*, what Williams himself describes as "an escape into reality" as well as pain and joy. The clarity of the prose is in itself an unadulterated joy.'

John had never met Williams, only becoming familiar with his work several years after the Texan's 1994 death. For Williams' widow, Nancy, still living in Fayetteville when the novels were reissued, the whole experience of seeing her late husband suddenly catapulted into the first rank of English-language novelists was deeply affecting. 'I am moved by your two introductions', she wrote to John, 'I'll never forget your efforts on behalf of two good books.' Inspired by what John had done for the novels, she began to read his work, treasuring *The Dark* and *Amongst Women* especially, before moving on to what would prove his final novel:

> I dearly loved *By the Lake*. It's one of those rare books that one reads slowly so as not to come to the end of it. Every night at my son's house I read more slowly than I had the night before. I came to love those people, Jamesie and Mary, Ruttledge and Kate and the rest . . . it's gratifying that younger readers are taking up *Stoner* . . . I am so very pleased about the interest you have stirred up.

By the Lake had, much to John's chagrin, become the American title of *That They May Face the Rising Sun*, Knopf feeling that the longer title might impede US sales. Perhaps they were right: the American volume was reprinted three times within months of first publication, far outstripping in sales any of his other books – including *Amongst Women* – on that side of the Atlantic.

That said, the original title, with its prayerful wish, had been carefully chosen by its author. 'It is a very old pagan burial tradition in Ireland', he told one French interviewer.

> When somebody dies, he is buried towards the East, so that on the last day he is facing the rising sun. There is an ancient Gaelic poem that goes: 'Bury me at Ros na Rí and set me down that I may face the rising sun,' Ros na Rí being the burial ground of kings in Ireland. In the 19th century, some priests tried to modify this practice and have people buried facing the church. But people thought that the Sun mattered more than the church.

But death on a terrifying scale had overtaken the whole question of an American title, with the 11 September 2001 attacks by Al-Qaeda on New York and Washington, DC. As the hijacked aeroplanes crashed into the World Trade Center that bright Tuesday morning, Madeline was 40,000 feet over the Atlantic, having taken off from Heathrow for New York. Her flight turned back, and she spent several unplanned days in London before eventually joining John in Colgate for what would be his final stint teaching there. Among the decisions the couple had to make over the phone during this enforced separation was the choice of an American name for the new novel. It could have been worse: the other title presented to John was *In the Village*.

'I think it probably *is* my best work', John declared of *That They May Face the Rising Sun* in a late interview, 'but it's not for me to say.' Pressed on a feeling that the novel seems to exist outside of history, he expanded on the book's origins:

I suppose as you get more connected you're less tied to your society and you're more closely connected with your language. I think there's quite a bit of history in *That They May Face the Rising Sun*, but it's by suggestion and innuendo, which I think is always more powerful than statement.

It would have gone through many drafts. It basically grew out of this story 'Love of the World.' I find that as I get older, I can't write *short* short stories any more, and that all the stories are growing into novels.

There is nothing new about a writer believing that whatever he has most recently written is his best work – why else would you write it after all? But there is a definite valedictory quality to this novel, a rich perfection that makes analysis feel superfluous. Little wonder that one recent American critic should declare it 'One of the great novels of the twenty-first century'. The book proved another notable success, selling 27,000 Faber hardbacks on release in January 2002 and over 100,000 paperbacks the following year. Though for the most part rapturously received by the critics, it failed to make the Booker Prize shortlist.

'Once I saw the list of judges', John tells Frances Byrnes, 'I knew the novel had no chance.' One can see why John might have been pessimistic: one of the judges, the British novelist Russell Celyn Jones, opens his *Times* review of the novel by damning it with faint praise: 'John McGahern's big hearted, old-fashioned pastoral novel incorporates several deaths and entrances of men, women and livestock in rural Ireland and ends more or less where it begins, after one year's farming cycle.' John saw little to encourage him in the other judges. Among them were Erica Wagner, then literary editor at *The Times*, and Jeanette Winterson ('she found it trivial'). John remarked that Lisa Jardine, chairperson of the panel, 'is also in the same group'. He finished, 'Everybody has an agenda. In fact, as I knew the book had no chance, I'm glad to be out of it early.'

In truth, John was more than comfortable enough both monetarily and within his own skin to ride out such perceived dismissals and misreadings. He was more irritated by the novel's cover than by its misfire with the Booker panel. 'Terrible. Totally out of whack', he tells Will Cohu of the *Daily Telegraph* over tea in Soho a week before the book is released to the public. The design, featuring a black-and-white photograph of leaves by Paul Strand, titled *Leaves, Orgeval, France, 1965*, was not approved by John, and Cohu sees why: 'The gloomy jacket underscores a commonplace assumption about McGahern: that he's a fine writer without a joke in the house. In fact, it's a funny as well as beautiful book, with a slowly contagious sense of the ridiculous.'

The cover, if botched, did not prevent the critics from rhapsodising about the quality of what was contained within. Eileen Battersby in the *Irish Times* considered it superb: 'McGahern, a supreme chronicler of the ordinary as well as of the closing chapters of traditional Irish rural life, has created a novel that lives and breathes as convincingly as the characters who inhabit it.' On the same day, John Boland of the *Irish Independent* was reminded of the nineteenth-century Russian tradition, seeing the book as in a whole different class from anything else then being published: 'while there's nothing self-consciously poetic about this book, the insights enshrined in its unassuming lyricism provide that unmistakeable poetic sense of truths being told about the tragi-comedy in which everyone of us is helplessly implicated. It's a masterpiece.' The *Belfast Telegraph* was similarly uplifted by the reading experience, with the reviewer also inclined towards thinking of the great Russians:

> John McGahern's first novel in over a decade brings to mind the theory of incarnation. Just as each life is said to more closely approximate nirvana, McGahern's books are nudging closer, and closer still, to technical perfection . . . I had forgotten how wonderful, and Chekhovian, McGahern can be. To read him is to step into a forgotten world of emotional nuance and integrity.

In the USA, *By the Lake* was also positively received, though with several reviewers puzzled by the absence of plot. John wrote to Joe

Kennedy: 'There were complaints: no plot, uncouth people, too much demands on the attention span of the modern reader etc. but they were in a minority, luckily.' Typical in this regard was the *Boston Globe*:

> The narrative thrust of a novel, by necessity and technique, must be both larger and faster than real life; otherwise, what you have is merely the story of a Sunday morning that takes all of Sunday morning to tell. And so *By the Lake* ambles on, no more concerned with fleshing out a dramatic story line than Ruttledge is with whether or not the shed on his land ever gets built.

Thankfully, others were more forgiving of the book's pace. For Malcolm Jones of *Newsweek*, *By the Lake* was 'the most perfect novel I've read in years. By perfect I mean composed, or built, like a handcrafted table, with everything mortised and sanded and finished to a T.' As with Nancy Williams, this reviewer wished the novel would never end: 'I saved the last 20 pages of the book for two weeks, unread: as long as I did not finish, I could stay in that world beside the lake.'

The British reviewers – with the notable exception of Sam Phipps in the *Spectator*, who thought that with this novel 'the blarney detectors appear to be running out of batteries' – were equally in thrall to the quality on display. *The Economist*, far from seeing the prose as silver-tongued Irish hokum, found itself moved by the novel's slow magic: 'This is a book to surrender yourself to. If you give in to its measured ebb and flow, you will find yourself in an intense, poetic world in which the simplest objects . . . take on a quiet but magical luminosity.' The *Sunday Telegraph* was similarly spellbound:

> *That They May Face the Rising Sun* is a tour de force, but not of the brash, eye-catching kind that a younger writer might have achieved. Think of an old man telling a story by the fireside, taking his time, but choosing each word with extraordinary care, and you will get the flavour of the writing.

Ultimately, the most perceptive review of the novel was written by Hermione Lee, whose 1996 biography of Virginia Woolf John so admired. She summarised the book's concerns:

> But this great and moving novel, which looks so quiet and provincial, opens out through its small frame to our most troubling and essential questions. How well do we remember? How do we make our choices in life? Why do we need repetition? What is to remain of us? Above all, what can happiness consist in?

Lee, as doubtless pleased John, had perhaps understood the work better than anyone else outside of Madeline. The possibility of 'happiness', that most dangerous of words, is what the book is primarily about. Interviewed by Lee at a prize-giving in Santa Fe, New Mexico in 2004, John was asked whether the darkness in his work came from himself or from Ireland's history. 'Somebody said about me recently in Ireland', he responded, 'that I had everything wrong, that when I should have been enjoying myself I was full of darkness and violence and now when I should be saying my prayers I'm beginning to enjoy myself.'

Asked by *Libération* what he had wanted to express in the work, John was unusually certain: 'I think that it is a novel about happiness. And happiness happens when nothing happens. And the most precious things in life are what is insignificant. There is such abundance around us. But it is difficult to capture.' When John would read from the book in public, he tended always to turn to a passage that takes place in the aftermath of Ruttledge's annual watching of the All Ireland football final with Jamesie, a character based on his dearest neighbour, Francie McGarty. As he returns to his own house across the lake having bid Jamesie goodbye, Ruttledge hears the voices of Kate and his uncle, the Shah, coming from within:

> They were discussing the sale and transfer of the business. As he listened to the two voices he was so attached to and thought back to the afternoon, the striking of the clocks, the easy, pleasant company,

the walk round the shore, with a rush of feeling he felt that this must be happiness. As soon as the thought came to him, he fought it back, blaming the whiskey. The very idea was as dangerous as presumptive speech: happiness could not be sought or worried into being, or even fully grasped; it should be allowed its own slow pace so that it passes unnoticed, if it ever comes at all.

'I think happiness is the most fascinating subject in the world', John declared in front of a paying crowd of over 1,200 at the Dublin music venue Vicar Street in the weeks after his novel's publication. Not since reading with Robert Lowell in Harvard twenty-five years earlier had he been exposed to such a large and eager public. Back then, it was the great Boston poet who had drawn the crowd, but now John alone was the star, and, before everyone had had their book signed, the restaurant that had been booked for the post-show dinner had closed.

* * *

By the time John was shortlisted, in April 2002, for the €10,000 Kerry Ingredients Irish Fiction Award at the annual Listowel Writers' Week Literary Festival, winning and losing meant less than ever. He had been diagnosed with colon cancer on his return from Colgate, having known for a while that something was not right with his body. He had delayed taking action until he was back in Foxfield and the novel was published.

'I knew there was something wrong with me for about a year', he writes to his friend Michael Gorman, 'though a doctor discounted the symptoms and when the publicity rounds were done I got myself into the Mater':

> I had a tumour in the colon. There was an uncertain 24 hours or so until they discovered the cancer hadn't spread and was easily operable. This was a success but a mistake was made with a catheter during surgery that led to trauma and septicaemia and kept me in hospital for 5 weeks. My own feeling is that I was fairly lucky. I go in now for

> mild chemotherapy, an hour every Thursday, 4 Thursdays in a row, two Thursdays free, and it'll last till November. It's not pleasant but it's not too bad either.

With characteristic professionalism, John was keen to go to Kerry. If he were to win, it would mean reading on Thursday, 30 May, a day for which chemotherapy was scheduled. He wrote in confidence to the committee:

> I would be honoured to read from the novel at 12.30 but am reluctant to ask for the therapy to be rescheduled to Tuesday or Friday unless I know I'll be required to read on Thursday. I feel very uneasy requesting this, not least out of respect to the other Finalists, the Judges, the Committee: but my position as regards the hospital and treatment is delicate. Any information you would choose to give me I would hold in strict confidence and would be grateful for the same concerning my medical situation.

John was quietly told the good news that judges Eileen Battersby and Eugene McCabe had chosen him as the winner, and he and Madeline arranged their trip to Listowel accordingly.

That They May Face the Rising Sun proved to be John's last novel, and that finish feels right: the Ruttledges have lived a life together, and they have learnt from that life. 'Nothing so profoundly human and so unvarnishedly honest has ever been written about rural Irish society', wrote Michel Déon. 'It rises above the blackness with which Irish literature usually speaks about its world.'

While the book is still, like most of John's works, permeated by cruelty and violence, it is appropriate that his final fictional lead should be Joe Ruttledge. He believes that value lies in a world not of cut and thrust but of more tender understandings, as a pivotal exchange with Patrick Ryan makes clear:

> 'Patrick shows none of us any mercy,' Ruttledge said by way of comfort.
>
> 'I tell the truth and ask no favours.'

'The truth isn't always useful.'

'Tell me what is.'

'Kindness . . . understanding . . . sympathy maybe.'

For this novel is the work of a mature man who, born into love and tempered through suffering, has arrived at his end with insight and dignity.

17
Ready to Die
2003–06

When you have no imagination, dying is small beer;
when you do have an imagination, dying is too much.

CÉLINE, *Journey to the End of the Night*

One day we all run out of luck. Yeats, Rilke and Proust, John's three great instructors, all had much to say about death and dying. The first of them thought of death as a completion, a place where one could finally understand, to 'know it all'. The latter two understood that we each are born with our death implanted, like a seed. The living are, remarked Proust, 'only the dead who have not yet assumed our roles'. Underlined in John's heavily thumbed and annotated copy of Rilke's *The Notebooks of Malte Laurids Brigge* is the narrator's realisation that 'one had one's death within one, as a fruit its kernel'. To carry that knowledge 'gave one a singular dignity and a quiet pride'. All three writers had made accommodation with the great mystery.

As John sat at his desk on 26 October 2003 to write to his old friend Niall Walsh, it was with settled equanimity that he laid out his predicament. This missive was one of several letters written that year in which those he had known longest were told the difficult news that his cancer was now terminal and that there was no way back. Walsh's medical background, the fact that he was himself a cancer survivor and the longevity of the friendship allowed John to write with straightforward candour:

> The cancer news is bad. I had the colon check last April, which was perfect. A scan wasn't due for another 3 months and so convinced were they that I was all right that it was only at David Legge's

> insistence that a scan was done then. 7 lesions showed on the liver, and there was no cancer elsewhere then or since. The statistics were 98% in my favour. The original tumour was very slow growing, and those cells were able to hide from the chemo, and 2% became my case.

John bore the news with characteristic stoicism, though he confessed to Madeline that he felt he could have written well into his eighties had he been given the luck of health. In the wake of the diagnosis, he began to cut down on engagements and found himself filled with a new writing energy. 'I used always look for ways to avoid writing', he confessed to Walsh, turning again to one of his favourite poems, Larkin's 'Show Saturday', for sustenance: 'but now I find it's there like hidden strength or those obdurate cells. It was probably always that way but it was more obscured. What is but trying to deal with reality?' John concluded the letter with thoughts of friends and family already passed from the world, knowing that he was soon to join their ranks:

> I suppose you saw that my dear friend Dick Walsh died. He should have died many years ago but somehow survived through will and spirit as much as medicine. Tom Jordan, who taught with me in Clontarf, died. I'm fairly sure you met him here. My sister Breedge died suddenly on a holiday in New Zealand. It is that season, like that charming late ode of Auden's to the cuckoo.

A week later, he would think again of Auden's cuckoo while writing to Neill and Mary Joy. The poem ends in meditative mood about the ways in which the bird's simple and evocative two-note cry marks the passing of time:

> Science, Aesthetics, Ethics, may huff and puff but they
> cannot extinguish your magic: you marvel
> the commuter as you wondered the savage.
>   Hence, in my diary,
>
> where I normally enter nothing but social

engagements and, lately, the death of friends, I
scribble year after year when I first hear you,
of a holy moment.

Every April, Foxfield could be guaranteed a visit from the calling migrant, sometimes to the point of distraction. As in so many country townlands, it was a matter of pride to be the first to hear it, the surest marker of spring's arrival and the promise of better days to come.

The finest of John's letters from this period of terminal diagnosis, capturing as it does his calm realism and surprising artistic energy, was written to his friend Michael Gorman in Galway:

> There is not too much difference here, other than the adjustment to a different reality, a reality we always knew was there, and unavoidable, but is still different when it comes. I used to have ways of avoiding going to the room to write, disliking the intensity and total absorption, but now I'm glad of it, it belongs more to now than when we felt free in acres of time; and that too was necessary, and is. I find I have to be socially more careful: all society excludes this knowledge, in order to function. There was a do for an old friend of mine, Alf Rowley, a barman in Mohill, two years ago. He was dying, and the function was to help pay bills. He lived less than a week afterwards. He had a fine singing voice, and at the end, before The Soldier's Song, he rose and thanked them, and then sang I Bid You All a Fond Goodbye. There wasn't a stampede for the door, but it was the next best thing, and mutterings about the poor man not being in his right mind, the Leitrim way of describing a lack of tact.

John busied himself in the face of his end. As well as writing every day, no longer afraid of the blank wall and white page before him, he did something few expected from a man who had built a reputation on the solitary toil of the clerk: he allowed himself to be persuaded into the most public role of his career, writing to the Joys about the move with a certain degree of mirth.

> I'm now a member of the Arts Council, and drink pints with the Minister, a nice man, John O'Donoghue, who isn't refined enough for some of the Elite. I have caused trouble already. Of the 53 million the Government spends on the Arts only 7% gets to artists: singers, actors, writers, painters etc.

Minister O'Donoghue and John had got along well at the Shelbourne Hotel presentation of the Irish PEN Award in March, and he was appointed to be a member of the Arts Council with effect from 14 August 2003 for a period of five years. For as long as his health would permit, he enjoyed travelling to Dublin by train to attend Council meetings in Merrion Square, arguing for increased and fairly awarded funding.

'I was reluctant to accept the Nomination for a number of reasons', he explained to Caroline Walsh, literary editor at the *Irish Times*, 'but we haven't the right to complain if we aren't willing to do something, and it is our country.' The musician, film producer and radio host Philip King, who served with John on the Council, recalled for me his rigour and passion: 'On a national level we miss him, we miss what he can tell us about ourselves.'

To join a large public body such as the Arts Council was just one of several uncharacteristic things John did in the knowledge that he was dying. Perhaps even more surprising was his decision to write something like an autobiography, or, more accurately, a series of memories, largely of his childhood and youth and of the lives of his parents. The resultant book, published in 2005, would be called, simply, *Memoir*, though John struggled, as so often, to name it. 'The Lanes' or 'Summer Lanes' had been considered. When John suggested 'The Moons of Gloria' to Neil Belton, his editor quickly emailed to say that such a title made them all at Faber 'a bit frightened'. John could see the point: 'About a hundred titles have been thrown at the book, and none of them seem to stick. Memoir might be the right title.'

Writing the actual book proved easier than coming up with a title. As John had told friends, he now found himself more concentrated on the writing, less inclined to find excuses or distractions. Starting work around the summer of 2003, he made what, for him, was spectacular progress and writes to Neill Joy in March 2004 of 'wonderfully quiet months of work'. This run soon got interrupted by a spate of travel to San Francisco, Santa Fe (where he was awarded the Lannan Literary Award for Fiction, worth $125,000, and interviewed publicly by Hermione Lee) and once more to Colgate, where he was conferred with an honorary doctorate of letters on 16 May.

By the following month, he was sufficiently advanced with the book to send a full manuscript to Ian Jack at *Granta* magazine, who would publish the opening section under the title 'The Lanes' in November. Jack, a railway fanatic, had various useful suggestions to make about possible revisions and pointed out to John that he had misnamed the railway company in his memoir as the 'Sligo, Leitrim and Northern Counties' when it ought to be the 'Cavan and Leitrim'. Jack further pointed out that the station John travelled from as a child was called Garradice Halt, not Aughawillan. John was more than happy to revise accordingly, Jack finding him 'a delight to work with'.

The editor wrote to me less than a year before his own death in open terms:

> His book editors may have had a different experience, but I never found him angry or irritable. In company, the little I saw of him in it, he enjoyed himself, talking freely and expressively. I gathered from people who knew him better, or at least longer, that he could be sharp and gossipy about the people he thought of as rivals. I never witnessed that but I don't disbelieve it. He liked gossip. The countryside is a gossipy place, after all.

In October, the book was sold to Knopf through John's London agent, Bill Hamilton at A. M. Heath, and published the following year in the USA under the title *All Will Be Well*. 'When I began the memoir', John wrote to Niall Walsh in January 2005, 'I didn't expect to have the time to finish. In some mysterious way these years have been more rich and full than any others.'

These months continued to be busy, at least for as long as John's health would permit. Early November 2004 saw filming around Foxfield and Cootehall for the Pat Collins-directed documentary on John's life, *A Private World*, a piece of film-making with a distinctly elegiac feel. John was visibly drawn and losing weight, though as mentally sharp as ever. Madeline, with a characteristic desire for privacy and feeling that she was not the subject of the film, did not wish to take part. As John told Walsh, 'Madeline tried to escape being filmed but the cameraman persuaded her to sit there. I'm glad he did.' When screened on RTÉ One on Tuesday, 11 January 2005, *A Private World* attracted viewing figures more usually associated with a championship football match, coming in north of 275,000.

Viewers were stumped by footage of John riding the Tokyo subway, a section of the film he disliked but which Collins retained. 'It's unpleasant watching yourself', he tells Walsh, 'but Madeline says he pulled it together all right.' John and Madeline's trip to Japan came just after the Foxfield filming as part of a cultural exchange supported by the Irish Department of Foreign Affairs.

Madeline kept a diary of their days:

> November 8: We walked to the venue/club, downstairs into a dimly lit space predominantly black. Groups sat around tables, a more brightly lit bar to the left. John is asked on the platform what is his favourite drink: whatever I can drink with one hand, he answered. He read Korea, the tiredness showing, not masking aggression in the reading, which sounded, especially toward the end, like a marching staccato rather than a controlled narrative. An actress in full regalia read the Japanese translation. Pat McCabe joins us. He is a benign presence.

> November 9: Interview in the hotel. Craft museum, lunch at Tim & P's with Murikami [*sic*] and a beautiful, discreetly pregnant journalist from the Japanese Times, from where Aisling took us to the train to Kyoto. Mt Fuji. Professor meets us. There is just time to shower and change and we are driven for half an hour to authentic Japanese dinner with 2 other profs. Professor Sano (Emeritus) reminded us

of Tom, dear Tom Jordan. We were grateful for the evening but exhausted. John fell asleep as soon as his head met the pillow. I've never seen that before. He looks well this morning.

The whole Japanese experience continued to prove compelling, with various hosts working hard to show off their homeland at its best and the McGaherns keen to make the most of their time so far from home in these marvellous surrounds:

> November 10: The hotel looks across to the imperial gardens. The city is a modern grid, with names not numbers. The limp grows pronounced. This morning at breakfast on seeing one of the guests I realized there is no strut here, which adds to the pleasant appearance of ease . . . Couldn't find a Starbucks and couldn't walk far, so I sit in a chic hotel lobby café listening to a Bach suite for harpsichord. It is balm . . . Back to the hotel where Prof. Sano meets us to take a train to the Imperial Palace. Two or three hours later he takes us to a covered market where we have a simple supper in the equivalent of a bistro or a café. We are then joined by the lady professor who took us to the previous evening's restaurant, and we set off to a popular theatre evening. The only thing of interest was the Japanese tea ceremony. The audience was made up of tourists who were constantly taking flash photographs. Unfortunately, after the show, as a special courtesy, we were taken backstage for an interminable amount of time, during which the actors spoke about their craft, which was translated.

As fascinating as this once-in-a-lifetime voyage proved, John's energy was inevitably low, and the travel proved sapping. Spring 2005 was spent in Foxfield, with John putting the finishing touches to *Memoir*. Not until May did the couple travel far, this time to Zurich, where John gave a reading at the James Joyce Foundation and the McGaherns stayed with the Irish ambassador and his wife.

The cancer treatments continued through that summer in an attempt to give John as many worthwhile days as possible. Niall Walsh remained the friend with whom he could be most open through these difficult times:

> I have been on a new treatment since before Christmas, a new stem cell drug, which ½ the time they mix with the chemo. The results vary from patient to patient but in my case it appears to have been unusually successful. How long this will last nobody seems to know: it is still just maintenance treatment.

And now the publication of *Memoir*, with all its attendant marketing, loomed large. 'I'm not looking forward to the next weeks,' he continues his letter to Walsh, 'when this will have to be juggled with the demands for publicity.'

John's final book was published on 1 September 2005 to huge public interest and critical acclaim, both the *Irish Times* and the *Guardian* having carried extracts in advance. John was given a month off from cancer treatment while he promoted *Memoir*. Trinity College Dublin held a launch event in the library's imposing Long Room on the 12th, followed by events in London, including a Faber dinner at The Ivy. John returned on the 18th, and on the 21st he launched a book of Liam Kelly's titled *Kiltubrid, County Leitrim: Snapshots of a Rural Parish in the 1890s*, having been invited to do so by the Carrick-on-Shannon Historical Society.

John had already by this time run into some difficulties with people who got unfavourable mentions in *Memoir* – his McGarry cousins, Bishop Francis MacKiernan, the family of Mrs McCann, the schoolteacher who 'kept a supply of bright yellow bamboo canes in the press, and when they splintered she used ash and sally and hazel from the hedges and plied them with zeal all through the day, for errors and mistakes, oral or written, for any straying of attention or the slightest indiscipline'. All this opposition led John to say to Kelly that evening: 'You were smart. It is much safer writing a book about the 1890s than it is about the 1990s.'

Despite these grumbles, there was a great crowd of Leitrim people present in the Bush Hotel that night. Kiltubrid, the parish being written about, had just won the Senior County Championship in football for the one and only time in the club's history, spirits were high, and the cup was brought to the launch. John enjoyed the evening, signing copies of *Memoir*, meeting and chatting with the locals. 'It was', recalls Kelly, 'a leavetaking of sorts – John saying farewell to Leitrim, and Leitrim, without being aware of it, saying farewell to John.'

The following evening, John appeared in a packed Galway Town Hall, introduced to the audience by Michael Gorman. At various times throughout the event there was uproarious laughter, one highlight being John's hilarious retelling of the Sergeant making a citizen's arrest of Ballinamore's parish priest for trying to stop young Seán from going to the Ulster Final with his father because he was expected to attend post-Mass religious instruction, the priest having Seán by the ear, the Sergeant having the priest by his ear. John always insisted that he had written the book primarily in an effort to understand his father, as is made clear within its pages:

> I knew him better by then than I knew any living person, and yet I had never felt I understood him, so changeable was he, so violent, so self-absorbed, so many-faced. If it is impossible to know oneself, since we cannot see ourselves as we are seen, then it may be almost as difficult to understand those close to us, whether that closeness be of enmity or love or their fluctuating tides. We may have an enormous store of experience and knowledge, psychological and otherwise, but we cannot see fully because we are too close, still too involved.

For that night in Galway, at least, the Sergeant was largely let off the hook, and tales of recalcitrance and remarriage were played for laughs.

At other moments, particularly as John concluded with the now celebrated closing passage of the book, people throughout the audience could be seen quietly weeping:

> We would leave the lanes and I would take her by the beaten path the otter takes under the thick hedges between the lakes. At the lake's edge I would show her the green lawns speckled with fish bones and

blue crayfish shells where the otter feeds and trains her young. The otter whistles down the waters for the male when she wants to mate and chases him back again to his own waters when his work is done; unlike the dear swans that paddle side by side and take turns on their high nest deep within the reeds. Above the lake we would follow the enormous sky until it reaches the low mountains where her life began.

I would want no shadow to fall on her joy and deep trust in God. She would face no false reproaches. As we retraced our steps, I would pick for her the wild orchid and the windflower.

The line of attendees waiting to have their copies of *Memoir* signed wound its way around the Town Hall lobby for well over an hour, everyone wanting to have their few moments with the author. The *Irish Times*' correspondent summed up how many there that night felt about what they had just witnessed:

> It was clear to everyone in the audience that we had happened upon a particularly rare and special evening. To be in the presence of one of the great writers that this or any country has known on a night when he delivered what seemed like a valedictory, recalling the dramas of an austere country existence with warmth and honesty and stunning clarity, was a very moving and powerful experience. The applause lasted a long time afterwards, the audience being reluctant to quit and to let go of the moment, which was fiercely poignant. It was a night that most people in the attendance will carry with them through the remainder of their lives.

That night would prove to be one of John's final public appearances.

Not everyone admired the book or the writer as much as the Galway audience. By the following January, Declan Lynch in the *Sunday Independent* had had enough of what he argued was unwarranted adulation. In a large spread, titled 'Herd Instinct' and dominated by a photograph of a Friesian cow with John's face superimposed over its head, Lynch sought to question the writer's place in the Irish literary pantheon. 'He has been a pariah and now he is a saint', wrote Lynch. 'He started out writing "dirty books"; now he writes books that are regarded almost as sacred texts.' He continued:

> Most newspaper articles about McGahern are written with a sense of awe, a feeling that every moment of an interview or a public reading must be treasured, the memory preserved as clearly as possible, and written down so that future generations may know what it was like to be in the same room as McGahern, to breathe the same air as this holy man.

The motivations for even writing *Memoir* are called into question:

> And for an artist of McGahern's integrity there was something oddly market-driven about *Memoir*, as if he was persuaded in a weak moment that people didn't know enough already about the man himself, though of course, like most major writers of fiction, McGahern has told us volumes about himself and all belonging to him in his short stories and novels.
>
> Anyway, it elevated him further into the realm of sainthood, providing enough tales of rural Ireland to keep the dinner parties of Dublin 6 well supplied, ensuring that they won't have to go back and read any of those collections of stories that sold 23 copies back in the day.

Others also wondered at the bona fides of the autobiographical turn. Seamus Heaney, having read through most of the book, writes to a friend of his impressions:

> I've taken a big chunk out of the middle of the book where the death gets ready to happen and the move is made to the barracks. John can do the thing truly and heartbreakingly, but B. Friel would more than share your unease. He thinks the mother hagiography is a derogation, almost a scandal. The writer/priesty fragrance is too much for him. And I know what he means, and why you had to take, as you say, 'an

obscure line' with the book. I feel – what shits we have to be – he's got too good at what he does.

But these were isolated voices, and *Memoir* was for the most part received enthusiastically by public and reviewers alike on both sides of the Atlantic. Colin Burrow in the *London Review of Books* dwelt on the intersection between autobiography and fiction:

> Fiction, we're sometimes told, is a way out of ourselves, or a way into other people. For McGahern it is not quite that, or if it is a way into other people it is a way that takes you so deep into the imprisonment that others experience that there is no way out on the far side.

The book was a worthwhile experiment, he thought, 'an important moment in McGahern's career and, perhaps, in the history of Irish fiction'.

The *Sunday Times* felt that John may even have superseded his fiction with this, his final book: 'McGahern's memoir can be bleak, but it is radiant with the absolute lucidity and humanity of his writing, and his sense that "the precious life is everything." It is actually better than his fiction, and that's saying something.' The *New York Times* was similarly in awe of John's gift for isolating the value of life itself: 'what makes this memoir so moving is its insistence . . . on the power of the single day that passes before us'.

In Ireland, the reviews were laudatory. 'Though primarily an artist', wrote Declan Kiberd in the *Irish Times*, 'McGahern emerges here as perhaps the profoundest of all sociologists of 20th century Ireland.' Emer O'Kelly in the *Sunday Independent* treasured the book's truth-telling quality: 'John McGahern, unyielding, uncompromising, sometimes unforgiving, is one of the blest and soaring few. He stands four square for truth and clarity of vision: in the service of his fellow human beings, he does not forgive the unforgivable.' One of the few reviews to comment on the almost complete absence of John's later life from *Memoir* came in the *Belfast Telegraph*: 'The fact that he takes us only up to the publication of his first collection of short stories, *Nightlines*, could mean there is more to come. There will be thousands, like me, who cannot wait.'

Alas, there would be no more. Christmas – a season always beloved of both John and Madeline – passed quietly in Foxfield. In late January, the couple travelled to London, where *Memoir* won the *South Bank Show* Award for Literature, the prize presented to John by Edna O'Brien at the South Bank Centre. The McGaherns dined afterwards at the Garrick Club with Melvyn Bragg, Matthew Evans and their partners before retiring to the Savoy. While in London, both McGaherns came down with food poisoning. On their return to Leitrim, they contracted flu, forcing them to cancel a planned trip to the USA to promote *All Will Be Well*.

'Madeline recovered easily enough', writes John to his solicitor on 24 March in what would be his penultimate missive, 'but since my own system has been shot up with chemotherapy for a number of years, I knew before I went into the Mater that I wouldn't make America.'

In his final days, John reread Freud's *The Future of an Illusion*, an essay on the origins of religious belief that seeks to understand 'man's need to make his helplessness tolerable'. John's last published essay, 'God and Me', had been commissioned by Ian Jack at *Granta* and was published posthumously in the *Guardian* a week after his funeral. He writes in this piece: 'Gradually, belief in those sacred stories and rituals fell away without my noticing until one day I awoke, like a character in a Gaelic poem, and realized I was no longer dreaming.'

As the end drew close, John was nursed, to his amusement, in what had once been Charles Haughey's room in the Mater Private Hospital on Eccles Street. He rose to the occasion when people visited, though in the final days requested that no more visitors come. He asked to be brought a copy of Jane Austen's *Mansfield Park*. He had a radio by him but did not listen to it much except for sports. Many cards and letters arrived from well-wishers, among them Hilary Mantel, Edna O'Brien and a host of complete strangers.

At about noon on Thursday, 30 March 2006, John McGahern died. Madeline was contacted, with unseemly haste, by RTÉ and asked to comment. Naturally, she refused. Once the necessary calls had been made and arrangements put in place, she returned to the McGaherns' small Stoneybatter house and, alone in Dublin and not knowing what to do with herself, went to the cinema to watch *Capote*, a film set around the composition of the author's 1965 classic *In Cold Blood*.

For months before his death, John had been making careful plans for his funeral and had secured permission to be buried alongside his mother in the churchyard of St Patrick's, Aughawillan. A fortnight before his death, he rang Fr Liam Kelly to ask if he would officiate at his funeral Mass. Kelly was a fourth cousin of John's. A native of Aughawillan, he trained as a Catholic priest at Maynooth in the mid-1970s and in the same period became friendly with the McGaherns after John and Madeline settled in Foxfield from 1974. Despite Kelly having noticed with sadness the obvious toll John's cancer was taking on him, and knowing for a year previously that the condition was terminal, he was shocked by the finality of the request.

Some months earlier, John had asked Kelly to check with the parish priest in charge of St Patrick's Church, Aughawillan to see if his funeral Mass could be held there and also to let the priest know that he wished to be buried alongside his mother in the adjacent cemetery. The telephone conversation on 9 March was short, and Kelly assured John that he would be honoured to celebrate his funeral Mass. Over the next three weeks, Kelly visited John twice at home and once in the Mater Private Hospital just three days before he died. Despite being very weak and unwell, John was lucid, and the two men talked openly about his final wishes. He was philosophical about his impending death at the relatively young age of seventy-one, and, during one of Kelly's visits to his house, John quoted from Yeats's *Oedipus at Colonus*: 'Endure what life God gives and ask no longer span.' Kelly was struck by this line and decided to use it and to add a few more lines from the same source in his homily a couple of weeks later.

During those visits, John talked in some detail about his funeral arrangements, and as he talked, it soon became clear that he wanted a traditional-style ceremony, a country funeral. John told Fr Kelly that he had asked Luke Early, the undertaker in whose Mohill pub he used to drink so contentedly, to look after the arrangements. He asked Kelly to contact Luke and select the simplest of coffins for him. John specified that he wanted the ceremony to be simple, with no music and no eulogies.

Kelly asked him if he wanted any of his sisters to take part in the funeral liturgy. John said that he did not want to give them, or indeed anyone else, any opportunity for 'self-expression'. Kelly, concerned about the wisdom of such a break with tradition, asked John to think carefully about the exclusion of family, and, in the end, the men agreed that John's four sisters – Monica, Margaret, Rosaleen and Dympna – would bring up the offertory gifts. Kelly composed the prayers of the faithful and read them. John's mother and father were remembered in these prayers as were his deceased siblings, Frankie and Breedge.

The readings for the funeral were selected by Kelly. The first was taken from Ecclesiastes: 'To every thing there is a season, and a time to every purpose under the heaven: A time to be born, and a time to die; a time to plant, and a time to pluck up that which is planted.' The second reading came from St Paul's First Letter to the Corinthians: 'There are different kinds of service, but the same Lord. There are different kinds of working, but in all of them and in everyone it is the same God at work.' Finally, the Beatitudes were read: 'Blessed are the poor in spirit, for theirs is the kingdom of heaven.' The first and second readings were taken, at John's request, by some young people from the Aughawillan area.

John warned Kelly in their chats over those final weeks that there was to be no artificial grass used at the graveside. He referred to it as 'butcher's grass' – that is, the livid green fakery some butchers use to display their meat. Kelly mentioned John's wishes on this to Luke Early the day before the funeral, and yet, to his surprise, there was artificial grass there at the open grave before Mass began. Kelly asked Luke to remove it, which he did. Luke and his wife Ann looked after all the details and were respectful and tactful in all that they did at the time of the funeral. In truth, they were grieving the death of a friend.

John also specified that the five decades of the rosary be said at his graveside and that some of the local Aughawillan men be asked to fill in his grave with shovels, in the traditional fashion, while the people were still present. He knew the age-old wisdom that saying the rosary and shovelling the clay into the grave would take about the same time, and he knew that something similar had happened at his mother's funeral at that same place some sixty-two years earlier. He did not want to sanitise what was happening in any way by covering the clay with artificial grass and filling in the grave after everyone had left. He wanted the thud of clay on the coffin to be heard by those present, even though he did not put words on this wish. Some of the bystanders tossed lumps of the wet clay onto the coffin with their bare hands as the skies opened up in typical Leitrim fashion.

Fr Kelly began his homily with references to John Donne before moving on to more personal thoughts:

> His death is a death in the family, not just for his own family and friends, but for the whole country which has come to know him through his writings and for people world-wide who hold him in great affection and high esteem. A great writer and a good man has died and we are all the poorer for his passing.
>
> Some of John's best writing, like the seasons, is cyclical in nature, ending up where it began. And so it seems appropriate that we should gather for this funeral here in St Patrick's Church in Aughawillan where John came to Mass as a small child. It was here that he learnt to serve Mass. It was here that he had his first brush with church authority when, as a small boy, he was denounced for rattling his beads too loudly during prayer. There would be other brushes with church authorities later – and even though he was treated badly he never held any grudges or traces of bitterness. He was bigger than that. The church was, he said, his first book and he had learnt much from it.

From here, Fr Kelly went into a longer meditation on John's changing relationship with the Catholic Church from childhood into maturity:

> He identified two parallel movements within Catholicism – one the fortress churches with their edicts, threats and punishments and the other the churches of the spires and brilliant windows that go towards love and life. The latter was his church and he lived his life on the river that led towards love and life. Today we remember that life, we celebrate it and give thanks to God for it.
>
> St Paul, in his first letter to the Corinthians, states that 'there is a variety of gifts but always the same Spirit' and 'that the particular way in which the Spirit is given to each person is for a good purpose.' John was a gifted writer and his work, like all good art, is essentially spiritual. He dedicated his life to writing about the local and the ordinary, the minutiae of life, the things that others see yet never notice. And through hard work, clear thinking and deep feeling he has produced works of art that are admired around the world, works of art that will survive the test of time.

That Fr Kelly turned to classical Greece as he came to conclude his reflection feels appropriate to the occasion and to the subject of this elegy:

> Over the past few weeks we had precious time together when John talked openly about his impending death and the arrangements for his funeral. He loved life but did not fear death. He had lived with the reality of death since he was a child and liked to quote Achilles: 'Speak not soothingly to me of death.' That was his way.

On the day of the funeral, Saturday, 1 April 2006, John's remains were removed by hearse from the hospital morgue after mourners had been given the opportunity to file past his coffin from 7 a.m. The cortège drove through the Midlands, and crowds, as it entered John's home county, began to gather. 'It was only when we crossed the borders of Leitrim', reported the next day's *Sunday Independent*,

> that you began to notice the small knots of people standing by the roadside, heads bowed in silence and respect. What started with a few people on the outskirts of Rooskey and a trickle along the roads

turned into hundreds of people lining the streets of Mohill, Fenagh, where the old ruined churchyard was one of his favourite places, and Ballinamore.

St Patrick's Church, Aughawillan is a small and intimate country chapel. It was full at least an hour before the funeral took place, and in the end there were more people standing outside than were seated inside. Fortunately, the parish priest, Fr Eamon Lynch, had made sure that there would be a speaker set up to relay the proceedings. President Mary McAleese was represented by Captain Lorraine Fahey and Taoiseach Bertie Ahern by Commandant Micheál Murray. Minister for Arts, Sport and Tourism John O'Donoghue represented the government. Among those from the world of the arts to be there included Seamus and Marie Heaney, Brian and Ann Friel, Michael and Edna Longley, Tom Murphy, Eugene McCabe, Declan Kiberd, Garry Hynes and Paula Meehan as well as members of the Arts Council. Faber & Faber was represented by Matthew Evans, Stephen Page and Robert McCrum.

The 3 April meeting of Leitrim County Council was adjourned for a short time as a mark of respect, with John being remembered as a great writer and a man 'with no airs and graces'. Obituaries were printed in all of the national newspapers and in the British broadsheets as well as in many provincial titles, some wishing to dwell on the character of the man, some on his work, and others delving into the banning of *The Dark* and the role John played in lifting a veil on past abuses and injustices.

Nobody caught John's spirit better than Nuala O'Faolain, one-time lover and friend, whose reflection appeared in the *Sunday Tribune* the day after he was buried. A native of Clontarf whose younger brothers had been taught by John, she begins with thoughts on the coming of spring once again to the Irish countryside as this friend of her youth is laid to rest: 'Yet when I think of him, I think of the rainy, shadowy, dark-grey Dublin of his youth and mine, where the golden light from pubs was almost the only light along the quiet streets.'

The year must have been 1961, after she had graduated from UCD and was readying herself to study medieval romance at the University of Hull and thence to Oxford on a travelling studentship. A letter survives from that period that casts light on the relationship, with John counselling her about life and love. Nuala was twenty-one, John twenty-seven: 'you have to be both careful and savage. The only world is the world of love, what you said, and if we're true we must be consumed in whatever reality there is. All the rest is really business.'

O'Faolain's obituary continues:

> I don't altogether trust my memory. Those days were such a chaos of emotion and learning and having no money and ignorance and drinking and falling in love and missing busses and always having wet shoes. I got things wrong back then. And I was so wrapped up in myself, I hardly saw other people. But I knew that John was extraordinary.

As much as she found John intriguing, she did not fall in love with him, nor he with her. 'No matter what happens we mustn't ever love one another totally', John appeals to her in November 1961. Another, undated, letter from the same period sees John cautious of where they might turn next:

> I think it's better for us not to meet on Monday, there's too much brokenness in our last evening and yesterday, a kind of inconsequence without joy, almost more pauses or waitings, both of us just coming out of our different lives and narcotics and going away after a kind of comical bowing. So let us wait apart for a while, it's better that way. I am sure. What is happening, since it's so careful – without risk – would only come to pallid and tolerant lyricism, and you are, at least, too beautiful and alive to deserve or want that pass.

These were two people meeting as equals who respected each other, who could see that there were things to learn from one another. 'I remember that we went out to Skerries on a bus one weekday, in summer', writes Nuala, 'and walked along a headland full of lightheartedness':

> We walked on Howth Head too, and we walked miles and miles around the middle of Dublin. Or we went to the afternoon movies or we sat in pubs, eking out one drink. The pub we used to meet in in Fairview turns up in the great story 'Sierra Leone'.

Though Nuala admits that she did not find John 'good-looking or attractive' and that there was 'no emotional connection' between them, the friendship was of enduring worth:

> Yet I valued every hour of our awkward friendship. I respected him, then and always. He had come out of childhood and youth a formidable person . . . He already knew what he meant by being a writer. He gave me, what he could ill afford, a copy of Rilke's *Letters to a Young Poet*. Now, I see that John, for all that he was shabby and unregarded and about to incur the hatred of the deathly Ireland of that time, had already absorbed Rilke's advice; 'that you may find in yourself enough patience to endure and enough simplicity to have faith; that you may gain more and more confidence in what is difficult and in your solitude among other people'.

'I don't think I've ever met anyone who so fully accepted the way things are', she concludes. 'In the simplest way, he was always ready to die.'

EPILOGUE
Hard Joy

> We live as we dream – alone . . .
>
> JOSEPH CONRAD, *Heart of Darkness*

'We get by on dreams', writes John on the first page of a green hard-backed Educational Company of Ireland copybook used during the composition of what was becoming *The Pornographer*. He continues: 'Sometimes life gives us a version of that dream, for if it was the dream complete it'd be the end of life. By the time we know it is a version and not the dream, the dream itself has changed or we have lost the energy to dream anew.'

This private note, written for his own consideration, is not dissimilar to what he had told his audience at the Rockefeller Institute, Manhattan a decade or more previously about the genesis and function of art:

> So we cannot live, we can only absurdly reign, but it is not possible to live when confronted with the immovable solidity of the world, so we transform it into another way because of nothing more than our distinctive need. And as we reign alone there on our cuckoo throne the subjects we summon up are images.

The scene brought to the surface in John's jagged, spidery, black biro over the following twelve pages of this notebook consists of an early draft describing the meeting in a dance hall and subsequent courtship of *The Pornographer*'s unnamed narrator with the dark-haired nurse who is caring for his dying aunt in a Dublin cancer hospital. It becomes one of the best scenes in the book, a lyrical yet raw meditation on mortality and its consequences for the human spirit. After dancing together, the couple take a taxi out to the nurses' quarters, the smell of freshly mown grass filling the air as they enter the grounds. In the midst of this plenitude, the narrator is conscious that in the looming hospital building beyond his beloved aunt lies dying:

> The taxi turned in the hospital gates, went past her window, the moonlight pale on the concrete framing the dark squares of glass. The wheel had many sections. She had reached that turn where she'd to lie beneath the window, stupefied by brandy and pain, dulling the sounds of the whole wheel of her life staggering to a stop. I was going past that same window in a taxi, a young woman by my side, my hand on her warm breast. I shivered as I thought how one day my wheel would turn into her section, and I would lie beneath that window while a man and woman as we were now went past into the young excitement of a life that might seem without end in this light of the moon.

The pair visit the sleeping aunt, return to the nurses' room, undress and hold each other close in the moonlight – it feels like as near to honest human connection as the narrator is capable. One wonders if love might even prove possible.

On his return to the hospital weeks later, having avoided any further contact with this young woman, the narrator wonders to himself what he has learnt from that clandestine night:

> The nothing that we always learn when we sink to learn something of ourselves or life from a poor other – our own shameful shallowness. We can no more learn from another than we can do their death for them or have them do ours. We have to go inland, in the solitude that is both pain and joy, and there make our own truth, and even if that proves nothing too, we have still that hard joy of having gone the hard and only way there is to go, we have not backed away or staggered to one side, but gone on and on and on even when there was nothing, knowing there was nothing on any other way.

John considered Joseph Conrad's *Heart of Darkness* 'a strange great poem'. Like Marlow, that novel's narrator, John believed that life had to be lived alone, that it is not possible to know another. But that did not stop him from trying, and his relationship with Madeline was as close as he would get to succeeding.

* * *

Madeline's mother, Kate Delafield, died in an Atascadero, California care facility in September 1995, aged eighty-two, after a long, meandering life. John could see how deeply this passing affected his wife, despite mother and daughter having seen very little of each other since Madeline's infancy. 'We were the only relatives present at the small funeral', John wrote to friends. 'Death is like another business deal there, more aesthetic than usual, formal, subdued, but still strictly business – The Chapel of the Roses.' The funeral taking place around Labor Day weekend meant that accommodation was hard to come by, and the couple ended up in a fleapit motel. John paid for lunch afterwards for Kate's elderly, trailer-park friends, who all took doggy bags away with them.

Madeline briefly felt overwhelmed with grief, a grief she has never processed: 'The feeling of freedom driving on up to Steinbeck Country afterwards was one of the happiest moments of my life. Onward to San Francisco.'

Notes

EPIGRAPH

vii *Some day men*: Rainer Maria Rilke, 'The Rodin Book: First Part', *Where Silence Reigns: Selected Prose*, trans. G. Craig Houston (New York: New Directions, 1978), p. 129.

PROLOGUE

xv *What part does*: John McGahern, 'The Creamery Manager', in *Creatures of the Earth: New and Selected Stories* (London: Faber & Faber, 2006), pp. 228–36, at p. 236.

xv *I especially remember*: John McGahern, 'Souveniers d'une Irlande en rouge et vert', trans. Florence Benoist, *Libération*, 11 and 12 June 1988. Translated back into English by Anne-Claire Leydier.

xvi *We have signified*: West Ham United v. Manchester United, Football League Division 1 match programme, 2 September 1967.

xvi *to show everyone*: Michael Green, 'And Go to Church on the Saturday, I Presume?', *Sunday Times*, 3 September 1967.

xviii *sauntered through it*: Brian Glanville, 'Diligent Charlton Is Still the Hero', *Sunday Times*, 3 September 1967.

xviii *How do you begin*: Brian James, 'Diary of a Strange Match', *Daily Mail*, 4 September 1967.

INTRODUCTION: TO WRITE A LIFE

1 *I think it is very*: Typed-up answers to unknown interview (1985), John McGahern Papers, University of Galway, P71/1205 (1).

1 *I can see how*: John McGahern, *The Pornographer* (London: Faber & Faber, 1979), p. 163.

1 *a monk's cell*: Michel Déon, *Horseman, Pass By! Irish Pages*, trans. Clíona Ní Ríordáin (Dublin: Lilliput Press, 2017), p. 138.

2 *Where anyone lives*: Ciaran Carty, 'John McGahern: "It Would Be an Insult to Be Called an Irish Writer"', *Sunday Independent*, 11 June 1978.

2 *All a writer*: Carty, 'John McGahern'.

3 *The second one formed*: For more on the provenance of this photograph, see Pádraig Óg Ó Ruairc, *Revolution: A Photographic History of Revolutionary Ireland 1913–1923* (Cork: Mercier Press, 2011), p. 151.

3 *The officer dispatched*: John McGahern, 'Korea', in *Creatures of the Earth: New and Selected Stories* (London: Faber & Faber, 2006), pp. 45–50, at p. 45.

3 *It was the stillness*: John McGahern, 'Sierra Leone', in *Creatures of the Earth: New and Selected Stories* (London: Faber & Faber, 2006), pp. 211–27, at p. 213.

4 *There is a definite*: Undated letter from John McGahern to Mary Lavin (August 1960), Mary Lavin Papers, UCD.

4 *inexact, misinterpreted*: Marie Nordlinger, 'On Reading *Marcel Proust: A Biography*', *X: A Quarterly Review*, 1 (3) (1960): 203–9, at p. 204.

4 *Even Ellmann's life*: Quoted in Joseph O'Neill, 'A Heartening Way with the Big Things', *Sunday Correspondent*, 6 May 1990.

5 *In the great*: John McGahern, 'The Life, the Work and the Hurt', in *Love of the World: Essays*, edited by Stanley van der Ziel, with an introduction by Declan Kiberd (London: Faber & Faber, 2009), pp. 351–3, at pp. 352–3.

6 *I have read the biography*: Letter from John McGahern to Eibhear Walshe, 21 July 2001.

6 *generous, thorough and*: Eibhear Walshe, email to the author, 11 January 2022.

6 *The way one views*: Patrick Gilligan, 'Volunteer Frank McGahern', *John McGahern Yearbook*, 3 (2010): 58–73, at p. 73.

7 *I think it*: Typed-up answers to unknown interview (1985), John McGahern Papers, University of Galway, P71/1205 (1).

7 *His reputation is*: John Walsh, 'Illuminating the Dark Side of the Irish', *Sunday Times Books*, 29 April 1990.

CHAPTER 1: COLD SHADOW, 1934–53

9 *To grow up*: Halldór Laxness, *Salka Valka*, trans. Philip Roughton (New York: Archipelago Books, 2022), p. 78.

10 *A lurid light*: John Walsh, 'Illuminating the Dark Side of the Irish', *Sunday Times Books*, 29 April 1990.

11 *set great store*: John McGahern, *Memoir* (London: Faber & Faber, 2005), p. 5.

11 *I was in the eighth*: John McGahern, *Amongst Women* (London: Faber & Faber, 1990), p. 74.

11 *Such a possibility*: See Patrick Gilligan, 'Volunteer Frank McGahern', *John McGahern Yearbook*, 3 (2010): 58–73.

11 *Thanks largely to*: Joe Kennedy, email to the author, 9 February 2022.

11 *The ledger detailing*: Civic Guard (Garda Síochána) temporary register (February 1922–September 1924), UCD digital archives. Francis McGahern, registered number 2074, is listed on p. 149.

12 *a gnawing resentment*: John McGahern, *The Barracks* (London: Faber & Faber, 1963), pp. 28–9.

12 *On one occasion*: *Memoir* erroneously recounts this story as involving the theft of a Crombie overcoat, one of many errors (whether accidental or deliberate) that pepper the book. I am grateful to Liam Kelly for the correction.

13 *During my father's*: McGahern, *Memoir*, pp. 53–4.

13 *The small fields*: McGahern, *Memoir*, p. 44.

14 *related their suffering*: Quoted in Liam Kelly, 'Seán MacDiarmada and the Tradition of Rebellion in County Leitrim', in Liam Kelly and Brendan Scott (eds), *Leitrim History and Society* (Dublin: Geography Publications, 2019), pp. 585–608, at p. 593.

14 *John's maternal grandmother*: Liam Kelly, *The First Fatality of the Land War: Philip Meehan (1845–1880)* (Cavan: Cumann Seanchais Bhreifne, 2021), p. 22.

14 *she was uprooted*: John McGahern, 'My Education', in *Love of the World: Essays*, edited by Stanley van der Ziel, with an introduction by Declan Kiberd (London: Faber & Faber, 2009), pp. 109–14, at p. 109.

14 *The Carysfort register*: Register of Students, 1911–25, Our Lady of Mercy, Carysfort, Blackrock. UCD Archives, C181/26/1.

14 *Through the sacrifice*: John McGahern, *The Leavetaking* (London: Faber & Faber, 1974), p. 85.

15 *I have nothing*: John McGahern, 'The Church and Its Spire', in *Love of the World: Essays*, pp. 133–48, at p. 133.

15 *My memories of her*: Fr Peter Dolan, letter to the author, 26 January 2025.

16 *One remarkable document*: Susan McManus nature notebook, John McGahern Papers, P71/1799.

16 *If we could walk*: McGahern, *Memoir*, p. 272.

17 *A silence came*: John McGahern, 'Love of the World', in *Creatures of the Earth: New and Selected Stories* (London: Faber & Faber, 2006), pp. 336–68, at p. 366.

17 *What would the people*: 'Burtonport Wake Outrage', *Derry Journal*, 14 November 1928.

18 *had dalliances with*: McGahern, *Memoir*, p. 54.

18 *Whether Frank was gallivanting*: On the marriage certificate, Frank is listed as living in Shanaglish, Beagh, Tubber, County Clare.

18 *No need to talk*: McGahern, *Memoir*, p. 55.

19 *She had seven*: John McGahern, 'My Education', in *Love of the World: Essays*, pp. 109–14, p. 109.

19 *No human being*: Thomas Kelly, 'On McGahern's People', *Sunday Independent*, 11 June 2006.

20 *There was always*: McGahern, *Memoir*, p. 23.

20 *she'd been warned*: McGahern, *The Leavetaking* (1974), p. 65.

20 *the cancer child*: McGahern, *The Leavetaking* (1974), p. 72.

20 *I started to move*: McGahern, *The Leavetaking* (1974), p. 49.

21 *That their father*: John McGahern, 'The Going', John McGahern Papers, P71/64.

21 *She watched him*: McGahern, *The Barracks*, p. 64.

22 *There was a church*: McGahern, *Memoir*, p. 25.

22 *My backgrounds are*: Undated letter (1975) from John McGahern to Elisabeth Schnack, John McGahern Papers, P71/1795.

22 *shadow was to fall*: McGahern, *The Leavetaking* (1974), p. 71.

22 *Susan McCaffrey*: Memories of Anna Kennedy, daughter of Susan McCaffrey, supplied in email from Liam Kelly to the author, 14 September 2023.

23 *I watched the hands*: McGahern, *The Leavetaking* (1974), p. 79.

23 *A child*: McGahern, *Memoir*, p. 23.

23 *I write because*: John McGahern, 'Playing with Words', in *Love of the World: Essays*, pp. 9–10, at p. 9.

24 *The barracks itself*: McGahern, *Memoir*, p. 32.

25 *10/6/58: While driving*: Sergeant Frank McGahern's final garda notebook, Madeline McGahern Papers.

25 *did what they did*: Gilligan, 'Volunteer Frank McGahern', p. 71.
26 *When my father*: McGahern, *Memoir*, p. 188.
27 *Each move he made*: John McGahern, 'Korea', in *Creatures of the Earth: New and Selected Stories* (London: Faber & Faber, 2006), pp. 45–50, at p. 50.
27 *Then late one evening*: McGahern, *Memoir*, p. 191.
28 *I was planting*: John McGahern, 'Schooldays: A Time of Grace', in *Love of the World: Essays*, pp. 103–8, at p. 104.
28 *John sat the entrance*: See *Presentation College 1948–1953* (Carrick-on-Shannon: Carrick-on-Shannon & District Historical Society, n.d.).
29 *Brother Placid took*: McGahern, 'Schooldays', p. 107.
29 *John repaid Brother*: See *Connacht Tribune*, 3 October 1953.
29 *without realizing it*: McGahern, 'Schooldays', p. 108.
29 *the ramrod-straight*: McGahern, *Memoir*, p. 171.
29 *Mr. Mannion was*: Lionel Gallagher, 'Sean and I: A Tale of Two Barracks', unpublished typescript, Madeline McGahern Papers.
30 *There were few books*: John McGahern, 'The Solitary Reader', in *Love of the World: Essays*, pp. 87–95, p. 87.
30 *I read books, Father*: Patrick Kavanagh, *Tarry Flynn* (Harmondsworth: Penguin Books, 1978), p. 43.
31 *Time was filled*: McGahern, 'The Solitary Reader', p. 87.
31 *surrounded by a huge*: McGahern, 'The Solitary Reader', p. 88.
31 *many, many books*: McGahern, 'The Solitary Reader', p. 89.
32 *If I didn't want*: McGahern, *Memoir*, p. 205.
32 *The winning of*: See Séamus O'Grady, 'John McGahern and the University', *John McGahern at NUI Galway* (Galway: National University of Ireland, Galway, 2007), pp. 13–14.
32 *Nobody from your*: John McGahern, *The Dark* (London: Faber & Faber, 1965), p. 167.
33 *If there are*: McGahern, *The Dark*, p. 173.
33 *These were all*: McGahern, *Memoir*, pp. 208–9.
34 *She had been*: McGahern, *Memoir*, p. 5.
34 *There were rumours*: McGahern, *Memoir*, p. 16.
34 *For some years*: McGahern, *The Leavetaking* (1974), p. 53.
35 *hereditary melancholia*: 'Return of Lunatics and Idiots in Public Institutions and Private Lunatic Asylums' (Mullingar, 1911).
35 *the poorhouse*: McGahern, *Memoir*, p. 15.
36 *I was never any good*: McGahern, *Amongst Women*, p. 6.
36 *Once the seniors*: John McGahern, 'The Creamery Manager', in *Creatures of the Earth: New and Selected Stories* (London: Faber & Faber, 2006), pp. 228–36, at pp. 230–1.
36 *Team lists in*: Gilligan, 'Volunteer Frank McGahern', p. 72.
37 *There was more caution*: John McGahern, 'Gold Watch', in *Creatures of the Earth: New and Selected Stories* (London: Faber & Faber, 2006), pp. 134–50, at p. 139.

CHAPTER 2: A SECRET LIFE, 1953–60

38 *only in Dublin*: John McGahern, *Memoir* (London: Faber & Faber, 2005), p. 217.

38 *The cinema was demolished*: See https://cinematreasures.org/theaters/52049 (accessed 10 November 2025).

39 *If you're at all*: www.criterion.com/current/posts/679-casque-dor-tenderness-and-violence (accessed 10 November 2025).

39 *John was thirteen*: See Ciaran Carty, 'Out of the Dark', *Sunday Tribune*, 6 September 1987.

39 *And then with relief*: John McGahern, *The Dark* (London: Faber & Faber, 1965), p. 168.

40 *I remember seeing*: John McGahern, 'The Solitary Reader', in *Love of the World: Essays*, edited by Stanley van der Ziel, with an introduction by Declan Kiberd (London: Faber & Faber, 2009), pp. 87–95, at p. 91.

40 *It would be a brave*: Quoted in Carty, 'Out of the Dark'.

40 *So much is done*: Quoted in Ciaran Carty, 'John McGahern: "It Would Be an Insult to Be Called an Irish Writer"', *Sunday Independent*, 11 June 1978.

40 *We were being groomed*: '*Ní bheidh sibh ar ais*: St Patrick's College Drumcondra', in *Love of the World: Essays*, pp. 115–16, at p. 115.

41 *I saw people beaten*: Interview with Mike Murphy, in Clíodhna Ní Anluain (ed.), *Reading the Future* (Dublin: Lilliput, 2000), pp. 136–55, at p. 142.

41 *Between classes and study*: John McGahern, *The Leavetaking* (London: Faber & Faber, 1974), p. 85.

41 *The queue in Granby*: McGahern, *The Leavetaking* (1974), pp. 85–6.

42 *When I walked off*: McGahern, *Memoir*, p. 213.

42 *Marge and Kathleen*: John McGahern, 'Hearts of Oak and Bellies of Brass', in *Creatures of the Earth: New and Selected Stories* (London: Faber & Faber, 2006), pp. 26–37, at pp. 29, 35–6.

43 *McGahern's stripped style*: John Montague, 'John McGahern', in D. L. Kirkpatrick (ed.), *Contemporary Novelists*, 4th edn (New York: St Martin's Press, 1986), pp. 592–3, at p. 593.

43 *male sweat and boiled*: Tony Whelan, 'Working at the Mill', *John McGahern Yearbook*, 2 (2009): 28–41, at p. 29.

43 *I still teach*: John McGahern to Tony Whelan, 16 July 1958, in *The Letters of John McGahern*, ed. Frank Shovlin (London: Faber & Faber, 2021), pp. 8–14, at p. 9.

43 *No faith or love*: John McGahern to Tony Whelan, 16 July 1958, *The Letters of John McGahern*, p. 14.

45 *confused and unhappy*: McGahern, *Memoir*, p. 216.

45 *He was at*: McGahern, *Memoir*, p. 215.

45 *A characteristically contrary*: Last Will and Testament of Francis McGahern, 16 November 1955, Madeline McGahern Papers.

45 *When I wrote*: John Donohoe, 'Athboy Community Remember Former Teacher McGahern', *Meath Chronicle*, 17 September 2016.

46 *Dempsey's restricted itself*: Treasa MacManus, email to the author, 7 October 2020.

46 *John's story 'A Ballad'*: Donohoe, 'Athboy Community Remember'.

46 *Not owning a car*: See Treasa MacManus, 'Encountering John McGahern', *Comhnasc: The Journal of the Retired Teachers' Association of Ireland*, 28 (summer 2020): 28.

46 *Nurses, students, actors*: John McGahern, 'Like All Other Men', in *Creatures of the Earth: New and Selected Stories* (London: Faber & Faber, 2006), pp. 201–10, at p. 201.

47 *Seán was only*: Joan Dempsey interview with Maurice O'Keefe, 6 February 2010 (Meath Oral History Collection). Thanks to Tom French for drawing my attention to this interview.

47 *These people had*: John McGahern, 'A Ballad', in *Creatures of the Earth: New and Selected Stories* (London: Faber & Faber, 2006), pp. 166–76, at p. 170.

47 *both wearing sheepskin*: McGahern, 'A Ballad', p. 176.

48 *An old man who*: Liliane Louvel and Ben Forkner, 'Interview with John McGahern', *Journal of the Short Story in English*, 41 (autumn 2003): 123–41.

48 *Years later, he confessed*: See Declan Kiberd, 'Foreword: John McGahern, Impossible Things', in Derek Hand and Eamon Maher (eds), *Essays on John McGahern: Assessing a Literary Legacy* (Cork: Cork University Press, 2019), pp. xii–xvii, at p. xiii.

48 *The Presentation Brothers*: John McGahern, 'My Education', in *Love of the World: Essays*, pp. 109–14, at p. 111.

49 *Actually, my wife*: McGahern, *The Leavetaking* (1974), p. 14.

49 *Old fanatical peasant*: McGahern, *The Leavetaking* (1974), pp. 12–13.

50 *This poor old devil*: Interview with Dónal and Dolores Cleary, 6 October 2018. *Duine le Dia* translates literally as 'a person with God'. It is a term sometimes applied in Irish to a person with a mental disability.

50 *There is great tolerance*: John McGahern, *The Leavetaking*, revised paperback edition (London: Faber & Faber, 1984), p. 153. This edition, published a decade after the original publication, contains substantial revisions to the original, particularly in Part Two of the novel. *Buiochas le Dia* translates as 'thank God'.

51 *I grew ashamed*: *The Leavetaking* (1974), p. 176.

51 *the lower-middle-class*: John McGahern, *The Pornographer* (London: Faber & Faber, 1979), p. 51.

51 *John makes his official*: Interview with Dónal and Dolores Cleary, 6 October 2018.

52 *The school was*: Fiona O'Connor, 'That Kind of School', *London Review of Books*, 10 February 2022.

52 *To everyone at Belgrove*: Des Dockery, email to the author, 18 January 2019.

53 *I saw him once*: Interview with Michael Carter, 1 February 2019.

54 *He would stand*: John Rogers, email to the author, 18 September 2024.

54 *A good teacher*: Declan Kiberd, 'Foreword: John McGahern, Impossible Things', in Derek Hand and Eamon Maher (eds), *Essays on John McGahern: Assessing a Literary Legacy* (Cork: Cork University Press, 2019), pp. xi–xvii, at pp. xiii–xv.

55 *Although most of*: John McGahern to Michael McLaverty, 9 March 1960, *The Letters of John McGahern*, pp. 23–5, at pp. 24–5.

55 *I didn't enjoy*: McGahern, 'My Education', p. 113.

56 *The long velvet*: McGahern, *The Pornographer*, p. 20.

56 *The more we read*: McGahern, 'The Solitary Reader', p. 92.

56 *A 1954 Bodley Head*: McGahern, '*Ní bheidh sibh ar ais*: St Patrick's College Drumcondra', p. 115.

57 *Britain could no*: John McGahern, 'Censorship', in *Love of the World: Essays*, pp. 96–102, at pp. 97–8.

57 *In many ways*: McGahern, 'The Solitary Reader', pp. 92–3.

57 *The next Saturday*: John McGahern, 'Along the Edges', *The Collected Stories* (London: Faber & Faber, 1992), pp. 188–99, at p. 189.

58 *Spring was late*: McGahern, *The Pornographer*, p. 105.

58 *For several months*: John McGahern, 'Sierra Leone', in *Creatures of the Earth: New and Selected Stories* (London: Faber & Faber, 2006), pp. 211–27, at p. 211.

58 *Indeed, there is no*: Colm Tóibín, 'Out of the Dark: A Profile of John McGahern', in *The Trial of the Generals: Selected Journalism, 1980–1990* (Dublin: Raven Arts Press, 1990), pp. 94–102, at pp. 97–8.

59 *The life of a teacher*: McGahern, *Memoir*, p. 217.

59 *There were many good*: McGahern, 'The Solitary Reader', p. 91.

60 *as yet I did not understand*: Rainer Maria Rilke, *The Notebooks of Malte Laurids Brigge*, trans. M. D. Herter Norton (New York: W. W. Norton & Company, 1964), p. 74.

60 *The next day*: McGahern, *The Pornographer*, pp. 62–3.

61 *We went to dancehalls*: McGahern, *Memoir*, p. 240.

61 *The distractions of*: McGahern, *The Leavetaking* (1974), p. 92.

61 *huge gatherings of young*: I am grateful to Treasa MacManus for sharing her memories of the Dublin social scene of the late 1950s and early 1960s over several emails in autumn 2020. The wearing of a gold *fáinne*, or ring, indicates fluency in the Irish language. A Pioneer badge indicates membership of the Pioneer Total Abstinence Association. The wearer does not drink alcohol.

63 *Across the low flat roofs*: McGahern, *The Leavetaking* (1974), p. 10.

63 *the cattle light*: McGahern, *The Pornographer*, p. 31.

64 *I am writing on*: John McGahern to Tony Swift, 14 December 1957, *The Letters of John McGahern*, pp. 4–7, at pp. 5–6.

65 *And it was actually*: John McGahern interview with Belinda McKeon, *Trinity News* (April 2000).

65 *The McDaid world*: John McGahern to Patrick Gregory, 25 October 1964, *The Letters of John McGahern*, pp. 135–6, at p. 135.

66 *not worth describing*: John McGahern to Tony Whelan, 18 December 1963, *The Letters of John McGahern*, pp. 98–9.

66 *There was a sense*: John McGahern, 'Bank Holiday', in *Creatures of the Earth: New and Selected Stories* (London: Faber & Faber, 2006), pp. 301–18, at p. 309.

66 *The door of the bar*: McGahern, 'Bank Holiday', pp. 311–12.

66 *Dublin is too small*: Daniel Rondeau, 'John McGahern: "Une forme de vie intense"', in *Les Fêtes partagées: Lectures et autres voyages* (Paris: NIL Editions, 1994), pp. 198–201, at pp. 198–9.

67 *I'm afraid I do not*: John McGahern to Mary Keelan, 6 April 1964, *The Letters of John McGahern*, p. 112.

67 *They met at eight-thirty*: McGahern, 'Bank Holiday', p. 304.

68 *They'd fill the trolley*: John McGahern, 'Wheels', in *Creatures of the Earth: New and Selected Stories* (London: Faber & Faber, 2006), pp. 3–12, at p. 3.

68 *Lightfoot, not my friend*: McGahern, *The Leavetaking* (1974), pp. 30–1.

69 *Now he could hardly*: McGahern, 'Bank Holiday', p. 304.

69 *He was splendid*: Patrick Gregory to John McGahern, 26 July 1965, *The Letters of John McGahern*, p. 169.

70 *The cinema in question*: Joe Kennedy, emails to the author, 31 March and 2 April 2022.

70 *The Dublin social*: Tom Corkery (Kevin Lehane), *Tom Corkery's Dublin* (Dublin: Anvil Books, 1980), p. 13.

71 *This is a lovely*: John McGahern, 'A Book of Non-Sequiturs', in *Love of the World: Essays*, pp. 302–4, at p. 302.

71 *Old Cogger dithered*: John McGahern, 'The Recruiting Officer', in *Creatures of the Earth: New and Selected Stories* (London: Faber & Faber, 2006), pp. 69–82, at p. 81.

72 *Instructions were sent*: Letter from Tom Jordan to John McGahern, 3 December 1968, John McGahern Papers, P71/1174.

73 *The sum total*: Frank McGahern to John McGahern, 8 January 1960, John McGahern Papers, P71/1201.

73 *The one important thing*: McGahern, 'Wheels', p. 9.

74 *I know a way*: McGahern, *Memoir*, pp. 234–5.

75 *the university could not*: McGahern, *Memoir*, p. 243.

CHAPTER 3: *X* MARKS THE SPOT, 1960–63

76 *writing is always*: Quoted in Daniel Rondeau, 'John McGahern: "Une forme de vie intense"', in *Les Fêtes partagées: Lectures et autres voyages* (Paris: NIL Editions, 1994), pp. 198–201, at p. 199.

76 *Ah, there you are*: Interview with Uinsin O'Donovan, 5 October 2018.

77 *I remember being*: Deirdre Madden, 'Book of a Lifetime: *The Barracks* by John McGahern', *Independent*, 15 August 2008.

77 *John McGahern's first*: Andrew O'Hagan, 'I Wish I'd Written . . .', *Guardian*, 3 April 1999.

78 *What was new and*: John Montague, 'John McGahern', in D. L. Kirkpatrick (ed.), *Contemporary Novelists*, 4th edn (New York: St Martin's Press, 1986), pp. 592–3, at p. 592.

79 *I was born in*: John McGahern to Mary O'Malley, 17 January 1960, *The Letters of John McGahern*, ed. Frank Shovlin (London: Faber & Faber, 2021), p. 22.

79 *It is a trying time*: John McGahern to Michael McLaverty, 22 August 1959, *The Letters of John McGahern*, pp. 16–18, at p. 18.

80 *The insistence that*: Undated letter (5 September 1960) from John McGahern to Patrick Swift, *The Letters of John McGahern*, pp. 31–2.

81 *born in that Bohemian*: David Wright, 'An Introduction', *An Anthology from* X: *A Quarterly Review of Literature and the Arts, 1959–1962* (Oxford: Oxford University Press, 1988), pp. xi–xix, at p. xiii.

81 *proved an ideal*: Wright, 'An Introduction', p. xv.

81 *move and to dance*: Virginia Woolf, *The Waves* (Oxford: Oxford University Press, 2015), p. 24; Wright, 'An Introduction'.

82 *The one person*: Letter from John McGahern to Hermione Lee, 20 April 2002.

82 *There was not a page*: Wright, 'An Introduction', p. xix.

83 *like a man about*: Anthony Cronin, 'Getting Wurred In', *X*, 2 (1) (1961): 64–71, at p. 64.

83 *When Cronin's Riley*: John McGahern to Patrick Gregory, 25 October 1964, in *The Letters of John McGahern*, pp. 135–6.

84 *The unstated object*: Wright, 'An Introduction', p. xi.

84 *The beats are*: Anonymous (Patrick Swift), 'On the Margin', *X: A Quarterly Review*, 1 (1) (1959): 79–80.

85 *of that order*: Helen Lessore, 'A Note on the Development of Francis Bacon's Painting', *X: A Quarterly Review*, 2 (1) (1961): 23–6, at p. 26.

85 *Mr John McGahern's*: 'On the Margin', *X: A Quarterly Review*, 2 (1) (1961): 78–9, at p. 79.

85 *I'm just trying*: Quoted in David Sylvester, *Interviews with Francis Bacon, 1962–1979*, new and enlarged edition (London: Thames & Hudson, 1980), pp. 88, 166, 29.

86 *the whole mortal*: John McGahern, 'The Image (Prologue to a Reading at the Rockefeller University)', *Honest Ulsterman: Monthly Handbook for a Revolution*, 8 (December 1968), p. 10.

86 *As we sat in the heat*: John McGahern, 'The Bird Swift', in *Love of the World: Essays*, edited by Stanley van der Ziel, with an introduction by Declan Kiberd (London: Faber & Faber, 2009), pp. 65–74, at p. 74.

87 *O God, O God*: John McGahern, 'The End or the Beginning of Love', John McGahern Papers, P71/9, pp. 36–46.

89 *Paddy Swift gave me*: John Bunting telegram to John McGahern, 31 January 1961, *The Letters of John McGahern*, p. 44n.

89 *No question, by*: Undated letter (April 1961) from Patrick Swift to John McGahern, *The Letters of John McGahern*, p. 44.

89 *Yr. original MSS*: Undated letter (April 1961) from Patrick Swift to John McGahern, *The Letters of John McGahern*, p. 44.

90 *I was very interested*: Charles Monteith to John McGahern, 14 March 1961, *The Letters of John McGahern*, p. 41n.

90 *Thank you for your*: John McGahern to Charles Monteith, 16 March 1961, *The Letters of John McGahern*, pp. 41–2.

91 *After the examinations*: Handwritten draft of sections from 'The End or the Beginning of Love', John McGahern Papers, P71/1.

92 *He would take a nun*: Handwritten draft of sections from 'The End or the Beginning of Love', John McGahern Papers, P71/1.

93 *The literary Ireland:* John McGahern to Charles Monteith, 5 July 1961, *The Letters of John McGahern*, p. 50.

93 *Later awards were*: John McGahern, 'Why the Booker Is Such a Hard Bet', in *Love of the World: Essays*, edited by Stanley van der Ziel, with an introduction by Declan Kiberd (London: Faber & Faber, 2009), pp. 99–102, at p. 100.

94 *For a little while*: John McGahern to Michael McLaverty, 23 February 1962, *The Letters of John McGahern*, p. 57.

94 *It would be easier*: See www.sheppardranbom.com/blog/small-comedies-the-letters-of-john-mcgahern (accessed 10 November 2025).

94 *He is a shy man*: 'Won Literary Award', *Roscommon Herald*, 10 March 1962.

94 *All last week*: Frank McGahern to John McGahern, 27 February 1962, Madeline McGahern Papers.

95 *think up a bit of influence*: Undated letter from Frank McGahern to John McGahern, Madeline McGahern Papers.

95 *My father had never*: John McGahern, 'Gold Watch', in *Creatures of the Earth: New and Selected Stories* (London: Faber & Faber, 2006), pp. 134–50, at p. 138.

95 *All his people*: John McGahern, *The Barracks* (London: Faber & Faber, 1963), p. 109.

96 *like a drug*: McGahern, *The Barracks*, p. 24.

96 *Then* Our Fathers: McGahern, *The Barracks*, p. 33.

97 *She was less*: McGahern, *The Barracks*, pp. 86–7.

97 *She had loved*: McGahern, *The Barracks*, p. 87.

97 *A time comes*: John McGahern, 'The Solitary Reader', in *Love of the World: Essays*, pp. 87–95, at p. 90.

98 *The most thing*: John McGahern to Charles Monteith, 8 February 1963, *The Letters of John McGahern*, pp. 79–80, at p. 80.

98 *I know nobody*: Anthony Burgess, 'Escaping from the Madhouse', *Observer*, 24 February 1963.

98 *of mesmeric power*: Michael Ratcliffe, 'New Fiction', *Sunday Times*, 17 March 1963.

98 *there is a quiet*: Paul Scott, 'Stress', *Times Literary Supplement*, 22 February 1963.

99 *Seldom do we read*: Kate O'Brien, '*The Barracks* by John McGahern', *University Review*, 3 (4) (spring 1964): 59–60, at p. 59.

99 *His sentences move*: Benedict Kiely, 'Life Is a Barracks', *Irish Press*, 23 February 1963.

99 *Mr. McGahren's*: John D. Sheridan, 'Classic Tragedy in *The Barracks*', *Irish Independent*, 16 March 1963.

100 *A section of this book*: Anonymous, 'Life in the West of Ireland', *Cork Examiner*, 21 March 1963.

100 *The* fucking *can*: Undated letter (December 1961) from John McGahern to John Montague, *The Letters of John McGahern*, pp. 51–3, at p. 51.

100 *We have no objection*: Charles Monteith to John McGahern, 6 July 1962, *The Letters of John McGahern*, pp. 62–4, at p. 63n.

101 *He saw she was shocked*: McGahern, *The Barracks*, p. 90.

102 *I thought Gore Grimes*: Undated letter (11 September 1962) from John McGahern to Charles Monteith, *The Letters of John McGahern*, pp. 67–8, at p. 67.

102 *When* The Barracks: Quoted in Julia Carlson, 'John McGahern', in Julia Carlson (ed.), *Banned in Ireland: Censorship and the Irish Writer* (Athens, Ga.: University of Georgia Press, 1990), pp. 53–67, at p. 56.

102 *THE BARRACKS really*: Charles Monteith to John McGahern, 23 April 1963, *The Letters of John McGahern*, pp. 85–7, at p. 85n.

103 *John McGahern, to congratulate*: Note from Pat O'Keefe (30 June 2020) informing me that he had purchased this inscribed copy of *The Barracks* in a Dublin bookshop. The copy in question is still in his possession.

103 *To a certain extent*: John McGahern to Rosemary Goad, 10 April 1963, *The Letters of John McGahern*, pp. 83–4, at p. 84.

104 *an immoral disgrace*: John McGahern to Charles Monteith, 22 February 1963, *The Letters of John McGahern*, p. 81.

104 *He made speeches*: John McGahern to Charles Monteith, 3 May 1963, *The Letters of John McGahern*, pp. 85–7, at p. 86.

104 *Apologetic acknowledgment*: Undated letter from Frank McGahern to John McGahern, Madeline McGahern Papers.

CHAPTER 4: A CALAMITY OF LOVE, 1960–64

105 *Sex is difficult, true*: Rainer Maria Rilke, *Letters to a Young Poet and The Letter from the Young Worker*, translated, edited by Charlie Louth (London: Penguin, 2011), p. 28.

105 *Elizabeth Smart, the*: Rosemary Sullivan, *By Heart: The Life of Elizabeth Smart* (London: Flamingo, 1992), p. 274.

105 *She would race around*: Christopher Barker, 'Rhymes of Passion', *Observer*, 20 August 2006.

106 *Later we would climb*: John McGahern, 'The Bird Swift', in *Love of the World: Essays*, edited by Stanley van der Ziel, with an introduction by Declan Kiberd (London: Faber & Faber, 2009), pp. 65–74, at pp. 66–7.

106 *It was Elinor who*: John McGahern, *The Leavetaking* (London: Faber & Faber, 1974), pp. 92–3.

107 *He and Elizabeth remained*: John McGahern to Jimmy Swift, 2 February 1965, *The Letters of John McGahern*, ed. Frank Shovlin (London: Faber & Faber, 2021), pp. 145–6, at p. 145.

107 *Patrick Kavanagh writes*: Elizabeth Smart, 'Books: Nine Bright Shiners', *Queen*, 24 March 1965, pp. 34–5, at p. 34.

107 *It was that same*: McGahern, *The Leavetaking* (1974), p. 94.

108 *'But why don't you*: Typescript draft of sections from 'The End or the Beginning of Love', John McGahern Papers, P71/8.

108 *We are sexual from*: John McGahern, 'Five Drafts', in *Love of the World: Essays*, pp. 3–4, at p. 4.

109 *I see sexuality as*: Quoted in Eamon Maher, 'Religion and Art', *John McGahern Yearbook*, 1 (2008): 116–25, at p. 117.

109 *The experience of coming*: Undated letter (21 March 1963) from John McGahern to Michael McLaverty, *The Letters of John McGahern*, p. 83.

110 *own private enjoyment*: Quoted in John Killen (ed.), *Dear Mr McLaverty: The Literary Correspondence of John McGahern and Michael McLaverty, 1959–1980* (Belfast: The Linen Hall Library, 2006), p. 17.

110 *I rang Mrs Walshe*: John McGahern to Michael McLaverty, 9 March 1960, *The Letters of John McGahern*, pp. 23–5, at p. 24.

110 *the harsh truth*: John McGahern to Mary Lavin, 9 May (1960), Mary Lavin Papers, UCD.

111 *I despair that*: John McGahern to Mary Lavin, 15 June 1960, Mary Lavin Papers, UCD.

111 *I have met many*: John McGahern to Mary Lavin (August 1960), Mary Lavin Papers, UCD.

111 *Why should you linger*: John McGahern to Mary Lavin (autumn 1960), Mary Lavin Papers, UCD.

112 *While my sisters*: Quoted in John Donohoe, 'Athboy Remembers Former Teacher John McGahern on Culture Night', *Westmeath Independent*, 16 September 2016.

112 *I was introduced*: John McGahern to Stanley van der Ziel, 14 February 2006, *The Letters of John McGahern*, pp. 796–9, at p. 797.

112 *you must now revise*: Undated letter from William Maxwell to Elizabeth Cullinan, John McGahern Papers, P71/1171.

112 *verbatim like an actor*: Joe Kennedy, email to the author, 6 March 2024.

113 *The evening had turned*: Elizabeth Cullinan, 'A Swim', *The Time of Adam* (Boston, Mass.: Houghton Mifflin, 1971), pp. 138–58, at p. 151.

114 *when they went out*: Cullinan, 'A Swim', pp. 141–2.

114 *on a magazine in New York*: John McGahern, 'Doorways', in *The Collected Stories* (London: Faber & Faber, 1992), pp. 158–77, at pp. 159, 161.

115 *Betty came to a party*: Frank O'Connor to William Maxwell, 6 January 1963, *The Happiness of Getting It Down Right*, ed. Michael Steinman (New York: Alfred A. Knopf, 1996), p. 194.

115 *It was the one time*: John McGahern to Joe Kennedy, 7 February 1999, *The Letters of John McGahern*, pp. 719–21, at pp. 719–20.

116 *We began to read*: McGahern, 'Doorways', p. 170.

116 *Joseph Conrad, you*: Undated letter (1960) from John McGahern to Dympna McGahern, *The Letters of John McGahern*, pp. 36–7.

117 *I understood nothing*: McGahern, 'Doorways', p. 177.

117 *I've just read*: Elizabeth Cullinan to John McGahern, 24 March 1971, John McGahern Papers, P71/1598.

118 *It was in one*: McGahern, *The Leavetaking* (1974), p. 94.

118 *We assemble a love*: John McGahern, 'Along the Edges', in *The Collected Stories* (London: Faber & Faber, 1992), pp. 188–99, at p. 193.

118 *I waited and waited*: Unpublished letter, MS 51,191/188, Correspondence from John McGahern, 1961–1963, Nuala O'Faolain Papers, National Library of Ireland.

118 *He had come out*: Nuala O'Faolain, 'He Was Already Embarked on a Life of Heroic Honesty', *Sunday Tribune*, 2 April 2006.

119 *it was kind*: John McGahern to Mary Lavin (summer 1962), Mary Lavin Papers, UCD.

119 *These days are so*: Undated letter (July 1962) from John McGahern to Jimmy Swift, *The Letters of John McGahern*, pp. 61–2, at p. 62.

119 *This girl didn't*: John McGahern to Jimmy Swift, 24 July 1962, *The Letters of John McGahern*, pp. 65–6, at p. 66.

120 *I write little*: Undated letter (20 September 1962) from John McGahern to Michael McLaverty, *The Letters of John McGahern*, p. 69.

120 *It was in the warm*: McGahern, *The Leavetaking* (1974), p. 103.

120 *My life will be*: John McGahern to Michael McLaverty, 7 December 1962, *The Letters of John McGahern*, pp. 75–6, at p. 76.

120 *You saw it years*: Undated letter (July 1962) from John McGahern to Jimmy Swift, *The Letters of John McGahern*, pp. 61–2, at p. 62.

121 *They're in love*: John McGahern, 'Coming into His Kingdom', in *The Collected Stories* (London: Faber & Faber, 1992), pp. 16–22, at pp. 16, 18, 21–2.

122 *One could say*: 'Darina' (Joan Kelly), 'Young Man on His Way Up in the World', *Irish Press*, 22 February 1963.

124 *She was an attractive*: This quotation and subsequent ones are taken from a handwritten account of McGahern's relationship with Joan Kelly and its fallout, Madeline McGahern Papers.

125 *I do not get much work*: John McGahern to Michael McLaverty, 24 May 1963, *The Letters of John McGahern*, p. 88.

125 *I'm afraid that*: John McGahern to Joe Kennedy, 31 May 1963, *The Letters of John McGahern*, pp. 88–9, at p. 89.

127 *the razor story*: John McGahern to Frances Kiernan, 30 January 1981, *The Letters of John McGahern*, pp. 524–5, at p. 524. McGahern could not fix the story to the *New Yorker*'s satisfaction, and it was ultimately first published in the *Irish Times*, 9 August 1985.

127 *The following days*: John McGahern, 'Bank Holiday', in *Creatures of the Earth: New and Selected Stories* (London: Faber & Faber, 2006), pp. 301–18, at pp. 315, 316.

128 *I thought you very*: John McGahern to Mary Keelan, 17 October 1963, *The Letters of John McGahern*, p. 90.

128 *It's a world*: Undated letter (7 November 1963) from John McGahern to Mary Keelan, *The Letters of John McGahern*, pp. 92–3, at p. 92.

128 *All my days*: Undated letter (December 1963) from John McGahern to Mary Keelan, *The Letters of John McGahern*, pp. 96–7, at p. 96.

128 *So write to me*: Undated letter (December 1963) from John McGahern to Mary Keelan, *The Letters of John McGahern*, pp. 97–8, at p. 98.

128 *My will is the*: John McGahern to Mary Keelan, 1 March 1964, *The Letters of John McGahern*, pp. 107–9, at pp. 107–8.

129 *Drained of every*: John McGahern to Mary Keelan, 6 April 1964, *The Letters of John McGahern*, p. 112.

129 *I almost hate*: Undated letter (6 May 1964) from John McGahern to Mary Keelan, *The Letters of John McGahern*, pp. 115–16, at p. 116.

129 *the loveliest city*: John McGahern to Mary Keelan, 15 May 1964, *The Letters of John McGahern*, pp. 117–18, at p. 118.

130 *Peter's almost manic*: Mary Keelan, email to the author, 8 August 2022.

131 *blood curdling evil*: Mary Keelan, email to the author, 1 January 2022.

131 *people were dancing*: Eeva Lennon, *Eeva Lennon, Lontoo* (Tallin: Karisto Oy, 2018), p. 206. With thanks to translator Maija Salokangas.

131 *It is very beautiful*: Undated postcard (26 July 1964) from John McGahern to Charles Monteith, *The Letters of John McGahern*, p. 124.

131 *I often think of*: Undated letter (October 1964) from John McGahern to Mary Keelan, *The Letters of John McGahern*, p. 130.

132 *On John's return to Dublin*: For this correspondence, see file of letters from Annikki Laaksi, John McGahern Papers, P71/13/1/1672.

133 *I liked it very much*: Undated letter (6 October 1964) from John McGahern to Charles Monteith, *The Letters of John McGahern*, pp. 127–8.

133 *I went down last*: John McGahern to Rosemary Goad, 14 October 1964, *The Letters of John McGahern*, p. 128.

133 *It's rather beautiful here*: John McGahern to Charles Monteith, 24 October 1964, *The Letters of John McGahern*, pp. 133–4.

134 *When they were called*: John McGahern, 'Peaches', in *The Collected Stories* (London: Faber & Faber, 1992), pp. 75–99, at p. 83.

134 *I would like to get*: Frank McGahern to John McGahern and Annikki Laaksi, 17 December 1964, Madeline McGahern Papers.

134 *After the harshness*: John McGahern, 'High Ground', in *Creatures of the Earth: New and Selected Stories* (London: Faber & Faber, 2006), pp. 190–200, at pp. 190–1.

135 *any more valid*: Interview with Eamon Maher, 22 August 2002; corrected version, P71/1215.

CHAPTER 5: DARKNESS VISIBLE, 1963–67

136 *Fame, when it came*: Rainer Maria Rilke, 'The Rodin Book: First Part' (1903), *Where Silence Reigns: Selected Prose*, trans. G. Craig Houston (New York: New Directions, 1978), pp. 89–129, at p. 89.

136 *God so loved*: Undated handwritten note (January 1965) on Stockholm hotel envelope, John McGahern Papers, P71/1263.

137 The Dark *is often*: Patrick Maume, 'John McGahern', *Dictionary of Irish Biography*, 2011, www.dib.ie/biography/mcgahern-john-a9414 (accessed 2 December 2025).

137 *In Dublin in*: John McGahern, *Memoir* (London: Faber & Faber, 2005), p. 249.

137 *What I will soon*: Undated letter (December 1963) from John McGahern to Mary Keelan, *The Letters of John McGahern*, ed. Frank Shovlin (London: Faber & Faber, 2021), pp. 96–7, at p. 97.

137 *Things are looking*: Joe Kennedy, 'An Afternoon with an Author', *Evening Herald*, 14 May 1963.

138 *he in good suit*: Joe Kennedy, email to the author, 8 January 2021.

138 *I washed and*: John McGahern, *The Pornographer* (London: Faber & Faber, 1979), pp. 20–1.

138 *For all art*: John McGahern to Michael McLaverty, 23 February 1962, *The Letters of John McGahern*, p. 57.

138 *The proofs came*: John McGahern to Jimmy Swift, 2 February 1965, *The Letters of John McGahern*, pp. 145–6, at p. 145.

139 *The moment I*: See Isobel Conway, '"A Calculating, Control Freak", Claims the First Wife of Late Author John McGahern', *Sunday Independent*, 28 May 2006.

139 *Dublin gave Anu*: Undated letter (April 1965) from John McGahern to Patrick Gregory, *The Letters of John McGahern*, pp. 151–2, at p. 152.

140 *Between the end*: Philip Larkin, 'Annus Mirabilis', *High Windows* (London: Faber & Faber, 1974), p. 34.

140 *Much to his delight*: Interview with Colm Tóibín, 8 July 2022.

140 *it seems to me*: Julian Jebb, 'Heart of the Matter', *Sunday Times*, 9 May 1965.

141 *I was more disturbed*: John McGahern to Charles Monteith, 19 May 1965, *The Letters of John McGahern*, pp. 158–9, at p. 158.

141 *Yesterday, Friday*: John McGahern to Patrick Gregory, 20 May 1965, *The Letters of John McGahern*, p. 159.

141 *Mr Lynch said*: Dáil Éireann debate, Tuesday, 18 May 1965, vol. 215, no. 11, www.oireachtas.ie/en/debates/debate/dail/1965-05-18/8 (accessed 23 November 2025).

142 *We do not know*: 'The Wise Monkeys', *Irish Times*, 19 May 1965.

142 *I am terribly glad*: Quoted in Andrew Hamilton, 'McGahern Claims He Was Dismissed Because of *The Dark*', *Irish Times*, 7 February 1966.

143 *The growing hotness*: John McGahern, *The Dark* (London: Faber & Faber, 1965), pp. 20–1.

143 *He didn't care much*: Early typescript draft of 'The Pit' (later *The Dark*), John McGahern Papers, P71/31.

144 *I feel as if*: John McGahern to Mary Keelan, 6 April 1964, *The Letters of John McGahern*, p. 112.

144 *I feel pretty lousy*: John McGahern to Charles Monteith, 28 April 1964, *The Letters of John McGahern*, p. 114.

145 *He and John*: Interview with Niall Walsh, April 2016.

145 *I didn't really care*: Quoted in Julia Carlson, 'John McGahern', in Julia Carlson (ed.), *Banned in Ireland: Censorship and the Irish Writer* (Athens, Ga.: University of Georgia Press, 1990), pp. 53–67, p. 55.

145 *I think it would be*: Cecil Scott to Peter H. Matson, 24 September 1964, *The Letters of John McGahern*, p. 129, at p. 129n.

146 *'Say what you*: McGahern, *The Dark*, p. 7.

147 *Change the fuck*: Undated letter (10 April 1965) from John McGahern to Patrick Gregory, *The Letters of John McGahern*, pp. 152–3, at p. 152.

147 *What disturbs me*: John McGahern to Michael McLaverty, 8 August 1965, *The Letters of John McGahern*, pp. 170–1, at p. 170.

147 *'You find it hard*: McGahern, *The Dark*, pp. 70–1.

148 *'The only thing*: McGahern, *The Dark*, p. 74.

148 *Most of the lads*: John McGahern Papers, P71/37.

149 *the religious life*: John McGahern, 'Doorways', in *The Collected Stories* (London: Faber & Faber, 1992), pp. 158–77, at p. 158.

149 *it was out of fear*: John McGahern, 'The Wine Breath', in *Creatures of the Earth: New and Selected Stories* (London: Faber & Faber, 2006), pp. 110–20, at p. 116.

149 *Somewhere, outside this*: McGahern, 'The Wine Breath', p. 120.

150 *went about their sensible*: John McGahern, 'The Solitary Reader', in *Love of the World: Essays*, edited by Stanley van der Ziel, with an introduction by Declan Kiberd (London: Faber & Faber, 2009), pp. 87–95, at p. 87.

150 *The true life*: John McGahern, *The Leavetaking*, revised paperback edition (London: Faber & Faber, 1984), p. 156.

150 *My love waits*: McGahern, *The Leavetaking* (1984), pp. 168–9.

151 *In a half-circle*: John McGahern, 'The Recruiting Officer', in *Creatures of the Earth: New and Selected Stories* (London: Faber & Faber, 2006), pp. 69–82, at p. 72.

151 *no religious feeling*: Seamus Deane, *A Short History of Irish Literature* (London: Hutchinson, 1986), p. 221.

151 *As it is not a novel*: Quoted in Denis Sampson, 'The Solitary Hero', *John McGahern Yearbook*, 3 (2010): 74–80, at pp. 75–6.

151 *a religious activity*: Quoted in Hamilton, 'McGahern Claims He Was Dismissed Because of *The Dark*'.

152 *I grew up*: John McGahern, 'God and Me', in *Love of the World: Essays*, pp. 149–51, at p. 149.

152 *As in other churches*: John McGahern, 'Oldfashioned', in *Creatures of the Earth: New and Selected Stories* (London: Faber & Faber, 2006), pp. 237–62, at p. 260.

152 *I can tell*: John McGahern, 'The Church and Its Spire', in *Love of the World: Essays*, pp. 133–48, at p. 133.

153 *I never found*: McGahern, 'The Church and Its Spire', p. 137.

153 *allowed back to*: Undated letter (31 May 1965) from John McGahern to Michael McLaverty, *The Letters of John McGahern*, pp. 160–1, at p. 160.

153 *On 10 June*: Charles Monteith to John McGahern, 10 June 1965, *The Letters of John McGahern*, p. 161, at p. 161n.

153 *The appeal failure*: John McGahern to Charles Monteith, 27 July 1965, *The Letters of John McGahern*, p. 167.

154 *It had not seemed*: John McGahern, 'Peaches', in *The Collected Stories* (London: Faber & Faber, 1992), pp. 75–99, at p. 87.

154 *What I plan*: John McGahern to Brian Friel, 30 July 1965, *The Letters of John McGahern*, p. 168.

155 *Much rumbles of*: John McGahern to Patrick Gregory, 2 October 1965, *The Letters of John McGahern*, pp. 172–3, at p. 172.

156 *I saw that*: Quoted in Carlson, 'John McGahern', p. 56.

156 *The headmaster read*: John McGahern to Patrick Gregory, 17 October 1965, *The Letters of John McGahern*, pp. 173–4.

157 *What the priest*: John McGahern to Patrick Gregory, 25 October 1965, *The Letters of John McGahern*, pp. 174–5, at p. 174.

157 *And I'm almost*: John McGahern to Patrick Gregory, 1 November 1965, *The Letters of John McGahern*, pp. 175–6, at p. 175.

157 *What entered your*: Quoted in Hamilton, 'McGahern Claims He Was Dismissed Because of *The Dark*'.

158 *And the old parish*: Interview with Mary Holland, *States of Mind*, RTÉ, 18 July 1979.

158 *My own belief*: Quoted in Hamilton, 'McGahern Claims He Was Dismissed Because of *The Dark*'.

158 *The net result*: Editorial, *Irish Independent*, 3 June 1965.

159 *This is that stone-breaker's*: Christopher Wordsworth, 'Shades of the Prison House', *Guardian*, 7 May 1965.

159 *distracting and unnecessary*: Jebb, 'Heart of the Matter'.

159 *he simply could not*: Bruce Cook, 'Irish Censorship: The Case of John McGahern', *Catholic World*, 206 (1967): 176–9.

159 *a Dublin public*: Undated letter (31 May 1965) from John McGahern to Michael McLaverty, *The Letters of John McGahern*, pp. 160–1, at p. 160.

159 *slightly too repetitive*: (Anthony Cronin), 'Swotting Out of the Farm', *Times Literary Supplement*, 13 May 1965.

160 *It was never easy*: McGahern, 'Peaches', p. 89.

160 *Well, if you haven't*: Treasa MacManus, email to the author, 7 October 2020.

160 *The whole business*: John McGahern to Michael McLaverty, 22 November 1965, *The Letters of John McGahern*, pp. 177–8, at p. 177.

161 *Mr McGahern*: Andrew Hamilton, 'McGahern Claims He Was Dismissed Because of *The Dark*', *Irish Times*, 7 February 1966.

161 *The Union spent*: Undated letter (January 1966) from John McGahern to Jimmy Swift, *The Letters of John McGahern*, pp. 181–2, at p. 181.

161 *I did not believe*: John McGahern, 'Censorship', in *Love of the World: Essays*, pp. 96–8, at p. 96.

161 *Remorseless fog, blue*: Undated letter (January 1966) from John McGahern to Jimmy Swift, *The Letters of John McGahern*, pp. 181–2.

161 *I didn't think*: Quoted in Joseph O'Neill, 'A Heartening Way with the Big Things', 161 *Correspondent*, 6 May 1990.

161 *physically and financially*: John McGahern to Patrick Gregory, 17 October 1965, *The Letters of John McGahern*, pp. 173–4, at p. 174.

162 *Not only did*: Joan and Joseph Kelly document, Madeline McGahern Papers.

163 *I liked California*: John McGahern to Alain Delahaye, 16 April 1984, *The Letters of John McGahern*, pp. 558–9, at p. 559.

165 *I met Niels Groen*: Deposition made by John McGahern in support of Kika Gron's suit for divorce from Niels Gron, 25 October 1982, Madeline McGahern Papers.

CHAPTER 6: FEROCIOUS SILENCE, 1966–68

168 *I would prefer not to*: Hermann Melville, *Billy Budd, Sailor and other stories*, selected and edited with an introduction by Harold Beaver (London: Penguin Classics, 1985), p. 72.

168 *a writer of courage*: Quoted in Ray Rosenfield, 'John McGahern Gives Insight on Melville', *Irish Times*, 25 November 1967.

168 *I am only interested*: Quoted in Seamus Heaney, 'Shedding the Skin of Youth', *Sunday Independent*, 26 January 1975.

168 *had the gift*: Rosenfield, 'John McGahern Gives Insight on Melville'.

168 *transfixed*: Conversation with Marie Heaney, 7 December 2022.

169 *It may be that*: Rosenfield, 'John McGahern Gives Insight on Melville'.

169 *Glasgow was then*: Ian Jack, email to the author, 26 November 2021.

170 *I admired it*: John McGahern to Charles Monteith, 3 May 1963, *The Letters of John McGahern*, ed. Frank Shovlin (London: Faber & Faber, 2021), pp. 85–7, at pp. 86–7.

170 *he made an oral poem*: Richard Murphy, *The Kick: A Life Among Writers* (London and New York: Granta Books, 2002), pp. 261–2.

171 *We write to please*: Quoted in Murphy, *The Kick*, p. 262.

171 *Sitting on the edge*: Phone conversation with Richard Murphy, 26 January 2018.

171 *The lecture was*: From reference written by Charles Monteith on behalf of McGahern, who was applying for a creative-writing post at Western Washington State College, Bellingham, Washington, 15 December 1967. Faber Archives.

171 *as powerful as*: Partial script of the lecture in author's possession. Other possible fragments can be found in the John McGahern Papers, P71/1293, P71/1294 and P71/1295.

172 *Politeness is a protection*: Neill Joy, letter to the author, 27 March 2019.

173 *since it leans*: Michael McLaverty to John McGahern, 25 November 1962, *The Letters of John McGahern*, pp. 75–6, at p. 75n.

173 *it seems to me*: John McGahern to Michael McLaverty, 7 December 1962, *The Letters of John McGahern*, pp. 75–6, at p. 75.

173 *For all men who*: Quoted in John McGahern Papers, P71/1293.

173 *I call Melville*: Lecture fragment, Madeline McGahern Papers.

173 *'Whatever you'd prefer*: John McGahern, 'Christmas', in *Creatures of the Earth: New and Selected Stories* (London: Faber & Faber, 2006), pp. 18–25, at p. 21.

173 *'He's a survivor*: John McGahern, 'Oldfashioned', in *Creatures of the Earth: New and Selected Stories* (London: Faber & Faber, 2006), pp. 237–62, at p. 249.

174 *They never answer*: John McGahern, 'Doorways', in *The Collected Stories* (London: Faber & Faber, 1992), pp. 158–77, at p. 159.

174 *You should try*: Undated letter (late 1950s to early 1960s) from John McGahern to Dympna McGahern, *The Letters of John McGahern*, pp. 18–20, at p. 19.

175 *I find the statement*: John McGahern, 'Mr Joyce and Mr Yeats: Foreword to a James Joyce Exhibition Catalogue at Colgate University', in *Love of the World: Essays*, edited by Stanley van der Ziel, with an introduction by Declan Kiberd (London: Faber & Faber, 2009), pp. 185–7, at p. 186.

175 *It often takes*: Joe Joyce, 'Fiction Farmer', *Guardian*, 26 April 1990.

176 *If you like*: 'John McGahern – Forum: The Image', 8 February 1966, Box 1, Tape AV 15020, FA953, Rockefeller University Press, Audiovisual Materials, Lectures and Assorted Events, Rockefeller University records, Rockefeller Archive Center.

177 *nature and experience*: D. J. Gordon and Ian Fletcher, 'Persons and Places', in D. J. Gordon, Ian Fletcher, Frank Kermode and Robin Skelton, *W. B. Yeats, Images of a Poet: My Permanent Impermanent Images* (Manchester: Manchester University Press, 1961), pp. 25–55, at p. 25.

177 *art that abolishes*: Gordon and Fletcher, 'Persons and Places', p. 43.

178 *All Art that is*: W. B. Yeats, 'Introduction', in W. T. Horton, *A Book of Images* (London: Unicorn Press, 1898), p. 10.

178 *Most good writing*: John McGahern, 'Playing with Words', in *Love of the World: Essays*, pp. 9–10, at pp. 9–10.

178 *art is immature*: Yeats, 'Introduction' to *A Book of Images*, p. 16.

178 *Horton's the first*: W. B. Yeats, 'All Souls Night', *The Poems*, ed. Daniel Albright (London: Everyman, 2001), pp. 279–82.

179 *Image after image*: John McGahern, 'The Image (Prologue to a Reading at the Rockefeller University)', *Honest Ulsterman: Monthly Handbook for a Revolution*, no. 8 (December 1968), p. 10.

179 *Because I seek*: W. B. Yeats, 'Per Amica Silentia Lunae', *Mythologies* (New York: Macmillan, 1959), pp. 344–5.

179 *Some single, magical*: 'John McGahern – Forum: The Image'.

180 *I see the whole*: Quoted in James Whyte, *History, Myth, and Ritual in the Fiction of John McGahern: Strategies of Transcendence* (Lewiston, Maine: Edwin Mellen Press, 2002), p. 229.

180 *I am very disturbed*: John McGahern to Mercure de France, 14 October 1971, *The Letters of John McGahern*, p. 316.

181 *Stupid vanity had*: McGahern, *The Dark*, p. 131.

182 *Things I have*: 'John McGahern – Forum: The Image'.

182 *I pass over*: Rainer Maria Rilke, 'Some Reflections on Dolls', *Where Silence Reigns: Selected Prose*, trans. G. Craig Houston (New York: New Directions, 1978), pp. 43–50, at p. 45.

182 *Hardly able to wag*: John McGahern to Seán Brehony, 2 March 1966, *The Letters of John McGahern*, pp. 185–6, at p. 185.

183 *Oh Lord, here*: Vivian Mercier, 'Growing Up in Ireland', *New York Times*, 6 March 1966.

183 *We've installed ourselves*: John McGahern to Patrick Gregory, 6 March 1966, *The Letters of John McGahern*, pp. 186–7, at p. 186.

184 *Nothing seems to*: John McGahern to Patrick Gregory, 10 July 1966, *The Letters of John McGahern*, p. 196.

184 *deliberately putting one's*: John McGahern to Patrick Gregory, 31 July 1966, *The Letters of John McGahern*, pp. 199–200, at p. 200.

184 *Persecuted with people*: Undated letter (early September 1966) from John McGahern to Patrick Gregory, *The Letters of John McGahern*, pp. 201–2, at p. 202.

185 *What I find disturbing*: Undated letter (September 1966) from John McGahern to Patrick Gregory, *The Letters of John McGahern*, p. 203.

186 *On the 17th*: Letter from Annikki Laaksi to John McGahern, 17 August 1966. File of letters from Annikki Laaksi, John McGahern Papers, P71/13/1/1672.

186 *Anu always complained*: Undated letter (late August to early September 1966) from John McGahern to Patrick Gregory, *The Letters of John McGahern*, pp. 200–1, at p. 201.

186 *I teach every day*: Undated letter (September 1966) from John McGahern to Patrick Gregory, *The Letters of John McGahern*, p. 203.

186 *Where you have*: John McGahern, 'My Education', in *Love of the World: Essays*, pp. 109–14, at p. 114.

187 *I was to learn of*: Murphy, *The Kick*, pp. 258–9.

188 *Things going rapidly*: Undated letter (October 1966) from John McGahern to Patrick Gregory, *The Letters of John McGahern*, pp. 208–9, at p. 209.

188 *We almost bought*: Undated letter (23 February 1967) from John McGahern to Patrick Gregory, *The Letters of John McGahern*, pp. 217–18, at p. 217. The property in question is now valued at over £6 million.

188 *Through spring 1967*: See 'McGahern Named for Award', *Irish Times*, 2 December 1966.

188 *I got into unholy*: Undated letter (23 February 1967) from John McGahern to Patrick Gregory, *The Letters of John McGahern*, pp. 217–18, at p. 218.

189 *We're about settled*: John McGahern to Patrick Gregory, 18 July 1967, *The Letters of John McGahern*, p. 224.

190 *I am conscious*: Undated letter (18 October 1967) from John McGahern to Madeline Green, *The Letters of John McGahern*, pp. 225–6, at p. 226.

191 *Write to me all*: Undated letter (14 November 1967) from John McGahern to Madeline Green, *The Letters of John McGahern*, pp. 227–8.

192 *an amusing experience*: John McGahern, 'Life as It Is and Life as It Ought to Be', in *Love of the World: Essays*, pp. 160–5, at p. 163.

192 *Among the other*: I am grateful to Clíodhna Ní Anluain for her help in identifying these guests; email, 16 November 2021.

192 *In the* Irish Times: Undated letter from Frank McGahern to John McGahern, Madeline McGahern Papers.

192 *It was gruesome*: John McGahern to Jimmy Swift, 20 December 1967, *The Letters of John McGahern*, p. 230.

193 *The most striking*: Owen Sheehy-Skeffington, 'The McGahern Affair', *Censorship*, 6 (spring 1966): 27–30.

193 *McGahern offended God*: Quoted in Sheehy-Skeffington, 'The McGahern Affair', p. 30.

193 *It looks more*: Undated letter (spring 1968) from John McGahern to Madeline Green, *The Letters of John McGahern*, p. 233.

193 *I have signed*: John McGahern to Patrick Gregory, 28 March 1968, *The Letters of John McGahern*, pp. 235–6, at p. 235.

194 *Can you write*: John McGahern to Patrick Gregory, 5 April 1968, *The Letters of John McGahern*, pp. 236–7, at p. 235.

194 *The reason for*: John McGahern to Patrick Gregory, 5 April 1968, *The Letters of John McGahern*, pp. 236–7, at p. 237.

194 *She writes in one letter*: Undated letter from Annikki Laaksi to John McGahern. Likely summer 1968, John McGahern Papers, P71/13/1/1672.

194 *the dinner seemed*: Undated letter (7 May 1968) from John McGahern to Madeline Green, *The Letters of John McGahern*, pp. 238–9, at p. 238.

196 *Stroll back towards*: Undated letter (spring 1973) from John McGahern to Niall Walsh, *The Letters of John McGahern*, pp. 343–5, at pp. 344–5.

197 *He was far*: Melvyn Bragg, 'John McGahern', in Željka Doljanin and Máire Doyle (eds), *John McGahern: Authority and Vision* (Manchester: Manchester University Press, 2017), pp. 191–4.

CHAPTER 7: LOST IN TRANSLATION, 1968–70

199 *I am happy*: Undated letter (May 1970) from John McGahern to Patrick Gregory, *The Letters of John McGahern*, ed. Frank Shovlin (London: Faber & Faber, 2021), p. 279.

199 *could be hurtful*: Phone conversation with Richard Murphy, 26 January 2018.

199 *I was given*: John McGahern, *Memoir* (London: Faber & Faber, 2005), p. 255.

200 *He had been approached*: See Richard Murphy, *The Kick: A Life Among Writers* (London and New York: Granta Books, 2002), p. 273.

200 *An outline letter*: Undated letter (January 1969) from John McGahern to Colgate University Library, *The Letters of John McGahern*, pp. 245–6.

201 *I believe it to be*: John McGahern, 'What Is My Language?', in *Love of the World: Essays*, edited by Stanley van der Ziel, with an introduction by Declan Kiberd (London: Faber & Faber, 2009), pp. 260–74.

202 *It's beautiful here*: John McGahern to Charles Monteith, 25 February 1969, *The Letters of John McGahern*, pp. 248–9, at p. 248.

202 *I finished the*: John McGahern to Patrick Gregory, 24 February 1969, *The Letters of John McGahern*, p. 248.

203 *we've got the benediction*: Undated letter (February 1969) from John McGahern to Madeline Green, *The Letters of John McGahern*, pp. 250–1, at p. 250.

204 *Through these letters*: Annikki Laaksi letters to John McGahern, John McGahern Papers, P71/13/1/1672.

204 *'Were you upset*: John McGahern, 'Bank Holiday', in *Creatures of the Earth: New and Selected Stories* (London: Faber & Faber, 2006), pp. 301–18, at p. 313.

204 *Those who believe*: McGahern, *Memoir*, p. 255.

204 *sending her husband*: Annikki Laaksi to John McGahern, undated (July 1969), John McGahern Papers, P71/13/1/1672.

204 *As the apartment*: McGahern, *Memoir*, p. 255.

205 *I was never more*: John McGahern to Patrick Gregory, 23 July 1969, *The Letters of John McGahern*, p. 255.

205 *I work every day*: Undated letter (late July 1969) from John McGahern to Patrick Gregory, *The Letters of John McGahern*, pp. 255–6, at p. 256.

205 *Two stories by*: Patrick Gregory to John McGahern, 28 July 1969, *The Letters of John McGahern*, p. 256, at p. 256n.

206 *I am tired*: John McGahern to Patrick Gregory, 14 September 1969, *The Letters of John McGahern*, pp. 258–9, at p. 258.

206 *By early October*: See Annikki Laaksi to John McGahern, 6 October 1969, John McGahern Papers, P71/13/1/1672.

206 *In February 1970*: See Annikki Laaksi to John McGahern, 26 February 1970, John McGahern Papers, P71/13/1/1672. The final piece of correspondence from Annikki to John among his papers is friendly and dated 11 November 1977.

206 *a story that was*: John McGahern to Charles Monteith, 6 November 1969, *The Letters of John McGahern*, p. 263.

206 *I cannot tell*: On the *Nightlines* dedication, see John McGahern to Charles Monteith, 10 November 1969, *The Letters of John McGahern*, pp. 263–4, at p. 263. Donald Gordon to Charles Monteith, 23 November 1970, Faber Archives.

207 *Lavin still baffles*: Patrick Gregory to John McGahern, 20 November 1969, *The Letters of John McGahern*, p. 266, at p. 266n.

207 *The piece strikes*: Patrick Gregory to McGahern, 1 December 1969, *Letters of John McGahern*, p. 266, at p. 266n.

207 *You have a key*: John McGahern, 'Bomb Box', *Nightlines* (London: Faber & Faber, 1970), pp. 71–84, at p. 79.

208 *The lawyer secured*: John McGahern to Charles Monteith, 26 January 1970, *The Letters of John McGahern*, p. 272.

208 *We moved upstairs*: John McGahern to Charles Monteith, 2 February 1970, *The Letters of John McGahern*, pp. 273–4, at p. 273.

208 *Madeline owns a very*: John McGahern to Patrick Gregory, 9 February 1970, *The Letters of John McGahern*, pp. 274–5, at p. 274.

209 *in the most sordid*: John McGahern to Patrick Gregory, 9 February 1970, p. 274.

209 *We moved upstairs*: Undated letter (early March 1970) from John McGahern to Patrick Gregory, *The Letters of John McGahern*, p. 275.

209 *I was sufficiently*: John McGahern to Charles Monteith, 16 April 1970, *The Letters of John McGahern*, p. 276.

209 *Among its many*: John McGahern, 'Preface', in *Creatures of the Earth: New and Selected Stories* (London: Faber & Faber, 2006), pp. vii–viii, at p. vii.

210 *I knew Beckett*: October 2004 interview with Stanley van der Ziel, in Željka Doljanin and Máire Doyle (eds), *John McGahern: Authority and Vision* (Manchester: Manchester University Press, 2017), pp. 195–212, at pp. 202–3.

210 *Madeline is well*: Undated letter (May 1970) from John McGahern to Patrick Gregory, *The Letters of John McGahern*, p. 279.

CHAPTER 8: THE TEMPLE OF THE HOLY GHOST, 1970–71

211 *I shall fight*: Undated letter (23 July 1882) from Vincent van Gogh to Theo van Gogh, *The Letters of Vincent van Gogh*, edited by Ronald de Leeuw, translated by Arnold Pomerans (London: Penguin Books, 1997), pp. 181–2, at p. 182.

211 *Nothing but dust*: John McGahern to Charles Monteith, 5 May 1970, *The Letters of John McGahern*, ed. Frank Shovlin (London: Faber & Faber, 2021), p. 278.

211 *That is why I like*: Daniel Rondeau, 'John McGahern: "Une forme de vie intense"', *Les Fêtes partagées: Lectures et autres voyages* (Paris: NIL Editions, 1994), pp. 198–201, at p. 198.

212 *I did so*: Fran O'Rourke, email to the author, 23 January 2018.

212 *On 11 August 1970*: See '*The Dark* to Be Unexpurgated', *Irish Times*, 11 August 1970.

212 *deserves banning*: John McGahern to Charles Monteith, 11 August 1970, *The Letters of John McGahern*, pp. 282–3, at p. 282.

212 *Years later when*: John McGahern, 'The Solitary Reader', in *Love of the World: Essays*, edited by Stanley van der Ziel, with an introduction by Declan Kiberd (London: Faber & Faber, 2009), pp. 87–95, at p. 94.

213 *My heart fell*: John McGahern to Peter Davison, 19 September 1970, *The Letters of John McGahern*, pp. 284–5, at p. 284.

215 *When I showed John*: Richard Murphy, *The Kick: A Life Among Writers* (London and New York: Granta Books, 2002), p. 294.

215 *The shadow had fallen*: John McGahern, *The Leavetaking* (London: Faber & Faber, 1974), p. 82.

216 *He has hired*: Mary Kenny, 'McGahern Takes a Cottage in Connemara', *Irish Press*, 30 November 1970.

216 *The roof leaks*: John McGahern to Rosemary Goad, 2 December 1970, *The Letters of John McGahern*, pp. 290–1, at p. 291. Eileen O'Malley ran the local pub.

217 *College Week*: Collegian, 'Town-Gown Week at UCG', *Connacht Sentinel*, 1 December 1970.

217 *Our lips moved*: John McGahern, 'My Love, My Umbrella', in *Creatures of the Earth: New and Selected Stories* (London: Faber & Faber, 2006), pp. 58–68, at p. 61.

218 *Tall, statuesque, Nordic*: Mick Gibbons' reminiscences come from a letter written to the author in January 2019.

220 *A Mr Powell*: Frank McGahern to John McGahern, 28 March 1966, Madeline McGahern Papers.

220 *A Mr Kiley*: Undated letter from Frank McGahern to John McGahern, Madeline McGahern Papers.

221 *I'll never forget it*: Phone conversation with Thomas O'Malley, 10 October 2024.

222 *I always get*: Mary Hutchinson to John McGahern, 31 August 1971, John McGahern Papers, P71/1636.

223 *The land offers*: Undated letter from Emmet McGarry, *c.*1971, John McGahern Papers, P71/9178.

223 *After a stop-over*: Joe Kennedy, email to the author, 31 January 2024.

223 *one room for*: John Walsh, 'Illuminating the Dark Side of the Irish', *Sunday Times Books*, 29 April 1990.

224 *the most disturbing*: Michel Déon, *Horseman, Pass By! Irish Pages*, trans. Clíona Ní Ríordáin (Dublin: Lilliput Press, 2017), p. 138.

224 *in the great tradition*: Bernard Share, 'Forests of the Night', *Irish Times*, 24 October 1970.

225 *I saw the Fuller*: John McGahern to Charles Monteith, 5 December 1970, *The Letters of John McGahern*, pp. 291–2, at p. 292.

225 *Reviewers confronted suddenly*: Roy Fuller, 'Lifelines', *Listener*, 26 November 1970, p. 755.

225 *a garrulous old bastard*: John McGahern to Charles Monteith, 5 January 1971, *The Letters of John McGahern*, pp. 296–8, at p. 296.

225 *Is there no escape?*: Derek Mahon, 'Is There No Escape?', *The Times*, 12 November 1970.

225 *if one critic*: Terence de Vere White, 'Year of Bestsellers', *Irish Times*, 1 January 1971.

226 *The real purpose*: Horace Gregory to John McGahern, 26 November 1970, Madeline McGahern Papers.

CHAPTER 9: DARK AND INLAND, 1971–75

227 *I shuddered as*: John McGahern, *The Leavetaking* (London: Faber & Faber, 1974), pp. 62–3.

227 *A week before*: *Irish Independent*, 5 March 1921.

228 *feeling a happiness*: Quoted in Liam Kelly, 'The Making of a Revolutionary: Seán MacDiarmada and His County Leitrim Background', *Breifne*, 3 (51) (2016): 851–71, at p. 871.

228 *We could see*: Frank McGrail, 'Eyewitness Account of Selton Hill Ambush', *Leitrim Guardian*, 1992.

229 *Bernie Sweeney from*: See Michael Whelan, 'The Tragedy of Selton Hill', *Leitrim Guardian: Leitrim's Annual County Magazine* (1970): 30–40.

229 *I looked through*: Quoted in Whelan, 'The Tragedy of Selton Hill', p. 33.

230 *It was very evident*: Bernard Sweeney Witness Statement, Document No. WS 1194, Bureau of Military History, 1913–21.

231 *William Lattimer was*: For an excellent account of Selton Hill, see Padraig Leyden, *Selton Hill* (Leitrim: Selton Hill Centenary Committee, 2021).

231 *They shot him*: John McGahern, *That They May Face the Rising Sun* (London: Faber & Faber, 2002), pp. 242–3.

231 *He was on every*: McGahern, *That They May Face the Rising Sun*, p. 243.

232 *They were a separate*: Interview with Declan Kiberd, *Exhibit A: The Arts Show*, RTÉ Television, 16 December 1985.

232 *I always found*: Undated letter (late 1950s to early 1960s) from John McGahern to Dympna McGahern, *The Letters of John McGahern*, ed. Frank Shovlin (London: Faber & Faber, 2021), pp. 20–1.

233 *What is so extraordinary*: John McGahern, 'In Pursuit of a Single Flame: Ernie O'Malley', in *Love of the World: Essays*, edited by Stanley van der Ziel, with an introduction by Declan Kiberd (London: Faber & Faber, 2009), pp. 248–59, at p. 259.

233 *They would probably*: Ernie O'Malley, *Rising Out: Seán Connolly of Longford* (Dublin: University College Dublin Press, 2008), pp. 160, 162.

234 *I am not a pacifist*: Quoted in Rachel Ray, 'Irish Writer Sees a Lost World Anew', *Albuquerque Journal*, 2 April 2004.

234 *They wore black shoes*: McGahern, *That They May Face the Rising Sun*, p. 245.

236 *Did you see about*: John McGahern to Charles Monteith, 1 February 1984, *The Letters of John McGahern*, p. 556.

236 *Generally, the Irish*: John McGahern, 'County Leitrim: The Sky Above Us', in *Love of the World: Essays*, edited by Stanley van der Ziel, with an introduction by Declan Kiberd (London: Faber & Faber, 2009), pp. 19–26, at pp. 21–2.

237 *a whole culture of silence*: John McGahern fax to Tom Hayden, 23 January 1996, John McGahern Papers, P71/1211. The Blueshirts were a fascist-leaning Irish paramilitary organisation of the mid-1930s.

238 *Both sides of the family*: Colm Tóibín, 'Out of the Dark: A Profile of John McGahern', *The Trial of the Generals: Selected Journalism, 1980–1990* (Dublin: Raven Arts Press, 1990), pp. 94–102, at pp. 94–5.

238 *the goodness and kindness*: John McGahern, 'Introduction', in John Butler Yeats, *Letters to His Son W. B. Yeats and Others, 1869–1922* (London: Faber & Faber, 1999), pp. 1–24.

238 *little rebels known*: Quoted in Liam Kelly, 'Seán MacDiarmada and the Tradition of Rebellion in County Leitrim', in Liam Kelly and Brendan Scott (eds), *Leitrim History and Society* (Dublin: Geography Publications, 2019), pp. 585–608, at p. 593.

238 *Gorvagh, one of*: Leyden, *Selton Hill*, p. 5.

239 *Ireland's resurrection would*: Quoted in Leyden, *Selton Hill*, p. 11.

239 The Leavetaking *had*: October 2004 interview with Stanley van der Ziel, in Željka

Doljanin and Máire Doyle (eds), *John McGahern: Authority and Vision* (Manchester: Manchester University Press, 2017), pp. 195–212, at p. 208.

239 *the work lacked*: John McGahern, 'Preface to the Second Edition', in *The Leavetaking* (London: Faber & Faber, 1984), n.p. (p. 5).

240 *Old fanatical peasant*: McGahern, *The Leavetaking* (1974), p. 19. These orders, though slightly misspelt, translate as 'hands up' and 'hands down'.

240 *The lavatories and*: McGahern, *The Leavetaking* (1974), p. 10.

240 *James takes up*: I am grateful to Dónal Cleary, John's one-time colleague, for sharing his Belgrove memories with me. Quotation from *The Leavetaking* (1974), p. 20.

241 *'Doesn't poetry remain*: McGahern, *The Leavetaking* (1984), p. 38.

241 *What a small country*: McGahern, *The Leavetaking* (1974), p. 182.

241 *The thronged vastness*: McGahern, *The Leavetaking* (1974), p. 108.

242 *He arranged a meeting*: McGahern, *The Leavetaking* (1984), p. 102.

242 *I blush still*: McGahern, *The Leavetaking* (1974), p. 174.

243 *a hard man*: Al Alvarez, 'Ian Hamilton', in David Harsent (ed.), *Another Round at the Pillars: Essays, Poems and Reflections on Ian Hamilton* (Tregarne: Cargo Press, 1999), p. 34.

243 *John had a similar*: John McGahern, 'The Beginning of an Idea', *New Review*, 1 (5) (August 1974): 43–8; John McGahern, 'Faith, Hope and Charity', *New Review*, 2 (19) (October 1975): 44–6; John McGahern, 'Doorways', *New Review*, 4 (41) (August 1977): 9–17; John McGahern, 'Along the Edges', *New Review*, 4 (45–6) (December 1977–January 1978): 19–24.

243 *It is plain that*: Michael Irwin, 'Sorrowful Pipings', *Times Literary Supplement*, 16 June 1978.

244 une comédie humaine: Pierre Leyris, 'Préface du traducteur', *Lignes de fond* (Paris: Mercure de France, 1971), p. 13.

244 *the ignorance and*: Abbey Theatre, anonymous readers' reports on *The Power of Darkness*, 28 September 1972, quoted in Susanna Capon letter to John McGahern, 16 October 1972, *The Letters of John McGahern*, p. 335, at p. 335n.

245 *very good to work*: John McGahern to Susanna Capon, 9 October 1972, *The Letters of John McGahern*, p. 335.

245 *Stephen Frears and I*: Interview with Stanley van der Ziel, p. 201.

245 *When I saw the actors*: Interview with Stanley van der Ziel, p. 201.

246 *It depresses me:* John McGahern to Niall Walsh, 6 January 1972, *The Letters of John McGahern*, p. 324.

246 *It's not that the work*: John McGahern to Niall Walsh, 25 March 1972, *The Letters of John McGahern*, pp. 326–7, at p. 326.

247 *Both of us are*: John McGahern to Niall Walsh, 20 March 1973, *The Letters of John McGahern*, p. 343.

248 *It is very lovely*: John McGahern to Charles Monteith, 15 April 1973, *The Letters of John McGahern*, pp. 345–6, at p. 345.

248 *With one reservation*: Charles Monteith to John McGahern, 19 July 1973, Faber Archives.

249 *Thank you for such*: John McGahern to Charles Monteith, 22 July 1973, *The Letters of John McGahern*, p. 348.

250 *the poetry fades*: John Mellors, 'Island Styles', *Listener*, 23 January 1975.
250 *It is written with*: Jonathan Raban, 'Exiles', *Encounter*, June 1975.
251 *there is another practicing*: Peter Prescott, 'Super-Soap: *The Leavetaking* by John McGahern', *Newsweek*, 17 February 1975.
251 The Leavetaking *represents*: Julian Jebb, 'The Call of the Deep', *Times Literary Supplement*, 10 January 1975.
251 *McGahern's imagination*: Seamus Heaney, 'Shedding the Skin of Youth', *Sunday Independent*, 26 January 1975.
252 *The making of martyrs*: Terence de Vere White, 'The Sack Race', *Irish Times*, 4 January 1975.
252 *If this was the first*: Terence de Vere White, 'The Lights That Failed', *Irish Times*, 3 January 1976.
252 *It was very right*: Brian Friel to John McGahern, 11 April 1975, John McGahern Papers, P71/1642.
253 *A writer can only*: John McGahern to Brian Friel, 20 April 1975, *The Letters of John McGahern*, p. 388.

CHAPTER 10: GEORDIELAND, 1974–76

254 *Manchester, Leeds, Newcastle*: John McGahern, 'Eddie Mac', in *Creatures of the Earth: New and Selected Stories* (London: Faber & Faber, 2006), pp. 263–78, at pp. 277–8.
254 *It's very hard*: John McGahern to Niall Walsh, 11 January 1975, *The Letters of John McGahern*, ed. Frank Shovlin (London: Faber & Faber, 2021), pp. 382–3, at p. 383.
254 *We were at the sea*: John McGahern to Niall Walsh, 21 April 1975, *The Letters of John McGahern*, pp. 388–9, at p. 389.
254 *The pale blue*: John McGahern, 'Just a Little Bit of Ireland . . .', *Sunday World*, 25 April 1976.
255 *John had been recommended*: Interview with Paul Bailey, 16 September 2022.
256 *Troubled by my own*: John McGahern, *The Pornographer* (London: Faber & Faber, 1979), p. 137.
256 *The quotation that*: See Thomas de Quincey, *Recollections of the Lakes and the Lake Poets*, ed. David Wright (Harmondsworth: Penguin, 1970), p. 361.
256 *like a monk's cell*: Bob White, email to the author, 2 February 2022.
257 *It was the start*: Richard Taylor, email to the author, 10 June 2022.
257 *I never did meet*: Richard Taylor, email to the author, 10 June 2022.
259 *The Murphy saga*: John McGahern to Niall Walsh, 26 December 1974, *The Letters of John McGahern*, pp. 379–80, at p. 379.
259 *The Poet Murphy*: John McGahern to Niall Walsh, 1 May 1976, *The Letters of John McGahern*, pp. 413–14, at p. 414.
259 *he told me he*: Sam Milne, email to the author, 1 April 2022.
259 *Among friends and*: See undated letter (spring 1976) from John McGahern to Madeline McGahern, *The Letters of John McGahern*, p. 412.
260 *shrewd, hurtful, ironic*: John McGahern, 'Memories of Newcastle', in *Love of the World: Essays*, edited by Stanley van der Ziel, with an introduction by Declan Kiberd (London: Faber & Faber, 2009), pp. 298–301, at pp. 299–300.

261 *I have never seen*: John McGahern, 'Doorways', in *The Collected Stories* (London: Faber & Faber, 1992), pp. 158–77, at p. 158.

261 *An earlier draft*: Typescript draft of 'Getting Through', p. 1. In possession of Bob White.

261 *everything seemed*: McGahern, 'Doorways', p. 177.

262 *nature, having started*: McGahern, 'Doorways', p. 158.

263 *I stirred uneasily*: McGahern, 'Doorways', p. 173.

264 *one has then*: Marcel Proust, *On Reading*, trans. and ed. Jean Autret and William Burford (London: Souvenir Press, 1972), p. 19.

264 *very beautiful and*: Bob White, email to the author, 1 May 2023.

265 *Bruce Babington recalls*: Bruce Babington, email to the author, 8 December 2021.

265 *I'm sorry not*: Undated letter (October 1975) from John McGahern to Seamus Heaney, *The Letters of John McGahern*, pp. 406–7, at p. 406.

265 *left shaken by excess*: Seamus Heaney to John McGahern, 13 October 1975, *The Letters of John McGahern*, p. 406, at p. 406n.

265 *John discovered in*: Bob White, emails to the author, 1 November 2021 and 16 January 2023.

266 *By way of Nun Street*: McGahern, 'Just a little bit of Ireland . . .'.

267 *Manchester, Leeds, Newcastle*: John McGahern, 'Eddie Mac', in *Creatures of the Earth: New and Selected Stories* (London: Faber & Faber, 2006), pp. 263–78, at pp. 277–8.

267 *The Empire in Woolwich*: McGahern, 'Just a little bit of Ireland . . .'.

267 *Between 1951 and 1961*: John McGahern, 'Whatever You Say, Say Nothing', in *Love of the World: Essays*, edited by Stanley van der Ziel, with an introduction by Declan Kiberd (London: Faber & Faber, 2009), pp. 128–32, at p. 129.

268 *When you were with*: Sam Milne, email to the author, 1 April 2022.

269 *harsh teaching style*: Emer Nolan, 'Farewell to the Saint: A Liberal Novelist's Harder-Edged Correspondence', *Times Literary Supplement*, 17 December 2021.

269 *As an undergraduate*: Sam Milne, letter to *Times Literary Supplement*, 24 December 2021.

270 *At one point*: Sam Milne, email to the author, 8 April 2022.

271 *John read one*: Email from Sam Milne to Bob White, 17 March 2022.

271 *There was nothing furtive*: Eamonn McCann, 'The Road to Monasterevin: Part Two of the Marion Coyle Story', *Sunday World*, 25 April 1976.

272 *John writes to Monteith*: See John McGahern to Charles Monteith, 6 December 1975, *The Letters of John McGahern*, pp. 409–10, at p. 409.

273 *After Val and Kelsey*: John McGahern to Madeline McGahern, 8 June 1976, *The Letters of John McGahern*, pp. 416–17, at p. 416.

273 *It must be the quietest*: Undated letter from Bob White to his parents (June 1976).

274 *I think what I value*: Bob White, email to the author, 18 October 2024.

274 *Madeline, as well*: John McGahern to Jonathan Coleman, 14 October 1975, *The Letters of John McGahern*, pp. 402–4, at p. 403.

CHAPTER 11: GETTING THROUGH, 1976–78

275 *But McGahern lures*: Nuala O'Faolain, 'Worlds Apart', *Hibernia*, 6 July 1978.

275 *Robert Booth came*: John McGahern, *That They May Face the Rising Sun* (London: Faber & Faber, 2002), p. 151.

275 *like an English bishop*: Conversation with Tom Paulin, 26 July 2019.
276 *That's not the point!*: Joanna Mackle, 'The Publishing of *Amongst Women*', *The John McGahern Yearbook*, 1 (2008): 88–91, at p. 91.
276 *I'd be glad*: John McGahern to Frances Kiernan, 22 September 1976, *The Letters of John McGahern*, ed. Frank Shovlin (London: Faber & Faber, 2021), p. 423.
276 *much spoiled by editors*: Undated letter (16 November 1963) from John McGahern to Charles Monteith, *The Letters of John McGahern*, pp. 93–4, at p. 93.
277 *I've had one easy*: John McGahern to Niall Walsh, 18 February 1977, *The Letters of John McGahern*, pp. 431–2.
277 *One such figure*: All quotations from Shep Ranbom and his Colgate friends are taken from a series of emails sent to me by Shep between November 2022 and March 2023.
280 *all out of our spiritual*: Quoted in Shep Ranbom, 'Conversations in the Hallway Still Linger', *Colgate Magazine* (winter 2023), news.colgate.edu/magazine/2023/02/13/conversations-in-the-hallway-still-linger/ (accessed 2 December 2025).
280 *all the vivid sections*: W. B. Yeats, *Autobiographies* (London: Macmillan, 1979), p. 106; John McGahern, 'Wheels', in *Creatures of the Earth: New and Selected Stories* (London: Faber & Faber, 2006), pp. 3–12, at p. 12.
280 *As life goes on*: Shep Ranbom, email to the author, 9 October 2022. See Yeats, *Autobiographies*, p. 189.
282 *brought this horrible excitement*: John McGahern to Madeline McGahern, 2 May 1977, *The Letters of John McGahern*, pp. 438–9, at p. 438.
283 *never before or since*: Neill Joy, letter to the author, 27 March 2019.
283 *I have the treasured memory*: (Anthony Glavin), 'Small Is Beautiful: Some Thoughts in Praise of the Literary Journal', *Irish Independent*, 2 May 2012.
284 *Faber has always*: John McGahern to Tim Seldes, 24 June 1977, *The Letters of John McGahern*, pp. 442–3.
284 *Me and my classmates*: Conversation with Tom O'Grady, 26 September 2024.
285 *He looks an unlikely*: Mary Leland, 'McGahern Spell', *Irish Times*, 30 December 1977.
285 *Quite apart from*: Charles Monteith to John McGahern, 2 November 1976, *The Letters of John McGahern*, p. 426, at p. 426n.
286 *Obviously his work*: Ciaran Carty, 'John McGahern: "It Would Be an Insult to Be Called an Irish Writer"', *Sunday Independent*, 11 June 1978.
286 *one can see something*: Neil Jordan, 'A Rural Irony', *Irish Times*, 17 June 1978.
286 *the familiar attributes*: Mary Sullivan, 'Real Irish Flavour', *Sunday Telegraph*, 11 June 1978.
286 *John McGahern is a new*: John Fowles, 'Irish Keys', *Irish Press*, 15 June 1978.
287 *Running through McGahern's*: Tom Paulin, 'Evidence of Neglect', *Encounter*, June 1978.
287 *a flavour so subtle*: Anthony Thwaite, 'Brief Encounters', *Observer*, 11 June 1978.
287 *McGahern appears to be*: Ulick O'Connor, 'Evoking the Past', *Sunday Independent*, 11 June 1978.
287 *They could as well*: Bruce Arnold, 'Has John McGahern Lost His Way in This New Collection?', *Irish Independent*, 26 June 1978.
287 *Even if McGahern*: Nuala O'Faolain, 'Worlds Apart', *Hibernia*, 6 July 1978.
288 *now I have to go*: John McGahern to Neill and Mary Joy, 2 October 1976, *The Letters of John McGahern*, pp. 423–4, at p. 424.

289 *a bit depressed*: John McGahern to Frances Kiernan, 2 June 1977, *The Letters of John McGahern*, pp. 441–2, at p. 442.

289 *It was the heart*: John McGahern to Niall Walsh, 10 July 1977, *The Letters of John McGahern*, p. 444.

CHAPTER 12: THE SILKWORM, 1978–80

290 *Art is art*: W. B. Yeats, 'At Stratford-on-Avon', *Essays and Introductions* (London: Macmillan, 1961), pp. 96–110, at p. 101.

290 *No member of the*: Anthony Thwaite, 'Irish Tragi-comedy', *Observer*, 14 October 1979.

290 *McGahern has adopted*: Michael J. Toolan, 'John McGahern: The Historian and the Pornographer', *Canadian Journal of Irish Studies*, 7 (2) (1981): 39–55, at p. 54.

290 *John McGahern is probably*: Peter Donnelly, 'McGahern Now a Porn Story-Teller', *Irish Independent*, 13 October 1979.

290 *worked but was*: Letter from Thomas Kilroy to Brian Friel, n.d. (early 1980s). Brian Friel Archive, National Library of Ireland, MS37,254.

292 *believe me we're glad*: (John Coughlan), 'Introduction', *Man Alive*, 1 (4) (October 1974): 3.

292 *a good demonstration*: John McGahern to Joe Kennedy, 12 August 1975, *The Letters of John McGahern*, ed. Frank Shovlin (London: Faber & Faber, 2021), pp. 396–7, at p. 397.

294 *Maloney was at breakfast*: John McGahern, *The Pornographer* (London: Faber & Faber, 1979), p. 243.

294 *Art is the distance*: I am grateful to Shep Ranbom for this insight. The quotation is from Albert Camus, *Notebooks, 1942–1951* (New York: Knopf, 1965), p. 84.

294 *For art is, out*: John McGahern, 'The Image', in *Love of the World: Essays*, edited by Stanley van der Ziel, with an introduction by Declan Kiberd (London: Faber & Faber, 2009), pp. 5–6, at p. 5.

295 *Art is not life*: Shep Ranbom, email to the author, 13 October 2022.

295 *Art is art*: W. B. Yeats, 'At Stratford-on-Avon', *Essays and Introductions* (London: Macmillan, 1961), pp. 96–110, at p. 101.

295 *It brings us near*: Yeats, 'At Stratford-on-Avon', p. 102.

295 *He warned against*: McGahern, *The Pornographer*, p. 27.

296 *But before he had*: Nathanael West, *Miss Lonelyhearts* (New York: New Directions, 2013), p. 9.

297 *The full tide surges*: John McGahern, *The Leavetaking* (London: Faber & Faber, 1974), p. 193.

297 *I sat and typed*: McGahern, *The Pornographer*, p. 50.

298 *Have you ever seen*: Stendhal, *Memoirs of an Egotist*, trans. Andrew Brown (London: Hesperus Press, 2003), p. 91.

298 *a charming man*: Stendhal, *Memoirs of an Egotist*, pp. 97–8.

299 *And here is the tribe*: Douglas Stewart, 'The Silkworms', *Collected Poems, 1936–1967* (Sydney: Angus & Robertson, 1967), pp. 49–50.

299 *All around us*: McGahern, *The Pornographer*, p. 33.

299 *the curse that domesticity*: Patrick Kavanagh, 'Untitled', *West47*, 4 (July 2001), p. 23.

299 *the ancestral voice*: Stewart, 'The Silkworms', p. 50.

300 *Not to have a reason*: McGahern, *The Pornographer*, pp. 252, 39.

301 *On a level it's*: John McGahern to Jonathan Coleman, 14 October 1975, *The Letters of John McGahern*, pp. 402–4, at pp. 403–4.

302 *By coincidence, just*: See 'Man's World Virtuoso', *Irish Press*, 10 October 1969.

302 *I'm not at all sure*: Tom Paulin, 'The Fire Monster: Recent Fiction', *Encounter*, January 1980, p. 61.

302 *The writing is crisp*: Lucille Redmond, 'The Fork on the Road', *Irish Times*, 20 October 1979.

302 *The reason that*: Interview with Eamon Maher, August 2005; corrected version, John McGahern Papers, P71/1215.

303 *The book was read*: Colm Tóibín, 'Amongst Shadows', *Irish Times*, 1 April 2006.

304 *ground breaker, trail*: Paula Meehan, 'Inside McGahern's Workshop', in Željka Doljanin and Máire Doyle (eds), *John McGahern: Authority and Vision* (Manchester: Manchester University Press, 2017), pp. 180–90, at pp. 182, 183.

304 *a real advance*: John Montague, 'John McGahern', in D. L. Kirkpatrick (ed.), *Contemporary Novelists*, 4th edn (New York: St Martin's Press, 1986), pp. 592–3, at p. 593.

304 *I don't think I could*: Interview with Eamon Maher, August 2005; corrected version, John McGahern Papers, P71/1215.

305 *It's as though*: Paulin, 'The Fire Monster', pp. 60–1.

305 The Pornographer *is without*: Redmond, 'The Fork on the Road'.

305 *able to write better*: Quoted in Paul Hennessy, 'A Great Gael's Return', *Colgate Scene*, January 1979.

306 *John told us, too*: Meehan, 'Inside McGahern's Workshop', pp. 180–90.

307 *And McGahern!*: Letter from Thomas Kilroy to Brian Friel, Brian Friel Archive, National Library of Ireland, MS37,254.

CHAPTER 13: A SORT OF HAPPINESS, 1979–85

308 *A style is the outcome*: Paolo Vivante, *The Homeric Imagination: A Study of Homer's Poetic Perception of Reality* (Bloomington, Ind.: Indiana University Press, 1970), p. 106.

308 *I think and I have*: Frank McGahern to John McGahern, 6 January 1961, Madeline McGahern Papers.

308 *I hasten to thank*: Frank McGahern to John McGahern, 2 February 1961, Madeline McGahern Papers.

309 *that had fallen from*: John McGahern, 'Gold Watch', in *Creatures of the Earth: New and Selected Stories* (London: Faber & Faber, 2006), pp. 134–50, at p. 148.

309 *There was extraordinary*: McGahern, 'Gold Watch', pp. 135, 138.

310 *Too bad you saw*: Undated letter from Frank McGahern to John McGahern, Madeline McGahern Papers.

311 *Francis is extremely*: Henry J. Wynne (solicitor, Boyle) to John McGahern (6 November 1980), Madeline McGahern Papers.

311 *I came back straight*: Letter from John McGahern to Linck Johnson, 16 July 1984.

312 *I cut hedges*: John McGahern to Neill Joy, 8 November 1980, *The Letters of John McGahern*, ed. Frank Shovlin (London: Faber & Faber, 2021), p. 518.

312 *Two bars watch*: John McGahern, 'County Leitrim: The Sky Above Us', in *Love of the World: Essays*, edited by Stanley van der Ziel, with an introduction by Declan Kiberd (London: Faber & Faber, 2009), pp. 19–26, at pp. 25–6.

313 *We're sick of the rain*: John McGahern to Brian Friel, 9 August 1993, *The Letters of John McGahern*, p. 668.

314 *Nothing seems to run*: Letter to Eoghain Ó Tuaraisc, 18 April 1982, Ó Tuaraisc Papers, University of Galway, G17/761.

315 *The government fell here*: Undated letter (March 1982) from John McGahern to Frances Kiernan, *The Letters of John McGahern*, p. 539.

315 *The Government fell last night*: John McGahern to Neill and Mary Joy, 28 January 1982, *The Letters of John McGahern*, pp. 538–9, at p. 538.

316 *No one beats a path*: John McGahern, 'Oldfashioned', in *Creatures of the Earth: New and Selected Stories* (London: Faber & Faber, 2006), pp. 237–62, at pp. 260–1.

316 *was here and shot*: John McGahern to Fran McCullough, 23 August 1978, *The Letters of John McGahern*, p. 462.

316 *entrancingly, with a*: John Updike, 'An Old-Fashioned Novel', *New Yorker*, 24 December 1979.

317 *My editor at Harper*: John McGahern to Charles Monteith, 30 January 1980, *The Letters of John McGahern*, pp. 500–1, at p. 501.

317 *a priggish, grudging*: Undated letter (spring 1980) from Fran McCullough to John McGahern, *The Letters of John McGahern*, p. 502, at p. 502n.

317 *Just the other night*: John Updike to John McGahern, 15 April 1980, *The Letters of John McGahern*, p. 506, at p. 506n.

318 *a semi-state body*: John McGahern to Alain Delahaye, 14 May 1980, *The Letters of John McGahern*, pp. 509–10, at p. 510.

318 *like to go through*: John McGahern to Alain Delahaye, 28 January 1982, *The Letters of John McGahern*, p. 537.

318 *That the second part*: John McGahern, 'Preface to the Second Edition of *The Leavetaking*', in *Love of the World: Essays*, pp. 277–8, at pp. 277–8.

319 *There was the usual*: The *modh múinte* translates from Irish as 'the teaching method'. McGahern describes it to Delahaye as a 'Pedantic Handbook for teachers'. John McGahern to Alain Delahaye, 20 April 1983, *The Letters of John McGahern*, p. 549.

319 *You won't die*: John McGahern, *The Leavetaking* (London: Faber & Faber, 1974), p. 27. Quoted by Alain Delahaye in letter to John McGahern, 11 April 1983, *The Letters of John McGahern*, p. 549, at p. 549n.

320 *Master Leddy and*: Undated letter (early 1982) from John McGahern to Frances Kiernan, *The Letters of John McGahern*, p. 536.

320 *Mr McGahern is more*: Joel Connaroe, 'Strong Women, Dreamy Men', *New York Times*, 8 February 1987.

321 *Can any story*: Vivante, *The Homeric Imagination*, pp. 128–9.

321 *McDonough had come*: Handwritten eight-page draft of 'Bank Holiday', John McGahern Papers, P71/569.

321 *What is he doing*: Vivante, *The Homeric Imagination*, p. 186.

322 *The manager moved away*: John McGahern, 'Bank Holiday', in *Creatures of the Earth: New and Selected Stories* (London: Faber & Faber, 2006), pp. 301–18, at pp. 302–3.

322 *A whole day was*: McGahern, 'Bank Holiday', p. 317.

322 *I have taken*: John McGahern, 'What Is My Language?' in *Love of the World: Essays*, pp. 260–74, at p. 272.

323 *The morning was clear*: John McGahern, *That They May Face the Rising Sun* (London: Faber & Faber, 2002), p. 1.

323 *a pervasive subjective*: Vivante, *The Homeric Imagination*, pp. 127, 133.

323 *that did not have to run*: McGahern, 'Gold Watch', p. 150.

323 *The holy pictures and*: McGahern, *That They May Face the Rising Sun*, p. 4.

324 *McGahern has an exceptionally*: David Sexton, 'The Search for Permanence', *Sunday Times*, 13 October 1985.

324 *I must confess to*: Terence de Vere White, 'The Conscious Artist', *Irish Times*, 14 September 1985.

324 *writing with the accuracy*: Seamus Deane, 'Looking for the High Ground', *Irish Press*, 9 November 1985.

324 *As always, the melody*: Seamus Heaney, 'A Chronicle of Middle Ireland', *Sunday Tribune*, 6 October 1985.

324 *Tonight he is funny*: Colm Tóibín, 'Out of the Dark: A Profile of John McGahern', *The Trial of the Generals: Selected Journalism, 1980–1990* (Dublin: Raven Arts Press, 1990), pp. 94–102, at p. 94.

325 *I'm interested in*: Some answers to an unknown 1985 interview, John McGahern Papers, P71/1205 (1).

CHAPTER 14: PLAIN ORDINARY WORK, 1985–90

326 *A writer knows*: John McGahern, 'My Education', in *Love of the World: Essays*, edited by Stanley van der Ziel, with an introduction by Declan Kiberd (London: Faber & Faber, 2009), pp. 109–14, at p. 114.

326 *a love story set*: Internal Faber memo from Charles Monteith, 5 November 1979, Faber Archives.

326 *When I came to write*: Interview with Mike Murphy, in Clíodhna Ní Anluain (ed.), *Reading the Future* (Dublin: Lilliput, 2000), pp. 136–55, at p. 149.

326 *When he hands the book over*: Quoted in Brian Lavery, 'From Rural Ireland, Prose Carved with Precise Simplicity', *New York Times*, 1 May 2003.

327 *I owe you too many*: John McGahern to Charles Monteith, 17 November 1980, *The Letters of John McGahern*, ed. Frank Shovlin (London: Faber & Faber, 2021), p. 520.

327 *I have ideas, maybe*: Undated letter (18 November 1982) from John McGahern to Frances Kiernan, *The Letters of John McGahern*, pp. 520–1, at p. 521.

327 *one knows that*: RTÉ Radio interview with Theo Dorgan, re-broadcast on *Bowman: Sunday: 8.30*, 24 November 2024.

328 *It will be in two volumes*: John McGahern to Charles Monteith, 10 November 1980, *The Letters of John McGahern*, pp. 519–20.

329 *I'd include* Purgatory: John McGahern to Charles Monteith, 22 November 1980, *The Letters of John McGahern*, pp. 521–2, at p. 522.

329 *In its starkness of symbol*: John McGahern, 'Introduction', in John Butler Yeats, *Letters to His Son W. B. Yeats and Others* (London: Faber & Faber, 1999), pp. 1–24, at p. 20.

330 *lately done real work*: John McGahern to Alain Delahaye, 30 November 1986, *The Letters of John McGahern*, p. 589.

330 *I took the bus out*: Details of the Victoria sojourn are taken from a letter from John McGahern to Linck Johnson, 14 July 1987.

331 *To justify the climate*: John McGahern to Tim Seldes, 28 July 1987, *The Letters of John McGahern*, pp. 594–5, at p. 595.

331 *The cheque for £2,000*: I am grateful to Ollie Jennings for sharing his memories of McGahern's connection with the festival.

331 *Trinity is pleasant*: John McGahern to Tom and Julia Kilroy, 28 April 1988, *The Letters of John McGahern*, pp. 605–6, at p. 605.

332 *I remember my first*: Nicky Grene, email to the author, 20 November 2024.

333 *I was a bit depressed*: John McGahern to Robin Robertson, 16 July 1989, *The Letters of John McGahern*, pp. 611–12, at p. 612.

334 *I finished the novel*: John McGahern to Alain Delahaye, 12 October 1989, *The Letters of John McGahern*, pp. 613–14, at p. 614.

334 *kindness and extraordinary generosity*: John McGahern to Colm Tóibín, 18 February 1990, *The Letters of John McGahern*, pp. 620–1, at p. 620.

334 *It is a work of heart-breaking*: Seamus Heaney to John McGahern, 22 January 1990, *The Letters of John McGahern*, p. 621, at p. 621n.

334 *There's not much news*: John McGahern to Seamus Heaney, 20 February 1990, *The Letters of John McGahern*, pp. 621–2.

335 *John and Pat had*: See undated letter (April 1943) from John McGahern to Frank McGahern, *The Letters of John McGahern*, p. 3.

335 *Uncle Pat died*: John McGahern to Neill Joy, 10 February 1988, *The Letters of John McGahern*, pp. 604–5.

336 *We had no idea*: John McGahern to Nicky Grene, 22 May 1990, *The Letters of John McGahern*, p. 626.

337 *There's a reading*: John McGahern to Alain Delahaye, 15 April 1990, *The Letters of John McGahern*, pp. 624–5, p. 625.

337 *John developed a good*: See Joanna Mackle, 'The Publishing of *Amongst Women*', *John McGahern Yearbook*, 1 (2008): 88–91.

337 *His fifth novel*: See John Walsh, 'Illuminating the Dark Side of the Irish', *Sunday Times Books*, 29 April 1990.

338 *most profound statement*: Paul Bailey interview with John McGahern for *Kaleidoscope*, BBC Radio 4, 27 April 1990.

339 *'O'Neill and O'Donnell*: John McGahern, *Amongst Women* (London: Faber & Faber, 1990), pp. 57–8.

340 *so poised on the edge*: McGahern, *Amongst Women*, p. 80.

340 *It was a horrible evening*: John McGahern to Sue and Bill Dumbleton, 14 January 1993, *The Letters of John McGahern*, pp. 662–3, at p. 663.

340 *In the end I had*: John Updike, 'Judging the Battle of the Books', *Irish Times*, 2 January 1993.

341 *I read* Amongst Women: Donal Ryan, '*Amongst Women* Almost Finished Me. How Could a Book Be This Good?', *Irish Times*, 30 March 2017.

342 *McGahern brings all*: John Boland, 'A Tyrant's Home Rule', *Evening Press*, 10 May 1990.

342 *Do not let the plain*: John Banville, 'To Have Is to Hold, and Hate', *Observer*, 6 May 1990.

342 Amongst Women *is much*: Nicola Murphy, 'Violence, Veiled by Ritual', *The Times*, 10 May 1990.

342 *whom the reader is*: Dominique Durand, review of *Entre toutes les femmes* by John McGahern (Presses de la Renaissance), *Le Canard enchaîné*. Translated by Anne-Claire Leydier. In John McGahern Papers, University of Galway P71/1220(6).

343 *His reputation in France*: Hilary Mantel, 'Breaking Away from Home Rule', *Sunday Telegraph*, 6 May 1990.

343 *Before we go any further*: Mary Hope, 'Cries for Ireland', *Financial Times*, 9 June 1990; John Banville, '12 of the Best', *Irish Times*, 11 December 1990; Douglas Kennedy, 'Land Girls', *Listener*, 24 May 1990; Bruce Arnold, 'Rich and Truthful Despair', *Irish Independent*, 12 May 1990; Patrick Skene Catling, 'Out of His Shell', *Daily Telegraph*, 10 May 1990.

343 *You left out Beckett*: See Mackle, 'The Publishing of *Amongst Women*', p. 91.

343 *The Guildhall itself*: John McGahern, 'The Solitary Reader', in *Love of the World: Essays*, pp. 87–95, at pp. 94–5.

344 *I'm secretly glad*: John McGahern to Alain Delahaye, 25 October 1990, *The Letters of John McGahern*, ed. Frank Shovlin (London: Faber & Faber, 2021), pp. 632–3, at p. 633.

CHAPTER 15: THE DAY OF THE RABBLEMENT, 1990–95

345 *No man, said the Nolan*: James Joyce, 'The Day of the Rabblement', in James Joyce, *Occasional, Critical, and Political Writing*, ed. Kevin Barry (Oxford: Oxford University Press, 2000), pp. 50–2, at p. 50.

345 *I'm apolitical*: In Gerry Moriarty, 'A Class of an Optimistic Fatalist', *Irish Press*, 2 September 1985.

345 *haven't an idea*: Interview with Pat Shaw, 'Ireland: A Discussion with John McGahern', *Colgate Maroon*, 19 November 1991.

345 *The lorries drawing*: On this controversy, see Gerry Moriarty, 'Author McGahern Joins Protest over Pet Food Plant', *Irish Press*, 13 August 1985.

346 *Nationhood is not*: In Moriarty, 'A Class of an Optimistic Fatalist'.

346 *The Catholic church's*: In Shaw, 'Ireland: A Discussion with John McGahern'.

346 *I have been going*: John McGahern, 'Blake's of the Hollow', in *Love of the World: Essays*, edited by Stanley van der Ziel, with an introduction by Declan Kiberd (London: Faber & Faber, 2009), pp. 41–4, at p. 41.

346 *Did the story of*: Undated letter (May 1992) from John McGahern to Alain Delahaye, *The Letters of John McGahern*, ed. Frank Shovlin (London: Faber & Faber, 2021), pp. 654–5, at p. 655.

347 *Ireland is changing*: In Shaw, 'Ireland: A Discussion with John McGahern'.

348 *their experience is plainly*: In Moriarty, 'A Class of an Optimistic Fatalist'.

348 *To be honest*: Michel Déon, *Horseman, Pass By! Irish Pages*, trans. Clíona Ní Ríordáin (Dublin: Lilliput Press, 2017), pp. 133–4.

348 *I ran into*: Undated letter (December 1980) from John McGahern to Neill Joy, *The Letters of John McGahern*, pp. 522–3.

349 *John intended* Amongst: John McGahern to Alain Delahaye, 30 November 1986, *The Letters of John McGahern*, p. 589.

349 *After an initial*: John McGahern undated correspondence (autumn 1986) with BBC. See John McGahern Papers, P71/1180.

350 *I've forgotten every*: John McGahern, *The Rockingham Shoot and Other Dramatic Writings*, ed. Stanley van der Ziel (London: Faber & Faber, 2018), pp. 226–7.

350 *it was like*: Quoted in Ciaran Carty, 'Out of the Dark', *Sunday Tribune*, 6 September 1987.

351 *One mutilated infant*: John McGahern to Matthew Evans, 12 May 1985, *The Letters of John McGahern*, pp. 570–1, at p. 570.

351 *The grim and primitive*: Abbey Theatre, anonymous readers' reports on *The Power of Darkness*, 28 September 1972, in Susanna Capon letter to John McGahern, 16 October 1972, *The Letters of John McGahern*, p. 335, at p. 335n.

351 *the sad lusting*: John McGahern, 'Introduction', *The Power of Darkness* (London: Faber & Faber, 1991), pp. vii–viii, at p. vii.

352 *the response was very warm*: Letter from Brian Friel to John McGahern, 20 April 1988, John McGahern Papers, P71/1183.

352 *Have just finished*: Undated letter (August 1988) from Tom Kilroy to John McGahern, John McGahern Papers, P71/1184.

353 *moral voice*: McGahern, 'Introduction' to *The Power of Darkness*, p. ix.

353 *Whether it ever*: Quoted in Christopher Murray, 'The "Fallen World" of *The Power of Darkness*', *John McGahern Yearbook*, 2 (2009): 78–91, at p. 83.

353 *hugely impressed*: Fintan O'Toole, email to the author, 16 January 2025.

354 *we try to set up*: Brian Friel to John McGahern, 29 May 1991, *The Letters of John McGahern*, p. 645, at p. 645n.

354 *Before I received*: John McGahern to Brian Friel, 2 June 1991, *The Letters of John McGahern*, pp. 645–6, at p. 645.

354 *met with such hostility*: John McGahern, 'Introduction to *The Power of Darkness* [2005]', in *Love of the World: Essays*, pp. 283–4, at p. 284.

355 *Only the first*: John McGahern to Alain Delahaye, 12 November 1991, *The Letters of John McGahern*, pp. 649–50, at p. 649.

355 *It was a debacle*: Gerry Colgan, 'A Tough Act to Follow', *Irish Times*, 26 October 1991.

355 *Maybe it's a*: Quoted in Murray, 'The "Fallen World" of *The Power of Darkness*', p. 87.

355 *ludicrous and hysterical*: Paddy Woodworth, 'Fine Finale for a Premature Exit', *Irish Times*, 29 December 1993.

355 *This sock-in-the-face*: Michael Coveney, 'Mortality and a Sock in the Face', *Observer*, 20 October 1991.

356 *This is a most curious*: Paddy Woodworth, 'Drama at the Abbey', *Irish Times*, 26 October 1991.

356 *Last night I was*: Angela Douglas, letter to *Irish Times*, 9 November 1991.

357 *theatre in this country*: John Mahony, 'McGahern', *Irish Press*, 21 October 1991.

357 *plays by ageing*: John McGahern to Brian Friel, 2 June 1991, *The Letters of John McGahern*, pp. 645–6, at p. 645.

357 *That is why drama*: Rainer Maria Rilke, *Diaries of a Young Poet*, translated and annotated by Edward Snow and Michael Winkler (New York: W. W. Norton & Company, 1998), p. 28.

357 *It was very hard*: John McGahern to Alain Delahaye, 12 November 1991, *The Letters of John McGahern*, pp. 649–50, at p. 650.

357 *I didn't mind*: John McGahern to Peter Fallon, 14 November 1991, *The Letters of John McGahern*, p. 650.

358 *Though we know*: John McGahern to Alain Delahaye, 29 January 1992, *The Letters of John McGahern*, p. 653.

359 *McGahern is good*: Assorted, undated rejection slips for 'The Country Funeral', *The Letters of John McGahern*, p. 595, at p. 595n.

359 *I've been going*: John McGahern to Alain Delahaye, 10 December 1991, *The Letters of John McGahern*, pp. 651–2, at p. 652.

359 *I think it is very*: In Moriarty, 'A Class of an Optimistic Fatalist'.

359 *John, I think*: Fintan O'Toole, email to the author, 16 January 2025.

360 *The football practised*: John McGahern, 'Souveniers d'une Irlande en rouge et vert', trans. Florence Benoist, *Libération*, 11 and 12 June 1988. Translated back into English by Anne-Claire Leydier.

362 *In June 1989*: I am grateful to Linda de Nazelle for sharing with me her memories of the event in an email of 30 July 2022.

362 *Rich, extremely closed*: John McGahern to Jimmy Swift, 16 November 1994, *The Letters of John McGahern*, p. 679.

362 *They have put*: John McGahern to Alain Delahaye, 21 July 1994, *The Letters of John McGahern*, pp. 674–6, at p. 675. CAPES stands for Certificat d'aptitude au professorat de l'enseignement du second degré, the diploma that allows one to become a certified secondary-school teacher in France.

363 *I got back last*: John McGahern to Luke Dodd, 28 January 1995, *The Letters of John McGahern*, pp. 681–2, at p. 682.

363 *During* L'Irlandais: Colm Tóibín, email to the author, 22 January 2021.

363 *The teaching is fairly*: John McGahern to Niall Walsh, 15 February 1993, *The Letters of John McGahern*, pp. 664–5.

364 *The day I left*: John McGahern to Neill Joy, 2 May 1993, *The Letters of John McGahern*, pp. 665–6, at p. 665.

364 *The circle of*: Gearóid Ó Tuathaigh, 'Honouring John McGahern', *John McGahern at NUI Galway*, compiled and edited by Liz McConnell, John Kenny and Riana O'Dwyer (Galway: Office of the President, NUI Galway), p. 44.

364 *One day, one day*: John McGahern, *The Dark* (London: Faber & Faber, 1965), p. 188.

365 *Good weather came*: John McGahern to Alain Delahaye, 21 July 1994, *The Letters of John McGahern*, pp. 674–6, at p. 675.
365 *What reason could*: John McGahern, *The Power of Darkness* (London: Faber & Faber, 1991), pp. 50–1.

CHAPTER 16: AN INTENSE FORM OF LIFE, 1996–2003

366 *I believe that*: John McGahern to Michael McLaverty, 13 January 1959, *The Letters of John McGahern*, ed. Frank Shovlin (London: Faber & Faber, 2021), pp. 15–16, at p. 16.
366 *The evening was setting*: Daniel Rondeau, 'John McGahern: "Une forme de vie intense"', *Les Fêtes partagées: Lectures et autres voyages* (Paris: NIL Editions, 1994), pp. 198–201, at p. 199.
367 *As well as a railway*: John McGahern, 'Christmas', in *Creatures of the Earth: New and Selected Stories* (London: Faber & Faber, 2006), pp. 18–25, at pp. 18, 20, 24–5.
368 *There was this girl*: John McGahern, *The Power of Darkness* (London: Faber & Faber, 1991), pp. 6, 9.
368 *a chapter of the moral*: James Joyce to Grant Richards, 5 May 1906, in James Joyce, *Letters*, vol. II, ed. Richard Ellmann (London: Faber & Faber, 1966), pp. 132–5, at p. 134.
368 *He would have known*: See John McGahern, *That They May Face the Rising Sun* (London: Faber & Faber, 2002), pp. 7–14.
370 *I was sitting here*: Thanks to Liam and Frankie Kelly for this anecdote.
370 *John took to him*: I am grateful to Liam Kelly and Peter Dolan for sharing their memories of Fr Frank McCabe over several emails and phone conversations.
370 *Father Conroy is plain*: McGahern, *That They May Face the Rising Sun*, p. 82.
370 *In one sense*: Seamus Deane, 'A New Dawn', *Guardian*, 12 January 2002.
371 *I have said*: Rondeau, 'John McGahern', p. 199.
371 *is never the bundle*: W. B. Yeats, 'A General Introduction for My Work', *Essays and Introductions* (London: Macmillan, 1961), pp. 509–26, p. 509.
371 *Michel, thanks for*: Letter from John McGahern to Michel Gresset, 14 September 1999.
372 *In my opinion, no*: John McGahern to Frances Byrnes, 20 August 1995, *The Letters of John McGahern*, p. 686.
372 *I have written a*: John McGahern to Frances Byrnes, 3 January 1996, *The Letters of John McGahern*, p. 690.
373 *Thanks for the kind*: John McGahern to Neill Joy, 4 March 1997, *The Letters of John McGahern*, pp. 699–701, at p. 700.
373 *It is very quiet here*: John McGahern, 'Love of the World', in *Creatures of the Earth: New and Selected Stories* (London: Faber & Faber, 2006), pp. 336–68, at p. 336.
373 *what I would like*: Letter from Gustave Flaubert to Louise Colet, 16 January 1852. Quoted in Frederick Brown, *Flaubert: A Biography* (Cambridge, Mass.: Harvard University Press, 2006), p. 289.
374 *A silence came down*: McGahern, 'Love of the World', p. 366.
374 *We both go to Morocco*: John McGahern to Neill Joy, 4 March 1997, *The Letters of John McGahern*, pp. 699–701, at p. 700.

375 *used to frequent*: John McGahern, 'Dreaming at Julien's', in *Love of the World: Essays*, edited by Stanley van der Ziel, with an introduction by Declan Kiberd (London: Faber & Faber, 2009), pp. 45–51, at pp. 46, 47.

375 *I write in English*: *Le Cercle de minuit*, directed by Pierre Desfons, France 2, 12 March 1996.

376 *I crossed the river*: McGahern, 'Dreaming at Julien's', p. 48.

377 *Enter lightly, Kate*: McGahern, *That They May Face the Rising Sun*, p. 7.

377 *The timid, gentle*: McGahern, *That They May Face the Rising Sun*, pp. 186, 188.

378 *magnificently courteous attention*: Penelope Fitzgerald, 'The Great Importance of Small Things', *Times Literary Supplement*, 9 October 1992.

378 *On a Sunday*: John McGahern to Neill Joy, 14 October 1997, *The Letters of John McGahern*, pp. 704–5, at p. 705.

378 *the last or second*: John McGahern to Frances Byrnes, 25 February 1998, *The Letters of John McGahern*, pp. 711–12, at p. 712.

378 *I'm working on*: John McGahern to Neill Joy, 14 January 2000, *The Letters of John McGahern*, pp. 727–8, at p. 727.

379 *The daffodils are*: John McGahern to Frances Byrnes, 25 February 1998, *The Letters of John McGahern*, pp. 711–12, at p. 712.

379 *It was very beautiful*: John McGahern to Frances Byrnes, 2 April 1998, *The Letters of John McGahern*, pp. 712–13, at p. 713.

379 *It seems art is almost*: John McGahern to Neill and Mary Joy, 16 December 1999, *The Letters of John McGahern*, pp. 725–6, at p. 726.

379 *I think of the novel*: John McGahern, 'The Stories of Alistair MacLeod', in *Love of the World: Essays*, pp. 208–12, at p. 212.

380 *I read a marvellous*: McGahern to Neill and Mary Joy, 16 December 1999, *The Letters of John McGahern*, p. 726.

380 *Skip introduced him*: Skip Hays, email to the author, 12 November 2018.

380 *in the hope it*: John McGahern to Caroline Walsh, 4 February 2003, *The Letters of John McGahern*, p. 763.

380 *Amidst his family*: John McGahern, 'Knowledge of the World: John Williams's *Augustus*', in *Love of the World: Essays*, pp. 213–18.

381 *There is entertainment*: John McGahern, 'A Matter of Love: John Williams's *Stoner*', in *Love of the World: Essays*, pp. 219–24, at p. 223.

381 *I am moved*: Nancy Williams to John McGahern, 19 June 2003, John McGahern Papers, P71/1749.

381 *I dearly loved*: Nancy Williams to John McGahern, 18 January 2004, John McGahern Papers, P71/1749.

382 *It is a very old*: John McGahern interview with Frédérique Roussel, *Libération*, 4 December 2003.

382 *I think it probably*: October 2004 interview with Stanley van der Ziel, in Željka Doljanin and Máire Doyle (eds), *John McGahern: Authority and Vision* (Manchester: Manchester University Press, 2017), pp. 195–212, at pp. 209–10.

383 *One of the great novels*: Sam Sacks, 'Such a Schemozzle: The Beauty of John McGahern's Prose', *Harper's Magazine*, February 2025.

383 *Once I saw the*: John McGahern to Frances Byrnes, 27 August 2002, *The Letters of John McGahern*, p. 756.

383 *John McGahern's big*: Russell Celyn Jones, 'An Earthly Tale of Love and Hate', *The Times*, 9 January 2002.

383 *she found it trivial*: McGahern to Byrnes, 27 August 2002, *The Letters of John McGahern*, p. 756.

384 *Terrible. Totally out*: Will Cohu, 'From Reviled to Revered', *Daily Telegraph*, 15 January 2002.

384 *McGahern, a supreme*: Eileen Battersby, 'A Superb, Earthy Pastoral', *Irish Times*, 8 December 2001.

384 *while there's nothing*: John Boland, '12 Years On, McGahern Delivers a Masterpiece', *Irish Independent*, 8 December 2001.

384 *John McGahern's first*: Una Bradley, 'Still Life in the Irish Countryside', *Belfast Telegraph*, 20 April 2002.

385 *There were complaints*: John McGahern to Joe Kennedy, 7 June 2002, *The Letters of John McGahern*, pp. 751–2, at p. 751.

385 *The narrative thrust*: Gail Caldwell, 'Still Life', *Boston Globe*, 10 March 2002.

385 *the most perfect novel*: Malcolm Jones, 'A Perfect Visit "By the Lake"', *Newsweek*, 19 May 2002.

385 *the blarney detectors*: Sam Phipps, 'The Curse of the Gab', *Spectator*, 19 January 2002.

385 *This is a book*: 'Green Horizons', *The Economist*, 12 January 2002.

385 That They May Face: David Robson, 'A Year in the Country', *Sunday Telegraph*, 13 January 2002.

386 *But this great and*: Hermione Lee, 'Everything Under the Sun', *Observer*, 6 January 2002.

386 *Somebody said about me*: Interview with Hermione Lee for the Lannan Foundation, Santa Fe, New Mexico, 7 April 2004.

386 *I think that it*: John McGahern interview with Frédérique Roussel, *Libération*, 4 December 2003.

386 *They were discussing*: McGahern, *That They May Face the Rising Sun*, pp. 182–3.

387 *I think happiness*: Interview with Myles Dungan, Vicar Street, 22 January 2002.

387 *I knew there was something*: John McGahern to Michael Gorman, 17 May 2002, *The Letters of John McGahern*, pp. 747–8, at p. 747.

388 *I would be honoured*: John McGahern to Maria O'Connor, 26 April 2002, *The Letters of John McGahern*, p. 746.

388 *Nothing so profoundly*: Michel Déon, *Horseman, Pass By! Irish Pages*, trans. Clíona Ní Ríordáin (Dublin: Lilliput Press, 2017), p. 134.

388 *'Patrick shows none*: McGahern, *That They May Face the Rising Sun*, pp. 75–6.

CHAPTER 17: READY TO DIE, 2003–06

390 *When you have no*: Louis-Ferdinand Céline, *Journey to the End of the Night*, trans. Ralph Manheim (New York: New Directions, 1983), p. 14.

390 *know it all*: W. B. Yeats, 'In Memory of Eva Gore-Booth and Con Markievicz', *The Poems*, ed. Daniel Albright (London: Everyman, 1994), pp. 283–4, at p. 283.

390 *only the dead*: Marcel Proust, *On Reading*, trans. and ed. Jean Autret and William Burford (London: Souvenir Press, 1972), p. 53.

390 *one had one's death*: Rainer Maria Rilke, *The Notebooks of Malte Laurids Brigge*, trans. M. D. Herter Norton (New York: W. W. Norton & Company, 1964), p. 18.

390 *The cancer news*: John McGahern to Niall Walsh, 26 October 2003, *The Letters of John McGahern*, ed. Frank Shovlin (London: Faber & Faber, 2021), pp. 768–70, at pp. 769–70.

391 *Science, Aesthetics, Ethics*: W. H. Auden, 'Short Ode to the Cuckoo', *Collected Poems*, ed. Edward Mendelson (London: Faber & Faber, 2007), p. 863.

392 *There is not too much*: John McGahern to Michael Gorman, 14 June 2003, *The Letters of John McGahern*, p. 766.

393 *I'm now a member*: John McGahern to Neill and Mary Joy, 16 November 2003, *The Letters of John McGahern*, pp. 770–1, at p. 771.

393 *I was reluctant to*: John McGahern to Caroline Walsh, 24 August 2003, *The Letters of John McGahern*, p. 767.

393 *On a national level*: Interview with Philip King, 10 March 2025.

393 *a bit frightened*: Neil Belton to John McGahern, 4 April 2005, *The Letters of John McGahern*, p. 787, at p. 787n.

393 *About a hundred*: John McGahern to Neil Belton, 5 April 2005, *The Letters of John McGahern*, p. 787.

394 *wonderfully quiet months*: John McGahern to Neill Joy, 12 March 2004, *The Letters of John McGahern*, pp. 774–5, at p. 775.

394 *a delight to work with*: Ian Jack, email to the author, 27 November 2021.

394 *When I began*: John McGahern to Niall Walsh, 20 January 2005, *The Letters of John McGahern*, pp. 783–4.

395 *November 8: We*: Madeline's Japanese notes, November 2004, Madeline McGahern Papers.

397 *I have been on*: John McGahern to Niall Walsh, 4 August 2005, *The Letters of John McGahern*, p. 789.

397 *kept a supply*: John McGahern, *Memoir* (London: Faber & Faber, 2005), p. 17.

397 *You were smart*: Liam Kelly, email to the author, 21 May 2020.

398 *I knew him better*: McGahern, *Memoir*, p. 226.

398 *We would leave*: McGahern, *Memoir*, p. 272.

399 *It was clear to*: Keith Duggan, 'Sideline Cut', *Irish Times*, 24 September 2005.

399 *He has been a pariah*: Declan Lynch, 'Herd Instinct: John McGahern', *Sunday Independent*, 22 January 2006.

400 *I've taken a big chunk*: Seamus Heaney to George O'Brien, 15 February 2005, *The Letters of Seamus Heaney* (London: Faber and Faber, 2023), p. 651.

401 *Fiction, we're sometimes*: Colin Burrow, 'No Way Out', *London Review of Books*, 20 October 2005.

401 *McGahern's memoir can*: Phil Baker, 'Paperbacks', *Sunday Times*, 21 May 2006.

401 *what makes this memoir*: Verlyn Klinkenborg, 'Safe in Her Shadow', *New York Times*, 26 February 2006.

401 *Though primarily an*: Declan Kiberd, 'Portraits of a Paradise Lost', *Irish Times*, 3 September 2005.

401 *John McGahern, unyielding*: Emer O'Kelly, 'Miracle of Tolerance Amid Prayer-Fuelled Barbarism of Home', *Sunday Independent*, 11 September 2005.

401 *The fact that he takes*: Noel McAdam, 'The Odyssey from Darkness into Light', *Belfast Telegraph*, 24 September 2005.

402 *Madeline recovered easily*: John McGahern to Tom Callan, 24 March 2006, *The Letters of John McGahern*, pp. 800–3, at p. 800.

402 *man's need to make*: Sigmund Freud, *The Future of an Illusion*, trans. and ed. James Strachey (New York: W. W. Norton & Company, 1989), p. 23.

402 *Gradually, belief in*: John McGahern, 'God and Me', in *Love of the World: Essays*, edited by Stanley van der Ziel, with an introduction by Declan Kiberd (London: Faber & Faber, 2009), pp. 149–51, at p. 149.

405 *His death is a death*: See Liam Kelly, 'Endure What Life Gives and Ask No Longer Span . . .', *Furrow*, May 2006.

406 *It was only when*: Liam Collins, 'McGahern's Final Send-off Echoes the Spirit of the Man', *Sunday Independent*, 2 April 2006.

407 *with no airs and*: Donal O'Grady, 'Council Meeting Adjourned as Mark of Respect to John McGahern', *Leitrim Observer*, 7 April 2006.

407 *Yet when I think*: Nuala O'Faolain, 'He Was Already Embarked on a Life of Heroic Honesty', *Sunday Tribune*, 2 April 2006.

408 *you have to be both*: Correspondence from John McGahern, 1961–1963, Nuala O'Faolain papers, National Library of Ireland, MS 51,191/188/3.

408 *I don't altogether trust*: Correspondence from John McGahern, 1961–1963, Nuala O'Faolain papers, National Library of Ireland, MS 51,191/188/2.

408 *I remember that we went*: Nuala O'Faolain, 'He Was Already Embarked on a Life of Heroic Honesty'.

EPILOGUE: HARD JOY

411 *We live as we dream*: Joseph Conrad, *Heart of Darkness* (London: Oneworld Classics, 2009), p. 29.

411 *We get by on dreams*: Notebook with draft of passage from *The Pornographer*, Madeline McGahern Papers.

411 *So we cannot live*: John McGahern, 'The Image', in *Love of the World: Essays*, edited by Stanley van der Ziel, with an introduction by Declan Kiberd (London: Faber & Faber, 2009), pp. 5–6, at p. 5.

412 *The taxi turned*: John McGahern, *The Pornographer* (London: Faber & Faber, 1979), pp. 172, 203.

412 *a strange great poem*: John McGahern to Neill Joy, 14 October 1997, *The Letters of John McGahern*, ed. Frank Shovlin (London: Faber & Faber, 2021), pp. 704–5, at p. 704.

413 *We were the only*: John McGahern to Margaret and Michael Gorman, 14 September 1995, *The Letters of John McGahern*, pp. 688–9, at p. 689.

Selected Bibliography

ARCHIVES

Brian Friel Archive
Eoghain Ó Tuaraisc Papers
Faber Archives
John McGahern Papers
Madeline McGahern Papers
Mary Lavin Papers
Nuala O'Faolain Papers
UCD Archives

BOOKS AND ARTICLES

Bragg, Melvyn, 'John McGahern', in Željka Doljanin and Máire Doyle (eds), *John McGahern: Authority and Vision* (Manchester: Manchester University Press, 2017), pp. 191–4.

Carlson, Julia, 'John McGahern', in Julia Carlson (ed.), *Banned in Ireland: Censorship and the Irish Writer* (Athens, Ga.: University of Georgia Press, 1990), pp. 53–67.

Cullinan, Elizabeth, 'A Swim', *The Time of Adam* (Boston, Mass.: Houghton Mifflin, 1971), pp. 138–58.

de Quincey, Thomas, *Recollections of the Lakes and the Lake Poets*, ed. David Wright (Harmondsworth: Penguin, 1970).

Déon, Michel, *Horseman, Pass By! Irish Pages*, trans. Clíona Ní Ríordáin (Dublin: Lilliput Press, 2017).

Gilligan, Patrick, 'Volunteer Frank McGahern', *John McGahern Yearbook*, 3 (2010): 58–73.

Gordon, D. J., and Ian Fletcher, 'Persons and Places', in D. J. Gordon, Ian Fletcher, Frank Kermode and Robin Skelton, *W. B. Yeats, Images of a Poet: My Permanent Impermanent Images* (Manchester: Manchester University Press, 1961), pp. 25–55.

Kelly, Joan (Darina), 'Young Man on His Way Up in the World', *Irish Press*, 22 February 1963.

Kelly, Liam, 'Endure What Life Gives and Ask No Longer Span . . .', *Furrow*, May 2006.

Kiberd, Declan, 'Foreword: John McGahern, Impossible Things', in Derek Hand and Eamon Maher (eds), *Essays on John McGahern: Assessing a Literary Legacy* (Cork: Cork University Press, 2019), pp. xi–xvii.

Killen, John (ed.), *Dear Mr McLaverty: The Literary Correspondence of John McGahern and Michael McLaverty, 1959–1980* (Belfast: The Linen Hall Library, 2006).

Leyris, Pierre, 'Préface du traducteur', *Lignes de fond* (Paris: Mercure de France, 1971).

Louvel, Liliane, and Ben Forkner, 'Interview with John McGahern', *Journal of the Short Story in English*, 41 (autumn 2003): 123–41.

Mackle, Joanna, 'The Publishing of *Amongst Women*', *John McGahern Yearbook*, 1 (2008): 88–91.

McGahern, John, 'A Slip-up', *Stand*, 16 (3) (1975): 21–4.

—— 'Along the Edges', *New Review*, 4 (45–6) (1977–8): 19–24.

—— 'Bomb Box', *Listener*, December 1969, pp. 885–7.

—— 'Doorways', *New Review*, 4 (41) (August 1977): 9–17.

—— 'Faith, Hope and Charity', *New Review*, 2 (19) (October 1975): 44–6.

—— 'Introduction', in John Butler Yeats, *Letters to His Son W. B. Yeats and Others, 1869–1922* (London: Faber & Faber, 1999), pp. 1–24.

—— 'Just a Little Bit of Ireland . . .', *Sunday World*, 25 April 1976.

—— 'Souveniers d'une Irlande en rouge et vert', trans. Florence Benoist, *Libération*, 11 and 12 June 1988.

—— 'The Beginning of an Idea', *New Review*, 1 (5) (August 1974): 43–8.

—— 'The Image (Prologue to a Reading at the Rockefeller University)', *Honest Ulsterman: Monthly Handbook for a Revolution*, 8 (December 1968), p. 10.

—— *Amongst Women* (London: Faber & Faber, 1990).

—— *Creatures of the Earth: New and Selected Stories* (London: Faber & Faber, 2006).

—— *Love of the World: Essays*, edited by Stanley van der Ziel, with an introduction by Declan Kiberd (London: Faber & Faber, 2009).

—— *Memoir* (London: Faber & Faber, 2005).

—— *Nightlines* (London: Faber & Faber, 1970).

—— *That They May Face the Rising Sun* (London: Faber & Faber, 2002).

—— *The Barracks* (London: Faber & Faber, 1963).

—— *The Collected Stories* (London: Faber & Faber, 1992).

—— *The Dark* (London: Faber & Faber, 1965).

—— *The Leavetaking* (London: Faber & Faber, 1974).

—— *The Leavetaking*, revised paperback edition (London: Faber & Faber, 1984).

—— *The Letters of John McGahern*, ed. Frank Shovlin (London: Faber & Faber, 2021).

—— *The Pornographer* (London: Faber & Faber, 1979).

—— *The Power of Darkness* (London: Faber & Faber, 1991).

—— *The Rockingham Shoot and Other Dramatic Writings*, ed. Stanley van der Ziel (London: Faber & Faber, 2018).

Meehan, Paula, 'Inside McGahern's Workshop', in Željka Doljanin and Máire Doyle (eds), *John McGahern: Authority and Vision* (Manchester: Manchester University Press, 2017), pp. 180–90.

Murphy, Mike, interview with John McGahern, in Clíodhna Ní Anluain (ed.), *Reading the Future* (Dublin: Lilliput, 2000), pp. 136–55.

Murphy, Richard, *The Kick: A Life Among Writers* (London and New York: Granta Books, 2002).

Murray, Christopher, 'The "Fallen World" of *The Power of Darkness*', *John McGahern Yearbook*, 2 (2009): 78–91.

Ó Tuathaigh, Gearóid, 'Honouring John McGahern', *John McGahern at NUI Galway*, compiled and edited by Liz McConnell, John Kenny and Riana O'Dwyer (Galway: Office of the President, NUI Galway).

O'Faolain, Nuala, 'He Was Already Embarked on a Life of Heroic Honesty', *Sunday Tribune*, 2 April 2006.

O'Grady, Séamus, 'John McGahern and the University', *John McGahern at NUI Galway* (Galway: National University of Ireland, Galway, 2007), pp. 13–14.

Ranbom, Shep, 'Conversations in the Hallway Still Linger', *Colgate Magazine* (winter 2023), news.colgate.edu/magazine/2023/02/13/conversations-in-the-hallway-still-linger/ (accessed 2 December 2025).

Rondeau, Daniel, 'John McGahern: "Une forme de vie intense"', in *Les Fêtes partagées: Lectures et autres voyages* (Paris: NIL Editions, 1994), pp. 198–201.

Rosenfield, Ray, 'John McGahern Gives Insight on Melville', *Irish Times*, 25 November 1967.

Sampson, Denis, 'The Solitary Hero', *John McGahern Yearbook*, 3 (2010): 74–80.

Shaw, Pat, 'Ireland: A Discussion with John McGahern', *Colgate Maroon*, 19 November 1991.

Sheehy-Skeffington, Owen, 'The McGahern Affair', *Censorship*, 6 (spring 1966): 27–30.

Tóibín, Colm, 'Out of the Dark: A Profile of John McGahern', in *The Trial of the Generals: Selected Journalism, 1980–1990* (Dublin: Raven Arts Press, 1990), pp. 94–102.

van der Ziel, Stanley, interview with John McGahern (October 2004), in Željka Doljanin and Máire Doyle (eds), *John McGahern: Authority and Vision* (Manchester: Manchester University Press, 2017), pp. 195–212.

Whelan, Tony, 'Working at the Mill', *John McGahern Yearbook*, 2 (2009): 28–41.

Wright, David, 'An Introduction', *An Anthology from* X: A Quarterly Review of Literature and the Arts, *1959–1962* (Oxford: Oxford University Press, 1988), pp. xi–xix.

Picture Credits

Every reasonable effort has been made to trace copyright holders. Any copyright holder who has not been correctly acknowledged is requested to contact the publisher.

Page 1

Frank McGahern and his Garda Síochána class, *c.* 1922; McGahern family with Aunt Maggie, *c.* 1945 (photographers unknown).

Page 2

Illustrations drawn by Susan McManus in her 'Nature Study Record Book', *c.* 1918–20 (McGahern Papers, University of Galway). Susan McGahern with friends; Annikki Laaksi and John McGahern, *c.* 1964–5 (photographers unknown).

Page 3

Portrait of John, *c.* 1963 (photographer: Alen MacWeeney).

Page 4

Portrait of Madeline Green, Paris, *c.* 1967 (photographer unknown). Photo-booth images with Madeline Green, Paris, *c.* 1968. John at work in 1 rue Christine, Paris, *c.* 1969–70 (photographer: Madeline Green).

Page 5

Peter Woods and Francie McGarty saving hay in the McGaherns' Foxfield shed; John's uncle Pat McManus at work in his Ballinamore garage; the McGahern home in Foxfield, 1980s (photographer: Madeline McGahern).

Page 6

Patrick O'Malley, Cleggan; Francie McGarty and John, the McGarty kitchen in the 1980s (photographer: Madeline McGahern).

Page 7

John and Jimmy Swift, the International Bar, Dublin, *c.* 1990; Tom Jordan; Neill Joy (photographer: Madeline McGahern).

Page 8

John with his boat at the lakeside, Foxfield, 1980s; John in his Foxfield home, mid-1990s (photographer: Madeline McGahern).

Index